Wasted Days and Wasted Nights

Freddy Fender

Volume I
A Meteoric Rise to Stardom
A Daughter's Story by

Tammy Lorraine Huerta Fender

Copyright © 2017 by Tammy Lorraine Huerta Fender.
TXU-1-793-304

Library of Congress Control Number: 2011900394
ISBN: Hardcover   978-1-4568-5105-7
          Softcover   978-1-4568-5104-0
          eBook   978-1-4771-8194-2

All rights reserved. No part of this book may be reproduced or transmitted in any form or by any means, electronic or mechanical, including photocopying, recording, or by any information storage and retrieval system, without permission in writing from the copyright owner.

Rev. date: 09/04/2019

To order additional copies of this book, contact:
Xlibris
1-888-795-4274
www.Xlibris.com
Orders@Xlibris.com
531819

Contents

Dedication vii
Inscription by Freddy Fender ix
Freddy Fender's Hometown xiii
Freddy Fender's Family Tree xv
Preface xix
Introduction xxv

Part I: The Rise

Chapter I	Don Benito	1
Chapter II	La Resaca	13
Chapter III	A Stepfather	24
Chapter IV	Private Huerta	40
Chapter V	Las Califas	55
Chapter VI	El Bebop Kid (1957)	77
Chapter VII	"Wasted Days and Wasted Nights"	95
Chapter VIII	Freddy Fender	110
Chapter IX	"A Man Can Cry"	131
Chapter X	New Orleans, 1960s	151
Chapter XI	Home Again in the Magical Rio Grande Valley	172
Chapter XII	RGV Girl	182
Chapter XIII	The Border Diablos	197
Chapter XIV	Broken Promises	206
Chapter XV	The Squeeze Inn	213
Chapter XVI	"Before the Next Teardrop Falls"	225
Chapter XVII	Star Makers	242
Chapter XVIII	The King of Tex-Mex	259
Chapter XIX	"To Our Favorite Son—Welcome Back Home!" ..	274
Chapter XX	The Mexican Hillbillies	294
Chapter XXI	A Powerhouse	315

Afterword 343
Interviewees 345
Acknowledgments 347
Freddy Fender Honors and Awards 351
Freddy Fender Discography 357
References 373
Credits 375
About the Author 383

*For Father, who
Lived life to the fullest,
Loved all people unconditionally,
Laughed and sang his blues away, and most importantly,
Learned to trust in a Higher Power—Jesus Christ.*

Freddy Fender and daughter Tammy during his first acting role as General Pancho Villa in the movie She Came To The Valley *(1979)*.

"From My Humble Beginnings To a Humble End"

Inscription by Freddy Fender

BALDEMAR GARZA HUERTA

THE FIRST HISPANIC SINGER TO RECORD ROCK & ROLL
IN SPANISH LANGUAGE IN AMERICAN MUSIC HISTORY
AKA
EL BEBOP KID (1957), FREDDY FENDER (1958–2006),
EDDIE MEDINA (1961), SCOTTY WAYNE (1962)

Freddy Fender's Hometown

The Rio Grande Valley

In 1904, a group of pioneers from the United States and Mexico founded the small town of San Benito, Texas. It was first named Díaz in honor of Mexico's president, Porfirio Díaz. On May 11, 1907, this pioneer vision of railroads across Texas and irrigation from the Rio Grande formed the land into a garden of Eden newly named San Benito.

Freddy Fender's Family Tree

(Maternal Ancestry-Garza)	(Paternal Ancestry-Huerta)
Freddy's Grandfather Benito Garza Born: March 21, 1875, Matamoros, Tamaulipas, Mexico Died: March 1, 1947, San Benito, Texas, USA *** **Freddy's Granduncles and Grandaunts** Víctor, Librada, Rafael, Ricardo, Manuela, Rosa, Paula, and Maria Garza Born: Matamoros, Mexico Died: Texas, USA	**Freddy's Grandfather** Ysidro Huerta Born: Soto La Marina, Tamaulipas, Mexico Died: Mexico
Freddy's Grandmother Dolores Delgado (married to Benito) Born: Matamoros, Tamaulipas, Mexico Died: 1925, Brownsville, Texas, USA	**Freddy's Grandmother** Tiburcia Medina (married to Ysidro) Born: Soto La Marina, Tamaulipas, Mexico Died: Mexico

Freddy's Uncles and Aunts
(Benito and Dolores' children)

Porfirio, Margarita, Serapio, Dolores, and Ovidio

***

All Born:
Las Yescas Ranch, Brownsville, Texas, USA

***

Serapio, Born: 1912; Died: 1977
Porfirio, Born: September 15, 1917; Died: December 13, 1988
San Benito, Texas, USA

***

Freddy's Mother
Margarita, a.k.a. Doña Máge Garza
(married to Serapio Huerta)
Born: June 11, 1919
Died: August 1, 1989
San Benito, Texas, USA

***

Dolores, Born: March 17, 1923
Died: March 24, 2018 San Benito, Texas
Ovidio, Born: August 24, 1925;
Died: September 10, 1993
Grand Prairie, Texas, USA

Freddy's Uncle
Casimiro Medina Huerta
Born: Soto La Marina, Tamaulipas, Mexico
Died: Mexico

Freddy's Father
Serapio "El Chapo" Medina Huerta
Born: March 3, 1907
Soto La Marina, Tamaulipas, Mexico
Died: January 15, 1945
San Benito, Texas, USA

Freddy's Siblings
(Margarita Huerta's Biological Children)
Isidro Garza-Huerta, Born: May 1, 1939
María Minerva Garza-Huerta, Born: February 20, 1941
Inocencio Garza-Ramírez, Born: December 28, 1942; Died: August 12, 2000
Juan José Garza-Huerta, Born: July 12, 1944; Died: September 13, 2007
José Luis Garza-Méndez, Born: November 27, 1945
Manuel Garza-Salazar, Born: October 29, 1948; Died: September 20, 2010
Sylvia Garza-Salazar, Born: February 24, 1958
Elvia Garza-Salazar, Born: June 28, 1961
All Born: San Benito, Texas, USA

Mr. and Mrs. Baldemar Garza Huerta
Married (49 years) 1957–2006

Baldemar Garza Huerta	Evangelina Nieto Muñiz-Huerta
Born: June 4, 1937 Died: October 14, 2006, San Benito, Texas, USA	Born: January 12, 1941 San Francisco, California, USA

Son	Daughter	Son	Daughter
Baldemar Huerta Jr. a.k.a. Sonny Born: May 18, 1958 San Benito, Texas	Tammy Lorraine Huerta Born: September 6, 1961 San Benito, Texas	Daniel Huerta Born: December 22, 1966 Harlingen, Texas	Marla Huerta Born: January 1, 1980 Corpus Christi, Texas

Grandchildren	**Grandchildren**
Sonny Huerta's family Daughter-in-law, Lupita Moody Huerta Born: May 3, 1958, San Benito, Texas Dectorio, a.k.a. Dexter Born: February 13, 1989, Corpus Christi, Texas Savannah Huerta Born: October 13, 1990, Harlingen, Texas	Marla Garcia and daughters Valencia, María, Mariela, and Alfreda Garcia Born: San Diego, California

Preface

With a distinctive voice and melody, Freddy Fender sang and bared his soul to us. His intellect encompassed the arts of culture, world history, and music. With a natural appeal and interest in people, he mastered the social science of communications across the globe.

Father attempted to write his life story various times without success. He would start talking about the most enchanting, picturesque place he had ever seen. While reminiscing, he would reflect upon his teenage years, recording memories of his hometown on paper and audio. However, on each attempt, he would quickly come to a dead halt. Then, like the comic superhero the Flash, Freddy would take off riding like the wind on his motorcycle, trying to recapture his youth and an old world he had left behind.

Freddy grew up in a majestic place and era. It was a place where time stood still for him. Before making his famous mark here and around the world, he would notoriously brand his birthplace. He concocted a beautiful world of fascination and fantasy, one that transcended the harsh reality of his childhood.

Father's hometown is a simple place, one where life made sense and was worth living. While traveling down south off US-77 onto Highway 83, one could easily miss this minute town with just the blink of an eye.

It was as though Freddy was born from a deep-seated, wild-rooted branch that allowed him to shoot up of his own accord. The magical rich soil, thick in humus, would cultivate in him an inner strength, allowing him to thrive beyond the confines of his provincial realm. The raw, uncooked stories of life in the magical Rio Grande Valley shaped and captivated Freddy. It bred in him a curiosity, and it became the catalyst for his unquenchable thirst for greater adventure. Freddy would take that journey to the unknown, yet remain true to his roots, promising to stay grounded, virtuous, and return home someday.

Father struggled in his effort to keep writing. Upon witnessing this, I assisted him by drawing a diagram of a brainstorming technique that I learned from my English professor back in college. Not long after this, I observed that he had attempted to continue his bio while using this effective technique. However, Father must have concluded that living life was much more invigorating and valuable to him than writing about it. As I had noticed, his efforts had only covered his early to adolescent years as a child migrant worker.

After Father's passing, he would not let me be. I found many others who felt the same way; he would speak to them in their dreams as though he was still running the show!

It was not until ten days later (on a Tuesday) that I felt his passing as I walked into my home while holding my groceries. Father had finally left us and gone on to another plane.

I had never really understood what the word *plane* or *dimension* meant, nor was I ever comfortable using this kind of terminology, until now.

I felt it in my chest, just like an air pocket being sucked out of me. It was a jolt (his spirit) leaving this world.

Father's death had punched a colossal hole into our hearts. Millions of fans worldwide kept writing on his Web site guest book, paralyzed and anxiously waiting for someone to retract the news of Freddy's death. They were hoping that perhaps it was just some malicious report transmitted by mistake.

We never did say the word *good-bye* or tell him that he was truly dying, nor could we. Nor was I able to let him go—not quite, or even as of yet.

Soon after, I came across one of the voice recordings from his memoirs. In it, he expressed a wish to write a biography titled *From My Eyes* by Freddy Fender.

With regard to his most important achievements, I would now like to set the record straight and immortalize him through this book, as it should be. Therefore, in this book, I have added multitudes of Freddy Fender's most humble and authentic quotes, which spanned a musical career extending nearly sixty years.

Since this is the first time our life story with Father will be revealed, I must share with you that it has weighed upon me something fierce. I deliberately went back in time and threw myself into the fires of memory as no one else in my family dared to do, except for Mother.

Keep in mind I'm just a storyteller. This is being told to you as compassionately and as best as I possibly can write. The book is raw yet authentic. It's real life! So, to understand my father (the man), Freddy Fender, we have to go back to the beginning.

When I first began this monster of a project, I spoke spiritually with Father. I told him that he was going to have to place certain people in my path in order to make this lonely task possible for me to withstand and accomplish.

Even before his death, I had mentally and emotionally detached myself. I remained disconnected from the present while thousands of electrifying flashbacks took me by force to the beginning. It was as if it were only yesterday.

At the initial start of my journey, mother handed over to me a hundred or so audiocassettes of Father's in which he recounted much of his musical career. In these tapes, he spoke of music history, different genres, and multitudes of great artists who came from across the globe into the United States. He commented on how these artists had influenced our society while developing new music genres with distinct sounds.

After two and a half years of extensive research and interviews, it felt right; I had more than enough insight into Freddy's personal and professional life. In piecing together his life, I discovered that his entire recording career reflected and paralleled his trials and tribulations (as is true of most artists).

In this book, I share our realities as they convey a personal message of beauty and truth. We witnessed firsthand all the dynamics that come with knowing an iconic persona. We lived with a man who was both a dreamer and a realist. His multitudes of extraordinary God-given gifts were beyond our normal human scope and comprehension.

As I was at the end of writing my father's biography, Mother gave me ten more cassettes, which recorded his last few months here on earth. The first few were phone interviews from music reporters from across the world. They were from countries in Europe as well as Mexico; they wanted to hear Freddy's last few words of wisdom. The conversations centered on other legendary artists such as Frank Sinatra, Elvis Presley, and more.

For the longest time, the last of the cassette tapes sat on my desk, as I dared not listen to them sooner than need be for fear of breaking my heart any further.

I had unbearable sleepless nights writing from dusk until dawn while doubt and fear began to creep up and overwhelm me. This was because of the sensitive nature of the true stories that were being shared by others and me.

The endless flashbacks of our lives with Father kept me up all hours of the night. They sent me running to my desk to jot down my memories of our love, our life, and what I had truly learned about him. It was as though I was not allowed to rest nor be free nor live in the moment.

No one understood my torment; I felt all alone. I assure you I had no choice other than to keep writing a story that needed to be told.

At last, there was an answer to my prayers. While drained and at my wit's end, I reached over late one night and grabbed hold of the remaining tapes. I began to listen to them while my husband, William, supportive of my relentless drive toward completion and peace, lay asleep.

There was Father, my angel, giving me what I had needed to hear all along. No one else other than God could have eased the anguish of my passion to write a wonderful and honest-to-goodness book about my father. It was the go-ahead to proceed. It was as though he had come back from the grave, while keeping his word to me that I would never feel or be alone again, no matter what.

"From My Eyes" by Freddy Fender

I would like them to write a book. Hopefully they will do a film on that!
But I do want them to write a real book, none of this lucky, hunky-dory poor-boy from
the Rio Grande Valley, and he did really well, that they could root for and all that.
No, I want the dark side, the bad things—about cocaine and the heroin shooting in my veins
with the bad stuff of drug issues, the penitentiary, divorcing my wife, and why and all that!
I want things written that were significant in my life!

Again, none of that hunky-dory poor-boy stuff—I would like that.
I would also like to do good things but that are in the eyes of God.
I don't want to be a priest or gospel singer, but I do want him happy with what I am doing.
Whoever gets to write the book, I hope is the right one—because if one
writes it another way, and with just any little change, it will not hit the
nail on the head! It is like a bad recording of a good song!
So, whoever writes this book—I just hope is the right one.
As far as being honored, honor to you might mean a lot of things.
But honor to me means that he or she would be the right one.
And I would appreciate them wishing me that.
(The Huerta Family Archives, 2006)

I was compelled to write from the start. This book is for our family's healing, especially for my own. Even more importantly, it is also for his fans—to continue his legacy—and because I promised Father I would bring this book to fruition.

There are people who just shine more than others do in families. Life is not always fair; they are born lucky and are considered "the chosen ones." In one way or another, they live amazing lives and are destined to be an example to others.

Freddy Fender, beaten down by misfortune, failure, and social prejudice, selflessly shared his whole life openly with us. He gave wholeheartedly, without reservations, and left us with many of his genuine talents.

As Freddy was busy living out his dreams, we all seemed to live ours through *his* life experiences. We were merely part of his wake from the beginning to the very end.

Both men and women wept when they lost their good friend Freddy Fender. Today the people who admired him have long passed on their memories through his music at family gatherings, weddings, funerals, and such. It gave Father much solace to know that the love and compassion he gave worldwide was returned to him tenfold.

This story is primarily about how Father affected and influenced our personal family life and his professional social recognition in the music world. Freddy Fender's voice transcended all musical genres; his multicultural fans are evidence of his universal appeal.

Freddy seized the opportunity that worldwide fame brought him. He learned about people, how they lived and struggled to survive. He became a part of their lives, bringing them a bit of joy and hope, as he expressed his compassion through what he knew best—his music.

His life was enriched more than he could ever have hoped or dreamed. He visited many foreign countries—such as Africa, Australia, Denmark, Germany, Hong Kong, Ireland, Italy, Japan, Malaysia, Mexico, Netherlands, Philippines, Russia, Shanghai, Singapore, Spain, Switzerland, and Vietnam.

Whenever—or wherever—people may remember Freddy's voice and intimate friendship (shared by his family, friends, and fans), he will always live on vicariously through them.

This book, which is the life story of Freddy Fender's rise to fame, is the first part of a two-part biography. It covers his music career until 1979, when he was in his early forties and at the peak of his success. The second volume covers "the fall" and "the redemption" of Freddy Fender. In the afterword, you can read a brief and vivid description of what's to come after "the rise."

In view of that, that is where we shall go to be with him. We will see it through his eyes, my mothers, and mine while trudging a road toward enlightenment, acceptance, and a new freedom from bondage. We shall seek peace and joy and embrace our lives once more with perhaps a brand-new set of eyes.

Tammy holding her Teddy Freddy Bear prototype (2009)
"With God as my mentor and a master trainer whipping me into physical shape, I was beyond prepared for the most important project of my life— a gift for you from my higher power, God, with his son and advocate, Jesus Christ."

"Found it!"
Father's CD titled Especially For You, track "Knocking on Heaven's Door"
Take it from the top—Hit it!

Introduction

I first met Father when I was about two and a half years old. On July 23, 1963, he was out on parole from DeQuincy prison, a correctional facility in Northwest Louisiana. He arrived back to his hometown of San Benito, Texas, on a Trailways bus.

In September of 1961, I too was born in the small town of San Benito. I came out with wild long black hair, just like Father's. It quickly grew down to my knees. My hair covered half of my face, and I had one eye peeking out—just like the character in *The Addams Family* television show. As a child, my family called me Cousin Itt.

On the day of his arrival, I walked up to him barefooted and stood behind him as he acquainted himself with *la palomia* (buddies) down the street. I placed my little hands on my boney hips, looked up at him, and said aloud, "I know who you are!"

At twenty-six years of age, Father stood there exasperated, with lackluster eyes. His spirit had been stripped away after over a thousand "wasted days and wasted nights" confined to one of Louisiana's finest prisons.

He turned to me; our eyes locked, staring as though we were in a Mexican standoff. I knew without a doubt that on this very day, he would know exactly who I was. I did not surrender or hesitate to inform him aloud, "You're my mother!"

He laughed at me and told me to get lost! I guess he figured I was just another *huerquita mocosa* (snotty-nosed kid) from El Jardín, the name of our humble barrio.

I must have sensed that this charismatic young man was related to me in some capacity. Who else would have the gall to talk to Freddy Fender like that but his own true daughter? Or to blurt out an introduction such as mine?

Everyone in the barrio was whispering about him because after a three-year absence, he was the center of everyone's attention and curiosity.

My elder brother, Sonny, had already seen him in prison and had cried at the sight of him. Sonny and I are fair-skinned like Mother. She is a Spaniard, and Father, well, he looked more like a Mexican bandit.

While I was growing up, Father always enjoyed a good laugh and teased me about how we first met—as father and daughter.

The stories I tell you are neither good nor bad. They are what they are, just that—our lives. There is no black or white in this book, only shades of gray. In the beginning of life, we are surrounded by the mystical whites of purity and innocence. In the midst of our lives, there are multitudes of brilliant colors as in a prism, shimmering all around, giving us a path of joy and hope for tomorrow.

However, for some of us, life can appear charcoal gray, a pitch-black darkness that envelops and blinds us. It can almost seem unbearable and horrific as it engulfs us whole. At times, it may seem almost impossible to penetrate as it prevents us from seeing beyond our human scope and power.

Having endured the impossible and having been tested as no other, a person must be fearless and have the purest of hearts in order to pierce through and embrace their darkest moments. A spiritual experience can arise from this, if one can only fall to one's knees and surrender with total humility.

Having crossed over, the light of truth enters the center of God's eye; we can become whole and lucid. God gives us new hope and purpose, as we see everything and everyone crystal clear as never before.

It is true that there is nothing to fear. At times, we may feel lonely, unloved, or perhaps even scared to live or die. However, I can assure you, there is no one and nothing to ever fear in this world again.

God is nothing but pure love! We have the power to heal within ourselves because God is in us all! Our physical bodies, emotions, and memories of broken hearts, some old, some new, have the capacity to heal, like a hardened scab that mends itself with time.

God gave us unconditional love and life. I say, "Life is for dreamers. Let the dreamers dream!"

"Now, where are you going?" Mother often asks of me.

I answer her, "I've got things to do, places to go, and people to meet. I'm going to go live my life, of course!"

I will make you glad, sad, mad, and perhaps even judgmental as you read about our personal lives. Yet I hope you will allow yourself to feel the same love and laughter and perhaps a divine kindness toward those who have affected your lives with such intensity.

You too, can reach the depths of your inner being and find compassion for others. With family and friends, we learn to "live and let live" for a new hope and a better tomorrow. We can also forgive and be forgiven. And as long as there is breath within us all, it is never too late to love or to be loved, all in the eyes of God.

I give you my tears, then some more tears; but they are teardrops of my spirited joy, renewed hope, and mercy. I now introduce you to my family and my father, Baldemar Garza Huerta, a.k.a. Freddy Fender.

Part 1

The Rise

*Freddy Fender at the Grand Ole Opry House, 50th Birthday Celebration, CMA Awards.
(October 13, 1975)*

Chapter I

Don Benito

Las Yescas Ranch
Los Castillos in La Palma
A Destiny Foreseen

My paternal great-grandfather, Don Benito Garza, crossed over the border from Matamoros, Mexico into Texas in the early 1900s. In our culture, we call our elders *Don* or *Doña* as a sign of respect, such as Mr. or Mrs. It was the norm for folks of all ethnicities to travel freely back and forth, even during one of the most fierce and chaotic periods in Mexican history. Self-elected Mexican president/tyrant Porfirio Díaz had created an unstable national climate, an uproar which began yet another shattering and unyielding revolution for the Mexican people.

Don Benito's father, Apolinar Garza, had passed away and left him as the head of their cattle ranch. However, because of authoritarian land disputes, no peasant or farmer could claim the land he occupied without formal legal title, as the Mexican government indiscriminately seized all property rights. Thus, Benito and his family had literally been run out of town. Rather than having their home burned to the ground or risk being killed, Benito had been forced into leaving their country and everything they owned behind.

This unforeseen circumstance is why Benito and his siblings were left to settle in the Rio Grande Valley. The Garza family moved into a town known as Brownsville at the tip of South Texas, which at the time was mostly *montes* (wooded areas). This is how Father (Baldemar G. Huerta aka Freddy Fender) and our family came to reside so close to the Mexican border.

During the revolt, people were in fear and unclear as to their future. However, Benito, who was a strong, burly man, had no problem finding work with local farmers or ranchers. Shortly after his arrival, a landowner from Las Yescas rode up in his wagon to meet him because the stranger had noted that Benito was a disciplined, hardworking man. He asked him, "Don Benito, I have much work for you. If you come to my ranch, I will build you a house!" He said it just like that.

Ranch owners built homes for all heads of families who lived and maintained their properties on site. Families at Las Yescas (which means fire-starter material) would have land large enough on which to flourish.

Benito couldn't resist a great offer, so he moved to Las Yescas ranch, which is in the vicinity of Brownsville. He quickly learned a new trade and became a well-known and respected lumberjack. He was hired to clear the land for both farming of small animals and crops. He would go out to *los montes* (the woods) and chop down mesquite and huisache trees. Then he would lug *la leña* (the firewood), which was in great demand for cooking and bathing, over to the various ranches and small towns to sell. He earned $50 a month; however, this amount would not be quite enough to sustain the large family he would soon have.

Across the street from his family's home on San Francisco Street, Benito had met and fallen in love with a young woman named Dolores Delgado. She too was from Matamoros, and both families were of strong Catholic faith and moral values. She was a beautiful, tall woman who stood up with self-assuredness and dignity. Yet she had a warm and gentle glow about her. Benito married my great-grandmother Dolores and they shared a life together at Las Yescas ranch. Altogether, she bore him nine children.

Freddy's aunts and uncles on his maternal side are (from the eldest to the youngest) Serapio, Carlos, Porfirio, Margarita, triplets Benito, María, and Dolores, and twins Ovidio and Julio. Of the triplets, only Dolores ("Lola") survived.

Meanwhile, blood was spilling on both sides of the Mexican border, and to combat the lawlessness, a group known as the Texas Rangers had been reorganized. They were hired to regulate the borderlines of South Texas and were well paid with land grants.

There was confusion in that neither the local folks nor the militia groups could distinguish between Mexican bandits and law-abiding citizens—or, should I say, a good Mexican from a bad one. It was a revolution! Sadly, many innocent people, including foreigners who traveled from afar to find work and settle along South Texas borders, died needlessly.

Therefore, when the *Federales* would ride up through Las Yescas, Benito would yell out, "Dolores, run and hide the children quickly!"

Without dismounting from their horses, they would ask Benito if they were harboring any Mexican bandits and giving them aid. The people had many doubts about whom to trust, so they kept to themselves, worked hard, and minded their own business. People lived hard lives and barely had the strength to complain or explain, especially to the children.

Unfortunately, Dolores died giving birth to a set of twins and one baby passed away in 1925. The surviving twin was given away to his maternal family to be raised in La Villa, Texas. Sadly, her son Carlos would also die young, but from a broken heart.

Freddy's grandmother Dolores Delgado Garza (center)
Wives and children of Las Yescas ranch (1920s)

Freddy's Aunt Dolores "Lola" Garza Huerta: *El Viejo* (The Old Man)

During my frequent visits to *Tía* Lola's home, who is my great aunt Dolores, she graciously shared our family's ancestry with me and we both found much comfort reminiscing about our beloved dead. She is a woman who has always been very religious, conservative, and happily married.

As she went back in time, she began to remember, "Well, there were many workers *aqui* (right here)! There were many wagons all around San Benito where we now live! *El viejo* (the old man, meaning her father Benito) would travel all over South Texas, and the landowners had been very nice to us." The landowners had given Benito a wagon with two huge horses so that he could haul loads of *leña*; he would chop it up into small squares and then stack it onto the wagon so that he would be ready to unload them faster for his customers.

As Benito began to travel, he left his children behind to be cared for by his sister Librada in Brownsville. While traveling through a small area called the Resaca City of San Benito, he was drawn to a quaint little *barrio* (a neighborhood) called El Jardín. Every week, Benito would ride into town and stop at the Díaz Post Office to send Librada money to care for his children.

Not long after his wife Dolores died, he met a woman named Elena and quickly married her. She already had grown boys of her own, and he felt she could help raise his children. Soon after, Benito sent for his children to live with him and Elena in the barrio of El Jardín, in San Benito, Texas.

As his own children got older, Benito did not believe it was necessary for his daughters to get an education; therefore, his daughters only completed the third grade. His primary reason was that he thought that boys only went to school to flirt with the girls. His eldest daughter, Margarita, born in 1919 (Freddy's mother), attempted to further her education without Benito knowing, but he soon found out and put a stop to it. From that point on, she was only allowed to attend catechism classes at Saint Vincent's Catholic School, located on Resaca Drive (now Freddy Fender Lane).

On the weekends, Don Benito would leave for work at Las Yescas, but before leaving he made sure the girls were safe and sleeping at his brother Víctor's house, which was only a few yards away. Most houses in El Jardín have several one or two-bedroom *casitas* (tiny homes) in one small lot.

Serapio, who was the eldest of Benito's children, had grown to resent his stepmother Elena because she neglected him and his siblings in comparison to the love and attention she gave her own children. After many arguments, Serapio took it upon himself to become the patriarch of his family, and what Serapio said became law. Thus, the siblings looked up to their big brother while their father, Benito, went off to work at Las Yescas ranch.

Freddy's Heritage: The Life of a Migrant Worker *Los Troqueros* (The Truckers) & *Los Patrones* (The Bosses)

The majority of *los Mexicanos,* as well as many other foreigners who came to live in South Texas, were uneducated and impoverished. Therefore, it was the norm to become a migrant worker, and Freddy would soon learn to follow the pack, while trying to survive one season to the next. The local workplace at the cotton mill was right across the street from Alexander's vegetable warehouse, which was also known to the locals as La Pricula. Both of these places were primary sources of work for the people of San Benito. They are both still standing on the corner of Stenger Street and Resaca Drive. It is also within walking distance to the barrio of El Jardín and located on one side of *la resaca* (a stream of water stemming from the Rio Grande that flows through to the barrios of the town.)

Freddy and his younger siblings began working as migrant workers as children; this occurred through the help of his distant cousins, who happened to be Elena's brothers-in-law. Generations of men in the Castillo family were local *troqueros* (truckers), who were especially known as *los patrones* (the big bosses). Elena and her sister, Clara, were often recruiting migrant workers for them. They gathered all the migrant workers in the area on time for seasonal harvest. When the migrant workers would give them a good hard day's work, *los patrones* would buy the men and teenage boys rounds of beer to celebrate a good crop. It was a big deal to be a *troquero*, and you were considered *somebody*!

Tía Lola remembers it as though it were only yesterday. "*Mi madrastra* (my stepmother) would tell me when to inform my siblings and neighbors on when to be ready to leave town and go to work *a las piscas* (gathering harvest)." Benito's children would load up into the extended beds of Mariano and his son Manuel's pick-up trucks and head to the nearest crop field. When the picking of cotton, vegetables, or fruit became scarce in town, they migrated up north to follow the crops to different states, according to the harvest and season. Some of the farmers provided homes for the workers to sleep in, and the women would be obligated to cook for their own families at each farmhouse, as a few of my cousins experienced while growing up.

Coincidently, the Castillos are distant relatives of my family through Teofila, the second wife of Apolinar (Freddy's great-grandfather), from Mexico. Although they are not related by blood, they are still considered family.

Across the railroad tracks is another humble barrio, called La Palma, where Clara lived with her husband, Manuel Castillo; they were an older couple and worked very hard. One morning, they made the thirty-minute trip across the border into Matamoros to visit their friends, Ysidro and Tiburcia Huerta. The Huertas had two sons, one named Casimiro and the other Serapio. Serapio Huerta was single and in his late twenties; however, he had a baby girl he helped raise and was in need of some work. The Castillos mentioned that they had migrant work for him in their family business, and invited Serapio to come live with them.

It was circa 1935 when Serapio Medina Huerta (Freddy's biological father) accepted the offer and crossed the Mexican border to live in San Benito. He slept in a one-room shack toward the back of the Castillo's home. In return, Serapio took good care of los Castillos while helping Manuel and Clara around the house. Clara would make him lunch, and every morning he'd jump into the back of Manuel's pick-up to go to *las piscas*.

Freddy's Parents Meet, Fall in Love, and Marry

One evening, when Elena took a walk to La Palma to visit her sister, Clara, she took Benito's sixteen-year-old daughter, Margarita, along with her. Margarita was a very humorous and passionate young lady with a zest for life and the local boys surely admired her.

This is when and where Baldemar Huerta's (Freddy Fender's) parents met, at the home of los Castillos in La Palma. Infatuated by her charm and wittiness, Serapio wasted no time becoming acquainted with Margarita. And when Margarita wanted to see Serapio, she would grab some rose petals and add a little color to her cheeks and lips. Then she would sneak out, as Lola yelled out to her father, *"Apá, Margarita se está saliendo por la ventana otra vez!"* ("Father, she's sneaking out through the window again!")

Serapio must have fallen in love with her because he paid the elders of La Palma to speak on his behalf to ask Benito's blessing to marry his daughter. However, each time Serapio would send one of the elders to go speak to him, Benito would avoid them by sneaking out the back way to go work at Las Yescas.

Eventually, Elena cornered him, and in their native Spanish language firmly said, "Benito, it has been three times already that you have left this house to avoid the elders. So, don't blame me if Margarita ends up running away with Serapio!"

"Well then, fine, tell them to get married," he replied.

On July 12, 1936, Serapio and Margarita were married. On the day of their wedding, Benito left for Las Yescas to work, but only to avoid his daughter's ceremony. They were married by a Catholic priest from Saint Vincent's Church, and their *madrastra*, Elena, held a small reception at her home. Serapio had given Margarita the money to buy herself a white dress. White cake and lemonade, made with juicy valley lemons, of course, were served. Margarita was seventeen and Serapio was in his early thirties when they married.

My *Tía* Lola sat in her chair staring at the television watching Mexican soap operas as she spoke to me—always saying nothing but positive things about her sister.

"Yes, Máge (short for Margarita) looked very pretty and ladylike that day. And she had such a beautiful voice. She just loved to sing and we never argued, not once."

I saw her hazel brown eyes fill up with tears of joy and admiration. She was moved by her sweet memories of her big sister, Margarita.

Freddy's Birth: June 4, 1937

Serapio Huerta began to work at Alexander's "La Pricula" packing vegetables and fruits. He boxed them up and filled them with layers of ice to keep them fresh. Then he would help load them into trucks for distribution throughout the Rio Grande Valley. Every morning, along la Resaca Drive, Serapio could be seen walking briskly and whistling on his way to work at La Pricula as though he did not have a care in the world.

He was not a shy person and loved telling *chistes* (jokes). He especially adored the ladies around town and enjoyed singing to them. He was known as El Chapo because he was stout, yet everyone agreed that he was very handsome. He had light brown skin and a full head of shiny, wavy black hair. He greased his hair every morning with a popular pomade product called Tres Flores. He wore khaki pants and long-sleeved shirts rolled up to his elbows. Serapio also loved wearing his fedora hat everywhere he went.

On June 4, 1937, Serapio and Margarita had their firstborn, a boy named Baldemar. The baby had a full head of black hair like both of his parents. Two weeks later, he was baptized at Saint Benedict's Church and his *padrinos* (godparents) were Isaac and Cecilia Martinez.

After his birth, Elena told them to come by and bring the baby so that Benito could see his grandson; she added that if Benito did not want to see the baby, they should still stop by anyway and visit.

So, they walked over to Benito's home and took little Baldemar with them. But when Margarita placed the baby in front of her father so that he could cuddle his first grandson, Benito shrugged his shoulders and said, *"¿Y que?"* (Well, so what?) Benito was still hurt because Margarita and Serapio had gotten married without his true blessing.

The look on my great *Tía* Lola's face said it all. I asked her how she felt about it. She looked down and in Spanish said sympathetically, "Well, I just felt very bad for them both on that day."

Baldemar, sitting, wearing a bonnet at 550 Biddle Street.
A cooking pot is hung outside the kitchen. (1939).

"From My Eyes" by Freddy Fender

My umbilical cord is buried in the yard of the house next to Doña Dominga's house,
before you get to one of her sons Lino Galván's home on Biddle Street.
Well, everything that is life giving has its roots—here are mine.

Freddy's Birthplace: Closest Vicinity to 550 Biddle Street

San Benito has many cornerstones; however, Biddle Street holds many memories for those who lived in the barrio of El Jardín. Baldemar was born and raised as a young boy on Biddle; his grandfather Benito also lived a few houses down with Elena and their children.

A well-respected woman by the name of Doña Dominga Galván and her family also have strong roots growing up on Biddle. You can still view her name engraved on the metal gateway in front of her home. Her daughter Catarina "Cata" Galván-Briones and Margarita Huerta lived side by side, directly across the street from Dominga's house. They became good friends.

Dominga's son was the owner of a small popular store that was right next to Dominga's home, on the corner of Biddle and Rockefeller streets. The stores in this small town are usually named after their owners, and his was called *la tienda de* (the store of) Pancho Galván. The Galván family also had a few grandsons who grew up playing with Baldemar.

However, Cata's daughter, Apolonia "Pola," remembers living next door to Margarita and Serapio as a young girl. She recalls how Baldemar often suffered as a baby because Margarita was a young mother who had to work out in the fields and leave him with Serapio.

At times, her mother would tell her to go and bring Baldemar to her because he might be hungry. Cata also had her own baby boy to care for, named Tomás. He was the same age as Baldemar. However, to pacify Baldemar, Cata would give him *pecho* (breast milk) as well.

Pola also recollects the good times, when her little brother Tomás and Baldemar would play in the muddy streets after each flood. There was no pavement, just dirt roads.

To be precise, Freddy was born in a tiny, one-room wooden shack next to Doña Dominga's home. These tiny shacks were often built, rebuilt, and torn down because of heavy rains and hurricanes.

Eventually, Pola purchased the property in which Serapio and Margarita once lived with their children and built a quaint home on it. Therefore, the original house Baldemar was raised in is no longer standing, but I have a clear picture of it in my mind today because of her.

Pola concluded the interview with a sigh. "Regardless of where Baldemar was born, Margarita and her family always rented, and never owned property. They merely lived here and there—all over El Jardín."

She was also gracious to allow us to place a historical marker, approved by the Texas Historical Commission, indicating her house as the closest vicinity of his official birthplace, at 550 Biddle Street.

A Close Bond Between Freddy and his Aunt Lola

Margarita gave all her children nicknames and Baldemar will be referred to as "Balde" for short; Isidro was "Cherín;" Maria Mínerva was "Míne;" Inocencio was "Chencho;" and Juan José was "Cáne." To help her elder sister, Lola moved in with Margarita and was often seen outside, sweeping the dirt away from the house. She helped bathe and care for Balde. At times, he would go for walks alongside his *Tía* Lola downtown to the Díaz post office. He would accompany her everywhere she went, and the two became very close.

Shortly thereafter, Lola began to date a strict and good family man (like her father) named Jesús "Chuy" Huerta. Balde would accompany them on their dates and became their regular chaperone. Thus, Balde grew to have a special bond with his aunt Lola.

Tía Lola Elopes

Tía **Lola continued** to reflect back on her youth and her father Benito. She explained aloud, "My father did not want me getting married either! *El viejo* treated us very well, but it was just that our father was very strict! So, *mi madrastra* Elena told me that if I wanted to marry Chuy, I was going to have to leave and do it without *el viejo* knowing about it. Therefore, when news of the matrimony came out in the newspaper, well then, it would already be out. He would then know, and it would have to be fine!"

That day, Chuy waited outside for Lola to arrive at Brownsville's courthouse. They got married and she never returned home.

When Benito arrived from Las Yescas, he sent Margarita looking for her; when she found Lola, she asked her, "Is it true? Did you really get married?"

Lola answered, "Si!" ("Yes!") Then she added, "And I'm seventeen years old!"

Though Jesús Huerta was not related to Serapio Huerta, he did work with him at Alexander's warehouse. Hence, there is a totally different Huerta lineage on Lola's husband's side of the family.

Her lengthy and blissful marriage to Uncle Chuy produced fifteen wonderful children, all of whom still reside on Resaca Drive (Freddy Fender Lane) and within the barrio of El Jardín.

At Eight Years Old, Freddy's Father Dies of Tuberculosis

In January 1945, Serapio became very ill and died. Sadly, Serapio never lived to see the day that the same street where he had first walked, whistled, sang, loved, and married would be named in honor of his firstborn son, Baldemar Huerta.

Balde was eight years old when he went to his father's funeral with his mother. As he stood there looking, he saw a woman (Serapio's mistress) place a hair comb in his father's suit pocket inside the casket. Serapio had always kept himself very well groomed; he was buried with a second hand black pinstriped suit and his fedora hat.

He is buried near Margarita at the city cemetery of San Benito. A tombstone was never provided for him and someday I hope to place a headstone for my grandfather Serapio Huerta, who was born in Soto la Marina, Tamaulipas, Mexico.

"From My Eyes" by Freddy Fender
My father, Serapio Huerta, had become very ill and was dying.
He was born in 1907 and died at the young age of thirty-eight years old in 1945 of tuberculosis.
This TB in the 1940s was known to our people—as consumption.
I was playing marbles, and some kids came and got me and said,
"Come on, your father is dying, and they want you!"
I was the oldest, and he had been having some problems with me, so I ran
to the house, and my brothers and sisters were lined up getting their blessing from him.
I am the last one, and I'm going, "Well, hurry up, man, come on!"
When it finally came to my turn, instead of giving me his blessing,
he was telling Mother what to do in case
I kept getting out of line. I said, "Wait a minute, you haven't blessed me yet!"
Finally, they took his hand, and he blessed me.
So, my life has been somewhat crazy from the very beginning, and I love it.
I don't think I would have it any other way.

Freddy and his Grandfather Don Benito

Don Benito's character had been strict, uncompromising, and overly moralistic, and he held the highest expectations of those he loved. He was also well respected and seen as a Good Samaritan around El Jardín, especially when the neighbors needed a good and strong lumberjack to cut down their trees and shrubs before the winter months.

Fortunately, Balde did have one treasured childhood memory of an unforgettable afternoon spent with his grandfather. One late afternoon, Benito had taken him to a carnival that came through town every year. The carnival would be held close by, either at Alexander's or the Lone Star brewery warehouse, which is located on the corner of Stenger Street by El Jardín. However, the festivities and live music could be heard throughout the various barrios. The clowns entertained them by blowing balloons and riding large bikes while juggling balls, bringing smiles to the children's faces. The carnies would also have pony rides for the kids to enjoy.

It was here at the carnival that Balde saw a female midget perform for the very first time. She had ruby colored cheeks, bright red lipstick, and wore a glittery sequined red, white, and blue dress with a white petticoat. The woman stood up high on top of a wooden platform, and as she began to sing, he noticed the sunlight shimmer and reflect off her costume.

With her little arms up high in the air, she kicked her right leg toward her left side, then switched to another leg while singing at the top of her lungs to a catchy, jazzy tune titled "Tain't What You Do, It's the Way That You Do It" (made popular by singer Ella Fitzgerald).

From the top of her head down to her little high-heeled boots, she swayed back and forth to the rhythm of the band's blasting trumpets, pounding drums, and crashing cymbals that could be heard throughout Resaca City of San Benito.

By the end of her performance, he stood mesmerized in a trancelike state. That is, until his grandfather had to wrench him away by force. This was perhaps his first glimpse of glitz and showbiz—Baldemar Huerta had foreseen his true destiny.

Baldemar "Balde" Huerta, a.k.a. Freddy Fender (1941)

Chapter II

La Resaca

Doña Máge and Balde
In Squalor
Three-String Guitar with No Backside

La Resaca (1940s)

"From My Eyes" by Freddy Fender
My life has been volatile from the very beginning.

After Serapio died, Doña Margarita "Máge" and her five children moved into a tin shack near Alexander's vegetable warehouse. Balde and his younger siblings stuck very close to their mother. They slept on the dirt floor and went without indoor running water. They used an outhouse that was directly behind the one-room shack, which also had an icebox placed in front of it. A large galvanized tub was used for bathing, boiling food and at times, to catch the rainwater pouring through the roof. Thus, the Huertas quickly came to live in squalor.

Freddy reminisces about his childhood and the harsh realities of their living conditions (1979).
(Still photo: Film Documentary *Comeback*. Producer/Director Boon Collins. 1979)

"From My Eyes" by Freddy Fender
This was perhaps the saddest place we ever lived. My dad had just died.
I guess it doesn't matter where you live—as long as you keep the family together.

Tammy Lorraine Huerta Fender

Survival: *El Robón*

There is poor, and then there is dirt poor, but Balde and his family were hungry poor. He went to school barefooted as many impoverished children did back then. And while some kids went home for lunch, Balde had no reason to do so.

On many occasions, Doña Máge and Balde were both seen walking around town in search of food. The Castillo family also owned a restaurant called El Tango. In fact, they owned a few restaurants around town. Both Máge and Balde would be seen entering El Tango, and the elders fed them.

Balde began to steal anything and everything; he was known as *el robón* (the robber). One day, Don Benito's neighbor told him that Balde had stolen his watch from his home. His grandfather wanted to beat him for taking it, but he had run away from the house. Upset and seeking to save his honor, Benito paid Balde's debt of $10 for the stolen watch.

He continued to steal, to the extent that when Balde and his siblings walked up to someone's home to play with their children, the neighbor would say, "Here comes one of Máge's kids, hurry up, let's get inside!" because the Huertas had begun to get a reputation in El Jardín as habitual beggars, tramps, and thieves. This was pretty much a daily occurrence and a way of life for him and his siblings to survive.

Because *los montes* were in close vicinity, and the fact that there were only a few houses nearby, the boys learned to hunt rabbits and chickens for food. Máge would snap off the necks, clean them, and then fry or boil the small animals.

To add to their meals, Balde would often go behind local grocery stores like Piggly Wiggly or Alexander's vegetable warehouse and jump into their dumpsters where he would find old vegetables like cabbage or lettuce. He would peel off the bad part and salvage the rest. The boys would take rotten, discarded food from the trash so that Máge could use it immediately for that one meal served.

Doña Máge Huerta (1940s)
Doña Máge: In Search of True Love & Acceptance

One afternoon, a relative from El Tango approached Máge as she stood outside smoking her hand-rolled Bugler cigarette while waiting for the bus. The woman offered her a job working in the kitchen at one of their smaller restaurants across *la resaca,* and Máge accepted her offer. The restaurant provided both breakfast and lunch for the locals and weary travelers. She prepared Mexican meals like *carne guisada* (stewed beef), frijoles (refried beans), and homemade tortillas. She also chopped plenty of lettuce, tomatoes, and onions for the tacos they served.

Máge was still young and hoped to find romance and another loving husband. However, with five children, it would be difficult to find someone who would be devoted to her. Times were very hard for Máge, and she became somewhat desperate. She came to believe smooth talkers who walked into the restaurant; one in particular, who was related to a political family, promised her the world. She entered into a relationship with him and soon had a beautiful baby boy. However, the promises the stranger had made to her were just that, empty promises.

The man's own mother came to love Máge, who also worked for his family as their domestic housekeeper. However, the father of the newborn (a politician) did not want anything else to do with Máge and kept the relationship and the baby hushed up. Afraid of the embarrassment and its political consequences for their family, the mother successfully convinced Máge to give the baby up for adoption.

The child ended up with a wonderful family, the Méndez family. His new father, Joe Méndez (who owned a tortilla business), named him José Luis. As a young boy, he and his father would deliver fresh, hot corn tortillas around el barrio food stores.

Many times, Doña Máge would see José Luis around El Jardín and long for her boy. He was so handsome and was such a kind person. She had also given her love child the nickname of El Tortillero.

Having to struggle and unable to cope without her husband, Máge did the best she could. She loved her children; so much so, that she didn't care what people thought of her. She would go to any extreme to feed and clothe them. El Jardín saw that she hustled and struggled to raise her children alone. Eventually, the barrio began to pitch in and help Máge out.

However, the beautiful thing about Balde's mother, my grandmother, was that she was a vibrant, hopeless romantic. She did have many gentleman callers in her youth, except that none of them were faithful to her. Nonetheless, Máge was still on a dire search for true love and acceptance.

Don Benito Passes Away

When Máge's father, Benito, became very ill, he called all of his children to his deathbed, including Ovidio, from La Villa, Texas. He revealed to Ovidio that he was his true father. He also explained to him that he was born with a twin and that his birth mother was Dolores Delgado. Benito went on to tell him that Dolores had died giving birth to him and his twin brother, Julio, who also died that day at Las Yescas ranch. Ovidio had been unaware of his biological family and was very happy to hear about the news. He clung tightly to his elder siblings, who welcomed him with open arms.

Don Benito Garza died March 1, 1947, brokenhearted and alone due to an unhappy marriage. However, he was loved and respected by his children. His eldest son Porfirio is buried next to him at the city cemetery of San Benito.

A Tight Bond Between Sisters: Doña Máge and Doña Lola

One could often see Doña Máge and Lola on their respective sides of *la resaca* sweeping the dusty porches and streets in front of their homes. At the end of the day, they would come together and sit on the porch reminiscing, joking, gossiping, and smoking their hand-rolled Bugler cigarettes. The two best friends had dominant personalities, were rather rough around the edges, and both enjoyed cussing like men when they were together. Rather than cry on the outside, when Máge spoke about her hardships to Lola, she would make light of it by joking and laughing aloud.

When they were done smoking, instead of flicking the cigarette ashes in the ashtray or ground, they would put out the cigarette with their wet tongues because they liked the taste of ashes.

Afterward, they would place the mashed cigarette butt inside the large front pocket of their homey Mexican-style floral dresses.

The fun part about being around Doña Máge was that she had this contagious laughter. All the Garzas and Huertas loved gathering around Máge to feel her warmth and enjoyed being entertained by her singing, spooky ghost stories, and jokes. In fact, all her children have her same laughter, humor, and singing voice as well. The two sisters were considered to be the strong and loving matriarchs of their families and were treated as such.

Máge Teaches Her Children Traditional Mexican Love Songs

In the still of the night, there would be hundreds of fireflies and locusts buzzing around Máge and her children. Night owls would listen in on their conversations as they sat calmly outdoors in pitch darkness. There were no streetlights, just the moon and stars glistening as they reflected light on top of *la resaca*. As Máge would begin to sing beautiful Mexican love ballads, her children would gather even closer. The music genres were boleros, *rancheras,* and polkas from the early 1930s and 1940s. The simplicity of the music and lyrics spoke of the people's hardships, long-lost loves, and yearning to taste a morsel of what life's sweet dreams were all about.

She sang and sang to her children until she soothed them to sleep. Her singing brought comfort to them when they were in doubt of tomorrow. I guess you could say that they lived like Mexican American gypsies, living from street to street around El Jardín. Naturally, the Huerta boys picked up her vocal talent and quickly learned to accompany her to escape the reality of their living conditions.

Tía Mínerva, "Míne," clearly remembers when they lived near Alexander's vegetable warehouse in the tin shack. She said that no matter what, Balde always found a way to pick up their spirits. He would first dig a hole in the ground, stack wood upright like a tepee, and build a great big fire. Then he would go into the fields to cut off corn and pull out carrots; he would then place the vegetables onto the fire to roast. They would sit around the fire to stay warm and enjoy the feast as they sang, just like Mexican Indians. Míne knew that as long as the family was together and had something to eat, it would have to be good enough for them to be happy.

Freddy's Mischievous Childhood

San Benito has many stories about the Huerta boys growing up. Some good, some not so good, but one thing for sure is that they all had beautiful singing voices, just like their parents. And when Balde and the boys weren't busy getting into trouble, Balde would play cowboys and Indians in the whole of El Jardín. His hometown of San Benito became his very own fantasy world.

On one occasion, Máge told Balde to go pay the rent. She gave him and his brother Cherín the rent money and they took off. A couple of hours later, her good friend Rufina Alvarado (the mother of Balde's playmates, Moisés and Alberto) went looking for Máge because she needed to talk to her immediately. Upon finding Máge, Rufina said, "I just saw Balde and Cherín at the bank and they had two guns!"

What happened is that instead of paying the rent, Balde and Cherín went shopping; they bought make-believe Roy Rogers brand guns and were standing on the street corner of the downtown bank on Sam Houston Road and Robertson Street, acting as if they were sheriffs.

Doña Máge went looking for them and when she found them playing by *la resaca*, she beat them both until they were black-and-blue for spending the rent money. They were tough, streetwise kids, and she had to be very tough on all of her children.

Her daughter Míne remembers an incident when her mother was very angry with her and Máge ran after her through the back alley of their home toward *la resaca*. Unable to catch up with her, Máge told Balde to go after her and bring her back home. He took off running and caught up with Míne. However, before she knew it, Balde had passed her by, looking back and laughing. He was just horsing around with her and wasn't being serious at all. He finally brought her back; Máge heard about Balde's silliness and sensitivity toward his sister, and she too began to laugh along with them.

As a young boy, Balde also liked riding horses and one morning mounted a neighbor's horse without permission. Then he rode it to their house, letting the horse poke his head through an open wooden window. Máge was asleep and woke up screaming as she felt the horse's breath and saw his large tongue over her face. Later, Balde broke his arm while trying to mount another horse without permission (he later wrote about the frightening fall for his English class at Del Mar College, in Corpus Christi, Texas).

After the fall, Balde could be seen wearing an arm cast and playing tag with his friends, jumping from one tree branch to another like Tarzan. His friends Cipriano Galván, Thomas Briones, Victor Ybarrra, Pepe Rodríguez, Joe López, and Benito Huerta all used *la resaca* as a swimming pool. One day, the boys dared Balde to swim across *la resaca*. Balde took the cast off his arm, swam across it and back, and then placed his cast back on. His friends swore nobody had ever done that before, only Balde. No one else ever dared again to swim across *la resaca,* either.

One Sunday afternoon, Balde took the galvanized tub that was used for cooking and washing and used it as a boat in the little *canalito* (small canal). The *canalito* was a small rivulet which had once flowed from *la resaca* into the barrio of El Jardín. He stopped a little girl named Betty, who was walking by on her way to church. She was dressed up that day and looking very *chula* (pretty). Balde asked her, "Betty, do you wanna get into my boat?" She said, "Yes." As she stepped into the make-believe boat, she fell into the water. Balde did not mean for her to fall, but Máge found out about it and whipped him anyway.

Betty also had a twin sister, and they both liked Balde. They also knew Balde was usually hungry, and so the girls told him that if he played with them, they would make him a food basket. Of course, Balde said yes, and all three played together by *la resaca*, while Balde got to enjoy eating his food basket. (Sixty years later, Betty's twin shared this story with us at our father's funeral.)

Balde's personality was bold, fun-loving and mischievous; he had a tender heart and was a sweet and kind jokester. He was also very helpful and a thoughtful young boy to everyone, especially his elders. Often, when heavy rains came, the *canalito* would overflow into the barrios. The streets would get muddied, and snakes would slither into *las casitas* (little houses). And as was often the case, Balde would hear mothers with babies in their homes shouting that there was a snake in the house. So, he would go into their homes and kill the snakes for them. The women liked the fact that Balde was always brave, fearless, and quick to react.

Marvel Comics: Freddy Learns of the Superhero "The Flash"

Balde was a new student at Frank Roberts Elementary when Jesús and María Villarreal and their son Louis moved into a house at 330 Commerce Street, which intersected with Biddle.

Almost immediately, the Villarreals met both Serapio and Máge and became close friends; they would often visit one another. Their son was tall (he was two years older than Balde), and as a result, they nicknamed him Big Lou.

What Jesús and Serapio had in common was that they loved reading comic books, among these were *Superman*, *Captain Marvel* (Shazam), *Captain America* and *The Flash;* they enjoyed swapping comic books. Lou was his father's middleman and when he arrived at the Huerta's home, Serapio would be seated on a small cot. Upon seeing Lou, he would grab three comic books from underneath the cot and swap them for three of Jesús' comics. This is how Balde learned about these fictional super heroes—from reading his father's comic book collection.

Needless to say, Balde then fantasized about doing everything at the speed of lightning, and of becoming fast and furious, just like *The Flash*!

Before Serapio passed away, Big Lou recalled how their fathers loved to sing songs together and whistle tunes. Sadly, Lou also remembered how quickly Serapio became thin when he became ill with tuberculosis as he spent his last few months resting on the cot.

After attending Serapio's funeral, Lou saw Balde playing at the school ground wearing a brand-new navy-blue suit. He said Balde really looked nice, and it made Balde feel good to wear something new. Then Big Lou thought, "*Wait a minute—I have a navy-*blue *suit just like that!*" So, when he went home, he asked his mother where his navy-blue suit was. His mother ignored his question. He asked her again, and she finally said to Lou, "Yes, *mijo* (son), his father died and was buried today. I gave Doña Máge some of your clothes for Balde because he needed them." With that said, Lou was okay. But Lou really liked and missed his navy-blue suit. He also said Balde was very quiet for a few days at school, but then he was okay.

Freddy becomes the Patriarch of the Huerta Family

At this point, with Serapio and Benito gone, Balde, being the eldest, knew he had his work cut out for him. He had always been seen as a disappointment in both his grandfather and father's eyes. However, he now knew that he had to carry out the responsibility of being the head of the family. He was going to have to grow up a little faster, step it up, and be more resourceful in looking out for his many siblings.

Máge was the matriarch and Balde became the new patriarch of the family. For the sake of his younger siblings, and for the rest of his life, Balde Huerta would try to keep up this role as patriarch. This obligation strengthened the bond between mother and son. Their personality traits were almost identical. And just like his mother, he too was resourceful, brave, and opportunistic.

The beauty about Balde's true nature was that he was very friendly, charismatic, and vocal. He also genuinely had a sweet sense of naiveté about him. He always smiled a lot, was charming, and was quick with his wits. He enjoyed communicating with everyone, especially the elders. And the word *no* was never part of his vocabulary.

Above all, Balde was an optimist! His great eagerness and determination (more of a hunger) had somehow become a passageway for him to survive. Though he would not know it, his many assets would come into play and serve him well in the most critical roles of his lifetime.

He began his first job by working, hustling and luring customers in front of downtown businesses such as restaurants and *cantinas* (beer joints) by singing the Mexican songs he had learned from his mother. Then he would ask strangers walking by if he could shine their shoes for a dime. The men also knew his father from working at Alexander's warehouse and were fond of Serapio, so they kindly allowed Balde to shine their shoes. The townspeople were also fully aware of the family's circumstances; therefore, the business owners allowed Balde and his brothers to work and sing for their customers. And at the end of each day, he would take his earnings home to Máge.

Across Pancho Galván's corner store, there was a business called Lola Tovar's *Restaurante*. They had a jukebox playing Mexican and English songs all day long; Balde was often seen, along with his friends, sitting on the corner of Biddle and Rockefeller streets singing along with the music at the top of his lungs. However, Pancho Galván would run Balde and his friends off because he did not want them disturbing his customers. He also thought Balde was serenading his daughters and would get upset with him. But Balde just kept returning to that same corner on Biddle Street to hear the latest records on the jukebox being played.

"From My Eyes" by Freddy Fender

I use to play on the corner of Pancho Galvan's grocery store.
I would play my guitar, which only had three strings and no back on it.
It had, uh, an Uncle Sam ring on a hat thing, you know,
like one of those Stella guitars my friend
gave to me. But before that, when I was nine or ten,
I would take a sardine can, one of those
flat ones, and take the lid off and put some screen wire on it,
and tie it up. Then I'd put a stick on it, so it would give it tension,
you know, so that I could pluck it!
It was hard to get a crowd when I was doing it because you could
still smell the sardines!
La Parranda (A Get-Together)

Balde's friend, Moisés Alvarado, gave Balde the aforementioned three-string guitar with no backside; he and his brother Alberto, Chencho García, and a few other boys from El Jardín would often sing along with him at the park by *la resaca*.

Since the people in the barrio couldn't afford radios or televisions, the boys would draw a crowd when entertaining. Everyone nearby, young and old, enjoyed walking through the park to listen to them sing. Soon after, the older teenage boys in the neighborhood began to pay Balde 50¢ to serenade their girlfriends.

By the time he was ten, Balde quickly picked up that singing and learning to play the guitar was beginning to pay off. So, from then on, he used his talent to hustle for money and food from whomever wanted to hear him sing.

Life in El Jardín is much like an ongoing *parranda* (a get-together or celebration) and a *pachanga* (fiesta or cookout) because there are many family gatherings and events held in these charming homes.

And today nothing has changed; it is still a lively and colorful neighborhood, rich with culture—a place where the people enjoy sitting outside in the early mornings drinking coffee and enjoying the scent of tropical flowers growing in their yard. Taking an evening stroll from street to street, you will see people's shadows in the windows as they visit friends and family. It is a sheer delight to hear them chatting on the patios outside their homes while sitting in pitch darkness, whispering tales that can be heard from one house to the other. Most wonderful is when one stops by to visit the elderly and they open their humble homes with joy, grateful that they have not been forgotten.

Freddy's Debut: *Los Aficionados* (Talent Contest)

Balde would visit his friend Benny Huerta in El Jardín and they would practice playing their used guitars. "It was like he was just born with that music," Benny recalled. "He would guide me on how to play guitar and with what tone." Big Lou would take his guitar there, too. And as soon as Balde would start singing, Lou would join in with his guitar. Except that Balde would have to stop Lou each time and say, "Big Lou, please! You can play with us on the next one, okay?" Then Balde and Benny would start all over, and Lou would come in and mess up the song again. Lou was a good singer, but the boys began to realize that Balde just had a different voice from the rest of the singers in El Jardín. They also knew that Balde was really preparing himself to compete at *los aficionados* (talent contest).

Baldemar, accompanied by Benny, made his singing debut at ten years old live on KGBT-AM radio in Harlingen.

Recalling how Balde introduced *himself* to legendary disc jockey Martín Rosales, Benny affirms, "I just want to clarify one thing. Nobody ever took Balde by the hand, anywhere! He took himself! Nobody ever helped push Balde's singing career, either!" He just went on his own and the boys just followed him wherever he went."

On the day of Balde's debut, all his friends, including Cipriano Galván, Tomás Galván-Briones and the other Galván boys, quickly called KGBT and voted for Balde to help him win the contest. The boys really enjoyed Balde's singing, and they truly liked their good friend Balde, period.

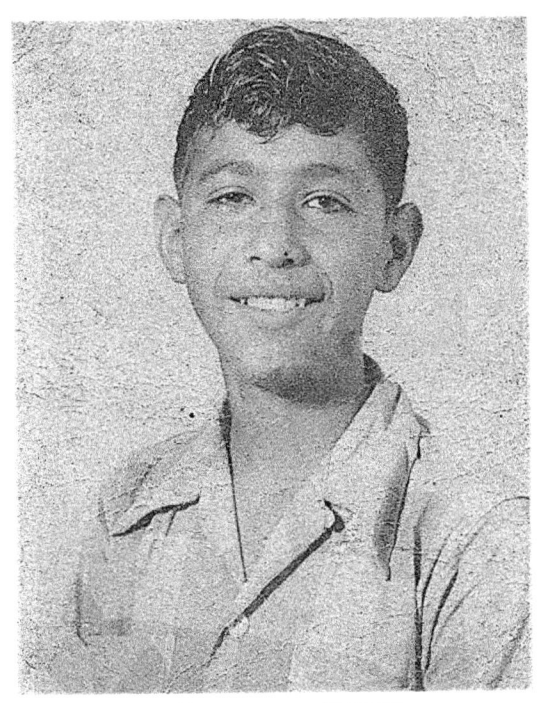

Balde at ten years old (1947)

"From My Eyes" by Freddy Fender

*At ten years old, I walked with a friend over to Harlingen City.
It was there that I entered my first talent show at El Grande Theatre de
Harlingen on Harrison Street, which is still standing. I wore* pantalones
de pechera [overalls] *and walked everywhere barefooted.
My friend won first prize of three dollars' cash, and I won second prize, which was a tub of food.
To me the food was worth more than money when you have a large family as we did.
I never forgot that day. Even my friend wanted to trade me the money for the tub of food.
I quickly took the food to Mother.
When I gave her the tub of food, she beat me. Then she asked me where I had stolen the food.
I told her that a man gave it to me, and I had won it.
So she made me take her and the tub of food all the way back to Harlingen.
She asked the man about it, and he told her that I had won it and that
I had sung a very popular song and that the kids really liked it!
I also had my first live broadcast performance on KGBS-AM radio and
KGBT-AM radio in Harlingen, where I sang that song "Paloma Querida"
("Beloved Dove").*

Chapter III

A Stepfather

Manuelon "El Aventurero" ("The Adventurer")
Migrant Student Workers "They're back!"
Freddy Soaks in Hillbilly and Soulful Music
Balde and Western Singer Luann Matlock
Good Ol' Hill Billy Jackson

Manuelon Salazar with cowboy hat—El Aventurero (The Adventurer)
Freddy's brother (Top left) Juan "Cáne," sister Minerva "Mine," and Manuelon's sons (1950s)

"From My Eyes" by Freddy Fender
At the age of ten, we migrated north to work beets in Michigan, pickles
in Indiana, and baled hay and picked tomatoes in Ohio. When that
was over, then came cotton-picking time in Arkansas.
We worked hard all year so that we can try to have a good Christmas.
That is all we ever looked forward to and coming back home to San Benito, Texas.

Manuelon Salazar was known around the Lower Rio Grande as an ambitious migrant *troquero* (trucker). He was the boss of his own crew and owner of a few fruit and vegetable stands. The workers were mainly his large family (of children) who worked the fields. He was a tall and brawny man who wore a cowboy hat and boots. His voice carried, and his robustness was more than intimidating.

He saw himself as *El Aventurero* (The Adventurer)! He was married, but he also saw many single ladies while traveling from town to town. Manuelon's zest for life while traveling could be compared to the song "Papa Was a Rolling Stone" (a heartbreaker).

One day, he stopped and had lunch at the same Mexican restaurant where Máge worked for a short time for the Castillos. She waited on him at the restaurant and noticed he was a real charmer. He too enjoyed her quick wit and sense of humor. Instantaneously, the two were attracted to one another, and before long, Máge fell deeply in love with *El Aventurero*.

"From My Eyes" by Freddy Fender

I remember Indiana for one specific event. I had a stepfather [Manuelon] *by then. Even though he never divorced his wife and only lived part-time with my mother. She loved him, and that was good enough for me. He kept his marriages together by sheer wit and charm. I learned enough to help me later on as I trudged my way through life and became a man. 'Thanks, Manny, wherever you may be. I hope the Good Lord embraces you, for even though you were a scoundrel and made Mother cry; you had some goodness within you that only the people who knew you can agree. Count me in as one of those. You know, Manny, I am taking into account that you are able to somehow hear me. I'm going to pretend that you can. After all, there is really no one to contradict me except for the Almighty. And if he does, I will be sure to know it. But I'm gonna tell a short mention of our lives when we were kids and you took us north to Indiana to pick* el pepino [cucumbers].' *As soon as my family got off your truck,* los patrones [bosses]—*all Anglos—pinned a small brooch type of relic on our shirts on the heart area. I will never forget that it was a badge in the image of a pickle with the word* Heinz. *I was so impressed at age ten. I could relate that name with a bottle of tomato ketchup that I had seen somewhere at some store. I shouted at my brothers and everyone else around, "Hey, we're working for Heinz!" We were all very happy of course except for the laborious task of harvesting the pricks of stinging* pepino *fields that waited the next day for all of us.*

Freddy at Thirteen Years Old: Working Up North in the Cotton Fields

It was the summer of 1950; Balde had just turned into a teenager while in Lapanto, Arkansas, hoeing cotton. Manuelon, *El Aventurero,* took Doña Máge and her children to work with him, along with his own children, in the heat during seasonal harvest.

Even though Máge and Manuelon were not married and lived apart, he was now head of her family. This is the closest person her children ever had to a father after Serapio died. As a result, Balde and his siblings referred to him as their stepfather.

Manuel Castillo was another one of *los patrones* (bosses); he had taken his own family up north to work the cotton fields. His son, Raúl Castillo, who was younger than Balde, was a water boy; Raúl recalls that if you were over twelve years old, you were old enough to pick cotton.

He remembered seeing Balde picking cotton from sunrise until sunset. He also recalled that Balde did not like having to pick cotton because it would scar his hands. So Balde would use a stick to separate the branches to keep the tiny thorns from pricking his fingers and making them bleed.

He also said that Balde's stepfather was abusive; Manuelon would often get drunk and start fighting with Doña Máge.

On a steaming hot day, Raúl saw Balde step in to defend his mother during a heated argument with Manuelon during which his stepfather broke out his shotgun. And to avoid Balde getting hurt, Raúl's father took Balde to a different campsite to work and stay with another family.

A few weeks later, Balde came back to the campsite. He began to play his guitar and sing and those around the camp gathered around him. Even Manuelon came out to join in and everything was tranquil and back to what was considered normal again.

"It was sad, but that was the reality of life back then," Raúl reflected.

After the seasonal harvest, Manuelon had Balde drive his mother and siblings all the way back to South Texas. Balde had never driven a vehicle before, but he quickly learned.

Out in the fields, Balde and his brothers had taken a lot of verbal and physical abuse from Manuelon's own sons because of the illicit love affair between their parents, and the boys fought frequently and furiously. However, as unbearable as it was, Balde and his siblings could not oppose their relationship knowing how their mother, Máge, felt about Manuelon. And Manuelon did love her in the best way he could for many, many years because to them, it was a real relationship.

"From My Eyes" by Freddy Fender

It was like being the captain of a ship.
The trucker, or troquero, kept a pocketbook and pencils, and the names of everyone in the family.
He loaned money and paid off the hands, settled family disputes.
It was a very important thing. I'll never forget on Saturday mornings when the heads of households would stand by the truck while the trucker paid them in brand new dollar bills.
He would call out a name, 'Jaun Garcia earned $48 and spent $16 at the company store,' and he would pay Juan $32 . . . although I never knew why, it was a very important ceremony.
And as long as the truck was around, the people knew they were being taking care of.

* * *

We were poor, but at the time, we didn't know we were poor,
and we had fun, especially outdoors when

conditions were nice. But then there were some places where
they only had a few shacks and the kids
had to sleep outside with the snakes and the hogs, where the drinking water was stagnant and
we had to bathe in the canals. But always there was the truck for shelter and shade.

From Field to Field and from State to State: Freddy Soaks in Hillbilly and Soulful Music

On his travels out of state with Manuelon, Balde listened to the latest music being played on the radio of his stepfather's truck. He quickly learned about different music genres and also realized that there were many other folks who were experiencing the same affliction of poverty that he and his family endured.

When Balde was a child laborer, he would often see many work trucks headed to other campgrounds. As they passed him by, he could hear hillbilly music being sung from the back of the pickups.

In Arkansas, he would listen to the radio and hear Western music such as Hank William's "Jambalaya," Gene Autry's version of "El Rancho Grande," and Hank Thompson's "Wild Side of Life," plus songs by Ernest Tubb and Grandpa Jones.

In other states, like Michigan, Balde had seen black folks singing across the fields as well. He heard heartrending blues and gospel melodies sung with such passion that they reached the core of his soul.

When his stepfather was not being a taskmaster, Balde would sneak away at sundown to pick his guitar with musicians from other campsites. Sometimes they would gather at the local beer joints, drink beer, and sing. They would play their guitar, banjo, and harmonica and blend their different music genres with each other—and to escape their reality of backbreaking toil.

Season after season, harvest after harvest, and the different melodies that echoed across the fields ingrained themselves into Balde's veins. He soaked in hillbilly and soulful music. As a young musician, this was perhaps the most developmentally rich time of Balde's musical career.

Traveling with *El Aventurero* from field-to-field and state-to-state, Balde worked hard picking cotton by day and guitar by night, while those experiences would one day pay off.

"From My Eyes" by Freddy Fender
On the weekends, I'd go to town with black people and try to be close to
the clubs and joints, and I'd hear some down-back-in-the-alley blues.
When we went to New Mexico to follow the onion crop, I'd only hear Spanish.
Then I'd hear Polish music when we picked the tomatoes in Ohio!
And I always managed to get Mother to buy me another guitar if the one I had was worn out.

The downtown Rivoli movie theatre (Middle-Right) on Sam Houston Road (1950s)

Los aficionados (Talent Shows)

***Los aficionados* were** amateur talent contests usually held for teenagers in the movie theatres. In between seasonal migrant work, Balde would be eager to return home and he looked forward to more work, but as a guitar player and singer. On foot, he would walk and enter every local talent show nearby.

Balde knew that if he won any prize, whether it was money or food, it would help his mother out, at least, until it was time to go back and work the crops. Above all, in spite of having a stepfather, he still considered himself as the bona fide patriarch of his family.

On certain days of the week, the movie theatres would fill up with teenagers watching the latest flicks. The theatre had a high platform in front of the big screen and the stage was used for live entertainment and to play Bingo during intermission between matinees.

The Rivoli movie theatre was mainly for *los Americanos,* and where old cowboy movies were shown. The *Palacio* (palace) Theatre showed Mexican movies with famous actors like Pedro Infante, Jorge Negrete, and Pedro Vargas. And during intermission, mariachis would perform for the audience. Local talented dancers, singers, and musicians and some artists from across the border also came to compete at talent contests where the prize was usually $3–$10, a tub of groceries, or a case of soda or popcorn.

The Ruenez theatre was another historical venue where talent contests were held on Friday nights; it is located on Díaz and W. Robertson streets. Next to the Ruenez was Castillo's Restaurant where Balde could be seen eating before walking over to the theatre to compete.

Balde would always win a prize by singing a traditional Mexican love song composed by Jose Alfredo Jimenez titled *"Paloma Querida"* ("Beloved Dove"). He was very young, and it was a very popular tune at the time, and the kids just liked the sound of his tender and unique voice, so it didn't matter if he sang the same song over and over.

Freddy Predicted His Future

Everyone was aware of Balde's talent, and when he was still a junior high school student, the San Benito High School faculty invited him to entertain during an assembly.

When Big Lou and Balde's junior high classmates found out, they all said aloud, "*orale!*" ("Let's hit it bro!") and crossed over the school ground to crash the assembly and see him perform. During that show, Balde walked from table to table; with his voice and guitar, he serenaded all the teachers, and even the principal.

The local boys from San Benito had a lot of fun growing up with Balde during their youth; when he had a gig at a *cantina,* the underage boys would hide their beers under the table.

One afternoon Balde, Big Lou and Benny Huerta went downtown to the Rivoli Theatre to see *Gone with the Wind*. When they walked out together, Balde turned back and pointed to the marquee and said, "You wait and see, one day it will say, BALDEMAR HUERTA!"

He added, "You know in my mind, I know I'm a celebrity, but I'm just the only one that knows it!" [Laughter]

"He was always telling everybody this," stated Big Lou.

Balde was supposed to sing for KGBT television the next day in Harlingen and he needed to look good for the show, so he asked the boys if they had a coat for him to wear, but none had one.

A quick thinker, Balde had spotted a nice coat hanging inside a pickup truck as they walked past a beer joint called The Hollywood club. So, he told his friends to keep on walking and that he would catch up with them. A few minutes later, Balde came running from behind and shouted, "Let's get out of here!"

The next morning, he looked sharp wearing his new, stolen black-and-white checkered jacket during his live television appearance for KGBT in Harlingen, Texas.

"From My Eyes" by Freddy Fender
I would talk the kids into clapping for me, so when I won, I would give them half of my winnings. I would give them a dollar and a half, and I would take the rest and quickly run and make it on home!

Freddy Gets Pounded to the Ground:
A Dedication "Don't Let the Stars Get in Your Eyes"

Another theatre where Balde competed was at the Azteca in Harlingen, Texas; he was fourteen years old. One evening, Big Lou, Benny Huerta and an older guy named Tampico, who lived across the border, accompanied him there. The contest would start at eight o'clock every Thursday night and the first-prize winner would receive $20.

Before the show, Balde's other buddies would already be waiting for him to arrive. However, since most of them didn't have money to get into the establishment, they would wait to walk in with him through the back door. They would bring their guitars and pretend to be contestants. This way, they could all get in free.

He told the boys that if they were going in with him, they'd better clap for him to win. He also told them that if he won, he would take them out to eat ice cream. You see, the way that they would measure the first-prize winner was by judging the audience's loud applause and the stomping of their feet.

At times, Balde would sing and play guitar against professional teenage boys and female singers from Mexico. He always felt that these young artists were so professional and had such amazing talent that they too could have been famous.

On this particular night, Balde wore blue jeans with a blue denim jacket and high army boots he had purchased from a second-hand store (they were cheaper and sometimes Balde would even get them for free).

Then it came time for Balde to compete, and the announcer, Ruben Benavides, would enthusiastically and with great fanfare introduce him: "Hee-re is Baldemar Huerta!"

He sang a few tunes, and then a rendition of a particular song he liked titled "Don't Let the Stars Get in Your Eyes." (Written by Winston L. Moore, whose stage name was "Slim Willet.") But before breaking into the song, Balde held the microphone close to his lips, looked up and said, "I dedicate this song to those tough guys up in the balcony, La Palomia Brava Del Falcón!"

Incidentally, those guys up in the balcony were *pachucos* (juvenile Mexican American gang members). There were many gangs in the Lower Rio Grande Valley, and Balde and his brothers often fought them in order to survive living in the barrio. Even though Balde was a sweet and friendly person who loved to smile, joke, and laugh with others, he lived in a tough neighborhood and he was not shy about defending himself. Freddy lived without fear, and was often known to be the first to provoke a fight.

That night, the winner of the first prize was Balde; as they walked out into the parking lot, a gang member named "El Bulto" and his gang surrounded Balde, Benny, Lou, and Tampico. As the gang took out their knives and chains, El Bulto stared Balde in the face and said, "So, you were sending a message to us, huh?"

Then one of their leaders swung his chain and hit Balde so fast and hard on his head and neck that he fell down to the ground! Balde was knocked out cold. Then the rest of the gang jumped on top of him and kept hitting and kicking him. Tampico jumped in to try to defend Balde, but they were outnumbered.

Luckily for Balde, Manuelon and Doña Máge had just driven up to pick Balde up from the Azteca. Seeing a commotion of people, they rushed into the crowd and saw Balde lying there; outraged and full of anger, Máge began yelling at the hoodlums.

Then Manuelon, who was bigger and tougher than any of them, angrily yelled out, "Who hit him?"

"I did!" El Bulto responded.

"Well, now you are going to hit me!" Manuleon said as he reached toward his back-hip belt and pulled out his knife.

Los *pachucos* saw Manuelon's knife; compared to theirs, his was actually a machete. Fearing for their lives, the gang members ran off! The next day, it was all over the local newspaper.

That night at the police station, nobody was talking, not even Balde; even though he had knots on his head; he knew it was better to stay quiet.

As it turned out, Balde was the one to see stars in his eyes that night. That incident created notoriety for Balde and, along with *los aficionados*, marked the start of Balde's teen fans following him throughout the valley. From then on, Balde began to stir up a commotion everywhere he went, even though he was just a local kid from El Jardín.

Freddy Sells his Baby Brother Manuel for *Tres Pesos* (Three Dollars)

No matter what Balde was going through while growing up, he just kept rolling with the punches; guitar or no guitar, Balde kept singing and pouring his heart out. It was almost as if he had shielded himself from whatever hurt. He did not care what people said to him. He had become desensitized to their living conditions and to the embarrassment regarding the relationship of his mother and stepfather. Right or wrong, Manuelon was the only living father he had.

Balde was hardheaded yet vulnerable, and sensitive to a fault. However, he must have had many angels protecting him because he did not let anyone deter him from his first love, which was playing his guitar and singing.

Nothing bothered him and the more Balde hurt or was disappointed, the more he sang. The more people turned him away, the harder he came at you. The more he played music, the more he could endure whatever was thrown at him just as long as he could play and sing for people. This is what gave him a sense of relief.

Something definitely drove Balde because he was not self-conscious; he did not care who was clapping for or booing him. Balde never had a shy bone in his body; I don't think the concept of fear ever existed in my father's mind, either.

Doña Máge eventually moved into a two-bedroom home with an outhouse in the backyard of 631 Rossiter Street. She gave birth to Manuela, named after her father, Manuelon. She would later die of tuberculosis. Then Máge had another baby, a boy, and she named him Manuel.

One morning, Balde overheard his mother expressing concern about how she was going to be able to afford to feed her new baby, Manuel. She had already given one baby, José Luis (El Tortillero), away. So Balde waited for his mother to leave the house to visit her friend Doña Santos—who lived on the corner of Francisco Madero

Street and Resaca Drive—to drink coffee and talk. Then he quickly grabbed baby Manuel, slipped out the back alley, and gave the baby to a couple who wanted a child.

When Máge returned, she noticed Balde eating popcorn, candy, and shooting cap guns. She asked him, "Where's Manuel?"

"Don't worry," Balde answered. "I already gave the baby away, and they gave me *tres pesos* (three dollars)!"

Upon hearing this, Máge grabbed her broom and began to beat him as he yelled and tried to explain. Poor Balde really thought he was helping his mother out by selling Manuel for $3. Besides, he got to buy candy and gave the rest of the money to his mother, so he thought he had made a smart transaction—problem solved.

To avoid getting hit with the broom again, he quickly hid from her underneath the bed. She swung her broom back and forth toward him but failed to see him. In a panic, Balde had grabbed on to the wire coils under the mattress and held himself to it like a spider.

In her desperation, Máge walked back to Doña Santos to ask for help. The two of them then took the whole bed apart. Meanwhile, Doña Santos was laughing because she knew that Balde was eventually going to have to tell his mother to whom he had sold his brother Manuel. After they took the bed apart, Máge got hold of Balde and began to beat him senseless. However, Balde managed to pull himself away from her! So, there went Doña Máge running through the park by *la resaca* after one of her kids once again.

Doña Santos and Doña Máge (smoking) in El Jardín on Resaca Drive (1960s)

Freddy Uses the Baby as a Shield

Singing for *gringos* (Anglo-Saxons) would prove to be easier than singing for Mexican Americans. Balde had learned many American hillbilly and Western songs while traveling up north with Manuelon. He would frequently walk up Business Highway 77 Sunshine Strip toward Harlingen and sing at country and Western music bars.

Even though Balde's voice was flavorful and romantic, he always sang with a heavy Mexican accent and he especially loved singing "Your Cheating Heart" by Hank Williams. However, when he sang it, it sounded more like "Your Shitting Heart."

Each time Balde attempted to enter white establishments, he would face different obstacles before he was allowed to perform because of his dark skin and heavy accent. But since Balde was a problem solver and had a great imagination, he always came up with some kind of brilliant scheme to overcome his obstacles, such as taking his baby brother Manuel along with him to sing to avoid getting beat up for being of Mexican descent.

In this scenario, he would walk into a bar and ask someone to please hold the baby while he sang for the customers. After he finished performing, he would quickly take his brother back into his arms, face everyone and say, "I have to hurry home to feed my baby brother and put him to sleep!" And it worked—problem solved!

At a young age, Balde quickly realized he had his work cut out for him as a singer. Working in the hot sun out in the fields made his complexion even darker, to the point that he looked like a black person. So, to break the ice, Balde used the quick wit, charm, and sense of humor he had acquired from his parents. After telling them a joke or two, he would be allowed inside the honky-tonks. And as soon as they heard him sing and play his guitar, well, that is all they needed to let him stay and entertain them. Balde was a solo act from the very start.

(Left-to-Right) Doña Máge, Lola's daughter María, Minerva "Mine," Manuel "Béke," Balde, and Cherín (1953)

Freddy's Youngest Brother, Manuel, Shares his Memories of their Youth

One evening, the boys went hunting on a stranger's ranch to kill a cow to eat. When the owner of the ranch saw his dead cow had been shot, he quickly called the police on the boys. When questioned, Balde and his brothers told the police that they thought they had shot a deer, which was a lie.

Then Manuel looked up to the policeman and gave his brothers away and shouted, "*Báke, báke,*" instead of *vaca*, which means cow. After the police released them, his brothers teased their baby bother and gave him the nickname of Béke.

The rancher kept the dead cow, and the boys were unable to bring the meat home to Máge. Back then, meat was so prized that you did not throw away any part of the cow. Normally, the people would go and buy meat at *las matanzas* (slaughterhouse). There they would even sell you the lungs, which is now illegal. Even our great-grandfather, Benito, went in his wagon door-to-door selling what remained of a carcass.

One morning, Béke saw his mother sweeping the dusty pavement outside her home when the police stopped by. They began to look around and she bluntly asked them, "What are you looking for, marijuana? Go to the backyard. There is a whole lot of marijuana back there!"

She was funny and to the point, just like her son Balde.

"No, Máge, I am looking for one of your sons. He was in a big fight last night," the police officer answered.

"Well, he is not here!" Máge said, and the officer left.

When Béke went to go look in the backyard, sure enough, there was a small field of marijuana.

Sometimes, when Manuelon would become abusive with Máge, Balde and his brothers would have to intervene until the cops arrived.

He had always beaten up on Máge's boys, but they were growing up and getting meaner. They would retaliate and gang up on their stepfather, but it was hard on Balde because he knew that his mom still loved Manuelon.

On the weekends, Máge's boys would get so drunk and would get into fights with local gang members in *las cantinas*. The boys would bring the violence home, continuing to fight but with one another. Furthermore, Máge would have to hide or find somewhere else to sleep and take Béke and Míne with her to avoid them getting harmed.

The boy's violence had escalated over the years and they now used weapons, especially knives, in streets and barroom fights. Máge lived in so much fear that at times she would tell her neighbors that she wanted to hang herself.

Uncle Béke simply added, "My brothers were just hoods."

"From My Eyes" by Freddy Fender

I spent the first fifteen years of my life in San Benito in a neighborhood called El Jardín.
If we wanted to go swimming, la resaca, *which was part of*
Rio Grande, was within walking distance.
Other neighborhoods were called La Palma, La Gallina, El Puente De Los Dos Amores, and

El Barrio Americano. You see, in those years, we called them Americanos *because they were white skinned and walked around as if they were the best that God could fabricate. We Mexicans looked the other way and didn't believe that it was worth it to protest our subservient way of life. The only thing we could do was to come together, and very few of us assimilated with* los Americanos. *The rest of us continued to live our lives by migrating up north and staying in good old San Benito, Texas.*

Benito's Ghost

In town, Máge and her brothers were often seen carrying their lunch pails and smoking their cigarettes as they headed across the street over Hwy 77 Sunshine Strip to go pick vegetables. As strange as this may sound, my Aunt Míne swore that while they were working there, their Uncle Porfirio looked up and saw his father Benito's ghost standing on top of the shed. He was smiling down at them; everyone there also saw Benito's ghost.

As for Manuelon *"El Aventurero,"* he did very well for himself and opened up several fruit stands and grocery stores for his own family. It was clear he never intended to leave his wife or children and he would never come to marry Máge, but he would stay with her on weekends and during harvesting seasons.

During one of his visits, Manuelon arrived with a truckload full of watermelons. He dropped off sacks of fruits to share with his second family and spent the night with Máge at the nearby motel across the street on 77 Sunshine Strip. And the next morning, he walked out to find his watermelons had all disappeared.

He never found out who took the watermelons. However, for the next few weeks, everyone in El Jardín enjoyed eating the best, most-mouthwatering valley watermelons around town, compliments of Manuelon.

"From My Eyes" by Freddy Fender
It is the Chicano way of life. For people to see Mexican Americans as they really are, a humorous people who have laughed in order to survive. To show their way of humor, way of language, values, customs, and show people that under the right conditions any flower can grow.

Luann Matlock: "When I Think about Balde, I Think about 'Alabama Jubilee.' He Had this 'Bebop' Beat Pat Down Even Way Back Then."

After following the crops, every fall, the Huertas would return home around mid-December. After missing the first three months of school, it was difficult and nearly impossible for them to catch up on their homework. And as the local migrant kids would walk into their classrooms, the full-time students would chorus aloud, "They're back!"

At San Benito Jr. High School, Balde's curriculum included taking choir and playing football with the San Benito Greyhounds.

A very special school friend named Luann Matlock met Balde during their lunch hour when she noticed him sitting outside, alone, playing his guitar and not eating lunch. She was a hillbilly singer and a very beautiful one at that. She had a pretty voice like Barbara Mandrell. Luann heard him singing hillbilly songs and joined him. During their lunch break, they would sing together, and she liked listening to him play his guitar.

They both had different styles of music, but since he knew all the songs she liked, they began to perform at San Benito's school assemblies. Other schools nearby had their own assemblies as well. This is when Luann and Balde would ride along together on the school bus to go and perform for other schools.

Balde would sing his favorite songs for the students. Then, when it was Luann's turn, she would sing and Balde would back her up on the guitar. They hit it off great!

"Balde just always had that guitar with him," she said.

Clear as a bell, she recalled, "Balde and I sang country songs, and he always sang 'Alabama Jubilee,' an old tune made popular by Red Foley (composed by George L. Cobb and Jack Yellen, 1915). And you could count on him to sing 'Alabama Jubilee,' which had this real good beat to it, and he had this 'bebop' beat down pat even way back then. Singing, 'You ought to see Deacon Jones when he rattles his bones, Old Parson Brown foolin' around like a clown. Aunt Jemima, whose past eighty-three, shouting I'm full of pep! Watch yo' step! Watch yo' step!'

"He would stop when he got to *'watch yo step,'* and everybody would go crazy! He would move to the music, and he was just so dramatic!

"When he went on that stage, he was very sure of himself. He had command even back then. So, when I think of Balde, I think of 'Alabama Jubilee' because it had a lively beat to it, and he'd get into that with that guitar. Next, I would sing 'Caribbean.'

"I remember it was about the last few months of junior high school. On these exchanges of assemblies that we went to, I noticed that Balde never took a lunch, and it took a few times for me to realize he never ate lunch, either. So, I told my mother, 'I don't think Balde ever has a lunch because he never takes a sack lunch.' Balde never said anything. He just didn't have one.

"Mother would pack an extra lunch, and I'd just say, 'Here, Balde, I have an extra sandwich. Do you want one?'

"Maybe it was a potted-meat sandwich or something like that because we were not exactly rich, but I always took him a sack lunch, and he took the lunch and he ate it. Balde was never the kind to say, 'Oh, what kind is this?' or anything like that, but he always told me, 'Oh, this is so good!'

He never met my mother because we didn't want to embarrass him or intimidate him so we addressed it rather gingerly.

Expanding on the music, Luann said, "Balde would always take his guitar to history class. The teacher would ask him questions, and he'd say, 'Miss, if I could sing, I could think better.'

"'You mean, I could do better,' the teacher replied. However, I think that Balde did mean 'I could think better.'

"So, the teacher would allow him to sing. He would get up and sing for us, and he was not bashful at all with his music, not at all!

"We used to talk about it all the time. Balde knew what he wanted and knew what he wanted to be!

"I lost contact with Balde after he dropped out of school in the ninth grade and went back out-of-state to work in the fields.

"All the things that I've heard about Balde since, I never knew. I never saw that side of him at all. He was a perfect gentleman when we went to these assemblies. I never saw anything bad in him, and I've heard so many people say he's had such a bad stretch in his life.

"My most memorable time with Balde will always be, I think, is when we would just sit and eat our lunch together. I regretted I never got to see him in concert after he became so famous. I used to tell my husband, 'I want to see him. I'm sure he would remember me!'"

Mrs. Luann, I am sure Balde would have remembered you. I bet my life on it. Father never, ever forgot a soul, especially one as kindhearted as you and your sweet mother. Thank you.

Luann went on to sing with a local band, won a talent contest in Corpus Christi, and landed a spot on a national television show. When Brenda Lee left the *Ozark Jubilee* out of Springfield, Missouri, Red Foley offered her the spot, but Matlock's father said no, and that put an end to her aspirations.

"From My Eyes" by Freddy Fender

I was plunkin' on the guitar and realized that people were really diggin' it.
I called it Chicano country [Mexican hillbilly]. *I just couldn't feel it* [Spanish] *in my youth.*
So why do something you just can't feel? I liked to listen to Chicano music—but not deliver it.
I've just always been into gringo music.

Balde's singing and playing the guitar started to dominate his time to the point that it was interfering with his concentration in school. To find out what transpired during this time, Mother and I went to visit Mrs. Pat Gossett in Mission, Texas. Gossett, who was his ninth-grade math teacher, was tall, a long blonde-haired beauty, and this is what she remembered.

"He did not like to do his math homework. He just didn't settle down, and we had some difficulty over this. And because I made him stay after school, this is how I got to know him very well.

"'First, I want to sing you a song,' Balde would tell me. Then he would do his math and that's how we would work it! In fact, Balde was so popular that some of his football teammates would sit and wait for him to get done with his homework. Then she paused and gave a short sigh before giving me her next statement.

"The worst advice I ever gave to a student is when I said, 'If you don't put down that guitar and learn some math, you're never going to amount to anything!' Thank goodness, he didn't listen to me and give up his guitar!" Mrs. Gossett said with a smile.

Thirty years later, Balde asked Mrs. Gossett to play a schoolteacher in the movie *She Came to The Valley* where he portrayed the starring role of Pancho Villa. It was a true story filmed in Mission, Texas. Balde must have felt Mrs. Gosset was very maternal as he also called her forty-five years later to tell her about his mother's passing.

"From My Eyes" by Freddy Fender
After returning home from migrating up north, I had a
difficult time keeping up with my classmates.
I was having trouble with math, and I thought I was dumb.
It got to where I was too embarrassed to ask the teacher for help.
I fell behind, and I could understand my comrades didn't have time to pick up the wounded.
So, I got this grand idea of joining the military to become big, like John Wayne.
Of course, two days after boot camp, I wanted to come home.

Good Ol' Hill Billy Jackson: "Yep! He was just living out his future!"

Another precious interviewee whom I had the pleasure to meet was an older gentleman by the name of William "Billy" K. Jackson, or shall I say, *Good Ol'* Hill Billy Jackson. The interview took place in a nursing home in the small town of Raymondville, Texas. I waited in anticipation in the conference room as he was brought in a wheelchair to greet me.

I knew right away, as I had done my homework, that he knew my dad in a special kind of way. Jackson referred to Father as Balde (his given name) rather than Freddy, his professional stage name. He was a gringo who knew Father as a young boy; therefore, he had my undivided attention.

He just stared at me, sitting quietly with anticipation and watching me set up my recording equipment. I placed a Freddy Fender Tour cap on his head and then pressed the play button on my oversized boom box disk player. The sound of Freddy's voice and old tunes from the 1950s and 1960s began to fill the room. I just knew it would spark up a memory or two. Then I sat down, studiously eyeballing him a little, and waited for his reaction.

It worked! I woke up the dead as his eyes literally lit up right in front of me. He had a big grin on his face from ear to ear. It is an awesome feeling to make people feel so doggone wonderful and alive again. Only Balde's voice could possibly make something like this happen in a split second. Just like that—it all came back to him. Jackson spoke up all right!

"I met Balde when he was very young," he said. "He had this shoe-shine box strapped over his shoulder. Yep, he started it out that way! He'd be singing in those bars. Yup, them gringos didn't care if he was Mexican because they all knew him.

"He would sing, and they'd ask one another how he learned to sing like that!

"He would just sit down and let it all come out, and them gringos would say, 'That son of a gun, I don't care if he is Mexican, he can sure damn sing!' Them gringos liked Balde, and they let him enter them bars, yup.

"He was just living out his future," old Jackson declared.

"Balde would just talk to everyone! The kids would ask him if we were going to get in some kind of trouble so that Balde would involve the students.

"He didn't talk about his past, he was just living out his future," Jackson again affirmed.

Balde came to Jackson one day and said, "Well, Jackson, I went and joined the marines!"

"Just like that!

"I told him, '*You* crazy son of gun, you are crazy,' and Balde just laughed. Balde was excited about leaving. He was just plain tired about being out on the streets." Jackson clearly remembers it just as if it were yesterday.

I left Jackson listening to Balde's unforgettable tunes, a compilation of 1950s and 1960s roots of Tejano rock songs. Freddy left us so many incredible Spanish rock songs and Spanish/English love ballads.

As I walked away, I could hear him down the hall singing along under his breath. That is all I knew to do for *Good Ol'* Hill Billy Jackson. And I knew in my heart that it was plenty. It was the first and last time that I saw Jackson alive. With much regret, I was a year too late in bringing him back a Texas barbeque sandwich that he so desired to taste once again.

As for Balde's education, because he had grown up in a family of migrant workers, he was unable to complete the ninth-grade level and eventually dropped out of school. The unfortunate circumstances had forced him to take a different avenue as he hungrily searched for direction and adventure.

Chapter IV

Private Huerta

A Marine's Guitar
Liberty
Get squared away!
First Composition "Ay Amor" ("Holy One")
Discharged Under Honorable Conditions

U.S. Marine at sixteen (1954)

Private Huerta kept up with all the latest hit songs regardless of where he was stationed, and he never stopped singing or playing guitar. However, he and a few other teenage marines also enjoyed cutting up just a little too much. As was evident the day he stood laughing at his buddy Leonard Encinas, who was stooped over the bar. Balde asked jokingly, "Why, Encinas, do you keep letting them knock you out like that?"

Encinas would constantly get into trouble and was thrown into the brig time after time, and Balde would inevitably follow him.

While locked up, the warden would ask Huerta, "Do you know how to play the guitar?"

"Yes, sir," Huerta responded.

"Do you know how to sing?"

"Yes sir!" Huerta answered.

"If you don't, I will break this guitar over your head!" the warden warned Huerta.

"They were tough on all of us," Encinas stated.

"From My Eyes" by Freddy Fender

I remember singing and playing my guitar for my drill instructors while in boot camp.
They would awaken me during the middle of the night and take me to platoon headquarters
to serenade everyone. I was only sixteen years old. I know that I was already picking and singing
before I got to the Marine Corps; but I honestly don't know how they found out!
This was a major part of my life as a marine; for later on, when I was stationed in Japan
and Okinawa, I was a tanker but unofficially,
I was allowed by the battalion commander to join Special Services.
Hey, little did I know I would be the future Freddy Fender, the singing marine, and proud of it.

Music Timeline by Music Archivist and Writer Ramón Hernández

As with most Americans of Mexican descent, Baldemar Huerta was weaned on Mexican music. However, his inquisitive, absorptive mind was beyond the norm, and he did not restrict himself to the music of his parents, especially after soaking up the tunes that he heard blacks and whites sing out in the fields during the day and the music he heard played around the campfire at night; every song expanded his knowledge of English-language tunes.

The early 1950s was a period known for the swinging orchestra sounds of the big-band era and, in rural America, bluegrass, hillbilly, Western swing or what was then generally called cowboy music. Ethnically, there was the blues, which derived from black spirituals and gospel music, and the African American style of danceable piano-based blues called boogie-woogie. Furthermore, black music was labeled "music of color," formerly called "race music,' and later referred to as rhythm and blues (plus soul music). This was also the musical era when Frank Sinatra, Bing Crosby, Andy Russell, Tony Bennett, Frankie Laine, Tennessee Ernie Ford, and other crooners reigned over radio's airwaves. Then there were the Caribbean calypso music tunes with a different beat and great lilt made popular by Harry Belafonte. These were the musical genres that Baldemar Huerta was exposed to and collectively influenced by.

Above all, one of his greatest inspirations was Elvis Presley—a musical rebel who combined hillbilly, pop, plus rhythm and blues to create a brand-new genre called rock 'n' roll. Elvis caught Balde's attention with his new, innovative sound. He was unlike any other singer. He was an original, and it was a quality that Balde admired because he too was to become an original.

Freddy Gets Sworn into the U.S. Marines

In late 1953, Balde got the grandiose idea of joining the U.S. Marines Corps; he got the idea from watching the movie *Sands of Iwo Jima*, starring John Wayne, at the Rivoli Theatre. Thereafter, he and his school friend *Good Ol'* Hill Billy Jackson decided to join the marines together.

Balde's stepfather Manuelon took Balde to the local recruiting station so that Balde could enlist in the marines. However, Manuelon arrived intoxicated and could not answer the appropriate questions asked by the recruiter. On top of that, the age shown on Balde's birth certificate was in question. There had been a typo stating he was born in 1938 when in fact he was born in 1937, making him younger than he really was. Ultimately, Doña Máge came to the station and signed the form, giving permission for Balde to join the military at sixteen years of age. *Good Ol'* Hill Billy Jackson did not pass his entry exams, but Balde was able to join and went to camp without a marine buddy.

U.S. Marine recruiters combined those who had enlisted in the Rio Grande Valley with those who signed up in San Antonio, Texas. The result was the formation of the newly formed 161-man Alamo Marine Platoon, which was the largest unit to be assembled within a six-month period.

On the day of the formal ceremony, the new recruits were photographed marching down North Alamo Street to the front of the famous Texas shrine, where on January 26, 1954, they were sworn into the U.S. Marine Corps. Balde's assigned service number was 145-44-03; he was five feet eight inches tall and weighed 139 pounds when he joined the marines.

That evening, they were flown to the beautiful city of San Diego, California. From there, they rode a bus to commence their ten-week boot camp training at Marine Corps Base Camp Pendleton near Oceanside, California, with their platoon's headquarters based in San Francisco, California.

Marine Baldemar Huerta (**Top-Left** First on second row)
U.S. Marine Corps Recruit Depot, Platoon 422, San Diego, California (1954)

Camp Fuji, Japan: Company "B" Marine Division Infantry

While stationed in Camp Pendleton, Huerta was not eligible for duty in combat area because he was still underaged, at least not until his upcoming birthday on June 4, 1954. However, prior to his birthday, he was promoted to private first class (PFC), and his primary duty was as a guardsman.

A year later, Huerta embarked aboard the USNS *General Brewster* (T-AP-155) from San Diego, California, and sailed to Kobe, Japan, arriving on February 14. He was assigned Baker Company, Third Tank Battalion, Marine Division Infantry (foot soldier), in Fujioka, a place they nicknamed Tin Camp (South Camp Fuji), where he stayed for six months as troops from the States were rotated back and forth.

There, Huerta learned to fire a .30-caliber M1, SS carbine, and worked in a mechanical maintenance area. In addition, he worked as a mess man, whose duties consisted of preparing meals in the kitchen for the servicemen and officers.

Ten months after making PFC, Huerta passed the test for advancement to lance corporal (L.Cpl.).

Wasted Days and Wasted Nights

Freddy Borrows a Guitar: Out on Liberty

Pete López, also in the Third Tank Battalion but assigned to the motor transport division of Charlie Company, was sitting under a tree and playing his guitar when Balde walked up, sat next to him, and asked if he could use his guitar. When López heard Balde play, he felt embarrassed because he paled in comparison. "To put it bluntly, I stunk at playing guitar," López said with a chuckle. They became friends, and Balde tried to teach López how to play guitar.

The barracks, which were attached to the transport division, were about half a block away from each other and near the mess hall. So, each evening, Balde would borrow Lopez's guitar and head for the mess hall or the slop shoot club to perform for the marines for a few hours, his friend recalled.

Then he added, "He just loved to play the guitar and if he did not have a guitar, he would go find a place where someone was playing music. But again, the guitar was always on his mind—all of the time. He just loved to play that thing, you know!"

One weekend, while on liberty from Tin Camp, Balde and López, along with two other marines, went into town to have a good time. They were Joe Estrada and John "Chief" Karate, a Native American from New Mexico. The problem was that the Indian would get drunk on just two beers and get wild and crazy. Afterward, they walked back to the barracks; but this time, Chief picked up a rock and threw it at a marine who was walking ahead of their group. His name was Guerra, and his complexion was so light that he looked like a white person, which must have bothered him.

"Who the hell threw that rock?" Guerra asked as he turned around.

Without hesitating, Chief quickly answered, "I did, and what are you going to do about it?"

In a snap, Guerra hit Chief and knocked him to the ground. Balde joined in, and he too was clobbered. Then López decided to join the fight, and he too got knocked out!

The next morning everyone (with the exception of Estrada) woke up with bruises and black eyes.

"How come you're not all black and blue?" the guys asked Estrada angrily.

"Well, someone had to hold and protect the guitar!" Estrada said as he held up everyone's favorite instrument. So, they let Estrada off the hook.

One of their favorite off-base hangouts was the Cherry Bar, a beer joint that catered to Mexican American marines. Of course, Balde would take López's guitar into the bars to sing and play for them. The joint did not have a jukebox, so the owner would buy the latest records to spin on a record player for the customers. The gootchi girls (friendly and social) would come by the Cherry Bar and meet up with the marines. Balde would sit and entertain them by playing his guitar while keeping up with the latest music he heard on the radio and jukebox.

Another bar, the Eden Club, catered to military officers and Balde was an enlisted man. However, the officers would frequently invite him inside just so they could listen to him sing with accompaniment by a fellow Texan on piano and a Japanese orchestra. Balde was very grateful to the musicians and would always thank them for backing him up. One favorite he enjoyed singing was "Cucurrucucú Paloma," a Mexican *huapango* (Composed by Tomas Méndez Sosa, 1954) made popular by Lola Beltran and later made famous by Harry Belafonte in the American market. Balde would hit those high notes without fail and each time, nobody knew how he was able to reach them.

Carlos Castillo, Balde Huerta, Reyes Quintero, Pete López at the Cherry Club in Fujioka, Japan (April 27, 1955)

You need to get squared away! Get squared away!"

Regrettably, military regulations became somewhat difficult for PFC Huerta to adhere to. He soon felt out of his element and became noncompliant, unable to conform to a restricted way of life. Records show that PFC Huerta was convicted by court martial for several violations while serving overseas in Japan. One of the violations was under Article 90. UCMJ, SP. when he willfully disobeyed a lawful command from his superior because he did not place his shoelaces back into his shoes when told.

On another instance, Balde was charged for appearing in an unclean uniform. When found guilty, he had to forfeit a range of $25–$50 pay per month, plus do several months of confinement and hard labor.

Furthermore, his rank of PFC was reduced to PVT (Private). In military terms, he was demoted from E-2 to E-1 pay grade.

On August 25, 1955, his marine division boarded LST 529 in Numazu, Honshu, Japan, sailed for five days, and disembarked in Naha Port, Okinawa, from Camp Fuji with the Fourth Tank Battalion and the newly arriving Third Marine Division.

Since Huerta's marine division had been transferred from Fujioka to Okinawa, Japan, López gave Balde his guitar as a parting gift, and because he couldn't play it as well.

While in Okinawa, PFC Huerta was competent and proficient in his new assigned military duties as an 1800 Tank Crewman. However, as both López and Carlos Castillo recalled, Balde had been feeling discontent and began to smoke excessively and drink liquor to the point that his buddies would often tell him, *'You need to get squared away! Get squared away!'* But it was to no avail.

Once more, Huerta was charged on another incident under the UCMJ of Article 91 (Insubordinate Conduct toward a Warrant Officer or NCO). While working in the mess hall, Balde was told to prepare a salad. However, Balde felt he was constantly being hassled by one of the noncommissioned officers (NCOs) and told him, "Don't rush me, you chicken shit," or words to that effect. The officer also reported that Balde had threatened him with a knife.

After the sentence, Huerta was found not guilty of the assault violation, but guilty of Article 92 (Uniform Code-Failure to Obey Any Lawful Order or Regulation). Again, he received hard labor for twenty days and forfeiture of $25 for one month.

"From My Eyes" by Freddy Fender

I had several encounters with my superiors. The first time this officer gave me an order, and I told him he could well, anyway, I got in a lot of trouble. The second time was in Okinawa.
I was drunk on duty. Then the third time was during the mess duty.
I was cutting salad; I was being punished for some other thing, you know.
A superior officer gave me a lot of sh—t and when
I turned around, he ran away hollering that I was trying to attack him with a knife.
Well—I mean, hell—how the hell you gonna cut a salad without a knife?

Balde had been sad and was homesick because when he had left home, he had had a crush on a young girl named Mary Alice Contreras. And when she'd walk by him at the park by *la resaca*, he would sing "Paloma Querida" at the top of his lungs. Although he never asked her out on a date, she was his first puppy love.

Feeling homesick, woeful, lovelorn and in the process of drowning his sorrows, he wrote his first song, a Spanish love ballad that he titled "Ay Amor." He later translated it into English and that version became legendary as the unforgettable tune known as "Holy One." His composition "Ay Amor" would become his first record ever to be released under his birth name of Baldemar G. Huerta.

Balde holding guitar with a Marine buddy (1955)

"From My Eyes" by Freddy Fender
*It was a song I wrote in 1955 for a girl I left behind. I gave it that title because
I thought she was holy, and in my mind, she was my first love.
Of course, I was too—holy, at that time.*

Marines in Camp Hansen, Okinawa, Japan (1956)
Balde holding a .30-caliber M1 rifle with Marines Joe Estrada and Pete López

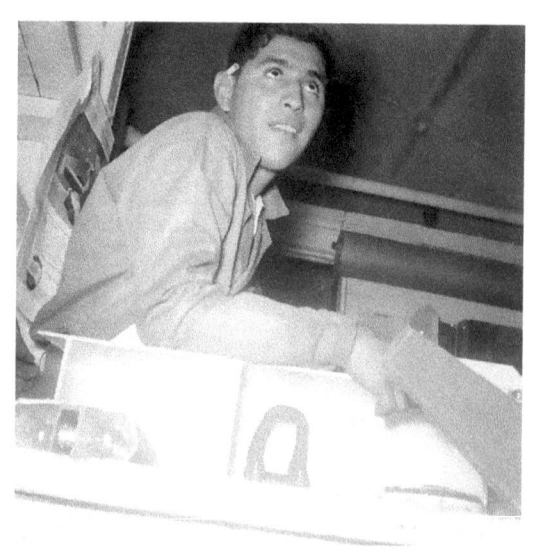

Balde with cigarette on his ear aboard ship cabin

Balde squatting (in center) with Marine buddies (1956)

"From My Eyes" by Freddy Fender

I was a gunner on an M-47—I was good too. I could hit an ant on the side of a mountain with the tank's 90 mm gun. I reported to Okinawa from Camp Fuji with the Fourth Tank Battalion. They shipped us from South Camp Fuji on landing ship tanks.
We arrived at Naha Port and drove our tanks to Easley Range [now Camp Hansen]. We had no camp, and we slept on the ground under tents while engineers built Quonset huts. One of the first huts was where officers and enlisted men dined and partied together. I remember one night I was standing guard duty when a couple of army friends from Camp Zukeran [now Foster] talked me into a little party. Well, I put down my rifle, picked up my guitar, and started to play. That performance landed me in the brig.
(Ron Appling, USMC Sgt. *Japan Pacific Stars and Stripes*. 1982)

* * *

I got my point of view from the time I spent in the brig.
It seemed that I just couldn't adjust myself to such a disciplined way of life.
I always liked to play the guitar in the barracks and drink so much that sometimes—
I forgot who and where I was.

Freddy Returns to the United States in a Brig

On May 13, 1956, Huerta boarded the USNS *General M.M. Patrick* and sailed back to the United States. For over two months, he was assigned to the H&S Company Marine barracks, U.S. Naval Station Treasure Island, San Francisco, California. However, unbeknownst to him, Carlos Castillo, also a marine buddy from Fujioka, had already been rotated back to the States prior to Balde's return.

Castillo's division was in charge of the brig at the port of San Francisco, and as he walked down to the brig, he saw Balde coming up the stairs with an MP walking behind him. Huerta gave Castillo a nod, as if to say hello, and then winked his eye at him as he passed him by. Later, Castillo was given the order to read and translate all of the love letters that Huerta had written to his puppy love.

He had been charged with the UCMJ of Article 128 (Assault), pulling the sergeant's pants down, and Article 134 (All Disorders and Neglects to the Prejudice of Good order and Discipline in the Military).

This is what actually occurred in Okinawa: Balde and another one of his marine buddies named Oliver were always playing jokes on each other; except this time one of them backfired! The incident involved a sergeant who looked just like Oliver from the back. What got Balde in trouble is that he ran behind the sergeant and pulled down his pants while under the impression that it was Oliver, a simple case of mistaken identity.

"It was a joke! We were all just kids, and he really thought it was Oliver!" Castillo and López confirmed the story, and both could only chuckle at the unfortunate circumstances of having to witness Balde struggle to be an obedient, orderly marine.

PVT. Huerta would continue adding to the list of charges upon his arrival in San Francisco. For unknown reasons, on the evening of July 25, Huerta went into town without permission and was thereupon charged with being AWOL.

"From My Eyes" by Freddy Fender
I regret what happened between the military and me.
If I had it to do over again, it would be different.
I would join today, but I'm afraid they'd use me for target practice.

Old Marine Buddies Reunited at the Famous Hollywood Palomino Club

Fast-forward to 1975 when Balde was scheduled to perform at the famous Palomino Club in Hollywood where Pete López and his spouse waited in the audience, Pete told his wife that he knew Freddy Fender.

"Aw, you're crazy," she responded.

"No, really, honey, we were in the marines together!" Pete assured her.

"Immediately, I became anxious and worried that I was not going to get to see Balde and prove to my wife that I knew Freddy. So, before the concert, I went backstage, and all of a sudden, there he was, sitting down tuning his guitar.

"I hollered, 'Huerta!'

"He looked right at me and questioned me, 'López?' Right away, he said, '*El Troquero!*'

"'Yeah, the trucker,' I answered.

"And the first thing he asked me was, 'Did you ever learn how to play the guitar?'" López chuckled again.

That memorable evening, 24 years later and at the Palomino Club, López proudly proved to his wife that he did know the famous Freddy Fender after all.

Furthermore, López never forgot how Balde would assist with writing to his mother for him. He recalled how Private Huerta would use the fancy words from his songs.

Thirty-five years later, marine buddies Freddy Fender and Carlos Castillo reunite in Hollywood, CA. (1990).

Discharged Under Honorable Conditions

For the record, a commanding officer did request for an immediate execution of discharge showing character of separation with the condition other than honorable; however, that was immediately cancelled. Authority: Title 10, U.S. Code, Section 1552 (The U.S. Secretary of a military department may correct any military record of the Secretary's department when the secretary considers it necessary to correct an error or remove an injustice.) As noted from the service secretary, the reason for his separation from the military was his misconduct discharge because of frequent board action.

Nonetheless, for almost forty years, Balde lived with the disappointment of his actions and the assumption that he was dishonorably discharged, period. The records show he was not available to sign, nor was he ever informed about the outcome either.

Wasted Days and Wasted Nights

Thanks to *Above & Beyond, "Former Marines Conquer the Civil War,"* a wonderful book published in 2003 and written by authors Rudy Socha and Carolyn Darrow, Freddy learned the truth that on August 8, 1956, Private Huerta had received a general discharge under honorable conditions. He had also earned the National Defense Service Medal for service to his country.

A "CAN DO" Attitude

Even though Balde did not experience any real gun battle while in the armed services, he did experience extensive military training shooting guns, using explosives, and whatnot. As a result, his eardrums were affected and somewhat damaged by the loud noise of explosions. For the rest of his life, Balde had difficulty hearing, which only made him speak louder, and people always thought he was shouting. However, when speaking, the sound of his voice became even more commanding.

I just want to say that on my late father's behalf, yes, he was very young, foolish, obtuse, and perhaps too free-spirited for his own good; however, these incidents were also the early signs of alcohol abuse.

With regard to his military stint, there are no excuses. Balde did disregard orders and disrespected several authority figures in the military. From day one, the military officers had him doing basically two jobs, carrying out his daily military duties and performing for them during their evening hour functions.

Balde learned discipline and the importance of a "CAN DO" attitude in the Marines Corps. It is what motivated him to later push himself to his limit in keeping commitments and following through on all aspects of his career. However, the real battle of his life would be when, one day, he would have to find the will (the courage) to fight and save his own life.

Yes, I am absolutely positive Father learned a lot because of the discipline that was instilled in him when he was in the marines. It would be an advantage that would assist him in becoming a great man toward the latter part of his life. And if you don't believe me, read the whole life story of Freddy Fender; let grown men, including his band members, tell you more about how Private Huerta taught them a thing or two about being a good soldier. He was a man of *true* honor who fulfilled his duty to God, family, friends, and fans around the globe.

U.S. Marine Corps Private Huerta (1956)

"From My Eyes" by Freddy Fender

*I love America! I would vow to fight for her causes at the drop of a sombrero!
We have a deep love for where we were born, like in Texas or
New Mexico. I am not a patriotic American.
I am a patriotic Mexican American. My roots are in
Mexico, but I am an American-born citizen.
That is why we remain here and the influence is still the same.
We know we belong here even though the government has changed hands.
I am an American, but like my people, my thoughts differ. We don't believe in women's lib.
We don't want for things we don't need. As long as there is
love and food in the home, everything is perfect.
We are extremely jealous and possessive of our women.
With Mexican people, there is no such thing as "girls' night out." That is taboo.
And I wouldn't think of letting my wife dance with another man.
We just don't go for that stuff. And we don't laugh at or joke with our elders.
We have too much respect for our elders. And we don't believe in an old folk's home.
These are just some of the qualities my people have.
By studying history, I have found that is the way the Americans are.
I think things are going so fast these days that Americans have forgotten how to be good.
Americans must learn to be humble and truthful even if it hurts.
I hope it never happens, but if a war broke out between
America and Mexico, I wouldn't give it a second thought. I'd fight for America!*

General Discharge

Under Honorable Conditions
from the Armed Forces of the United States of America

This is to certify that

PRIVATE BALDEMAR HUERTA 145 44 03

was Discharged from the

United States Marine Corps

on the 8TH *day of* AUGUST 1956 *under honorable conditions*

B. K. BANCROFT, CAPTAIN, USMC

DD 257 MC 1 MAY 1950 (1900)
S/N 0102-LF-002-4500
☆ U.S. GOVERNMENT PRINTING OFFICE: 1986-605-009/26990 2-1

Private Baldemar Huerta 145-44-03 was discharged "under honorable conditions." (1956)

Tammy Lorraine Huerta Fender

Chapter V

Las Califas

Balde and La Califa
"Slaying In Mission District"
La Villita known as The Town Talk
"Our lifestyle was called survival"
Honeymoon "You better take care of her"

My maternal grandmother, Pauline Nieto, and her family are originally from the Rio Grande Valley—Harlingen, Texas. She lost both parents at a young age and was only 13, barely a teenager, naive and trusting, when she met a man ten years older named Marcus Muñiz (my grandfather). Soon after, she became pregnant by him, and he insisted they both leave town immediately. Her brothers tried to catch up and stop Marcus from stealing their little sister away, but they were too late.

Her father, Simón Nieto, who was from Mexico, had been a successful store owner. He owned much land and a home in the Harlingen area. One evening, before closing up shop, he went to the back alley to empty out the trash bins and was brutally attacked by a few young men with knives. One of them held both his arms back and the other slashed him across his belly. Instead of walking home to his family, Nieto, holding his innards, walked to the hospital emergency clinic nearby, collapsed on their front door, and died.

Because she was too naive to know better, Pauline was unaware that Marcus was very close with the hoodlums who had killed her father. Marcus had a long criminal record and made the local newspapers each time he was caught. Nevertheless, the manner in which the murder transpired was suspicious. My great-grandfather had been a well-to-do businessman, but sadly, Pauline never prospered or saw a dime from her father's estate; it all went to her siblings, who lived back home in Harlingen, Texas.

After he snatched her away, Marcus drove Pauline to the West Coast, married her, and settled in the big city of San Francisco. They lived at 3153 Seventeenth Street in a Spanish-speaking area known as Mission District. Their upstairs apartment above the Three Pals Club boasted the distinction of being the site where, a year prior, a man had been killed at the bar during a gun battle with the police.

My grandfather Marcus was a short European Spaniard with medium brown hair and fair skin. He had been a migrant worker back in the Rio Grande Valley and then became a sheet metal laborer in the shipyards of San Francisco. My grandmother, Pauline, was a beautiful Spanish fair-skinned woman with big brown eyes. Together they had eight children, four boys and four girls. The boys' names, from the eldest to the youngest, are Michael, Gilbert, Jerry, and Paul. The girls' names are Mary, Evangelina (my mother), Beatrice, and Sylvia. Since Pauline was raised Catholic, their children also attended Saint Charles Catholic School; Pauline and the children would pray together every day.

Pauline worked hard to feed her children and toiled all day for long, exhausting hours at a laundromat washing and folding clothes. Then she would go home and repeat the same chores because she liked having everything neat and clean, even ironing the pillowcases and family undergarments.

Michael ("Mike") was born when his mother was only thirteen. Mike remembers watching his youthful mother playing jacks joyfully on the floor along with his sisters; she also relished cooking for them and taking good care of her eight children.

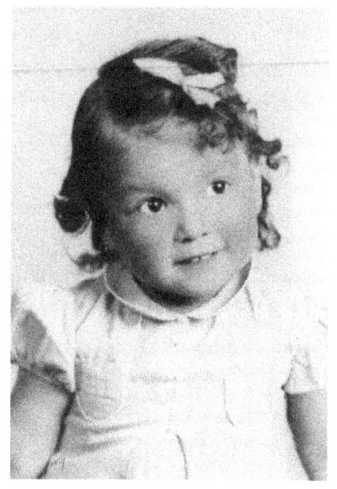

Evangelina Nieto Muñiz-Huerta

Evangelina

My mother, Evangelina Nieto Muñiz, was born on January 12, 1941. She is petite, has big brown eyes and a white porcelain-skinned face like a china doll. She is also reserved, shy, prissy, and always a lady.

My grandmother loved to dote over Evangelina. She enjoyed curling her hair with bows and setting it with hairpins every morning. However, fussing over her daughter's hair made Evangelina late for school each morning. At school, she would often stand in the hallway, crying in embarrassment at having been late for class again. Then the teacher would go out and get her to come inside. Furthermore, her schoolteacher would call her Eva, and that brought more unwanted attention to her. As a result, they held her back in the first grade for being constantly late. She also came to dislike the shortened name of Eva.

As a young girl, Evangelina became accustomed to primping and caring for herself as her mother had taught her. She would never be seen with a hair out of place, wearing pants or looking like a tomboy; instead, Evangelina wore dresses, earrings, bows, and long white gloves.

However, her father, Marcus, was very strict and kept the children confined inside their apartment. So, the children played indoors and became very close.

When Evangelina became a teenager, she noticed a pretty-faced boy who lived next door and she thought he looked so handsome, just like singer/heartthrob Ricky Nelson, whom she adored. From then on, Evangelina liked pretty-faced boys.

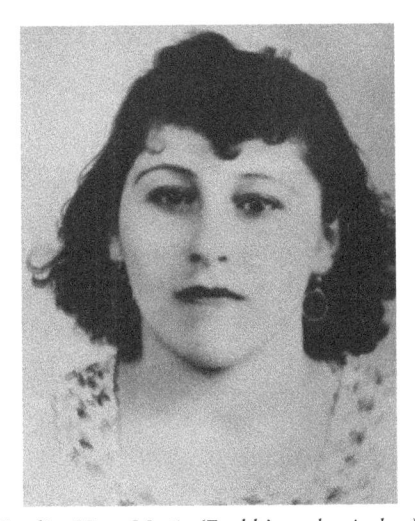

Pauline Nieto-Muñiz (Freddy's mother-in-law).

NOTE: I dedicate this recipe on my grandmother Pauline's behalf for the obvious reasons written below about her life.

Grandma Pauline's Soft-shell Corn Beef Tacos

1 lb. ground beef (fry and drain)
1 head of lettuce (thinly chopped)
Canola or Wesson oil
Corn tortillas

Sauce:

1 large can of Hunt's Whole Tomato (crushed by hand)
Add 1-2 pinches of garlic powder into the tomato sauce
Pinch of ground oregano into the tomato sauce
Pinch of salt to taste

Soft-shell Corn Tortillas: Fry corn tortilla, turn, and fold it in half before it hardens. Drain on a paper towel and add a dash of salt on tortillas (or not). While shells are hot, place tablespoon of beef inside soft shell, add lettuce, and spoonful of sauce. Delicious! Thanks, Grandma Pauline!

Grandfather Marcus Muñiz: Alcoholic, Abuser and Murderer

One terrible afternoon, Marcus came home after one of his drinking spells and threatened Pauline with a knife. Horrified and fearing for her life, Pauline looked at the girls and told them to pray for her. Then she jumped out their third-floor bedroom window to prevent Marcus from stabbing her. Frozen with fear, Evangelina held on tight to the iron bedpost. She was so scared that she peed on herself. The urine was running down her legs when she heard her mother hit the ground with a sickening thump. Then, Marcus threw the knife under the bed and took off.

Mary Josephine, the eldest daughter, called the police, and Pauline was taken to the hospital where doctors took some of her bones to reconfigure her jawbones (as seen on image). She also suffered a broken hip and ankle. After Pauline returned home to recover, she was very angry with God because he had not listened to her prayers after she had asked Him to protect her and the children from Marcus. So, she went to the shrine she had built for God, the place where she knelt and prayed every single day, and knocked over all the figurines and statues of saints, as well as the candles that were on the table.

Soon after, Pauline filed for a divorce because of Marcus' excessive drinking and increased abusive behavior toward her and the children. He had also become an unreliable provider. Pauline grew tired of having to support Marcus, his drinking habit, and being forced to endure his cruelty. Marcus did not take the divorce well.

Marcus grew more infuriated with Pauline because she was moving on with her life and had plans to marry another man. He also had been paying for child support and that made him even angrier.

Four years after the divorce, on Thursday, February 3, 1955, her friend Gladys Solórzano and her toddlers went to visit Pauline and her children. They went to a late matinee and did not return home until after ten o'clock; it was late so Gladys decided to spend the night with Pauline. They all went to bed, but before doing so,

Pauline, who feared that Marcus might show up without notice, made sure the front door to the apartment was shut closed with triple locks.

Gladys was half asleep when suddenly she heard a scream! She quickly ran down the hallway inside the apartment and saw Marcus. Then she saw Pauline's arms raised as if to shield herself, and sparks flaring out of Marcus' gun as three rounds were fired in Pauline's direction.

My grandfather Marcus had shot my grandmother dead! He shot her in the head, the chest, and her hand.

Careful not to make a noise, Gladys ran back to the bedroom with the children and hid in the closet until she heard him run down the stairs. Once again, Aunt Mary called the police, and was screaming with fear and tearfully uttering over the phone, "Hurry up and send the police. Daddy just shot Mommy!" (*The San Francisco Examiner/Call Bulletin*. "Father of 8 In S. F. Wife Murder," 1955.)

Their senses numbed, their physical bodies paralyzed, and with no understanding of what had just transpired, the children huddled in a corner of the apartment as the police took photos of the crime scene. Sadly, the younger kids were confused and upset as to why they wouldn't take Pauline to the hospital.

My *Tío* Mike told me he had gone looking for his father with a butcher knife; however, when the officers confronted him, he agreed to let the police locate his father.

Marcus was on the run; he already had a police record of arrests for vagrancy, a narcotics charge, assault upon Pauline, and now murder in San Francisco.

Marcus' face was plastered all over the news. After two days, the police found him hiding in an out of town motel in Tracy, California, where he was arrested. He was charged for murder; however, he served only five years in prison.

My grandmother, Pauline Nieto-Muñiz, whom I never got to meet and love, was thirty-one when she died and left behind eight innocent, orphaned children.

FATHER OF 8 IN S. F. WIFE

"Slaying in Mission District"
Evangelina Muñiz (seated) in shock with family friend Gladys Solórzano and babies
(Photo by Ingwerson, Henry. Reprinted with permission by *The San Francisco Examiner/Call Bulletin*. February 4, 1955.)

"Mate Held in Wife Killing. Heard Shots"
Evangelina Muñiz sitting quietly, stunned at the tragic death of her mother.
(Reprinted with permission by *The San Francisco Examiner*, pho. unk., Feb. 5, 1955)

As Documented: SNEERS AT VICTIM—"He Displayed Amazing Callousness to the Killing/Wife-Killer Suspect Calm in City Prison I Was drunk—I Wasn't Even There/Sneering Ex-Con Cold over Wife's Slaying/I wouldn't dirty my hands on her/She meant nothing to me."
(Reprinted with permission by *The San Francisco Examiner/ Call Bulletin*, pho. unk., Feb. 5, 1955)

Tammy Lorraine Huerta Fender

Evangelina "La Califa" at fourteen years old (1955- '56)

The Muñiz Siblings Return to South Texas: "The Town Talk" (*"La Villita"*)

My poor mother, Evangelina, only fourteen years old at the time, vividly remembers that night. "I just knew my mother was dead; I was just so frightened!" she said, feeling still the great loss as she recounted the memory.

On the day of the funeral, Mike attended their mother's burial, electing not to take his younger siblings to spare them from more grief. Thereafter, Mike and the children went to stay for a short while with his girlfriend (whom he eventually married). *Tío* Mike was of legal age and was able to care for his baby sister, Sylvia. Of course, social services stepped in and talked to their relatives (who lived in Harlingen, Texas) to take in the remaining six children. Otherwise, they would have wound up in an orphanage.

Once in Harlingen, the siblings Paul, Gilbert, and Jerry were split up among relatives; Evangelina, Beatrice, and Mary went to live with their *Tía* Simona.

However, moving to South Texas was a culture shock, especially considering that their grandmother, Marcus' mother, Josephine, was into some form of Santeria (Mexican voodoo) and would place candles all around the room in a circle. It would really scare the girls. As a little girl, I do remember meeting my great-grandmother; she had green eyes and long white hair down to her waist. Her complexion was white like an albino.

Evangelina recalled how they were forced to work very hard for food and shelter despite their young age. The siblings shared horror stories of the living conditions with a few of their relatives, such as going to bed without being fed, being told to sleep in the barn, or being beaten without reason. As a result, most of her siblings ran away from their relatives. My aunt Mary (the eldest) was raped by a few of her uncles. That is when she ran off to live in the closest town she knew, which was San Benito, Texas.

Speaking for my mother, the shock of losing her own mother, losing her siblings, living in a new state and city, attending a new school at Gay Jr. High School in Harlingen, facing a new culture, and living with cold, cruel strangers was just too much for a fourteen-year-old.

The Muñiz sisters, Mary, Evangelina, and Beatrice were the new girls in town and for that reason alone, the girls at her new school wanted to beat up Evangelina, who was the most girliest, timid and reserved of the three sisters. However, a tall and pretty friend of Evangelina's named Elida would stick up for her.

Every day, they would walk home together, but on one day, Elida had to turn back because she had forgotten her schoolbooks and Eva was left to walk alone. This is when the girls caught up with her behind the bleachers. Evangelina had been holding in all her frustrations; she had not had the time to mourn the loss of her mother nor to accept the fact that she had to learn to fend for herself without her siblings. Her repressed anger, sorrow, and torment finally broke loose, and her fury was unleashed.

Evangelina grabbed hold of one of the girls by her hair and rammed her head into the pavement. She just kept banging her head until she bled. The girls ran off, and Evangelina never went back to school again. Her education stopped at the eighth-grade level.

Frightened and overwhelmed, she got on the bus and left for San Benito to look for Mary. Her younger sister Beatrice stayed behind in Harlingen with other relatives. She was less than ten minutes away, but to Evangelina, San Benito was still a great distance.

In the summer of 1956, Evangelina moved in with Mary into an efficiency apartment on the second floor of 340 West Robertson Street. It is next door to businesses *La Zapateria* (shoe store) and *La Especial* (the specials) bakery, which still bakes the best Mexican *pan dulce* (sweet bread) in town.

Mary and Evangelina used a kerosene stove that emitted a lot of smoke when they cooked. Now teenagers, the girls remembered their mother's cooking skills, so they bought one pan and one pot and attempted to learn to cook. And across the street was La Villita Meat Market: the owner's name was Cesar Gonzales; Gonzales was also San Benito's Mayor. He would freely give the girls *chorizo Mexicano* (Mexican sausage) to cook and mix with scrambled eggs. The girls were very grateful to him.

Around the corner and virtually next door was La Villita, a popular outdoor dancehall. Then there was Pete Conseco's drugstore where teenagers enjoyed the taste of delicious mouth-watering hamburgers and ice cream floats and the nonstop sound of music records playing from the jukebox. Everyone in the valley knew this small area in San Benito as "The Town Talk" and "La Villita."

Mary and Evangelina's apartment (second floor) at 340 West Robertson Street in San Benito. Also, it is the apartment where Balde meets Evangelina (1950s). The Azteca building in the far background is where dances were held on the open rooftop.

"La Villita" Uptown, Robertson Street, also known as the Town Talk. (1950s)

Side street of meat market is La Villita dance hall.

Aunt Mary Muñiz: And the Stranger Who Stole a Kiss

My Aunt Mary was very beautiful and charismatic. She was also very mature for her age. She spoke to everyone with kindness, and they would often ask her for advice. She had very fair skin, loved to tease her hair, and wore lots of makeup. Men and women really enjoyed her company and laughter. She had a shapely body, and she loved to sing and dance. I mean she really loved to dance, almost as much as I do.

Mary was not shy and she would go to El Grande Theatre in Harlingen to compete in *los aficionados*. As attractive as Mary was, she was also a tomboy. She enjoyed hanging out with young men at local beer joints. She would often be seen laughing, drinking, and smoking cigarettes like them.

However, Mary was adamant about not wanting to be submissive and wind up dead like her mother. She was very sensitive on the inside and she would not let people see her vulnerable side. So, Mary would cry to Evangelina because she was pretty and vivacious, yet so lonely. But Mary was also a go-getter! She had a zest for life! She was also street smart and wise beyond her years.

She worked at a shrimp place and when she got off work, she would quickly get ready for her date. And if she smelled fishy, it's because she wouldn't go home to bathe and wash off the fish smell. She would just sprinkle on powder, put on her red lipstick, and take off.

Mary once liked this guy named Cervantes and even followed him all the way to Corpus Christi, which is a two-and-a-half-hour drive from San Benito. They had a relationship, but soon after, he told her he was going to marry someone else. Mary had put everything she had into the relationship and took it very hard. So hard that she got underneath his car and told Cervantes to run over her because she wasn't going to live without him.

Evangelina was the opposite of her sister Mary. So much so that Mary would have to tell the boys not to mess with or stare at Evangelina because she was so shy that she would start crying.

At fifteen, Evangelina started her first job as a babysitter for *La Casa de Cuna*, a nursery in Harlingen. She would take the city bus back and forth to San Benito.

In the apartment, the girls had put up a curtain to divide the kitchen from the sleeping area. One night, Evangelina came home dead tired and went to sleep early. Shortly after falling asleep, Evangelina woke up to sounds of laughter coming from the kitchen. She peeked from behind the curtain to see who it was. She saw Mary and some guy entering the apartment. He was wearing military pants with a button-down shirt, and squatted by the front door. He had a few pimples on his face and his hair was greasy, with long sideburns. He wore his shirt collar up, and looked really tough and mean.

As soon as he saw Evangelina, he quickly took out his pocketknife and began to clean the tip of his fingernails to look like a tough guy. But when she looked up at him, she got so scared that she quickly closed the curtains and went back to bed.

Mary must have met him at the talent contest held at the Grand Theatre that night and invited him over. Since she had many guy buddies, everyone knew Mary was friendly and outgoing. While Evangelina lay sleeping, the stranger gave her a kiss on the cheek before he left Mary's apartment that night.

But when Mary saw him steal a kiss, she whispered to him, "You will never be able to touch my sister because she is too good for you!"

My mother, Evangelina, made a comment to me, "Mary must have known what kind of guy he [my father] really was."

NOTE: After my father's passing in 2006, Mother, who is a private person, opened up and allowed me to interview her. I didn't even have to push because she was more than ready to release her painful emotions; for over a year, she held nothing back as she revealed her most intimate and heartfelt memories of her childhood and marriage to the only man she ever knew and loved, my Dad, Baldemar Huerta.

Las Califas (The Californians)

The Muñiz girls were quickly known around town as Las Califas because they were from California. They were nothing like San Benito Valley Girls. I know firsthand because I too am a Valley Girl, as were both my grandmothers.

Las Califas were very different from Southern girls because they dressed and spoke differently. So, they stood out a lot, especially in San Benito.

Because Las Califas were young and pretty, they were asked to help at the Vegas Café to attract the attention of customers. The girls would get an order, turn it in, and when the food was ready, they would serve it to the customers. When they got hungry, they would just sneak to a back room and get a quick bite to eat.

This was a difficult thing for Evangelina to do—to take orders and face people—because of her bashfulness. Evangelina was so timid that she could not look people in the eye.

About a week later, the same guy with the pimply face that visited Mary's apartment walked into Vegas Café holding a guitar. He came in with a friend named Tomás. His friend had a nice, smooth, and pretty face, just as Evangelina liked and preferred.

Tomás asked his greasy-haired *pachuco*-looking friend (who knew how to sing and play guitar) if he would serenade this cute girl for him because he wanted a way to break the ice so that he could ask her out.

As he began to play his guitar, he asked his friend which girl he was interested in asking out and Tomás pointed toward Evangelina. Without hesitating, he began to sing; however, when she turned around he took a good look at her and noticed she was one of the Califas. It was Mary's younger sister, Evangelina, from whom he had stolen a kiss while she lay sleeping.

So instead of serenading Evangelina for his friend Tomás, he began to serenade her for himself. When she saw that he was staring at her that made her feel uneasy. She got scared, turned red with embarrassment, and then went to the back of the restaurant. She kept ignoring him, so he stopped playing his guitar. Then he walked out of the restaurant and headed toward the outhouse in back of the building. He looked into the window and there she was sitting alone eating her lunch. He walked away without saying a word and let her be.

"From My Eyes" by Freddy Fender
Like a boxer or fighter, I always went for the jugular.

Freddy Returns Home Singing Rockabilly Music

Pérez Prado, who was famous for the song "Mambo No. 5," was an international singer from Cuba who found fame in Mexico City. He was about to perform at the civic center in Brownsville for a big show and dance. Therefore, almost every young adult in the Rio Grande Valley wanted to be there.

Early that evening, the crowd was getting anxious to see Pérez Prado. Everyone was in his or her best handmade dress and secondhand suit. The young women were all dolled up, ready to get on the dance floor. The locals looked around to see who had made it into the hall and who had not been so lucky. They were just ecstatic because they had saved enough money to enter the civic center that night.

Then the announcer introduced Pérez Prado, and the couples began to hit the dance floor. He was well into his performance and everything was grooving.

Suddenly, a pimply-faced teenager with a ducktail haircut, long sideburns, loose slacks, silk shirt, and white suede shoes jumped on stage and literally just grabbed the microphone away from Pérez Prado!

Who was it? It was none other than Baldemar Huerta, who had returned home from marine duty.

On August of 1956, Balde returned home through the port of San Francisco and was elated to finally be back in San Benito with his family, who were still residing at 631 Rossiter Street. Coincidently, he had made it just in time to meet Las Califas, who had also just arrived from San Francisco themselves.

Meantime, Pérez Prado didn't know who the heck Balde was because Prado was from Cuba! But Balde just did not have any better sense or a shy bone in his body. His impulsive move to show off in front of a crowd was electrifying to the locals.

Balde was singing bebop and rockabilly music. And Prado just stood there looking at Balde in amazement while the crowd went crazy! Impressed by Balde's singing, Prado actually enjoyed his performance and let him keep the microphone for a bit.

Balde took over, and they were thrilled to see and hear someone from the valley singing mainstream music.

Besides, *la palomia de* Balde (his buddies) had not heard him sing for a few years and they were in awe at the enthusiasm, cockiness, and coolness he brought to the valley. Balde would not let up onstage, and the crowd danced nonstop. Balde was digging it, and he reminded everyone that he was back in town!

Then he looked out into the audience and saw his friend Tomás having a good time on the dance floor. However, when he took a second look, he noticed Tomás was dancing with none other than La Califa, Mary's younger sister Evangelina.

Balde hastily put his guitar down, jumped offstage, and walked right up to them. He grabbed hold of Evangelina's arm and made her sit down and wait for him to finish playing and singing. Balde did not ask her; he told her to sit down. And he wouldn't let her dance with Tomás or anyone else.

She was scared of him. He also made her feel bad because everyone was dancing and having fun, while she had to stay in her place. She was only fifteen years old.

When he returned, he grabbed her again by the arm and pulled her out of the civic center. She began to scream! She quickly looked back to find her sister Mary, but Mary was already tipsy and singing and dancing on the stage with Pérez Prado! Prado liked Mary because she was very pretty and could really dance and shake her butt, too (like me!). Everyone liked Mary! She was nice and a lot of fun to be with!

Evangelina did not know Balde. But she remembered him; he was the same guy with the pimply face who had shown off for her back at Mary's apartment. He was also the same guy who tried to serenade her for Tomás at the Vegas Café. But she could not stand to look at him because she would start to cry. It was clear that she did not like Balde!

Without regard for her wishes, Balde had Tomás drive them both away from the dance hall; he and Evangelina sat in the backseat. [Recounting the memory, my mother noted humorously, "No kissing."] He meant business and took her away from the party scene.

"He just did everything by force," Mother said. Balde didn't ask Tomás questions either; Balde just did what he wanted to do! He told Tomás to drive them back to Mary's apartment in San Benito. So, they dropped her off, and then Balde went back to Brownsville's civic center—and that was that! This time, he claimed the Califa, Evangelina, for himself.

Eva is Raped

Underneath his rough facade, Balde found a soft spot for Evangelina and promptly began to butter her up with his wit and charm. After letting his guard down, he showed her his vulnerable side and told her how much he loved her. He then began to call her Eva. So, from this point on, Evangelina will be referred to as Eva for short.

One of her cousins from Harlingen had a boyfriend whom Eva knew. One evening, on the way back from babysitting at *La Casa de Cuna*, Eva was waiting at a bus stop in Harlingen and encountered the young man. He stopped to offer her a lift home; although he was with two other boys in the vehicle, Eva thought it was okay because it was her cousin's boyfriend. She got into the car with them.

However, instead of taking her home, the boys took her out into a field and told her to take off her panties. She did what they told her, and she cried as two of them raped her. The third guy told his friends to leave her alone, while another pulled her watch off her wrist. It was the one thing she had left that belonged to her mother.

After she tearfully told Balde, he wanted to do something bad to the young men, but Eva told him not to go after them. She did not think to call the cops, either.

To make her feel better, Balde went to his mother's house to get her some chicken tacos that Máge had just cooked on the stove. She ate the hot *taquitos* and stopped crying. Balde's gentle act of kindness dried up her tears.

Balde was impressed with Eva because she was so young and had endured so much. He was amazed at how strong-willed she was; she did not fall apart at the seams so easily.

Eva had no time to think about living a normal life like other teenage girls her age. She was too busy just trying to survive on a daily basis. He realized that his struggles were of no comparison to hers.

The pain and confusion of being lost without her mother and siblings was more than Balde could ever imagine or comprehend. He felt for her. At least he had his own family together and relatives nearby, he thought, while she had only her sister Mary around. But Mary was preoccupied, coping with the brutal loss of her mother and family in her own way.

Evangelina
I didn't have time to grieve for my mom. We were different; we were weird to them.
We just needed to eat like everyone else. Our lifestyle was called survival!
We were known as "Las Califas."

Eva Feels Out of Place

Las Califas wore makeup, and their hairstyles were different from Valley Girls. The Muñiz girls would roll their bobby socks down to their ankles, and the Valley Girls would wear them up. Las Califas wore tight skirts and body-fitting sweaters with scarves around their necks, while Valley Girls wore their petticoats with starch, making their skirts flare up over their knees. They also wore their hair teased with lots of hair spray and the Valley Girls wore their hair down with a tiny hairpin or bow to the side to look reserved. Las Califas also danced to mainstream music and rock 'n' roll, while the Valley Girls danced mostly to ethnic music, such as polkas and *rancheras*!

Las Califas just couldn't figure it all out! They were just different, like in the movie *Grease*. They clashed and tried their best to stay alive in the valley.

Since Eva's personality differed from Mary's, she really had nobody to talk with or complain to. Mary would just go out and have a good time while Eva stayed home. Mary had even gotten so mad at Eva for cramping her style that she threw her sister out of the apartment.

When this occurred, Balde took Eva straight to his mother's house on Rossiter Street and dropped her off. She thought he was going to take good care of her like a friend or sister, but no, he took her there for himself, as his girlfriend. Then, Balde took off into the night for the music, laughter, and pleasure to be found at La Villita. He did what came natural to him—to show off his talent and entertain.

Music Timeline by Music Archivist and Writer Ramón Hernández

El Patio La Villita is a historical treasure that is located in Downtown San Benito. From the 1950s to the 1970s, it was the premier dance hall in the entire Rio Grande Valley; people traveled from all over the valley to hear and dance to the music of the Beto Villa Orchestra (Villa is considered to be the father of Tejano orchestra), Isidro López, the founding father of Tejano Music, plus *conjunto* legends such as Narciso Martínez, Tony De La Rosa, Valerio Longoria, and many other musicians, bands and orchestras.

Dancing under the moonlit night and stars at La Villita. Falcón Orchestra of Falcón Records

La Villita dancehall has no rooftop (1950s)

Eva Humiliated

La Villita, as previously mentioned, was a local outdoor dance hall owned by Fernando Sánchez; it is located kitty-corner to what was formerly Mary's apartment on W. Robertson Street. It is still open today and is considered to hold many memories for the locals. To many others, La Villita was their life!

Balde went back to La Villita after he dropped Eva off on Rossiter. However, later that evening, Máge decided to take the teenage girls, Míne and Eva, to the dance. When they arrived, Doña Máge and the girls sat at an available sitting area by the dance floor. While the live band played, Míne was already dancing when a guy approached Eva and asked her to dance. Then she looked over to see that Balde was dancing with another girl. She knew something was wrong with this picture. She didn't know what to do! So, she handed Máge her purse and got up to dance. When the boy swirled her around the dance floor, Máge threw the purse at Eva's face. Eva was embarrassed and hurt, but she kept right on dancing. She wasn't interested in the young man at all. It was just an innocent dance.

When Balde saw her, he was on the stage about to sing in duet with Moy Gonzales. instead of making a scene since, he took a different approach. Moy, by the way, had once asked Eva to marry him, so imagine how she felt as they broke into "Mujer Paseada," a popular and risqué tune during that era.

Eva did not speak much Spanish, but she knew the lyrics were about a woman that liked to mess around. And as they sang together, they looked directly at Eva. When they stared at her, Eva ran out the door of La Villita and down Robertson Street. She stopped on the edge of *la resaca* and broke down crying because she had been embarrassed and humiliated.

She didn't know where to go, because Mary had kicked her out of the apartment that very same day. Balde had taken her back to his house, leaving her alone with his mother. And now, Máge had taken her to La Villita that very night and left her there. Eva felt lost and distraught.

Afterward, Balde and Moy went running after her, and upon reaching her, Balde took her in his arms. Balde's gentle act of kindness dried up her tears once again. Then he took Eva back to his mother's home on Rossiter Street, and they made up.

Freddy's First Three-Month Tour: Eva Left Alone with Doña Máge

Balde was nineteen when he left on his first out-of-state tour. He would be gone for three months traveling to towns in between Pueblo, Colorado and back. The reality was that Eva wasn't aware that Balde had already started his career as a professional singer, songwriter, and musician, which during his youth was more of a survival thing. He was grabbing and soaking up everything in sight, doing what had become second nature to him, but Eva did not like this fast lifestyle of his at all.

Furthermore, Balde wasn't asking anyone's permission; he was doing it! This is how *Good Ol'* Hill Billy Jackson had strongly put it: "Balde was just living out his future!"

So rather than worry about Eva, he just left her there at his mother's house to keep her safe and away from all the other guys who wanted to marry her.

Eva stayed with Máge, and she did have some memorable, good times living with his family. She and Míne became close friends and they would play along *la resaca* when they were just teenagers. She could still remember the fresh aroma of food (like *fideo* noodles with stewed meat and pinto beans) being cooked every morning at their home.

Máge had accepted Eva like her own daughter. She even made Eva her first petticoat dress. In fact, Máge bought her several petticoats. When Máge washed them, she would place them on the clothesline to dry. Then Míne would starch the petticoats, and they would flare up. Eva had worn tight skirts *a la pachuca chicana* but was now dressing Tex-Mex style and La Califa officially became a Valley Girl.

To my knowledge, the only risqué thing my mother has ever done was allowing *Tío* Cáne to give her a tattoo when she was fifteen. If you look very closely, right on the back of her left hand is a purple dot the size of a pin needle.

Eva also recalled a very close and dear friend of Máge's by the name of Ramona Mireles. She too, was a tough old broad like Doña Máge, who in her younger days would move Máge and her children all around El Jardín in her wagon.

They were so close that Ramona would go to the bread companies and ask them for free stale bread. She would tell them it was for the pigs, and take it to Máge. Then Máge would throw the bread into a midsize galvanized container, pour milk, sugar, and then bake it. The family, including Eva, would enjoy eating the fresh baked bread.

Ramona and Máge would also go to *la matanza* (stockyards where the cattle are killed), and there they would scrounge for leftover meat to take home.

When Eva lived with Máge, she remembers seeing Balde's mom hustle for food. Every morning Máge would put on her slippers and go to the outhouse to shower. Then she would slip on a casual dress, earrings, and Avon talc she loved using. She was a big woman, and she had this charming smile; however, Eva was still scared of her.

When ready and smelling sweet, Máge would go door-to-door around El Jardín and collect from the neighbors—a little bit of this and a little bit of that for the day's meal. And if Máge collected enough money, she would go buy a live chicken, kill it, clean it, and then fry it in oil. Eva was amazed at how Doña Máge could make such a simple meal taste so yummy.

Máge Beats the Crap Out of Manuelon!

Eva recalls vividly how Máge would keep an eye out to see Manuelon drive by on Highway 77 Sunshine Strip and Resaca Drive. When Manuelon saw that Tío Porfirio's truck was at her home, he would check himself into the motel across the street out of respect for her brother. Upon seeing his truck, Máge would quickly powder her face, sneak out, and walk across the street to meet him.

Eva was happy because she knew that every time Manuelon showed up, even if only for a while, Máge would be somewhat pacified with the few dollars he gave her. Then she would bring home a fresh chicken to fry. Máge would be content to feed everyone poultry and her family, including Eva, would get to enjoy eating a little bit of crispy, oiled chicken on that day.

On one memorable occasion during Manuelon and Doña Máge's long love affair, my mother recalled how furious Máge became with him when she found out about his infidelities. It was the final straw. He had cheated on her for the last time. To see him cheat on her with someone other than his legal wife was more than she could endure; especially after all she had put her children through being with him.

Taking Eva with her, Máge boarded a bus to Brownsville; when they arrived, they went to Manuelon's fruit and vegetable store. Máge stormed into the shop (while the "other woman" stood nearby) and beat the crap out of Manuelon! He didn't fight back or lash out; he just took it.

After the beating, Máge said a few choice words to him and walked out. Then she and Eva got back on the bus, went back home and that was the end of *that* romance and Freddy's so-called step-father!

Balde Claims La Califa

Doña Máge liked Eva living with her and treated her like a daughter; that is, just as long as Eva kept away from Balde. But as soon as he would return from wherever, the two would reunite and Máge would again be unkind to her.

Eva's reminiscences are filled with pain. "Balde was already a man. He would go out screwing around. But he would tell me straight out that I belonged to him! I didn't know what that really meant because I was just so shy and naive."

When Balde went to Pueblo Colorado, and left Eva with Máge, he didn't give her any money. He probably didn't have any and Eva was uncomfortable asking Máge for money.

While Eva lived on 631 Rossiter, she began to feel lonely and since she figured Balde was out screwing around anyway, she decided to move in with two young Anglo women.

When Máge heard gossip being spread around el barrio that Eva was going out with Anglo boys, she got word to Balde that Eva had also left the house.

So, when Balde finally returned from Colorado, he immediately went looking and found her at the house where she was rooming with the two women. He knocked on their door, and when Eva opened the door, he punched her in the stomach and face; she fell to the ground. "It's either you come back the right way, or I will bring you back by force." Eva never thought of reporting him to the cops. She was just a young girl who grew to like him, but she was still scared of him.

This time, Balde took Eva straight to go get a blood test and told her they were getting married. He dropped her back at her home, then lingered (off and on) outside their house for several days until the test results came in. Balde did attempt to soften Eva up by taking her hot food to eat; they would also go out and about and enjoy one another's company again.

Then on Saturday, August 10, 1957, Balde had his friend, Carlos Sifuentes, accompany him as his best man to the courthouse at Brownsville. On the way there, Balde had Sifuentes stop and pick up his new buddy, Louis René Moody, and Eva's sister, Mary. Eva was still black and blue when she stood before the judge to say "I do." She said she did have to wear heavy makeup to cover them up. Balde had just turned twenty years old and she was sixteen when he basically forced her to marry him. Right or wrong, she loved him when he claimed her as his wife.

On their honeymoon, they went to Club 13, a nightspot for young adults owned by Carlos Sifuentes and located on Stenger and Sam Houston streets. He and his friend Louis René Moody had been paid $5 by Sifuentes to be the opening act at the club that night.

Balde took his new bride there to show her off in front of all the other guys who wanted to date and marry her. Afterward, they continued the celebration and drove over the border into Matamoros.

They spent their honeymoon night inside a little shack of a skeleton house on 631 Rossiter where their bed was right by the window, and anyone could hear everything right through the walls.

In the morning, several guys came by to congratulate them. One of them was *Mosca* (The Fly) and the other was Bedinski. Another two sat on a swing while they waited and waited for them to come out. Running out of patience, the young men finally went and tapped on the window asking Balde, "Hey, are you through in there?"

Balde replied, *"¿Qué quieren?"* ("What do you want?")

"Well, we just came by to tell you that you better take care of her," they said.

Balde, Eva, her sister Mary, Louis René Moody, and wedding padrino Carlos Sifuentes. In Matamoros Café, a popular restaurant and nightclub, in Matamoros, Tamaulipas, Mexico (1957).

Evangelina

You couldn't help but love your dad because of the way he was. Balde was obnoxious. Your dad was very tough and malo [bad]. *He had pimples, and I couldn't stand your dad. Your dad wasn't handsome until he was older. He bothered me. He then grew on me. He was a teenager learning how to live with people. He had a very hard life.*

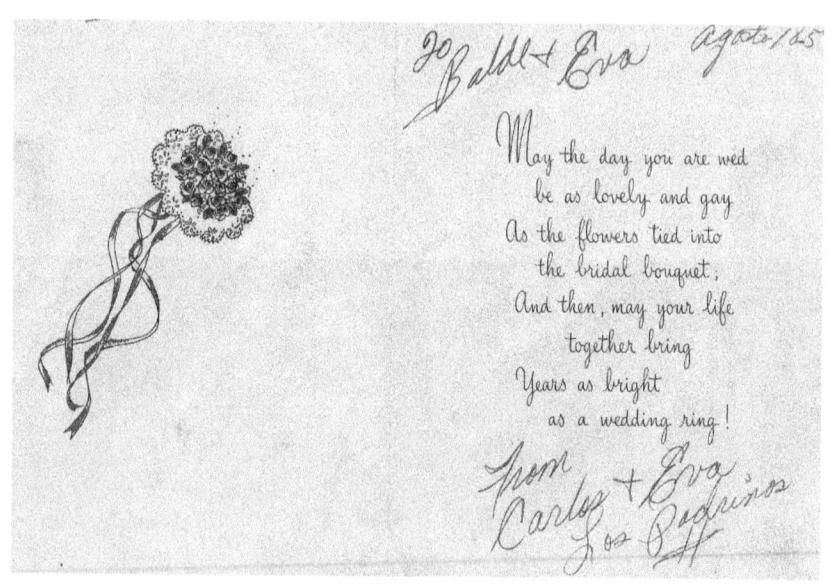

Wedding Cards, August 10, 1957
"To Balde & Eva From Carlos & Eva, Los Padrinos (The Godparents)."

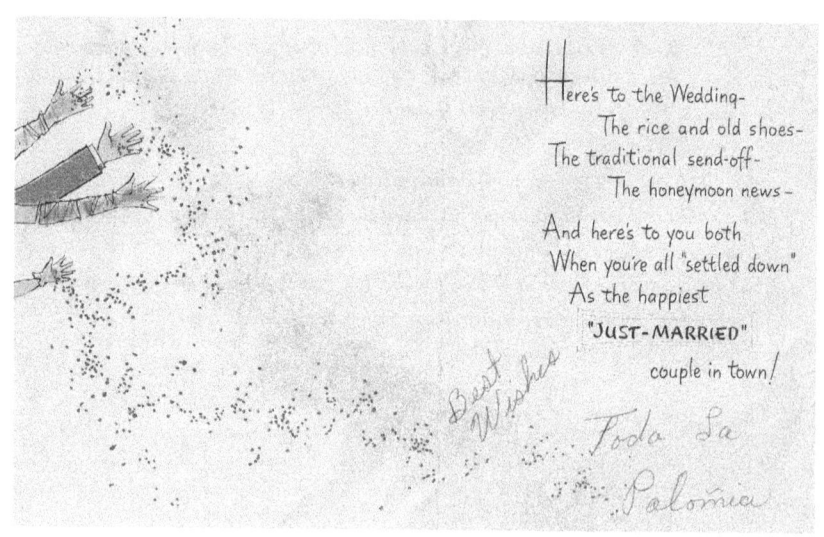

"Best Wishes from Toda La Palomia (From All Your Buddies)"

Tammy Lorraine Huerta Fender

Chapter VI

El Bebop Kid (1957)

"Ay Amor" ("Holy One")

Pseudonym "El Bebop Kid"
Father of Orquesta Tejano Band Leader, Beto Villa
Falcón Records
"I was the first! Mexican American rock 'n' roller …"
Tex-Mex Rockabilly

"From My Eyes" by Freddy Fender
I was playing rock 'n' roll and I started what you might say, Tex-Mex Rockabilly!

Club 13 was where *Good Ol'* Hill Billy Jackson met up with Balde once again. The newlyweds showed up to continue their celebration and because Balde had another gig there that following week. And Jackson, well, he just loved being in Balde's company.

Inside the club, Balde spoke to Jackson as they walked toward the table. Balde told him, "Jackson, I want to tell you something. Now I want you to sit right here with my wife and don't let any son of a bitch dance with my wife." Then Balde got up onstage and made the announcement, "For those guys that don't like me, I have crazy Jackson sitting over there watching over my wife."

Balde just laughed, but he meant it, Jackson recalled. What was even funnier was that Jackson was a big man, and yet he was a sweet guy, but the crowd didn't know otherwise.

Jackson also remembered club owners always having to have bouncers wherever Balde played because he brought so much energy and excitement to any club in San Benito, Harlingen, or Brownsville. He just knew how to liven up a joint.

On another occasion, Balde had a gig at a Mexican bar in Harlingen, and Jackson tagged along with him. When he started singing, the Mexicans began to boo him. They wanted Balde to sing traditional Mexican *rancheros* and polkas, but Balde stuck to his guns and sang his own style of music, Jackson recollected.

"This is for all my loudmouth friends out there that don't like me!" Balde responded. He sang the same song, "Don't Let the Stars Get in Your Eyes," that had provoked "Bulto" and his gang of hoodlums that got him beat up once before. When he was done playing, Balde laughed as the Mexicans booed him.

After he finished performing, the *Mexicanos* were waiting for Balde to get offstage. Then they got into a fistfight with him. That's how Balde always got started, stated Jackson.

Good Ol' Hill Billy Jackson just chuckled. "They were jealous of him because he was just that good! The Mexicans kept thinking that the song 'Don't Let the Stars Get in Your Eyes' meant Balde was going to punch them out. But the song was just a love ballad. On this night, Balde did provoke them on purpose, and he had never backed down from a fight unless he got knocked out first.

"Yep, they beat him up that night! Gringos never really bothered him too much though. The gringos just liked Balde," Jackson declared once again.

Club 13 *on Stenger Street (1950s)*

"From My Eyes" by Freddy Fender
I sang a lot of rock 'n' roll because I wanted to be a rebel!
My culture did not like me to sing rock 'n' roll.
They wanted me to sing conjunto, accordion, or norteño.
And I did not want to sing that kind of music!

Two Separate Lives

NOTE: Bear with me as I take you, the reader, back to 1956, when my parents were first dating; I will try to separate the artistic and personal aspects to give you a more vivid picture and examination of Freddy's earlier musical career. It will also shed more light on the uncertainties of both of my parents' youth and how they were destined to collide. Straight from the brig, Father returned home from marine duty to his first true love—his music.

Grande Theatre in Harlingen, Texas

Balde (with long side burns) and Louis René Moody rehearsing at Grande Theatre (1956).

Balde and Louis René Moody performing with electric guitars at the Grande Theatre (1956).

Freddy Wins First Prize Seventeen Weeks in a Row

A teenage girl named Elida Andaverde, who lived within view of the movie theatre, enjoyed entering *los aficionados* at the Grande Theatre in Harlingen. She entered the contest religiously and loved dancing to Elvis Presley music. Elida, who always looked forward to seeing Balde every Wednesday night, would normally win second or third prize.

The first-prize winner would always receive $20. And Balde was still in need of money for his family and would enter the talent contest with intentions of winning first prize every week. So, he would practice backstage to Elvis Presley songs on his guitar, and Elida would practice her dancing to Freddy's guitar playing.

"Valde was very handsome, and I really had a crush on him," Elida commented, "but he didn't know it. I was only fourteen years old, and I never saw him with anyone else. Valde was kind to me. He had never made a pass at me as other guys had."

As a side note, it was common for her and people closest to him in the valley to call him *Valde* (with the letter v) instead of Balde.

"He was around nineteen years old when he mentioned he was looking forward to recording and hoped and dreamed to record his first record someday.

"I also felt as though there was something special about his eyes. I can't explain it. He just had this twinkle in his eyes that drew you in. I also never saw him angry, disrespectful, or with a bad attitude. He was always friendly and always smiling.

"A year later, many of us teenage girls in San Benito and Harlingen were terribly saddened and upset to hear Valde was dating someone special and had gotten married."

Elida vividly remembered Balde onstage holding his guitar, wearing silky black shirt and black slacks. As Balde reached the microphone, you could hear the crowd of teens whispering, "Here comes first prize!"

She knew that the local kids were going there just to see Balde and to sing and clap for him. Balde had won first prize seventeen weeks in a row. When Balde couldn't make it to the contest, the other contestants would be so happy because someone else was going to win first prize. Elida was always hopeful to win that first prize. She remembers that the song Balde liked to perform was a popular new hit by Elvis Presley called "Hound Dog." It was the flip side of "Don't Be Cruel," another huge hit of Elvis Presley.

"From My Eyes" by Freddy Fender

I was going from theatre to theatre competing in these talent shows—
La Azteca and El Grande Theatre in Harlingen,
the Ruenez movie theatre in San Benito, plus the Victorian and Majestic in Brownsville.
A lot of those guys had enough talent to be professionals.
I sang songs like "Jambalaya" or whatever was popular!
The prizes weren't that much, but they added up.
I won about $50 a week; that was good money back in the '50s [laughing].
I made it a way of life. Finally, the theatre owners began to ask me not to compete.
They said I was too good and that I should let somebody else have a chance.

How Freddy and Louis René Moody First Met
(Eventual Partners in Crime)

Balde would be seen walking everywhere with his guitar in one hand and a little amplifier in the other. He was looking for someone to hire him to sing for a few dollars. This is how he lived from one day to the next hustling for a gig like a true musician.

One afternoon, a local teenager named Evaristo Moody went running toward Pete's Pharmacy near La Palma (The Palms) neighborhood to see his brother Louis René, best known as Louis. They lived on the other side of US-Highway 83 in the neighborhood known as La Gallina (The Chicken).

While Louis was standing outside Pete's drugstore, Evaristo ran up to his brother and told him, "You ought to come and hear this guy singing tonight at La Villita, he is really good!" So, they went to La Villita, and Louis saw that Balde was singing rock 'n' roll. Louis also noticed that he was onstage by himself, without backup. Louis, who had never picked up an instrument, thought this guy might be able to use some help. So, Louis jumped on the stage with him and attempted to play the drums that were already set up. Balde liked that he did that. Nobody then really knew much about rock 'n' roll, let alone how to play it, and surely not in San Benito!

Afterward, Louis asked Balde, "Hey, are you going to be singing in Spanish or English?"

Balde replied, "Why *vato* (dude)?"

"Well, because you have a hell of a Mexican accent, and you can't keep singing that song like, 'You nocing budda hun dog' ('You're Nothing but a Hound Dog')." After Louis backed him on drums, Louis and Balde started hanging out together and that is when Louis invited him to play at Club 13, which coincidently was Balde's wedding day, August 10, 1957.

NOTE: Today, if you hear Freddy's music, you will hear every word and every letter pronounced crystal clear. Freddy was very studious about listening to others when speaking. He was hard on himself and paid special attention to his voice when he spoke or sang. He may have had a strong Mexican accent, but he strove for excellence when speaking, as well as for his grammar usage. He also did not allow instruments to overpower his voice. His voice *was* the main instrument as can be heard in all the songs he recorded. Also, Father was very hard on us (his three children) and would scold us in front of anyone when we used incorrect grammar. Another thing about Father, he never spoke without knowing the facts. When he spoke, he knew *exactly* what he was talking about. That is why he always paused, prior to responding to a question during an interview and would first say, "The fact is. . . ." Freddy was always genuine, blunt, and to the point.

"From My Eyes" by Freddy Fender
I have always had this obsession to speak correct English.

Radio Personality Proclaims Balde Huerta "El Bebop Kid"

In the fall of 1956, when Balde arrived back from marine duty, his friend Ruben Aguirre and Balde's cousin Ysaúle Ysasi wanted Balde to go to KGBT radio and dedicate a tune to a particular girl Ysaúle had met. The popular song was "Traciónera," which means "the betrayer." However, when it came time to make Ysaúle's dedication, the disc jockey, Martín Rosales, got confused and dedicated "Tracionera" to Aguirre's girlfriend by mistake. Of course, Ruben had some explaining to do to his girlfriend, whom he eventually married.

At ten years old, Balde had already performed for KGBT radio; however, on this day, a musician was scheduled to play the marimbas for fifteen minutes on Martín Rosales' live radio show, but had problems crossing over the border. So, as luck and fate would have it, Balde wound up filling in for them for half an hour and got to sing "Kingston Town," "Jamaica Farewell," "Jambalaya," plus some rockabilly tunes by Elvis. Balde especially liked to sing the song by Little Richard entitled "Tutti Frutti."

Most important, this turned out to be the day in Balde's musical history that the popular radio personality referred to him as "El Bebop Kid." Thus, over the radio airwaves and before thousands of listeners, Martín Rosales christened Balde with his first stage name.

Father of Orquesta Tejano Band Leader, Beto Villa Hears "El Bebop Kid" On KGBT—The Mexican Elvis

Prominent, well-known Tejano orchestra leader Beto Villa (Google) had been listening to the KGBT radio. He liked Balde's voice, and Villa went to see him on Rossiter Street. He asked Máge and Balde if he would perform with his nationally known orchestra in *El Centro Civico* in Brownsville. Villa told her not to worry, that he would get him a tuxedo and he would take care of everything. Balde was already familiar and had performed with Japanese orchestras when he was stationed in Japan, so he looked forward to this opportunity, which also brought a touch of class and respect to rock 'n' roll.

That weekend, the civic center filled up quickly with young adults eager to hear the orchestra. Many of them had to stay outside, peeking through the windows. Aguirre also attended the show but was on the outside looking in. They were all in the same boat (dirt poor), chuckled Aguirre.

After the orchestra finished playing their music, Beto Villa announced a new and special talent to everyone as "El Bebop Kid."

Well, nobody had ever heard of The Bebop Kid before, not here or there! So, when this new talent, this skinny dark-skinned Mexican boy with ducktails, appeared, they all shouted, "Hey, that's Valde [Balde]!" They had a great time watching Balde. He was a big hit, and the kids loved him.

That night, Balde made his first public appearance as El Bebop Kid with Beto Villa's orchestra at the civic center in Brownsville.

Immediately after the show, Villa went back to Máge's to ask her if Balde would be willing to travel with him and his orchestra. Máge said he was a minor and that she would have to sign but it was up to him. Even though Balde was of legal age, back then, people still referred to teenagers as minors. Unfortunately, Balde declined the offer.

Aguirre remembered their conversation on Rossiter Street; Balde's siblings and the local kids from El Jardín gathered around Balde and Beto Villa as they spoke.

Singing with an orchestra wasn't really Balde's style, he told Beto Villa. However, Balde would have become a huge star to the people of Mexico had he agreed to sign and move there.

Balde continued to have several orchestras backing him in Harlingen and across the border into Matamoros, Mexico. This helped him get more exposure as a professional singer, but only in the southern borders of Texas.

It was then established that in late 1956-'57, the people of the Lower Rio Grande Valley had their very own Mexican Elvis, known as El Bebop Kid.

Winter of 1957, Matamoros, Tamaulipas, Mexico—Baldemar Huerta "The Bebop Kid" backed by Chucho Hernández and his orchestra (1957).

Ramón Piñon's Memories of Freddy's Father, Serapio: *"Hay viene Chapo Huerta!" Y la Parranda de Eden*

A dear friend named Ramón Piñon knew Balde's relatives very well. After Serapio's death, he had been somewhat of a father figure to Balde. Moreover, Piñon played a very special role at both the start and end of Balde's musical career. I would like to shed some light on their relationship and how this era would bring Freddy his very last Grammy at the end of his life. But it would be in the Latin Pop category, won for the CD titled *La Musica de Baldemar Huerta*. (It was toward the end of Freddy's life, his mind returned to childhood memories, filled with rooted songs that called to him to finally record *all* in Spanish. . . and beckoned him home.)

At times, Piñon would see Balde's grandfather, Benito, working alone across Highway 77 Sunshine Strip, taking care of farm animals. Benito seemed sad and distant, he recalled.

However, he vividly remembers how Balde's father, Serapio, was always *alegre y con chistes* (happy and joking). He claims Serapio was even more handsome than his son Balde. He was also hardworking and respectful to everyone, especially toward Doña Lola (his sister-in-law).

Piñon and Serapio worked together at Alexander's vegetable warehouse. The job involved packing vegetables. When the boxes were open and run through a conveyor belt, they would drop ice from above to keep the vegetables fresh. This was refreshing to the men because there was no air-conditioning.

They had to work fast, and Piñon, who was a musician, did not have much time to think about his music because there was loud noise coming from all the machinery. They could not even hear each other talking. They wore rubber boots, jeans, overalls, and a rubber apron.

Back then, they were paid 40¢ per hour, and Piñon worked day and night in order to make $40 a week. He worked one hundred hours icing down vegetables, packing vegetables, and loading and unloading the trucks. Piñon worked day and night and would get off work at 5:00 a.m. and clock back in at 8:00 a.m. But Piñon—all he could think about was his music. He also loved to write his own compositions.

Piñon recalls that Serapio loved to work *con gusto* (with delight). One morning, Piñon was at work waiting for Serapio to arrive. Piñon smiled as he saw Serapio and yelled to him, *"¿Ya estás listo?"* (Are you ready?) Serapio just grinned and nodded his head.

Every year on Mother's Day, Serapio would go to *la parranda* in El Jardín to serenade the ladies. For the locals, *la parranda* is an area where musicians sing and play their musical instruments.

Piñon remembers that Serapio "Chapo" had three other friends that were always around him, and Piñon nicknamed them *la parranda de Eden*. His inseparable friends were José "El Mocho" Contreras, Manuel Castillo (Balde's uncle), and Daniel Martínez. They liked to sing and never got into arguments. They just enjoyed singing and whistling. Not in bars, which they could not afford, but only in *la parranda en* El Jardín.

They drove around in a black 1939 pickup, and during the weekends, they would sit in the back singing songs. Serapio would stroll house-to-house serenading the ladies with special love songs. The people would yell out, *"Hay viene Chapo Huerta!"* (Here comes Chapo Huerta!)

Ramón Piñon's Memories of "Blinkie"

Piñon was younger than Serapio, but older than Balde. They did not go to school together, but they did hang out after school. He knew all of Balde's brothers and their nicknames. He recalls how the local boys would call Balde "Blinkie" because he would always close his eyes, squint, and blink his eyes every time he sang.

However, he first met Balde in front of Pancho Galván's Grocery Store. They were both barefooted and up to their ankles in mud. In fact, when it rained, they would make mud balls and throw them at each other.

Piñon recalled the first songs Balde learned were "Paloma Querida" ("Beloved Dove"), "Andando en La Parranda" ("Walking Among Friends while Out on a Spree"), "and "La Traicionera" ("The Betrayer").

One day, Balde asked him, "Hey, Piñon, don't be a bad guy, loan me your Fender guitar and your amplifier!"

"Sure, there it is, take it," Piñon would tell him.

Eventually, Máge bought Freddy his first Stella guitar for $9 from Tamayo's Furniture Store "It wasn't like today when there's so much opportunity. Balde worked a lot and suffered a lot. And many were envious of him," recalls Piñon. He said that as a young man, Balde would wear laced-up black Nunn Bush dress shoes that cost $1.99. At that time, a shirt cost 99¢ and a pair of dress pants was $1.50.

He shed some light on the small carnival that would come into town every year. They would set up the carnival alongside *la resaca* in front of the Lone Star warehouse. One year, there was a short, fat blonde woman at the carnival. They tried to pass her off as a mermaid while she sang and played a guitar. "But it was a scam," Piñon said. We both chuckled.

Piñon and Balde Learn to Sing Traditional Mexican Love Songs: *La Parranda* and *La Pachanga* in El Jardín

On occasions, Piñon and Balde would lie on their backs by *la resaca* looking up at the stars. Piñon would play *conjunto* music on his *bajo sexto*, and Balde would sing. They would just make up songs. As he spoke to me, Piñon began to laugh because as young men, they thought they knew everything, yet they knew nothing at all, he admitted.

Both enjoyed singing traditional Mexican love songs like "Lagrimas de Oro" ("Golden Tears") and "Indita Mia" ("My Indian Girl"). Piñon recalls how Balde used to sing these songs to his mother, Máge.

However, there were no fancy clubs in *el valle* (the valley). If somebody wanted to have a dance, they would just hang lamps on the clothesline in the backyard and dance on the dirt. There was no singing because of the dust—just music, music, and more music. The pay was not much; it was about $2 for the *bajo* players and $3 for the accordion player. Piñon added, "That was from 8:00 p.m. to 8:00 a.m." He would be on his way home the next morning and could still hear the music ringing in his ears. He said not everybody could play a *bajo sexto*. Almost all pretty songs are used with a *bajo sexto* because of the warm feeling the instrument expresses. That is mandatory for a romantic love song. This is what he played at *la parranda* and at *la pachanga* around here in El Jardín.

Piñon also played *requinto* music with a guitar and a *bajo sexto*. He would play at the Victoria and the Majestic theatres in Brownsville. He had gone up north to

Michigan, and they really liked his style of music, but the alluring tiny city of San Benito drew him back home.

Piñon knew many old-time musicians on a personal level, even musicians such as Narciso Martínez, who was a pioneer accordionist. He had a sharp mind when it came to pioneer musicians and old traditional Mexican music. Even though Balde and Piñon had very different styles of music, they were very good friends and respected each other. He and Balde never played together as a duet.

As Balde grew older, he looked up to Piñon. Balde was also very much like him; they both had tender souls and hearts of gold. They truly cherished one another's company, very much so, like father and son.

It was easy to fall in love with the old man Piñon. He was just so sweet and tender, and without any reservation, he let me into his musical world, which had meant so much to him. Like a bird, he sang to me, song after song, while he lay there, ill and disabled, in his bed. He reminded me so much of my father. The more they suffered, the more they'd write and sing heartfelt melodies aloud to soothe their souls.

As a child, I remembered Piñon wearing a light-colored hat and holding a cane while walking around El Jardín. I will always be grateful to him for spending time with me, visit after visit, while offering me valley fruit and Mexican sweetbread. He had so little to share with me in his humble home, and yet he had so much to offer. I felt his selfless heart. To me, he is a real man, like my father. Ramón Piñon became my dear friend. And I loved him dearly.

(A photo of him along with my other interviewees can be seen in back of this book. However, something horrific and unbelievable happens to poor Ramón after I interviewed my dear friend several times. It infuriated the townspeople of San Benito and me. I share this crushing blow to our very soul in Volume II: The Afterword.)

"From My Eyes" by Freddy Fender

I was just playing around, and I had ambitions about recording, so I went in to do harmony with a guy who was cutting a record. Nobody knew me then, really.
When we finished the recording session, the owner of the label wanted me to stay behind.
From that moment on, I was hogging the mic, playing and singing wherever I could.

Falcón Records: Freddy Gets Discovered as Spanish Rocker "The Bebop Kid"

Falcón Records was the only label in South Texas considered to be mainstream; it was based in McAllen, Texas and founded by Arnaldo Villarreal Ramírez, Sr. and his composer brother, Rafael Arnaldo Ramírez.

Ramón Piñon had written four beautiful Spanish songs and was going to Falcón to record on a Wednesday afternoon. One of the songs was called "Alegre Me Ando

Paseando" ("I Am Happily Passing My Time"). Again, his style of music was *conjunto* and he needed a backup on guitar and on harmony. So that day, Piñon asked Balde to help him out on a couple of numbers.

However, on Wednesday, Balde was nowhere to be found—Piñon had to track him down. He found him at the schoolyard flirting with the girls. Balde was nineteen years old. Piñon said, "*Oye* (listen), knucklehead, come on, we are going to be late." They caught a bus and headed to McAllen.

After Piñon recorded his four songs, the co-owners asked Piñon if he wouldn't mind taking the bus back home because they wanted to talk to Balde alone. Piñon did not mind and left Balde behind.

In fall of 1956, Arnaldo Villarreal Ramírez had been looking for someone who could sing Spanish rock 'n' roll. When they heard Balde on harmony with Piñon, Falcón knew that they had finally found the person they were looking for. Balde was a natural as their one and only "Mexican Elvis Presley."

Baldemar Huerta, The Bebop Kid (1957)

"From My Eyes" by Freddy Fender

Rafael Ramirez of Falcón Records called me Baldemar Huerta "The Bebop Kid."
He wanted me to sing like Elvis Presley.
You ever try to sing like Elvis Presley in Spanish? I was terrible!
He'd say, "No, no, get back." And send me back into the studio.
Finally, I did it like he wanted, so I could collect my twenty-five bucks and got out!

Tammy Lorraine Huerta Fender

Freddy Fender's first Spanish Rock song.
Baldemar Huerta con Los Romanceros "No Seas Cruel" ("Don't Be Cruel")
(Falcón label. November 6, 1956)

The First Chicano Singer to Record Rock and Roll in Spanish Language in American Music History

On November 6, 1956, Balde signed his first recording contract with Falcón. During the first recording session, Balde recorded the first composition he wrote while in the marines, "Ay Amor." For the flip side of this single, Falcón had Balde sing M. Rivera's Spanish translation of Elvis' hit "Don't Be Cruel."

Both tunes were recorded with Los Romanceros, his first band, which was Benny Huerta, guitar; Freddy Treviño, saxophone, and Louis René Moody on percussion.

However, because the drum noise was overpowering Freddy's voice in this tiny room, the percussion was left out. Afterward, they added the drums to the final cut.

On the day of the recording, Evaristo Moody drove his brother, Louis René, Balde and his new girlfriend "La Califa" Eva, to Falcón's studio. Louis and Eva had to sit out on the car and wait for them to finish the recording session.

Louis Moody stated, "I don't remember ever hearing anyone else singing Spanish rock 'n' roll before Balde and making a living at it in the mid 1950s in the United States or Mexico. Balde was living it! He was bebop, rockabilly, and rhythm and blues. Balde was the real deal!"

Evangelina

Pete Conseco, who was the drugstore owner, had given me a
dollar to go buy the record No Seas Cruel.
I remember it being a 78 single and with a purple label. I placed it in the jukebox.
Your father and I were dating. We were just teenagers.
We drank our root beer floats, and then we'd dance together to his record outside
on the sidewalk of La Villita (known as the Town Talk).

NOTE: Shown below are a few illustrations of Baldemar Huerta's first recordings with Falcón Records from 1956-1960. Popular rock and country songs were rewritten and recorded in Spanish. Freddy's ledgers and vinyls with Falcón Records (and Ideal Records) are found digitized online at www.arhooliefoundation.org under La Frontera Collection.

Baldemar Huerta's first recording session no. 381, November 6, 1956
Side One: F-2278 Title "No Seas Cruel" ("Don't Be Cruel")
Side Two: F-2279 Title "Ay Amor" ("Holy One")

Tammy Lorraine Huerta Fender

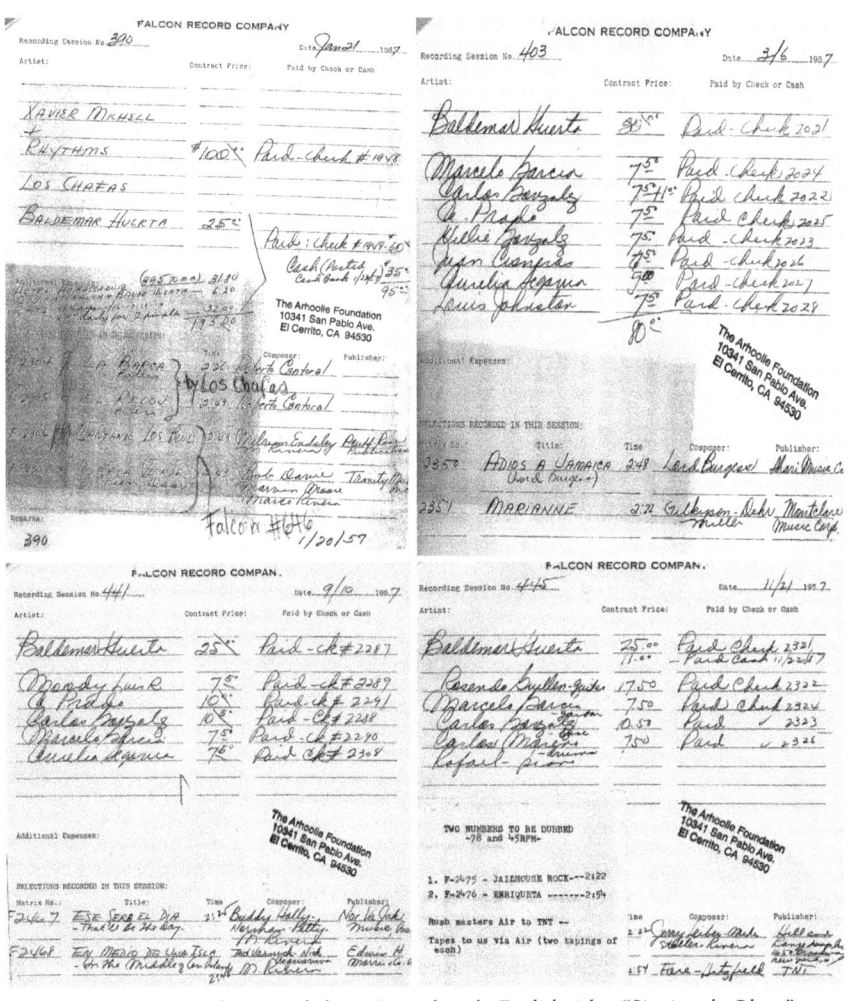

Mainstream rock hits recorded into Spanish rock. English titles: "Singing the Blues," "Green Door," "Farewell Jamaica," "Marianne," "That Will Be the Day," "In the Middle of the Island," "Jailhouse Rock," and "Henrietta" (1957)

Wasted Days and Wasted Nights

"El Twist," "I've Got a Tiger by the Tail," "You Lied to My Heart," and
"Your Cheating Heart" (1960)

"From My Eyes" by Freddy Fender

*I took the songs that were becoming popular on the Anglo
charts and translated them into Spanish.
I was the first Mexican American rock 'n' roller to sing south of the [Texas] border and
across the Rio Grande. I recorded many more records starting with Falcón in 1956.
It sold well into Mexico, Cuba, and many parts of South America.
Falcón Records was connected to Peerless Records, which had distribution all over Mexico.
"My people" in the valley billed me as "The Bebop Kid."
I had long sideburns and a greasy duck-ass haircut!*

Tammy Lorraine Huerta Fender

First early records with both names **Baldemar Huerta** *and* **El Bebop Kid**:
English Rock songs recorded in Spanish language
"Chantilly Lace," "Botecito De Vela," "Mala, Mala, Mala,"
and "El Twist" (Falcón label, 1958-1960)

Music Timeline by Music Archivist and Writer Ramón Hernández

"Ay Amor," which featured "No Seas Cruel" ("Don't Be Cruel") on the flip side, was first released as a 78-rpm single in April 1957, but it was the B Side that got the radio airplay in South Texas and Mexico and became a hit. Hence, the Elvis Presley hit recorded with Los Romanceros became the first existing and tangible Spanish-language rock 'n' roll song ever recorded by an American artist of Mexican descent in this country.

Rock 'n' roll was El Bebop Kid's first calling card, and according to McAllen, Texas-based Falcón Records and Discos Peerless label honchos in Monterrey, Mexico, it went on to sell over one million copies in the Latin Hemisphere. This was after "No Seas Cruel" was released as a 45-rpm single with airplay and distribution extending to the rest of the United States, over all of Mexico and as far as South America.

The fact that it was the first genuine rock 'n' roll record to peak and reach the top spot in those countries was quite a feat. It was a historical first as "No Seas Cruel" beat out trios, bands, orchestras and vocalists doing boleros, *rancheras, corridos,* rumbas, contemporary pop tunes, mambo, and the cha-cha.

In the United States, Pat Boone and other crooners had recorded some versions of Elvis' hits because rock 'n' roll was considered too wild and even vulgar to others. In Mexico, some orchestras had recorded boogie-woogie and jazzed-up versions of American rock 'n' roll hits, and these were first embraced by upper-class adults but not teenagers.

However, no one had exposed Mexican youth to such raw soul, power, and energy like the San Benito, Texas music rebel, who as El Bebop Kid deeply influenced teenagers across the Rio Grande to the tip of South America. When they heard Baldemar rocking in their own language, they went wild.

The result is that he unknowingly started a wave, a counterculture movement, the creation and establishment of a new music genre when Mexican teenagers started forming their own garage *rocanrol* (rock 'n' roll) bands and combos.

This same year, 1957, "Adios A Jamaica" and "En Medio De Una Isla" were also released. Shortly thereafter, both tunes were covered by Los Hooligans, who went on to make a name for themselves covering most of Freddy's rock-*en-Español* hits in Mexico. And they weren't the only ones becoming famous by riding Freddy's coattails.

Consequently, Baldemar could easily be considered the *Father of Rock 'n' Roll en Español* in Mexico.

Chapter VII

"Wasted Days and Wasted Nights"

The Bebop Kid
The Starlight Club
"Mean Woman"
Drugs and Rock 'n' roll
"Yo Mando!" ("I'm Boss!")
"Like King Kong with no fear:
I Want My F—king Wife!"

Balde was nineteen and Louis René Moody was twenty when The Bebop Kid was hired to bring in the New Year as the headline act at the civic center in Brownsville.

So, on New Year's Eve 1956, Balde, as El Bebop Kid, sold out the rock 'n' roll show in advance. Then he and the band—Rubén Pompa (acoustic guitar); (Louis, drums), and Alfred Serna ("doo wop, doo-wah" backup vocals)—brought down the house with "Ay Amor," "No Seas Cruel," "In the Still of the Night," and, of course, "Hound Dog."

And as Louise recalled, "We had a lot of fun, and it is a night that I will never forget."

"From My Eyes" by Freddy Fender
I was hogging the mic every time I went somewhere, just getting whoever was performing to back me up whether they wanted to or not, as I just stuck to the mic!

The Bebop Kid's Own Art: American Top 10 Rock Tunes
Translated into Spanish-Language Versions of Rock 'n' Roll

In early 1957, Musicians Rosendo "Chendo" and Louisiana-native Archie H. Pier were in a band called the Rhythmaires. Their band played both rock and country music on a regular basis at Jewels Country and Western Dance Hall in Harlingen, a club that catered to *los Americanos*.

One day, Balde, along with four other buddies, walked in on the Rhythmaires while they were performing; they liked their style of playing. So, he sent one of his buddies up to the bandstand to ask them if Balde could sing along with them. However, The Rhythmaires actually got off the stage because Balde accompanied himself (monopolizing the mic) and sang Spanish-language versions of "Hound Dog" and "Don't Be Cruel." Then Balde finished showing off with another rock tune "Roll over Beethoven." Guillén clearly remembers how everyone just went crazy over The Bebop Kid.

Guillén also recalled another incident that occurred when he was attending Brownsville High School.

"I was seated in a U.S. government class in the school's basement. It was about 2:00 p.m. when I saw Balde approaching, and he was on foot. Balde softly tapped on the window and stood outside the classroom. Then in a low voice, he asked me if I wanted to skip school, go to a nearby A&W stand, and entertain for free for root beer drinks."

Guillén responded that he could not go with him during school hours. Then Balde asked him if he could borrow his metallic green solid wood guitar. "I said, 'Just go over to the house and tell my mother I said that it was all right.'"

Six months went by, and Guillén had not seen Balde or his metallic green guitar. Until one afternoon, while cruising around town, he and Archie saw Balde playing the guitar in a parking lot by the civic center on Eighteenth Street. Guillén went up to him and said, "*¿Que pasó, Balde?* (What's up, Balde?) You never returned my guitar." Balde handed over the guitar and told him he had been "fine-tuning" it for him.

However, Balde did return the kind act shown to him; he told Guillén that he was recording with Falcón as El Bebop Kid and that he wanted to include him in his next recording. During this session, Guillén backed him up on "El Rock de la Carcel" ("Jailhouse Rock"), "Encaje de Chantilly" ("Chantilly Lace"), and "Tequila" an instrumental piece. Guillén was paid $25 for playing guitar for Balde.

After Guillén graduated from high school, Balde asked him to go on tour with him to Louisiana, but he turned him down; instead, he got married and joined the U.S. Air Force. He said he didn't want to face a rough life on the road.

Balde went on to record sixteen more mainstream rock songs in Spanish, like "Un Gato De La Cola" ("I've Got a Tiger by the Tail"), "El Twist" ("The Twist"), "Esa Sera el Dia" ("That Will Be the Day"), "Adios Jamaica" ("Jamaica Farewell"), "En Media de la Isla" ("In the Middle of an Island"), "Cantando Los Blues" ("Singing the Blues"), "Puerta Verde" ("Green Door"), "Te Acusa El Corazon" ("Your Cheating Heart"), and "Marianne."

These were all American top 10 rock tunes that Balde translated into Spanish-language versions of rock 'n' roll. This is an art, and The Bebop Kid had begun to make a living at it from then on.

Los Romanceros in front of San Benito civic center at 210 East Heywood Street, in San Benito, Texas. (February 1957) Freddy Trevino (saxophone), Benny Huerta (guitar), Baldemar Huerta (singer and lead guitar, wearing silk shirt), and Louis René Moody (drums) with wife Ofelia Garza

"From My Eyes" by Freddy Fender

I was playing around, but I think that subconsciously, I had a vision [superstardom].

Balde and Los Romanceros Kick Off Rock 'n' Roll at the San Benito Civic Center

Balde formed his first rockabilly band Los Romanceros with Benny Huerta on rhythm guitar, Freddy Trevino on saxophone, and Louis on drums. Of course, Freddy was their lead singer and played lead guitar. The site of their first gig was at the San Benito civic center.

They had just started playing rock 'n' roll in the Rio Grande Valley. All four band members were onstage, and Louis' girlfriend Ofelia and mother were collecting admission at the door.

That night an out-of-towner kept pestering Louis' girlfriend to dance, and in spite of her repeatedly brushing him off with a flat no, he continued to harass her.

Finally, Pete Maldonado, a large football player with the San Benito Greyhounds, stepped in and asked him to back off. Maldonado took him outside, and a fight broke out. The night ended with the high school football star getting stabbed; the young man would die.

Well, there went that. Louis sighed. "We just kept trying to keep rock 'n' roll alive, especially in *el valle,* where it had a rough crowd.

Most of the time, Balde did not have a car, so he had to walk everywhere or bum rides to get to his gigs. However, he was always dressed up for the occasion. His mother, Máge, had always shopped at secondhand stores and he learned to do the same.

Balde was a rail-thin *chuco* (hip dude) who had a knack for finding almost new, sleek, silky, cool-looking clothes in stores like Goodwill. When possible, he went shopping right before each gig. Then he would also grease up his hair with Tres Flores, just like his father Serapio.

Moreover, Balde would go anywhere to sing, even going as far as to play with black bands, which was unheard of back then. He did not care who said what to him. He was a true blue and loyal musician, first and last. Down in the Rio Grande Valley, black or Mexican, they were all in the same boat—dirt poor.

The Bebop Kid waiting to entertain the crowd at a club in Matamoros, Tamaulipas, Mexico. Louis, Ernest "Chapita" Chapa, and Balde (1957).

Music Timeline by Music Archivist and Writer Ramón Hernández

Thanks to super powered radio stations with as much as one million watts of power, programs directed at American audiences were transmitted from the Mexican side of *la frontera* (Texas-Mexico border). Hence their signal reached as far north as Chicago and the tri-state area of Michigan, Indiana and Ohio; it was at one of these stations, XERB, across from Del Rio, Texas, that Wolfman Jack introduced an entire generation of teenagers to rhythm and blues. Border radio was not only about music but also became a mecca for evangelists, medicine men, and others to sell their religion, cures, and wares. So, border radio was a springboard for all these genres and, most importantly, for Balde's music.

Freddy's first official music three-month tour.
Louis Moody, Ramiro "Ram" Rodriguez, Balde Huerta, and Marmolejo.
The Senator Bar in Pueblo, Colorado (1957).

"The Bebop Kid!" logo seen in print on the bass drum.
Marmolejo (saxophone), Louis (drums), Balde "The Bebop Kid" (guitar), and Ram (trumpet)
The Senator Bar in Pueblo, Colorado (1957)

Wasted Days and Wasted Nights

Freddy's First Three-Month Tour to Pueblo Colorado: Earning $75 Per Week

The Bebop Kid's rockabilly music was first heard on local radio stations in South Texas. As more locals began to listen in, a medicine man named Valadez heard Balde sing and asked him to accompany him on his travels. Thus, Balde's first tour was a three-month road trip with a medicine man that took him from Northwest Texas to Colorado. Valadez became Balde's short-term manager/booking agent, and began to promote him. He booked them in San Angelo, Dallas, Fort Worth, Lubbock, and Pueblo, Colorado. This is when Balde left Eva behind to stay with his mother on Rossiter Street while he went off to make a living as an entertainer.

Balde was able to carry the whole show on his own, stated Louis. However, Balde took Louis (from San Benito), Ramiro "Ram" Rodríguez (from Corpus Christi), and Marmolejo (from Robstown) with him on the road. Furthermore, Louis had never seen girls crowd the stage quite like the way they did there, when the Bebop Kid packed them in at a dance in San Angelo.

Louis said. "Yes, Balde and his valley boys were booked and filling venues every night except Mondays. However, they were in such high demand that they would be invited to play at local parties on their nights off and who is going to turn down extra cash?"

During their tour, they ran into the Texas queen, legendary artist Lydia Mendoza; they also got their first taste of discrimination. There were some prejudices back home, but not as in Lubbock, Texas! Balde and Louis soon found this out when they drove through a small West Texas town looking for a place to eat and they spotted a restaurant with a sign that stated, "No Blacks."

Balde told Louis to go check it out. Then as Louis approached the restaurant door and before he could open his mouth, the gringo restaurant owner snapped, "Yeah! That means you too!"

Balde was used to social prejudice and discrimination from both Mexicans and gringos, but to see Louis, who was Irish, be discriminated against was particularly funny. Louis laughed out loud as he repeated, "Yeah, you too, out!"

During the three months they were gone, the musicians made $75 per week; they earned a few hundred bucks more on other gigs they picked up along the way. Then they all packed into Ram's car and drove back to Texas.

After they dropped off Marmolejo, Ram drove home to Corpus Christi. Then Balde and Louis bought a cheap car in Robstown.

Next, they played two dances in Corpus Christi. For this gig, they had four horns, a bass, a piano, and Louis was still on drums. For that weekend, the medicine man rented the Armory Hall in the San Juan civic center. Balde was so popular in the area now that people slept in their cars the night prior to ensure that they would be able to get in. Sure enough, on Saturday night, the place was packed as tight as a can of sardines!

On Sunday, the guys drove up to the civic center parking lot to look for another gig. They waited, and when someone drove up, Louis asked them how they had found out about the dance the night before. They said it was all over the radio and there were posters all over town. The driver told them there was going to be a wedding and a reception that night, and so the band crashed that party and made some extra pocket money.

Evidently, the boys were very, very hungry for work. Balde was so happy to finally make some real money to take home to his mother, Máge, and his siblings.

Return to My Parents Wedding Blitz: Freddy Writes "Wasted Days and Wasted Nights"

Not long after their honeymoon, Eva realized that Balde's lifestyle and dream was not an ordinary one. She began to kick him out of the house because he was playing at local honky-tonks. He often played at a place called the Starlight Club, which was located in downtown Harlingen, not getting home until early the next morning. Balde wound up practically living there soon after he married.

Wayne Duncan owned the Starlight Club. Eva recalls him as being very tall, conservative, and businesslike; but in spite of his professional demeanor, he made her feel uneasy.

He hired Balde to sing on a weekly basis at the Starlight. Eva's brothers, Gilbert and baby Paul, would sometimes come by and hit Balde for a few bucks. They would wait in the parking lot and wait for Balde to come outside and give them a little pocket money.

On the home front, Eva liked to antagonize Balde, and she knew how to press his buttons. So, to avoid arguing with Eva about working late hours, he would sneak off early to the Starlight.

Soon after Eva kicked Balde out of the house, he started sleeping on a cot Duncan kept in the back for musicians who needed to stay overnight.

On the other side of the coin, Eva also knew how to win him back by playing hard to get or by giving him the silent treatment—and it always worked.

One evening, in 1958, Las Califas, Mary and Eva, went to the Starlight to see Balde sing. They went into the ladies' bathroom. They were still teenagers; therefore, they would still giggle and like to talk about boys.

Balde, who was in the men's bathroom, overheard Eva through the paper-thin walls. He started cussing at her out loud and yelling, "You better cut your shit out, Eva!"

It was that night, while sitting on the commode, that Balde wrote on a paper tissue the passionate tale of his "Wasted Days and Wasted Nights" spent over his young wife, Evangelina.

She recalls that he even sang the song to her on stage that night. The more Eva (the Spaniard) gave him a hard time or ignored him, the more he would write lyrics and melodies down on paper napkins, brown paper bags, cardboard, or anything that was at his disposal.

Balde wrote songs, "Wasted Days and Wasted Nights" and a killer rock tune called "Mean Woman" about La Califa (he later translated "Mean Woman" into Spanish and called it "Que Mala").

Baldemar Huerta, the Mexican Elvis

"From My Eyes" by Freddy Fender

I was separated from my wife, and a lot of people think I wrote it in prison ("Wasted Days and Wasted Nights"). It is about how wrongly I invested in a love affair. You see, I'm a romantic, and we romantics are more sensitive to the way people feel. We love more and we hurt more, and when we're hurt—we hurt for a long time.

The Starlight Club

Armando "Mando" Peña was Balde's first professional drummer. The *Cubano* (Cuban), who once backed up Sammy Davis Jr. in a movie, also lived in the Rio Grande Valley.

When Mando would have a drum solo, they would turn the lights out. You could see his white teeth in his pretty smile, his white gloves, his drumsticks with white-tip, and The Bebop Kid's name glowing in the dark written on his bass drum. Mando would just captivate the crowd with this effect, and girls went crazy over him because he was a very good-looking guy with dreamy eyes (I vividly remember him when I was a little girl.)

One evening, Mando called Louis and told him to go to the Starlight and back up Balde as a drummer because he could not find a ride. Instead, Louis told Balde, "Hey, Balde, I don't want to play backup for you on drums anymore. I want to be in the front."

Balde said, "Okay, well then, show me something!"

Louis grabbed someone else's electric guitar and began to play a little.

That night, Louis played guitar, and they ended up using a house drummer.

A week later, Balde and Louis went to La Villita, where a group from San Antonio was playing. It was a singer named Little Sammy, who was playing electric bass guitar and singing rock 'n' roll.

Balde and Louis just looked at each other, and when Monday morning arrived, they both went to the music store in Harlingen and bought an electric bass guitar and amplifier for Louis. Thereafter, the three of them would pack the crowds in.

They became a big hit in the clubs in *el valle*. No one else who lived in San Benito had an electric bass. Louis also played bass guitar with other groups; however, he liked playing rhythm and blues with Balde the most. He said Balde would teach him a lot more songs called "Peanuts."

However, when Mando could not appear to perform, Balde would use backup drummers like Little Herman, a black dude from San Antonio. Little Herman had been playing jazz music but now wanted to play rock 'n' roll. Little Herman stayed, and another drummer named Jackson, joined them. So now they had two very good black drummers, plus a Cuban.

During the late 1950s, musicians were performing for next to nothing since small-town-club pay scales were ridiculously low, so one night, Louis reproached Balde with "Hey, I want more than $6 a night!"

"What? You want to make more than me, or what?" Balde shot back.

"This is not enough money!" Louis complained. "I'm standing onstage looking at forty-four cases of beer and at 50¢ apiece. You can't tell me that we can't make more than six bucks!" Can you believe that $22 could buy forty-four cases of beer?

"Balde would have never asked for more money from anyone if I hadn't brought it up because he was always about the music and pleasing the crowd," Louis admitted. Duncan gave in and started paying Balde $10 and Louis $8 a night.

*Three-man rock band. Freddy playing every mainstream
rock, country, and blues hit under the sun.
Louis Rene Moody (bass guitar), Balde (lead guitar), and Mando Peña (on drums).*

"From My Eyes" by Freddy Fender
*By late 1956, I was definitely trying to keep a band together,
or as we called them back then, combos,
and get bookings during the holidays. We did instrumentals and little vocals, very simple stuff.
I played rhythm and lead guitar. I had a bass player and a drummer.
We were playing in the style of the Bill Black Combo.
That was me, very simple.
All our instruments and the microphone were connected to one Sears Silvertone amp!*

Evangelina Huerta (Mrs. Fender)
Balde was turning criminal!

Drugs and Spanglish Rock 'n' roll

Sure enough, Balde plus Louis, and his brother Evaristo began to earn extra money on the side by making drug runs as they crossed back and forth across the Mexican border. All three would sneak the drugs into the state by stashing them in the (Bebop Kid's) bass drum. On their way out of town to perform at certain cities and states, they would drop off the drugs at the predesignated places for the drug cartel.

Pill popping was the popular thing to do to get high back in the 1950s–1960s. And Balde was always the life of the party because he liked to sing, drink, and have fun, period! He also lived high on speed much of the time. Balde was quite the charismatic person and very friendly—but he was no angel. So, wherever Balde went, drugs were sure to follow him.

One night, Balde and his musicians were playing at Chip's Café, a local dive in Port Isabel, at South Padre Island, Texas, when they found out that the fill-in drummer was about to be arrested and charged with possession of drugs. The law enforcement officials searched them and found nothing on them. They couldn't blame it on just one person, so the police officers let them off the hook and allowed Balde to continue playing that evening. They got very lucky that night. Of course, the ordeal was posted in the *Port Isabel Press* newspapers the very next morning.

A Tragic Accident: On Speed Speeding

In December of 1958, Evaristo Moody had moved to the Windy City of Chicago Heights. He had gotten married and his wife was expecting a baby. However, he had just purchased a brand-new white Cadillac convertible, and drove back from Chicago to visit his brother. Louis was now working as a medic at the State Tuberculosis Hospital, which was outside city limits in Harlingen.

Evaristo, his cousin Roy Moody, and Balde decided to go party early that day while Louis was at work. They thought they would have some fun before having to pick Louis up at 4 o'clock pm.

By the time it was time to pick up Louis from work, Balde, Evaristo and Roy were all intoxicated and speeding on black mollies and whatnot. Roy lived in Los Indios not too far away from Harlingen, and so they dropped him off at home. Then on their way back, they drove through Rangerville city back toward Harlingen. That is when Evarista asked Balde, "Hey *vato* (dude) you want to drive my new convertible?" Of course, Balde took over the wheel and sped off on the way to pick up Louis.

It was on Rangerville Road that Balde came upon a sharp curve. Since it was a new car, the steering wheel was very touchy; Balde barely touched it to make the sharp turn at a high rate of speed. Still high as a kite, Evaristo placed his foot on top of Balde's foot, which was on the gas pedal, to make his new car go even faster and the car went out of control.

The convertible flipped repeatedly. Both were thrown out of the vehicle and Balde landed on soft ground. Then he quickly went toward Evaristo and placed his hand behind Evaristo's head, but it was all messed up. Evaristo had not been so lucky; he hit the pavement hard and died instantly. For many years, Balde felt bad about the accident.

Unfortunately, this tragic accident did not stop Balde's lifestyle of performing, partying, and making drug runs for the Rio Grande Valley *mafia* just to make some extra cash.

This would be just the first of many tragedies to come in the true life-story of the late Freddy Fender and his rise to redemption.

Freddy's Mentality: *"Yo mando!"* ("I'm boss!")

At the time, Louis had been dating Eva's sister, Beatrice, another one of the Califas. On one of these drug-runs up north to Chicago, Louis drove a white Chevrolet El Camino pickup while Balde and Eva drove the second vehicle, a black Bel Air convertible. The pickup had fiberglass from the tire wells to the back of the truck; it was in the wells that they stashed fifty pounds of marijuana on each side. In those days, this was a lot of pot.

Eva would go along with Balde because she loved him and wanted to be with him even though he was drinking or drugging.

As for Balde, things were going to get done his way, or else! He made that clear when he would tell her, *"Yo mando!"* ("I'm boss!")

Louis took note that instead of slapping a woman with an open hand, "Balde would [only] hit Eva with the back of his hand, or fist." He would tell Balde to lighten up on her but he wouldn't let up. It was like a love and hate relationship, Louis recalled.

Evangelina
I wound up with a guy like my dad, Marcus. He cheated on me and would lie about everything.
Your father was cruel to me, but your father loved me too.
But if he couldn't have me, nobody else was going to, either.
I was so scared to date or marry anybody or be in front of your dad or he would find out and hurt me or the other person. I had other guys wanting to marry me.
Mary would say, "Why don't you? He has hurt you!"
I would leave town, and Balde would just follow me anywhere.

"Like King Kong with No Fear: I Want My F—king Wife!"

Every time Balde would hit Eva, Mary would call the cops. But each time, Eva would get him right out of jail! Eva did try to get away from him. Once, she went as far as Corpus Christi to live with Mary in a small duplex home at the corner of Kenny and Port streets.

One day in 1958, Eva, with her hair now dyed blonde, was wearing a pretty blue shoulder-strap sundress. She looked very beautiful, but was still hiding from Balde. Suddenly, she sensed his presence. She peeked out the window just in time to see him pulling up to the duplex parking lot. Eva knew where Mary was and quickly went out the back door to ask her neighbor to take her to see Mary.

She knew that Mary was nearby at a local lounge with Lalo, a merchant marine with whom she would party each time he came into port. It was located on Port Street, which was known to be a rough area.

When Eva arrived, she quickly leaned over to whisper into Mary's ear that Balde was in town and that she was scared.

In San Benito, Lalo had already told Balde that if he continued to mess with Eva or show himself in Corpus Christi, he was going to have to deal with him.

Suddenly, Balde barged in and shouted, "I want my f—king wife!" Then Eva saw the owner of the lounge slowly pass a Budweiser blade to Lalo.

Maybe he did see Eva, and maybe he did follow her, or a neighbor may have told him where Eva was. Anyway, Balde should never have walked in, as she put it.

(While on the road doing some research at an Austin library, I interviewed my mother. She was sitting quietly on a bed in our motel room. She let go and told me the true story of how Father really got that scar on his neck. Until now, it has never been revealed.)

"You do not mess with people like these men," she said. They were the type of men the locals respected because they were important local businessmen. This was also a very dangerous area to live in, and those who came in to drink at this particular lounge were as equally dangerous; even the women were very violent.

Holding the blade in his hand, Lalo looked Balde straight in the eyes and said threateningly, "Remember what I told you in San Benito? That if you ever came to Corpus and hit her again, that your ass was going to be mine!"

Balde ignored his threats as he reached for Eva, backslapped her, and then tore off her dress strap.

Then the owner got hold of Balde's arms and held them back. Then Lalo quickly stood up from his chair and slashed him from the back of his neck to the front of his throat. Lalo and the owner really meant to kill him.

Eva recalled, "Lalo might have saved my life that night because your dad went there like King Kong, with no fear and knowing those guys were not going to take his bull!

"They could have finished the job. Instead, they got Balde and threw him out like an animal right out the front door and onto the sidewalk.

"My heart hurt me," she gasped. "But he had no compassion for me, either!"

So, Mary and Eva sneaked out the back door and went around to the front of the lounge. They knew what type of guys Lalo and the club owner were. They were good people, but if you asked for trouble, they were not going to back off.

In spite of what could have been a fatal cut, Balde got up and continued to bang on the lounge door. Again, he said, "I want my f—king wife!" He wouldn't stop! As usual, nothing fazed him. Luckily, for Balde, they had locked the door to keep him from entering again.

She did not know if he was high on drugs, but Mary called 911 for an ambulance.

"Again, my heart was breaking for him," Eva said. "We didn't want the guys seeing us going out the back door because we didn't want to be raped, not that we necessarily would be, but we just didn't know.

"I just didn't want them hurting your dad anymore! By the time I got to the front, he was bleeding all over the place. He was on the ground in front of the lounge, and before the ambulance arrived, Balde looked at me and turned his head around, just so that I could see his neck, bleeding profusely.

"He kept doing that because he wanted me to feel sorry for him. The blood was just gushing out! I was scared to death, crying and crying. I was very sentimental."

Las Califas did not report what had happened because they didn't want to get in trouble with Lalo and the bar owner. They just told the ambulance driver "Somebody must have cut him!"

Somehow the paramedic knew Eva was Balde's wife, so he let her ride in the ambulance with him to the hospital. It took many stitches to close up the five-inch gash. "Of course, your dad was acting like he was dying, and I really thought he was dying too, so I helped him out by staying with him."

The doctor told him that if the cut had severed his artery, he would have bled to death.

After they left the hospital that night, Las Califas took Balde to their house. Mary went out again, but not before asking Eva if it was all right that she be left alone with him. Eva said yes.

After Mary left, Balde pinned Eva down. He was hurting her. She was crying and grabbed on to the stitches on his neck, but he just wouldn't let go of her!

Eva remarked, "Your dad was the type of guy that wanted me, and then he didn't want me. But he hurt me, and he'd beat me up; each time I left him, he wanted me even more.

"I told him that if he wouldn't get off, I was not going to let go of his stitches. When he took me by force, I pulled out all of his stitches, which later left him a big scar. What could I do? He was like a wild animal on top of me! But you have to stop fighting because you want to get it over with.

"Then he started to bleed again, and I didn't have the heart to throw him out!

"It was a mixture of love and violence there. You don't understand that here I am, young and seventeen, but even after all that, I still had compassion for him. After he took me by force, he was okay.

"I saw that he was still bleeding, but he acted as if it didn't hurt. I got him a towel and asked him if he wanted to go to the hospital and get restitched. He said no and went to sleep.

"After that, he talked me into going back with him to San Benito, to Máge's, as Balde always did.

"I was too stupid to ask why he was doing these things to me. I was too scared and too timid.

"Later, Balde and the bar owner became good friends and would party together.

"Your dad was a very forgiving man, or he was just very stupid!

"As for Lalo, after Balde got famous, he also became a minister (like Moy Gonzales), and they too became very good friends. In fact, Balde even slept at Lalo's house."

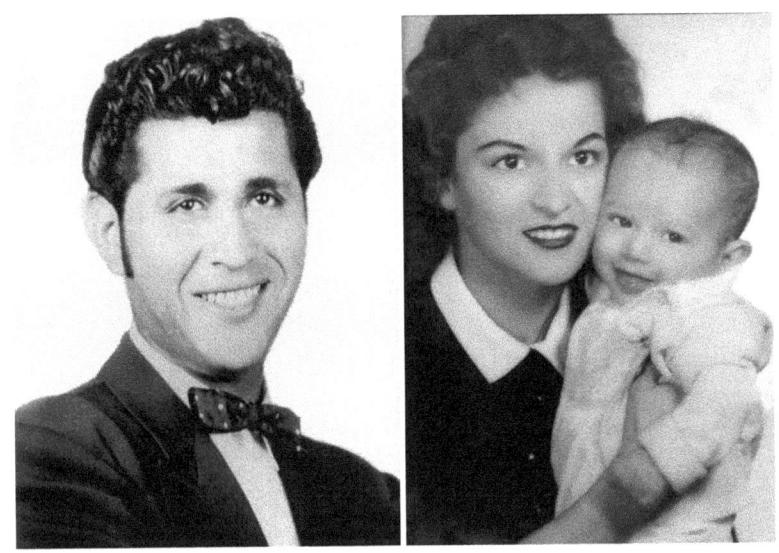

Evangelina Muñiz-Huerta holding Baldemar Jr. "Sonny Boy"/Baldemar Huerta

First Born: "Sonny Boy"

On May 18, 1958, Balde and Eva had their first baby. It was a boy and they named him Baldemar Jr., also known as Sonny Boy. He had blond hair, hazel eyes, curly eyelashes, and had very light skin. Prior to the birth, the women around El Jardín would come by and, per tradition, place large safety pins on Eva's clothes so that she would be sure to have a baby boy.

Sonny was three months old when he was baptized at Saint Benedict's Church. Ironically, his godparents were Lalo and Lalo's mother. He was so handsome; everybody wanted Sonny. Lalo and his mother really loved Sonny and took good care of him. As a kind gesture, they even had a portrait taken of Eva holding Sonny Boy.

Balde and Eva lived together as a small family in El Jardín where everyone in el barrio liked to dress Sonny as a cowboy, with a hat, shirt, and cowboy boots.

One morning, when Sonny Boy was a toddler, Eva woke up and saw that food had been thrown out of the refrigerator onto the floor. She looked for Sonny, but he was nowhere to be found. So, she woke Balde up, and they drove around looking for him.

They spotted Sonny walking along the road wearing his cowboy hat and shirt and Freddy's boots. When Eva asked Sonny where he was going, Sonny replied, "Ketchup, Mom, ketchup!"

Apparently, Sonny was trying to make it to the corner store to buy some ketchup with his good looks and no underpants.

Chapter VIII

Freddy Fender

Pseudonym "Freddy Fender"
"Holy One" and "Mean Woman"
Fame in Freddy's Reach: Imperial Records
Arrested in Baton Rouge
Pseudonym "Eddie Medina"

Freddy Fender (1959)

"From My Eyes" by Freddy Fender
Then I had glanced over to the amplifier, and it read, "Fender," so then I added Freddie.
Though, I always wanted to be called Flash, like Flash
Lightning [The comic book superhero]*!*

Wayne Duncan, who owned the Starlight Club, also owned a jukebox business route, which earned him a good living. He liked Balde's voice and knew he had potential, but he wanted him to change his birth name to an English-language name for marketing purposes. Balde was a dark-skinned Mexican with a heavy accent and too rough around the edges for the Anglo market.

In his quest to make Freddy a star, he went to Houston to visit The Crazy Cajun, a radio disc jockey and up and coming record producer, Huey Purvis Meaux, since he also wanted to learn the music business and needed some advice on how to start his own record label.

Even though Freddy still had a contract with Falcón Records as the Bebop Kid, Duncan became Balde's road manager and from this point onward, Baldemar Huerta began to record for the very first time under the moniker of *Freddie Fender* (with the letters ending in *ie*). His first 45-rpm single record with Duncan titled "Holy One," with "Mean Woman" on the flipside, has this alternate spelling. He also began to record English songs rather than just Spanish rock tunes.

At the time, Mexican names were not welcomed or embraced by the Anglo market; however, the regional market began to take notice of Freddy's voice and talent. For marketing purposes, the name *Freddy Fender* was soon adopted as it was simpler to advertise with twelve even letters.

As the story goes, this is how the name Freddy Fender became rapidly known and accepted in the music industry as an upcoming English-language recording artist.

"From My Eyes" by Freddy Fender
We recorded them [the 45-rpm singles] *in a little room in a home in Brownsville. We used a monaural machine just to do one track!*

Freddy Fender's English-language 45-RPM Singles

Duncan label finally made it possible for Freddy to record in English. Freddy wrote and recorded a catchy rock tune called "Mean Woman." For side B, he translated "Ay Amor" into "Holy One". Freddy's first single "Holy One" sold a few hundred thousand records in a few weeks within the South Texas region.

Freddy thought it was quite interesting that "Holy One," which was side B, became no. 1 in San Antonio; "Mean Woman," which was more rock, rhythm and blues, became no. 1 in Fort Worth and Dallas on KLIF radio. But the popularity of the songs must have been achieved by word of mouth. The fact that the disc jockeys were playing it was pretty darn good exposure, considering that Duncan Records was not a major label (Nelson. *Canciones de mi Barrio*. Roots of Tejano Rock. Arhoolie).

A year went by, and on one productive night, Freddy finally recorded "Wasted Days and Wasted Nights." Duncan paid Freddy $25 for the whole night of recordings. The first four 45-rpm singles were released on November 12, 1959, and the remaining four in 1960. Of the eight, Freddy composed "Holy One," "Mean Woman, "Wasted Days," and "Little Mama."

And what's so cool is that you can still find all of Freddy's vinyls/45-rpm records from the 1950s- '80s on Ebay. Beware, there are shrewd record collectors selling them at high bid.

"From My Eyes" by Freddy Fender
"Holy One" enabled me to do what I wanted to do.
It enabled me to get my first job in a club without getting fired the next week!
It was the first real proof that I could hold a job playing music in a club
and be able to depend upon it to make a living.
(Professor Fred Hopkins. *Blue Suede News* #47. Summer, 1999.)

"Holy One," "Mean Woman," "Wasted Days and Wasted Nights," and "San Antonio Rock"
(Duncan label, 1959)

"Crazy Baby," "Wild Side of Life," "Little Mama," and "Since I Met You Baby"
(Duncan label, 1960)

Freddy's Formula: Stripped Tunes Down to Bare Bones—Sheer Perfection!

Freddy was still doing his own thing as El Bebop Kid, still singing day to day at *los aficionados* and *cantinas*. And whoever was there, on the spot, got to play with The Bebop Kid on stage.

Once, Duncan got Freddy and Louis a spot on the *Ty Cobb Show* in Harlingen. The *Ty Cobb Show* was an afternoon valley-wide television program on KGBT and they got to play a couple of songs. It would be a collector's dream to find some video footage of The Bebop Kid in his early twenties, that's for sure.

As was his custom, Freddy liked to buy everything used and with its original parts intact. So, after his gigs picked up, he bought himself a used red Cadillac convertible, which he drove around the Rio Grande Valley to perform in the after-hour clubs in Matamoros, Mexico.

The Bebop Kid was also singing rhythm and blues tunes like "Ooh Poo Pah Doo," by Jessie Hill, which is one of my personal favorites. Then, when Chubby Checker hit radio airwaves with "The Twist," which became the new dance sensation, dancing the bebop started to taper off. Of course, Freddy also translated that hit into "El Twist."

This would become part of Freddy Fender's formula: taking an English-language hit, changing the lyrics into Spanish, and making each tune his own.

Freddy had a keen ear for music and would rearrange it to sheer perfection. He couldn't help but to strip tunes down to bare bones, right down to the melody as he saw fit.

Freddy's first vinyl The Only! Freddie Fender (Falcón label, 1959)

The Early 1960s in Baton Rouge, Louisiana: "Why Not?" "He's Black!"

Freddy Fender was first heard in Louisiana when "Holy One" became no. 1 at WAIL in Baton Rouge. It also became no. 1 on WNOE and WTAX in New Orleans. Both "Mean Woman" and "Holy One" were to continue to catch momentum rather quickly (Davia Nelson. Arhoolie Records. CD *Roots of Tejano Rock*, 1992.).

So when "Wasted Days and Wasted Nights" was released, it became an overnight hit at radio stations along the southern belt of Louisiana.

In Baton Rouge, folks didn't much care for Mexicans or blacks and they were not shy about letting you know it, either. New Orleans was a little more liberal than other towns in Louisiana.

Next, Henry Locke, a black Louisiana-native, who had just gotten out of the U.S. Air Force, became Freddy's drummer.

Since Freddy's records were hitting in Louisiana, Duncan decided to take the boys there. Along the way, Duncan stopped in Houston to visit Huey Meaux again. When Huey saw Locke, the first thing Huey told them was "You can't go to Louisiana with him!"

Louis abruptly asked, "Why not?"

"He's black! They don't allow that! As a matter a fact, they have shows on one night for the whites and the next for the blacks. You can't take him with you, and he can't even play with you," Huey warned them.

This was the 1960s. Freddy and Louis just looked at each other knowing that Huey was right and drove Locke back home.

Then, when they arrived in Baton Rouge, they hired a local teenage gringo drummer.

The way it was set up, Saturday's show was for whites, and Sunday was for black audiences only. That's the way it was, if you played in a band, it had to be all white or all black. If you played for a black crowd and you were white, then you would go back to your room during intermission, when bands were changing sets or musicians.

Many folks loved listening to "Wasted Days and Wasted Nights"—they just didn't like a Mexican singing it. Freddy stirred up a lot of commotion when he showed up in Baton Rouge as prejudiced crowds asked, "Who is he?" "Is he Mexican?" "Well, I thought he was Anglo!"

Yet Freddy Fender was rapidly drawing in crowds from all over the Southern Delta.

Fame in Freddy's Reach: Contract with Imperial Records in Los Angeles

In Baton Rouge, Duncan and Freddy stopped by to see S. J. Montebano, who owned M&S Record Shop. He doubled as a booking agent, and Duncan wanted Montebano to get Freddy to play at the CYO (Catholic Youth Organization).

"Holy One," "Wasted Days and Wasted Nights," and "Mean Woman" were his first three hot records, and they were selling like hotcakes in the Southern region.

Inside the record shop, Montebano introduced Freddy to a young beauty pageant queen of Baton Rouge (who shall remain anonymous—a last-minute request). She was working at the record shop and also attending Louisiana State University (LSU).

Miss beauty pageant queen, whom I interviewed, was gracious enough to share the happy and sad times she experienced while spending time with Freddy in the early 1960s. Interestingly, the beauty pageant queen also added that Freddy called her on the phone on that very same day.

"Freddy was very attractive. And when Freddy wanted someone, he really went after you! He was also very kind and sweet to me. We never really dated and were always among a group of people."

Meanwhile, Freddy was working hard promoting, singing, and doing one-nighters all over Louisiana trying to get some notoriety away from South Texas. Freddy's singles were circulating rather swiftly and the name *Freddy Fender* and voice was spreading like wildfire; Duncan and Freddy were on the move and weren't getting much sleep.

Meanwhile, Imperial Records released "Wasted Days and Wasted Nights" and it was rising on *Cashbox Magazine* top 100 singles at no. 82, along with the biggest artists of the 1960s. On top of that, Freddy and Duncan were about to sign a long-term record contract with Imperial Records in Los Angeles.

Finally, Freddy was being exposed to the Anglo audiences, getting noticed by mainstream music industries, and playing with other bebop bands.

Moreover, Freddy's dream as a young music composer, singer, and guitarist was finally coming to fruition; fame and stardom were now within his reach.

Music Timeline by Music Archivist and Writer Ramón Hernández

In 1959, Freddy was making enough waves to attract Imperial Records, one of the nation's biggest labels. So, Wayne Duncan capitalized on this and sold the licensing rights to all of Freddy's singles on Duncan Records to Lew Chudd, the president of this prestigious label in Hollywood. Hence, all of Freddy's singles were rereleased on Imperial and were distributed overseas and all over the United States.

This was a feather in his cap since Imperial is the company that released Fats Domino's "The Fat Man" and was the first major U.S. label to pioneer rock 'n' roll. They later also signed Ricky Nelson to their label, so this was a major *coup de maître* for Duncan.

The only thing Chudd asked of Freddy is that he cut off his sideburns because they made him look too Mexican. "Well, what do you think I am?" Freddy shot back. Despite his protests, he wound up shaving off the long sideburns. He also did away with the ducktail, waterfall hairstyle and toned down his flamboyant bluesman-of-the-barrio wardrobe. He was disgusted and detested the fact that it was really a "race" issue and that this was one way for Anglo-Saxons to force and squeeze Hispanics into a cookie-cutter mold. Worst of all, deep inside of him, he hated the aftertaste from giving in and swallowing his ethnic pride.

It was the ultimate sacrifice, but it also paid off because in 1960, the entire nation was exposed to the pain-filled tenor voice that propelled "Wasted Days and Wasted Nights" to *Cashbox Magazine*'s Top 100 Singles chart (http://cashboxmagazine.com/archives/60s_files/1960.html) on July 23, 1960. The tune moved up several more notches to no. 82 the week after, on July 30, 1960.

With this chart posting, Freddy had finally achieved national acclaim, since he was now in the same ranks as Elvis Presley, Rick Nelson, Roy Orbison, Connie Francis, Ray Charles, Fats Dominos, Chubby Checker, Sam Cooke, Lloyd Price, Paul Anka, Dion, Frankie Avalon, Frankie Valli, Bobby Darin, Bobby Rydell, Jackie Wilson, Little Willie John, B.B. King, Dinah Washington, the Coasters, the Platters, the Drifters, and others.

Furthermore, this is the proof that he had made it into the 'national' charts, one of the most-important requirements for nomination to the Rock and Roll Hall of Fame. Thereafter, Freddy shared the same stage with Fats Domino and B.B. King (who were two of his early inspirations) and a year later, he was rubbing elbows with Frankie Avalon and Roy Orbison.

Another very important point is that Freddy continued to make an impact in Mexico as whatever he recorded in the United States was reflected in the Latin Hemisphere. He did this with "Wasted Days and Wasted Nights," which numerous Mexican rock-n-roll bands recorded in Spanish. Again, thanks to the World Wide Web, the actual proof can be seen and heard through videos posted on YouTube by Los Reno, www.youtube.com/watch?v=8s7Ol5pod30; Los Zippers, www.youtube.com/watch?v=7n8HdiKW4UE; Los Rogers, www.youtube.com/watch?v=cdX0u8sZb6g, and Santos Guadalupe, www.youtube.com/watch?v=GdW08SECN-8, to cite a few.

Freddy Fender with Roy Orbison and rockabilly group the Tom Toms
Back row *(left to right):* *Leonard Walters, (Tom Toms), Freddy Fender, Tommy Brown (Tom Toms), Roy Orbison, Ronnie Dawson, Joel Colbert (Tom Toms), Eddie Wayne Hill (Tom Toms), David A. Martin (Tom Toms)* **Front row:** *Pete Antoniano (Carlos Brothers), Scotty Mckay, Bobby Rambo, Jimmy Carlos (Carlos Brothers), and Joe Donnell (Tom Toms). Guthrey Club, 214 Corinth Street, Dallas, Texas.*
(© Silicon Music PubCo., Gene Summers Archives, 1960)

"Holy One" and "Mean Woman" (Imperial label, 1960)
(Universal Music Enterprises of UMG Recordings, Inc.)

Wasted Days and Wasted Nights

"2 Rock'n Swingin' Sides! Billboard Spotlight Winner"
Fender's compositions "Holy One" ("Ay Amor") and "Mean Woman"
Cashbox-Imperial Records, April 9, 1960.

"Wasted Days and Wasted Nights" (Imperial label, 1960)
(Universal Music Enterprises of UMG Recordings, Inc.)

Tammy Lorraine Huerta Fender

Cashbox 1960 Index
Cashbox Main
Music Main

Cash Box
July 30, 1960

23-Jul-1960
6-Aug-1960

TW	Title	Artist	LW	Chg	2wks	3wks	4wks	#wks
1	I'm Sorry	Brenda Lee	1	--	2	3	5	8
2	Only The Lonely (Know How I Feel)	Roy Orbison	3	1	4	7	11	9
3	Itsy Bitsy Teenie Weenie Yellow Polkadot Bikini	Brian Hyland	4	1	29	64	--	4
4	Alley-Oop	Hollywood Argyles	2	-2	1	2	2	10
5	Mule Skinner Blues	Fendermen	7	2	7	9	10	9
6	Tell Laura I Love Her	Ray Peterson	10	4	14	19	41	6
7	Everybody's Somebody's Fool	Connie Francis	5	-2	3	1	1	12
8	It's Now Or Never	Elvis Presley	48	40	--	--	--	2
9	Because They're Young	Duane Eddy & The Rebels	6	-3	6	4	3	12
10	Please Help Me, I'm Falling	Hank Locklin	9	-1	10	15	21	9
11	Josephine	Bill Black's Combo	11	--	12	17	25	7
12	Walking To New Orleans	Fats Domino	13	1	25	32	72	5
13	Image Of A Girl	Safaris & The Phantom's Band	14	1	20	26	34	7
14	Look For A Star	Garry Miles	15	1	23	37	60	6
15	Feel So Fine	Johnny Preston	17	2	32	48	76	6
16	When Will I Be Loved	Everly Brothers	12	-4	9	13	19	8
17	(You Were Made For) All My Love	Jackie Wilson	28	11	64	86	--	4
18	A Rockin' Good Way (To Mess Around And Fall In Love)	Dinah Washington & Brook Benton	8	-10	5	5	6	11
19	There's Something On Your Mind (Pt. 2)	Bobby Marchan	19	--	28	38	45	6
20	Finger Poppin' Time	Hank Ballard & The Midnighters	37	17	56	67	87	7
21	Trouble In Paradise	Crests	24	3	40	49	64	6
22	A Woman, A Lover, A Friend	Jackie Wilson	34	12	45	74	--	4
23	That's All You Gotta Do	Brenda Lee	16	-7	13	11	15	9
24	Mission Bell	Donnie Brooks	35	11	46	50	58	7
25	Where Are You	Frankie Avalon	26	1	34	42	74	6
26	Big Boy Pete	Olympics	31	5	39	47	73	7
27	Wonderful World	Sam Cooke	21	-6	11	10	12	13
28	Theme From "The Unforgiven" (The Need For Love)	Don Costa & Orchestra	23	-5	18	22	28	13
29	Heartbreak (It's Hurtin' Me)	Little Willie John	29	--	36	44	49	7
30	This Bitter Earth	Dinah Washington	33	3	41	45	69	7
31	Question	Lloyd Price	44	13	52	61	75	6
32	Don't Come Knockin'	Fats Domino	41	9	57	62	86	6
33	Is A Blue Bird Blue	Conway Twitty	38	5	47	55	79	6
34	Cathy's Clown	Everly Brothers	18	-16	8	6	4	15
35	My Home Town	Paul Anka	25	--	15	8	8	12
36	One Of Us (Will Weep Tonight)	Patti Page	32	-4	35	36	54	8
37	Wake Me, Shake Me	Coasters	43	6	49	53	70	6
38	Sticks And Stones	Ray Charles	42	4	27	34	61	6
39	Walk--Don't Run	The Ventures	67	28	--	--	--	3
40	Love You So	Ron Holden With The Thunderbirds	36	-4	19	18	13	18
41	Volare	Bobby Rydell	--	New	--	--	--	1
42	The Twist	Chubby Checker	82	40	--	--	--	2
43	Runaround	Fleetwoods	22	-21	24	23	27	12
44	I'm Gettin' Better	Jim Reeves	47	3	50	57	68	5
45	I Really Don't Want To Know	Tommy Edwards	39	-6	21	21	22	12
46	In The Still Of The Night	Dion & The Belmonts	56	10	91	--	--	3
47	Burning Bridges	Jack Scott	27	-20	16	12	7	15
48	Clap Your Hands	Beau-Marks	45	-3	54	46	40	11
49	Pennies From Heaven	Skyliners	25	-24	26	24	29	13
50	Theme From "The Apartment"	Ferrante & Teicher	63	13	81	90	--	4
51	Won't You Come Home Bill Bailey	Bobby Darin	30	-21	17	16	16	10
52	Hey Little One	Dorsey Burnette	40	-12	43	41	50	8
53	Do You Mind?	Andy Williams	59	6	68	70	77	7
54	I Can't Help It	Adam Wade	31	3	59	60	67	8
55	Dreamin'	Johnny Burnette	65	10	89	100	--	4
56	All I Could Do Was Cry	Etta James	54	-2	55	27	24	15
57	Cool Water	Jack Scott	--	New	--	--	--	1
58	My Love	Nat "King" Cole & Stan Kenton	73	15	92	--	--	3
59	Down Yonder	Del Shannon (Johnny & The Hurricanes)	53	-6	48	31	32	9
60	In My Little Corner Of The World	Anita Bryant	70	10	--	--	--	2
61	Is There Any Chance	Marty Robbins	72	11	86	94	97	5
62	Banjo Boy	Jan & Kjeld	62	--	65	71	80	7
63	That's When I Cried	Jimmy Jones	76	13	99	--	--	3
64	Bad Man Blunder	Kingston Trio	64	--	63	68	78	6
65	Bongo Bongo Bongo	Preston Epps	83	18	90	92	99	5
66	Paper Roses	Anita Bryant	49	-17	22	14	9	16
67	All The Love I've Got	Mary Johnson	60	-7	58	65	84	6
68	My Tani	Brothers Four	4	1	71	75	71	7
69	One Boy	Joanie Sommers	86	17	100	--	--	3
70	Red Sails In The Sunset	Platters	98	28	--	--	--	2
71	Happy Shades Of Blue	Freddy "Boom Boom" Cannon	--	New	--	--	--	1
72	Little Bitty Pretty One	Frankie Lymon	--	New	--	--	--	1
73	Johnny Freedom	Johnny Horton	75	2	74	82	83	6
74	It Only Happened Yesterday	Jack Scott	--	New	--	--	--	1
75	Over The Rainbow	Demensions	93	18	--	--	--	2
76	Never On Sunday	Don Costa & Orchestra	--	New	--	--	--	1
77	Cat Nip	Dave "Baby" Cortez	79	2	80	83	89	7
78	Ta Ta	Clyde McPhatter	--	New	--	--	--	1
79	Lonely Little Robin	Browns	78	-1	85	97	--	4
80	I Shot Mr. Lee	Bobbettes	90	10	100	--	--	3
81	Mack The Knife	Ella Fitzgerald	52	-29	38	33	31	12
82	Wasted Days And Wasted Nights	Freddy Fender	84	2	93	95	--	4
83	Good Timin'	Jimmy Jones	46	-37	30	20	18	16
84	The Teacher	Felcons	85	1	94	98	--	4
85	Night Train	Viscounts	--	New	--	--	--	2
86	There's A Star Spangled Banner Waving #2 (The Ballad Of Francis Powers)	Red River Dave	87	1	95	--	--	3
87	Mio Amore	Flamingos	97	10	--	--	--	2
88	I Just Go For You	Jimmy Jones	92	4	--	--	--	2
89	Pardon Me	Billy Bland	91	2	96	--	--	3
90	Swingin' School	Bobby Rydell	50	-40	37	25	14	14
91	Theme From "Adventures In Paradise"	Jerry Byrd	95	4	97	--	--	3
92	Too Young To Go Steady	Connie Stevens	96	4	98	--	--	3
93	The Wreck Of The "John B"	Jimmie Rodgers	100	7	--	--	--	2
94	Tell The Truth	Ray Charles	--	New	--	--	--	1
95	Another Sleepless Night	Jimmy Clanton	58	-37	42	28	17	15
96	I've Been Loved Before	Shirley & Lee	100	4	100	--	--	4
97	Be Bop A-Lula	Everly Brothers	94	-3	84	89	100	5
98	I'll Fly Away	Lonnie Sattin	100	2	--	--	--	2
99	Young Emotions	Ricky Nelson	51	-48	33	30	23	15
100	Partin' Time	B.B. King	--	New	--	--	--	1
	We Go Together	Jan & Dean	--	New	--	--	--	1
	I Need You	Ted Taylor	--	New	--	--	--	1

"Wasted Days and Wasted Nights" climbing the charts at no. 82 http://cashboxmagazine.com/archives/60s_files/1960.html
(Cashbox Magazine Index, July, 23/30, 1960.)

Wasted Days and Wasted Nights ~119~

"From My Eyes" by Freddy Fender

At Rookies club someone [B.R. Detective] brought up a paper to me. I said no, I am not taking requests. The guy said no, this is not a request—it is a search warrant!

Warrant for Freddy's and Louis' Arrest in Baton Rouge, Louisiana

On a Friday the thirteenth in May of 1960, in the city of Baton Rouge, Louisiana, Freddy and Louis had a gig at Rookies Circle D Restaurant and Bar, at 2328 North Boulevard. It would be Freddy's and his bass player's most memorable performance of their lifetime (and one that they would never be able to forget!). Freddy was twenty-two, and Louis was twenty-three years old.

According to Louis, earlier that day, he met an Anglo woman in Baton Rouge; she liked him and gave him a bit of marijuana. He took it with him to smoke at their rented garage apartment at 2955 Calumet Street where they had a party with their newfound buddies, Coley Hudgenson and Ernie Hernández. The young men especially enjoyed tagging along and driving Balde to his gigs around town.

Later that day, Hudgenson invited a new guy named Castille over to the apartment. While Balde was dressing, the boys passed a lit joint around and smoked a little before the evening show. Louis then took the little leftover residue of pot and wrapped it in foil. He threw it into the oven, and the boys took off for Rookies Bar.

When Freddy and his buddies entered through the back door at Rookies, everybody except Castille walked in. Freddy, Louis, and the drummer (an Anglo kid) went up onstage, and they began playing music.

Then, while Freddy was entertaining the crowd, two undercover narcotic officers walked in. They stood right in front of the stage, and when Freddy was in the middle of a song, the detectives directed both Freddy and Louis to get down from the bandstand.

The drummer then asked Freddy, "What's going on?"

Freddy turned around and told the kid, "Just keep playing—we'll be right back!"

The officers followed Balde and Louis outside where they asked them, "We hear you boys brought marijuana in from Mexico, and we have warrants for your arrest!"

The officers then cuffed them, shoved them into the police car, and drove them to their apartment. There they sat them down on the sofa while they rummaged for illegal drugs.

"I couldn't find anything," one officer said.

"Me neither," another answered.

Then the detective that opened the oven said, "Lookit here what we found!"

"Excuse me," said Louis, "but you have to open the tinfoil before you can say something like that. I mean Superman can't see through foil, or is it just lead?" [Freddy kept quiet.]

Apparently, there was an ongoing narcotics investigation being conducted by the state police detective bureau and officers from the detective division of the sheriff's office in Baton Rouge.

Having found the evidence, the detectives needed to book them, they were taken downtown for more questioning. At the police station, they were even searched with a magnifying glass while the detectives shouted, "Now show us something green that is loose in your shirt or pants pocket! Whose pants, are they? Whose shirt is it?"

They were then searched thoroughly and made to turn their pockets inside out so the seams could be checked. Though nothing more than a few seeds and twigs could be found; they were still booked for the residue left in the foil.

An article in *The Advocate* newspaper read, "The detectives found a white handkerchief containing a tin foil of greenish vegetable material and some green seed in the stove oven. [And] The two men told them they planned to plant the marijuana seeds in Baton Rouge but were waiting for the weather to improve.... [And] The two purchased five cartons of marijuana in Mexico before coming to Baton Rouge." (*The Advocate*. 1960.) My interview with Louis confirmed that their statement was completely misinterpreted. However, he confirmed they were stoned on the evening of their arrest.

Back then, marijuana was considered a heavy drug, and having it in one's possession was a serious offense. *The Advocate*, as well as many other newspapers, followed the story of Freddy and Moody's arrest throughout the trial.

"From My Eyes" by Freddy Fender
I finally got my break. Only in this case it was a big break in my career!

* * *

"You got to remember that this was in 1960—one year after the '50s had ended—and the Louisiana legal system. Unlike the rest of the country, it is based on the Napoleonic Code: you're guilty until proven innocent!"
(Professor Fred Hopkins. *Blue Suede News* #47. Summer, 1999.)

* * *

"The kid (drummer) is probably still sitting there waiting wondering what happened!"

"On My Way to Compete for Miss Louisiana": Baton Rouge—Beauty Pageant Queen Blackballed

The beauty pageant queen's mother owned a popular diner, where cops would often stop by to eat breakfast and drink coffee. She said her mother didn't like her hanging out with Mexicans, so she gave her daughter a hard time about dating "them

Mexicans," as her mother called them. Her friends also wanted her to stop going out with both Freddy and Louis.

Prior to the arrest, the police had already been harassing Balde and Louis for being in Baton Rouge. This was before her mother had known she was going out with them and that the police would follow them all around town.

Inside the restaurant, she often overheard her mother talking to the local cops about "those two Mexicans." It was clear that her mother didn't want Freddy going out with her anymore.

The pageant queen said passionately to me, "Nobody was going to keep me from seeing Balde [Freddy]!"

Then she described the repercussions of dating a Mexican: "I had won a beauty pageant, and I was on the way to compete for Miss Louisiana, but I got blackballed out of the contest! The word had gotten around fast. Put it this way, they said it to me like this: 'If you continue to keep seeing him, you won't be able to be in the pageants.'"

She had already won many local pageants when she entered one sponsored by the American Veterans Association, and this is what she said happened next: "I was supposed to have gone to state! I won second runner-up, and I knew why! The other girls went to state, and I stayed local because I knew they were going to give me a hard time."

One evening, Jimmy, a local and popular and rising singer, asked the beauty pageant winner to go riding in his black Cadillac. When he tried to kiss her, she pushed him away.

"I thought we were just going for a ride," she said.

Jimmy told her, "You have been going out with that greasy Mexican. You mean I can't put my hands on you?"

"That was the end of that. I never saw Jimmy again," she affirmed. "I am not prejudiced toward anyone, so I was upset with the things people said about Balde and Mexicans. I did not understand it. I believe that Hispanics are not black. They are Spanish.

"When we were in a restaurant, you could hear people whispering about Balde. He thought it was funny and laughed it off, but I didn't think so.

"At that time, Freddy wore his shirts on the outside and buttoned down. I saw him onstage a few times. I also didn't drink alcohol at the time.

"I was not in town while Freddy was being arrested. When I got back home to Baton Rouge, Mother told me about it. But I already knew because it was in the paper and all! Mother said, 'I told you to stay away from him. I told you he was trouble. You just better be glad you weren't around at that time!'

"That is just being mean to get him off the stage like that. He wasn't a murderer. Couldn't they have waited until he got offstage?

"I was sad, and I couldn't see Freddy. I thought it was a trumped-up charge. Freddy was very conscientious about that stuff. He called it *junk* [marijuana].

"I was Miss Junior New Orleans, Miss Radio, and Rodeo Queen. I was just Miss Everything!

"Freddy always was in Texas and never got to see me in a pageant."

The beauty pageant queen was clearly upset and saddened about how Freddy and Louis had been treated in her hometown of Baton Rouge, Louisiana, in the early 1960s.

Freddy Pleads Not Guilty: Out on Bail with Drug Rehab Offer

At first, Freddy pleaded *not* guilty. The district attorney offered them a deal: they could go to a drug rehab center in Kentucky and pay their bail bond of $5,000 each. So, in order to raise money for bail and court fees, Duncan quickly drove to Chicago to try and lease a few of Freddy's songs to Checker Records, a subsidiary of Chess Records.

A few days later while they waited in jail for Duncan's return, they saw Castille walking by and placed in another cell. They glanced at one another. They weren't sure why he was there, but it looked pretty suspicious to Louis, since Castille was at the apartment when they had their little pot party on that fateful Friday the thirteenth. They did not communicate about the incident and Castille didn't stay in jail very long, either.

Upon Duncan's return, he only had a portion of the bond money for the two. So, Freddy asked Louis, "Do you think your dad can come up with the other fifteen hundred?"

Louis answered, "No! Besides, if he hocks the house, how am I going to repay my dad back with the type of jobs that I can do, like working at the grocery store or at a gas station in San Benito? The only thing backing me up is being a medic."

"Well then, if he doesn't get the money to get you out," Freddy told him, "I will go in and do the time and you can get out!"

Soon after, Louis' father drove up from San Benito and posted bond for him, and Duncan bailed Freddy out. Then they all left the state of Louisiana together and went back home to South Texas.

Freddy looking rather rough around the edges. Intimo Club (Intimate) in Matamoros, Mexico Mr. and Mrs. Wayne Duncan, Freddy, Betty Smith, Louis Moody, and Victoria Ford (February, 1961)

"From My Eyes" by Freddy Fender

*My grandfather's name was Benito, so I was also known as
Little Benny but I never recorded under the
name of "Benny." You see, in the '50s, everybody was known as "Little," like Little Richard,
Little Freddy, Little Benny, Little Johnny, Little Mickey, or Little Anthony.*

* * *

In January of 1961, I recorded the album Eddie con Los
Shades *under the name Eddie Medina.
I used that name because at the time I was still with Falcón
Records under my real name, Baldemar Huerta.
I chose Eddie Medina because my father's mother's last name was Medina.
And Eddie, I just like the name. The group was called
Los Shades because whoever played with me
on that very night, I just put sunglasses on them. We all wore them!*
(Davia Nelson. Arhoolie Records. CD *Roots of Tejano Rock*, 1992.)

Eddie con Los Shades: "One More Makes Ten—Let's Rock 'n' Roll!"

Eva was pregnant with a second child and Freddy didn't think twice about perjuring himself. At the time, he still had a contract with Falcón Records but he used the moniker of *Eddie Medina*. The name Medina was his paternal grandmother's last name. He wrote and recorded a whole album of Spanish rock songs for Ideal Records. He and Louis knew that they would most likely serve some time in prison; therefore, Freddy wanted to leave Eva with a little money. He felt badly about the whole arrest situation; Freddy quickly got his three-man band together.

Then Eddie Medina (Freddy) con Los Shades (two other band members) went into Ideal Records at 10:00 a.m. that morning. Louis was on bass guitar, while Little Herman and Henry Jackson alternated on drums and backup vocals.

However, whenever bands and vocalists such as Tony De La Rosa and/or Paulino Bernal were in town, they would stay over to get a recording session the next morning. This is what Tony De La Rosa had done. Freddy had no choice but to wait for him to finish recording. So, Eddie con Los Shades hung around listening to them record until noon.

This was a period when Isidro López, Sunny Ozuna and Little Joe, among others, were the biggest thing in South Texas.

Not one to waste idle time, Eddie Medina (Freddy) like "the Flash," was writing new lyrics and translating popular rock 'n' roll songs from English to Spanish until it was time for them to enter the recording studio.

Then Louis told Freddy to quickly come inside because he saw the other band unplugging their equipment and taking their setup apart. While Tony De La Rosa went out for lunch, Freddy saw an opportunity and seized it!

Eddie con Los Shades quickly recorded a song, "No Está Aquí" ("She's Not Here") using Henry Jackson and Little Herman as the backup singers. Altogether, they had nine songs down pat that were Freddy's!

When De La Rosa's musicians returned, they were busted! But instead of getting mad at Freddy, De La Rosa's saxophone player and guitarist picked up the maracas and claves and joined in.

By now, Freddy (as Eddie Medina) was on his ninth song and needed one more tune to make it ten.

One of the current hits was a *cumbia* with a Caribbean beat that contained the word Acapulco.

Freddy clearly remembered listening to it on the radio and said, "Hey, let's try this, man." And he came out with another one of his own rock'n compositions entitled "Acapulco Rock." No lines, no nothing—just "Let's go!"

They [Freddy] did it in *one take*, packed up, and left!

This is how Freddy came to record his first all-rock album at Ideal Records. The studio was behind Rio Grande Music Company on Sam Houston Road in San Benito where Paco Betancourt and Johnny Philips sold home appliances and jukeboxes. Next door, the senior citizens played dominos, and in the back was Ideal label's record studio.

Ideal's owner, Paco Betancourt, paid Eddie and the Shades $100 each for the ten recordings that make up this 1960 album (Ideal LP 109). Freddy wrote his best songs under pressure and havoc, and musically this album really rocks your feet off!

Freddy and Louis played their hearts out like there was no tomorrow and basically said *adios* to their friends and family.

Wasted Days and Wasted Nights

Freddy Fender as Eddie Medina (Ideal label, 1961)

45-rpm singles found with the pseudonym **Eddie Medina** *con Los Shades: "Acapulco Rock," "Desde Que Conosco" ("Since I Met You"), "Que Mala" (Song "Mean Woman" in Spanish), "No Está Aquí" ("She's Not Here"), "Que Soledad" ("Hello Loneliness," also in English), "No Quiero Nada Con Tu Amor" ("I Don't Want Anything to Do with Your Love"), "Dices Que Me Quieres" ("You Tell Me You Love Me"), "No La Vuelvo A Ver" ("Won't See Her Again"), "Dime Si Me Vas A Ver" ("Tell Me If You'll See Me"), and "Lucy Lucy"* (Ideal label, 1960s)

Offer off the Table: "No Money, No Deal! No Rehab": Jumped Bail: Go Straight to Jail and Do Not Pass Go!

At the time, Louis Moody went back to Baton Rouge to party with the local pageant queen and her friends for the weekend. However, when he went to the bus station to return home to San Benito, her mother had already called the neighborhood police to inform them of his whereabouts. Even though Louis was legally out on bail, he was hastily hauled back to the police station and locked up until his trial date.

As for Freddy, his trial had been set back because of an ongoing murder case that had continued over; Freddy's trial had been rescheduled and he was told to return that coming Monday. But Duncan and Freddy had been doing some traveling, trying to muster up enough money to pay their lawyer, Daniel Deblanc, to represent them.

Unfortunately, Freddy failed to appear in court on time, and so the District Attorney requested that the court raise his bail to $20,000 if they apprehended him. So, now Freddy had another charge on top of that for jumping bail. However, when Freddy arrived, he did turn himself in to the sheriff.

So, when Louis saw that Freddy and Duncan were present in the courtroom during their trial, he believed they were going to get them out of their mess. But when it came time to put up the money, Duncan and Freddy didn't quite have all of the funds to pay their court fees.

"Why did Duncan go and spend all the money? How can your manager make such a big mistake and sell all the rights to your songs?" Louis questioned Freddy.

"Why did you let that idiot spend all the money in New Orleans? You all just went to party! He didn't even care about you or about us! Why would he let you stay in prison?" Louis kept questioning Freddy.

Again, Louis shot back at Freddy. "Now we don't have the money to get the deal on rehab either!"

Louis remembers that Duncan would use anyone he ever came across. Duncan was raking in all the money, and they never saw any of it! Another reason Louis didn't like Duncan is because he owned jukeboxes; he had money and could easily have paid the lawyers to defend them, but he didn't.

They had to tell the lawyer that they were short of money and asked that this be accepted. He responded, "No money! No deal! No rehab!" The option for going to rehab in Kentucky was definitely off the table, period.

Sadly, Freddy had gone looking for work to sing and pay the court fees, but he was a just a little too late arriving to see the judge.

As Louis Moody summed it up, "We never had a fair trial and did ask to have a lawyer from the beginning, but we never really saw a lawyer until the last day, when the District Attorney requested more money. Freddy and Louis had no choice but to plead guilty to all charges.

With all the setbacks and fines during litigation, the court system, and their attorney, had no other choice but to follow through with the laws of Baton Rouge in the early 1960s.

Both Freddy and Moody were immediately handcuffed and taken straight to the Louisiana State Penitentiary in Angola, also known as the Alcatraz of the South.

Duncan's Side of the Story on Freddy's Arrest

Nonetheless, Wayne Duncan saw a lot of potential in Freddy and did the best he could for him at the time, considering the legal circumstances and troubles that Freddy often got himself into.

Sadly, the incident brought Freddy and Duncan's dream, of a career in the music industry to a shrieking halt.

Wayne Duncan shares his memories about his side of the story and the ordeal Freddy endured on his way to stardom at twenty-two years old. And I would like to thank Wayne Duncan and his family for believing and doing all they could for my late Father in 1960.

The following is a reprint of selected liner notes cited on back of the album cover *Since I Met You Baby* written by Wayne Duncan, (GRT Records, 1975):

> I decided to make a deal with Imperial Records. But "Holy One" was not the national hit we had hoped for, so Imperial released "Wasted Days and Wasted Nights." It started to climb the bestseller charts in *Cash Box* magazine. Imperial asked us to fly to Los Angeles to sign Freddy to an exclusive recording contract, but before we left, something happened that changed both our lives. He was living near Baton Rouge at the time, and suddenly, he was arrested for possession of marijuana. In the late '50s, that was a very serious offense, and I am convinced that Freddy was framed on the charges. I got Freddy out of jail on $20,000 bail, and we flew to Los Angeles. Suddenly, the story of Freddy's arrest hit the wire services and was in newspapers across the country.
>
> By the time we go in to see the head of Imperial Record's, the story of Freddy's arrest killed "Wasted Days and Wasted Nights." Imperial said there was nothing they could do and they wished us success with Freddy at whatever record company he might go to next. While Freddy was out on bail we recorded a great number of tunes including the songs in this album (*Since I Met You Baby*). We finally signed a contract with Chess Records out of Chicago

and they released one record. [Under pseudonym Jerry Glenn 45 single "Holy One"/ "You Can Take Me Like I Am"].

But the story of Freddy's arrest was still on the minds of both the disc jockeys and the public and so nothing happened. We even tried releasing his records under other names like Scotty Wayne [Duncan's son's name], but without success.

You might say that Freddy was a marked man. . . . He said you had to be "in" with the clique to come out alive. . . . A friend of his was killed in a crazy, silly argument over a TV channel, and worst of all to Freddy, the poor guy was buried at the prison.

Eventually the Louisiana governor, Jimmy Davis, helped us get Freddy out, but three years of his life had been wasted. . . .

Music Timeline by Music Archivist and Writer Ramón Hernández

Freddy's 1961 *Eddie con Los Shades* album made a huge impact in Mexico because his recording were genuine rock 'n' roll and his songs caught the immediate attention of Germán "Tin Tan" Valdés, one of Mexico's most popular comedic actors and singers.

Impressed by the San Benito-native's original lyrics and catchy rock 'n' roll beat, Tin Tan immediately recorded and included "No Está Aqui" in his "Pilotos de La Muerte" movie (www.youtube.com/watch?v=eB8YVZ6sbEs).

However, "Acapulco Rock," which Freddy also wrote, and which is in the *Eddie con Los Shades* album, had the greatest overall and most lasting impact since it was recorded by Miguel Ángel (www.youtube.com/watch?v=DR6tcL3sI_A) and Los Jokers (www.youtube.com/watch?v=dRvi4mdtsv8), who claimed it was an original tune.

Then there were versions by Manolo Muñoz (www.youtube.com/watch?v=OsN8yEHaeqM) and Los Hooligans (www.youtube.com/watch?v=XyGGrtu8oik), all before the year ended.

The covers continued with Los Súper Secos (www.youtube.com/watch?v=eVcfUAF7PGo), Rigo Tovar (www.youtube.com/watch?v=IkLwDjzGoK0), Tropical del Bravo (www.youtube.com/watch?v=leiuLAvo9Eg) (who did it as a cumbia), and Los Tatifans made it a kid's tune (www.youtube.com/watch?v=ej-sTsx9UU4).

The list of those who recorded "Acapulco Rock" continues with Chucho Pinto y sus Kassinos (www.youtube.com/watch?v=UZBaJtzuPE4), Tatiana (www.youtube.com/watch?v=whCgreVTG7k), Analu, Chiquinha/La Chilindrina, Musical Punto 7, La Banda del Recodo and most recently as a robotic electronic version by Maika and Vocaloid (www.youtube.com/watch?v=O_dwgd0DYCM).

A quick search of You Tube videos will also reveal that this tune continues to be performed by kids and bands from the Philippines to France and other parts of the world.

In spite of airplay around the world, Freddy Fender never received one cent in royalties for "Acapulco Rock." Perhaps this was due to the fact that Freddy—whose real name, as we know, is Baldemar Huerta—wrote them under the alias Eddie Medina.

Therefore, he is probably owed millions of dollars in Mexico because of the countless Freddy-penned rock-n-roll tunes that numerous Mexican bands recorded and sold in incredible numbers.

Another little known fact is that in Mexico, Freddy also recorded for Discos Peerless, Discos Flecha, Discos Dominante and other labels.

Furthermore, Mexican musicologist Arturo Lara and other sources state there are famous singers who can affirm that Freddy simply gave them new, unregistered handwritten original lyrics (while sitting at a bar enjoying a drink) without ever asking for a penny. Some of those compositions gave them a boost at the start of their success. However, there is no written proof of those transactions.

Chapter IX

"A Man Can Cry"

Angola Prison to DeQuincy
LA State Pen: "The Walk"
Pseudonym "Scotty Wayne"
Album "Recorded Inside Louisiana State Prison"

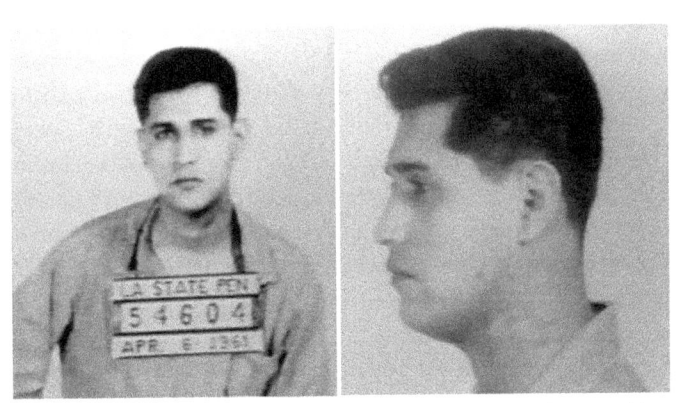

Angola, LA State Penitentiary (nicknamed the Alcatraz of the South)
Scar from knife wound seen on left side of neck (April 6, 1961).

"From My Eyes" by Freddy Fender
Prison for me was like a burial cemetery.
(Cook and Greenberg. "*Tex-Mex Troubadour.*" Newsweek Music Magazine, 1975.)

The Louisiana State Penitentiary of Angola is where Huddie William Ledbetter (best known as the legendary folk and blues singer Lead Belly) and many other talented musicians served time. Now Freddy Fender had to serve his turn and punishment there as well. As an inmate, he was forced back into migrant work, but this time, there were shotguns aimed and ready to fire if he were to escape his toil.

Each day, Freddy and Louis, along with their fellow inmates, walked the rows and did the hoeing. If they were caught cutting too much sugarcane instead of weeds, they would be written up and then placed in the hole. It was not until sometime between 7:00 p.m. and 9:00 p.m. that they were allowed to come in from the heat, beaten down from working the sugarcane crops all day long.

Freddy and Louis lucked out and got to share the same cell. One evening, Freddy sneaked out to play guitar with another inmate and was caught by a guard. Louis was totally unaware of this when he woke up and saw Freddy grabbing his bunk roll.

"Where are you going?" Louis asked.

Freddy responded, "Man, I was jamming with those guys, and they got me."

"Oh, okay." So, there went Freddy, back into the hole for another week.

A week later, Louis was in the warehouse eating an egg sandwich when a guard approached him and asked where he had gotten the sandwich. Louis told them he got it from the guys who delivered the food and he had thought nothing of it since they would always give him a little something extra. So, as Freddy was coming back out of the hole, Louis was going in for having eaten the unauthorized sandwich. As they passed each other, Louis turned to Freddy and said, "Hey, how did it go?"

Freddy answered, "It was all right. It was just a little cold at night."

Each day, the prisoners were loaded into big, long trucks and hauled off to work the fields. The prison guards would hold their rifles and trot alongside on their horses as they surveyed the field. As soon as the workers got off the truck, there were two guards on horses in front, and two more on every row of the field. One guard on each side at the end would start them off working, then the next two workers, and so on. Then the guards would rest and wait until the prisoners came out of the fields.

There was Freddy, under a blistering, hot sun, wielding a machete to cut weeds, having difficulty working, knowing he had three no. 1 regional hits— "Wasted Days and Wasted Nights," "Holy One," and "Mean Woman"—playing on the radio. And he couldn't do a damn thing about it!

At the time, Angola was the largest maximum-security prison in the United States. If Freddy had managed to escape, the prison was surrounded on three sides by the murky, muddy Mississippi River, which was riddled with water moccasins. The fourth side was an almost impenetrable, dense forest of trees, which was most likely inhabited by poisonous rattlesnakes.

Freddy sits in front center, playing claves and feeling defeated, as his dream of becoming a major recording artist has just been shot to hell. Louis Moody (playing bass guitar) is standing behind Freddy, still wearing his shades. Angola Prison, Louisiana. (1961-1962)

"From My Eyes" by Freddy Fender

I'd have to say I never got adjusted to, uh, confinement.
All I did was keep telling myself to keep on doing time, and just kept on doing it!
You get adjusted to a way of living with other convicts, compromising,
being diplomatic about things—smiling at people you don't like—
and having to dislike people you like because of the circumstances.
Racial tension was very heavy in the penitentiary at that time,
to the point that I was spotted by one of the guards playing guitar
with a black person and they put me in the hole for a week.
I always tried to get a benefit out of any situation.
I think I got a benefit being exposed to Southern music,
to be able to combine the frustrations and suffering of loneliness.
The separation from my family was hard.
I saw a lot of friends of mine cry like babies when they could not wait any longer for them.
So, I just took her [Eva] off the mailing list, and when I came out of the penitentiary,
I just got together with her and picked up the pieces again—go on forward and don't look back!

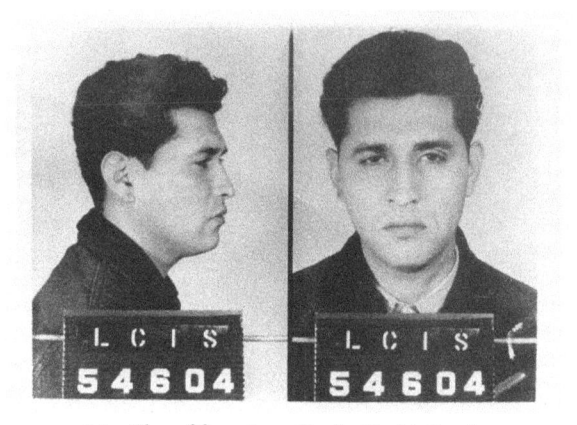

Mug Shot of first-time offender Freddy Fender.
(LCIS) Louisiana Correctional Industrustrial School in DeQuincy (1962)

Duncan's brother-in-law was a lieutenant at the prison, and he had the guards bring Freddy and Louis to his office to ask them how hard it was for them. Louis replied, "Very hard, get us out!"

Well, they did the second-best thing; after serving six months in Angola prison, a special place for hardened criminals, both were transferred to a correctional facility in the city of DeQuincy, an institution for first-time offenders, to serve out their five-year sentence.

The Walk
Freddy (third on left), *Louis* (far right), *with convict musicians at DeQuincy Correctional Institute (1962-1963).*

Freddy (second from left) *and Louis* (at the far right) *wearing sunglasses.*

"From My Eyes" by Freddy Fender

My time in prison was hard, but music made it better. I can remember when my bass player and I were busted together and walked into Angola carrying our guitar and bass instead of our clothes. Then every Saturday and Sunday, we would play on **The Walk** *for all my fellow convicts. I even recorded an album of Chicano songs on a portable tape recorder in prison. I guess I would have gone crazy if I hadn't had my guitar! (Freddy and Friends: "Freddy Salutes the Nation on this Bicentennial Year, 1776-1976")*

Racial Barriers: "The Walk"

At DeQuincy, skilled musicians would perform for the chamber of commerce. Afterward, the band would get to enjoy a cup of gumbo. At times, musicians were taken in state vehicles, like vans, to entertain Louisiana's state politicians. The city officials would inform them whether they were good or terrible musicians. They practiced hard, hoping and praying that they would be released as first-time offenders.

The Walk was held on visiting days each weekend. You got to do *The Walk* when the blacks got their visiting days on Saturdays. While the blacks visited their folks, the whites would have to walk to the playroom filled with musicians. On Sundays, it would be the opposite. *The Walk* would continue, but with the blacks walking to the music room and the whites walking the opposite direction to the visiting area. If you were Mexican or Puerto Rican, you were considered and classified as white. Freddy and Louis always tried sneaking into the music room after work on their days off.

Wasted Days and Wasted Nights

Both Freddy and Louis worked in the warehouse, and each morning, they received the orders for the day. They would fill them out and give them back to a guard named J. A. Puerta. The guard would stand there, look them over, and that was it! They were both also responsible for handing out the prison uniforms to the new inmates.

Again, they bunked across from each other, and Puerta gave Freddy a lot of leeway.

In DeQuincy, there were two honor cottages and each had twenty-eight rooms. There was a waiting list of who was next in line, but thanks to Puerta, Freddy would often get a room all to himself. They were supposed to lock him in at 5:00 p.m., but he would stay out until eight o'clock at night since he was in the honor cottage.

However, you really had to stay on your toes because if you were busted and placed in the hole, then you lost your turn, and the next inmate on the list would go in your place.

Freddy and Louis had the privilege to meet many professional musicians—among them a music instructor and his assistant, who taught them music lessons. Then there were jam sessions, which they would enjoy. Freddy learned more about music and new techniques from other professional musicians. Louis also became a talented guitar player and harmonized well with Freddy while they were doing time in prison.

"From My Eyes" by Freddy Fender

My manager was ashamed that I had been smoking pot, so he released some of these singles under this combination of his son's name [Scott Wayne].

Wayne Duncan: Talent Scout Label

Freddy was incarcerated when Duncan started a new label, which he named Talent Scout. His son's name was Scott, so in 1962, he took Freddy's unreleased recording and put them out under the new pseudonym of Scotty Wayne.

Some of the titles Freddy composed and released under Scotty Wayne are "Find Somebody New," "I'm Gonna Leave," "You're Something Else," and "Pretty Baby." They are all beautiful rhythm and blues tunes that really make you feel connected to Freddy's life.

As a kind gesture, Freddy put Louis' name as coauthor on a couple of songs that were written in prison. Years later, Louis received a royalty check for $250 in the mail and paid his father for the money he owed him for bailing him out of jail. "Not bad, considering both of us never received any tangible royalties for "Holy One," "Wasted Days and Wasted Nights," or one of Freddy's best songs he ever wrote, "A Man Can Cry," grunted Louis.

Two years later, in 1962, Duncan reissued "Holy One" as "Only One" on Talent Scout because disc jockeys thought it was about a saintly woman and had serious concerns about listeners interpreting it as a religious tune. Years later, Freddy changed it back to "Holy One."

I know he wrote a great many hits and lyrics, but there is nothing like your first love or your first anything. Freddy was writing more and more songs in prison, as he never wasted time or could stay idle. But for Freddy, they just kept on coming; one of those tunes was a beautiful love ballad titled "Sweet Summer Day."

For years now, I have noticed that many loyal fans like to use this particular song at weddings and funerals because it is both heartfelt yet soothing to the soul.

Freddy Fender compositions with the pseudonym **Scotty Wayne**: *"Sweet Summer Day," "Find Somebody New," "Pretty Baby," "I'm Gonna Leave," "Lonely Night," and "Only One"* (Talent Scout label, 1960-1962)

Prison Correspondence

Letter (1)

```
Mr. Paco Betancourt
P. O. Box 861
San Benito, Texas


Dear Sir:

    I hope that you are in the best of health. I want you
to be so advised as to my waiting for you to write Mr. Mar-
cantel and make a session proceding arrangement. I have
Looked into the material and have to my knowledge improved
it. I know now that you desire a clean and leveled sound.
I promise to do my best in meeting you requirements. Sir,
I also want to take the liberty of asking for $20.00 so as
to furnish our ciggarettes and utilities.

                                        Yours truly,

                                        Baldemar Huerta

P. S.  Mr. Chudd is supposed to call me up soon
       regarding the Imperial Contract.
```

Letter written by Freddy Fender from DeQuincy to
Paco Betancourt (Ideal Records) in San Benito

Freddy appeals to Mr. Paco Betancourt to get his support for rehabilitation (a job) when he comes out of prison. In addition, he asks Betancourt to write to Marcantel (the guard) to make a session arrangement (recording) while behind bars.

Tammy Lorraine Huerta Fender

Letter (2)

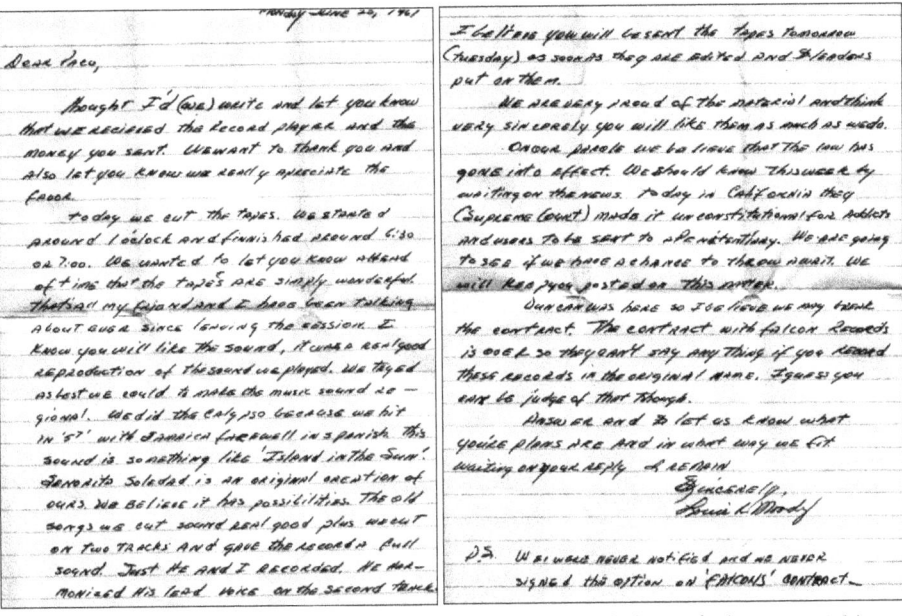

Letter written from Louis Moody to Paco Betancourt owner of Ideal Records. (June 20, 1961)

Excerpt: Letter by Freddy's Bass Player Louis Moody

We started around 1 o'clock and finished around 6:30 or 7:00. I know you will like the sound; it was a really good reproduction of the sound we played. We tried as best we could to make the music sound original. We did the calypso because we hit in '57 with "Jamaica Farewell" in Spanish. This sound is something like "Island in the Sun," and "Señorita Soledad" is an original creation of ours.

Letter (3)

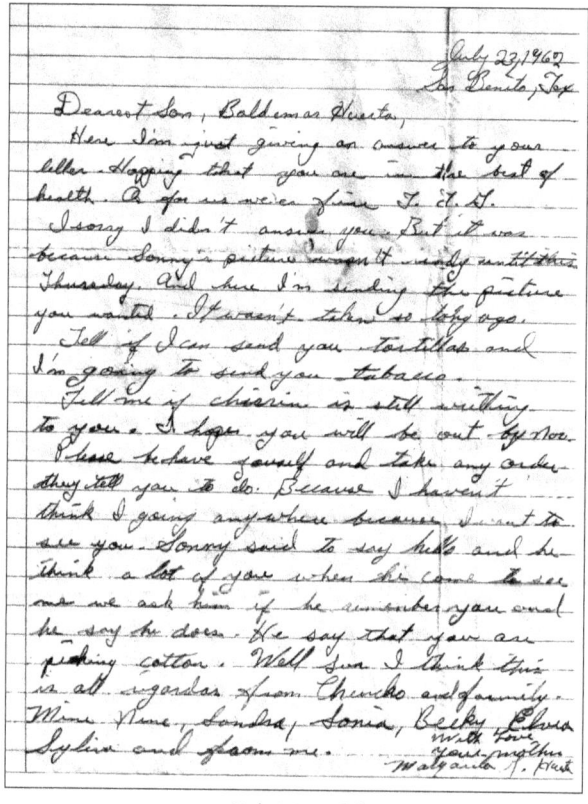

(July 23, 1962)

Excerpt: Letter from Freddy's Mother

Dearest Son,

    Tell them if I can send you tortillas. I am going to send you tobacco. I hope you will be out in November. Please behave yourself and take any order they tell you to do. Sonny said to say hello and he thinks of you a lot. We asked him if he remembers you, and he says he does. He says that you are picking cotton. Well, son, I think this is all.

With love,
Your mother, Margarita G. Huerta

Tammy Lorraine Huerta Fender

Letter (4)

Letter by Freddy Fender written to Paco Betancourt
(1962-1963)

Freddy is appealing to Mr. Betancourt to sign documents on his behalf attesting to the merit of his character. He also explains that things are "a mess" in Louisiana because of a new law for first-time drug and alcohol offenders. He states that some prisoners who were in prison before the law was passed can be released, and that those who have been incarcerated after the law was passed cannot get out. The men in prison are all threatening to throw a writ of habeas corpus, and Freddy is uncertain of the outcome. Freddy realizes that the only way out of his mess is to get a contract with Imperial Records, in order to hire a lawyer. Freddy is aware he has to write Chicano songs first before Betancourt will give him or his mother a few dollars.

Letter (5)

Excerpt: Freddy Fender letter to Paco Betancourt

Dear Sir,

   As you will know, it is doubtful that I will be released soon. I have recorded with your company with no financial interest whatsoever. I believe that you will agree with me on the fact that I should receive some currency for my future recordings. I have been working on some fast commercial twist numbers. I also have a good number of rhythm and blues. My material can be published by you, or I can get it published here. I will let you decide on that. If you want to put me under a contract on Spanish only, I will be glad to sign it for a period of one year with a one-year option. I'm sure that if you write to the superintendent, Mr. Cormier, he will consider the possibility of taking some glossy commercial photos so you can advertise. For singles, I am asking for $50 a record for session wager. For albums, I am asking for $150 as session money on each album cut.

P.S. Imperial is interested on giving me a contract for two years with a one-year option. I want you to give me whatever comments you may give. I will appreciate them.

Yours very truly,
Baldemar Huerta

Letter (6)

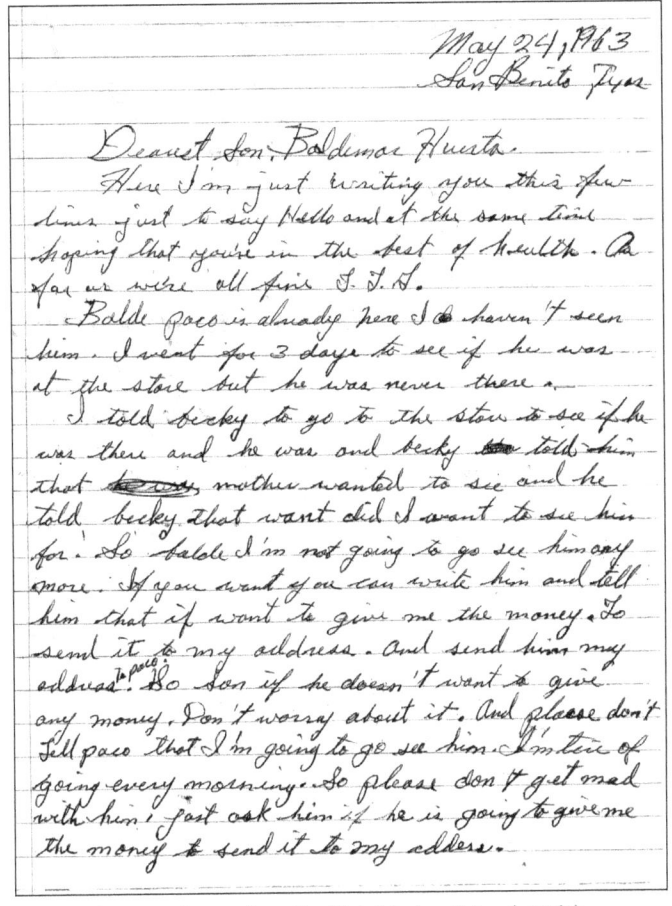

> May 24, 1963
> San Benito, Tixas
>
> Dearest Son, Baldemar Huerta.
> Here I'm just writing you this few lines just to say Hello and at the same time hoping that you're in the best of Health. As for us were all fine I. T. H.
> Balde paco is already here I haven't seen him. I went for 3 days to see if he was at the store but he was never there.
> I told becky to go to the store to see if he was there and he was and becky told him that mother wanted to see and he told becky that want did I want to see him for. So balde I'm not going to go see him any more. If you want you can write him and tell him that if want to give me the money. To send it to my address. And send him my address to paco. So son if he doesn't want to give any money. Don't worry about it. And please don't tell paco that I'm going to go see him. I'm tire of going every morning. So please don't get mad with him. just ask him if he is going to give me the money to send it to my address.

Excerpt: Letter from Freddy's Mother (May 4, 1963)

Freddy is still trying to help earn money for his mother and family from the penitentiary. Doña Máge went to see Betancourt hoping to receive money, but was unsuccessful. She writes to Freddy and pleads with him not to make her go see Betancourt anymore. If Betancourt wants to give her money, she asks that he mail it to her.

(On the official contract signed in 1964, Freddy did receive $40 for every single record he ever made from DeQuincy for Paco Betancourt of Ideal Records.)

Wasted Days and Wasted Nights

Letter (7)

> Tell me all about yourself, have you been doing well. I guess that you are "Wasted days and Wasted nites." Do you remember asking me to lock you up in the clothing room so you could write your songs. It seems like yesterday. Freddie We are all doing fine as of now. Thank God for that. Balde take care and write to me and let me know how you all doing. OK. te acuerdas de las "Morenitas" Mamacitas Portate bien hijo
>
> John A. Puerta
> Route-3- Box 1014
> DeQuincy Louisiana 70633

Quote: John A. Puerta

A dear and old friend, John A. Puerta, who worked as a guard at DeQuincy Correctional Facility in the 1960s, wrote to Freddy decades later.

Dear Balde, do you remember asking me to lock you up in the clothing room so you could write your songs? It seems like yesterday.

John A. Puerta
Album: Freddy Fender *Recorded Inside Louisiana State Prison*

In 1963, Gene Marcantel, a guard who ran the kitchen facility in DeQuincy, found out Freddy and Louis were assigned to kitchen duty. Marcantel quickly arranged a meeting with a guy named Eddie Shuler. Shuler was a local record producer for Goldband Records. So Marcantel requested permission for Freddy to record a musical jam session inside DeQuincy Correctional Facility. When Shuler heard Freddy's voice, he liked it and wanted to record him.

Both Freddy and Louis knew what they had to do if they wanted to get out of prison, and that was to knock out all the recordings (an album). Freddy had to quickly teach a new inmate how to play the drums because the drummer Jerry Bryan had gotten out on parole. Within a week, the new drummer was able to keep time and give him a rhythm and blues sound. Freddy wrote ten songs in just two hours, and "he made no mistakes" while singing. And Louis had his bass lines down pat!

However, Freddy was only given a minimum amount of equipment to use. He ended up having to use a Webcore tape recorder given to him by Lew Chudd from Imperial Records. (The prison recordings were later released on Goldband Records.).

The album *Freddy Fender Recorded Inside Louisiana State Prison* (recorded in 1962-63) included songs like "Hello Loneliness," "Carmela," "Oh My Love," "Bye Bye Little Angel," "The Village Queen," "My Happy Days Have Gone," "Quit Shucking Me Baby," and "I Hope Someday You'll Forgive me." (Released in 1964.)

Many talented musicians who were convicts actually did live in a real "Jailhouse Rock"—and it was no movie rehearsal, either!

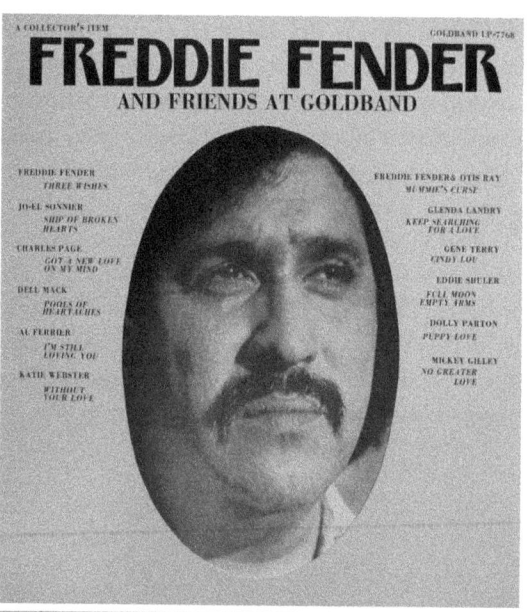

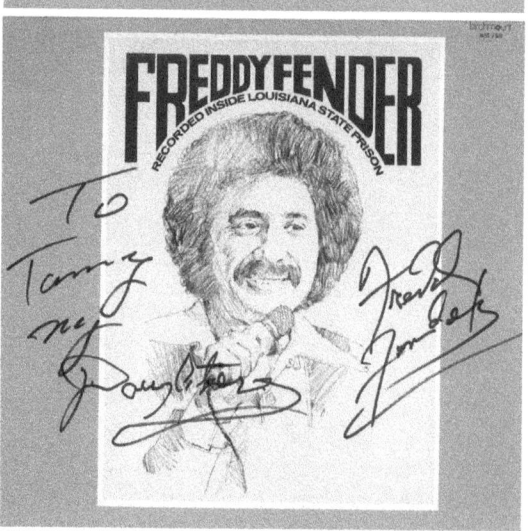

A Collector's Item: Freddie Fender and Friends at GoldBand, 1964/Freddy Fender Recorded Inside Louisiana State Prison, 1975. (Goldband label)

"Bye Bye Little Angel," "Carmela," and "Me and My Bottle of Rum"

"My Train of Love," "Oh My Love," "Oh, My Love," and "Three Wishes"
(Goldband label, 1964)

"From My Eyes" by Freddy Fender

We only received a minimum amount of equipment from [owner] Lew Chudd, so we eventually recorded my songs in prison with a Webcore tape recorder. The convicts played the instruments. It was actually one of the best albums I ever recorded! I recorded Spanish language versions of "Corrina, Corrina" and Little Richard's "Slippin' And A Sliding." I called it "Boracho y Resvalando," and I made up a story of a drunken guy trying to get in somewhere. It was released in 1961-62, and the cover of the album is in color with my face in the moon." [Another collector's item]
(Professor Fred Hopkins. *Blue Suede News* #47. Summer, 1999.)

It's a Girl: Freddy's Early Release

While incarcerated, Moody lost his lovely wife, and Freddy had only one visit from his family during his entire stay at the prison. On the positive side, Freddy took the GED (General Equivalent Diploma) test and received his high school diploma and, of course, spent much of his time in his cell writing music.

Louis' parents took Máge, Sonny Boy, and longtime family friend Jimmy "El Radio" Cortez to visit them both in DeQuincy. Sonny cried and was frightened when he saw our father. Once Freddy picked Sonny up, they bonded as father and son. They all sat outside together at a picnic table and talked for hours.

Máge gave her son a photo of his newborn child. Since his imprisonment, he had taken Eva (my mother) off the mailing list and was, therefore, unaware of her daily life. However, he knew very well that she no longer wanted anything to do with him and had moved on. With no education or skills, Eva had been forced to find work while she was pregnant.

The baby girl (me) had been born on September 6, 1961. Mother named me Tammy, after the popular television show from the 1960s called *Tammy*. Her sister, Aunt Beatrice, gave me my middle name of Lorraine. During this period, Doña Máge also had two other daughters with Manuelon, Sylvia and Elvia.

Freddy's incarceration ended when Governor Jimmy Davis helped his case for earlier release. At the age of twenty-six, Freddy was released from prison on July 23, 1963, having served a little over three years instead of five.

NOTE: Governor Davis was also known as a songwriter and singer before he became a politician. He was famous for writing "You Are My Sunshine," one of the most popular tunes of all time. Years prior, the governor of Louisiana had pardoned the legendary blues artist Huddie William "Lead Belly" Ledbetter. He loved music and musicians and tried to rehabilitate them to abide by the laws of the state of Louisiana.

On their day of The Walk, (left to right) Louis' parents and niece, Freddy, Sonny Boy, and Doña Máge at the outside grounds of the Correctional Facility in DeQuincy, Louisiana (1963).

Louis Moody, Jimmy "El Radio" Cortez, Freddy, and Sonny Boy, in DeQuincy (1963)

Still wearing their shades at DeQuincy (1963)

Music Artist Beatriz Llamas "La Paloma del Norte"

Twelve years later, when Freddy Fender became famous, he would come to meet an artist named Beatriz Llamas. Her fans know her as *La Paloma del Norte* (Northern Dove). And when he met this beautiful lady, he told her he was very angry with her.

La Paloma was taken aback that Freddy Fender would be mad at her since she had never met him before. It was then that he sat her down and explained how her music had made him feel while incarcerated. His mother, Doña Máge, had brought him Llamas' record albums for him to enjoy, and her music had had a profound impact on his emotional state.

He had to tell her that her lovely voice and sincere lyrics had really gotten to him. "You made me cry so much in prison," he said to her. Following their chat, they happily posed for a picture together to honor the moment.

Shortly, thereafter, he was inspired to write a beautiful love song (for La Califa) called "Aunque Me Hagas Llorar" ("Although You Made Me Cry"). Just hearing this melody, his voice, and its lyrics will make you cry.

Freddy Fender and Beatriz Llamas "La Paloma del Norte" (1975)

Freddy had finally let go and faced the harsh reality of his failure to be a good husband, father, and provider during the years he wasted locked up in prison. He finally allowed himself to release his sorrow and disappointments and wept while hearing Ms. Llamas' music lyrics. He knew very well that he had just lost the biggest opportunity to rise as a music artist and perhaps achieve stardom at the early age of twenty-three years old.

Naturally, Freddy continued to create many more tearjerkers and to captivate his audiences after his prison release. One can actually feel his deepest experiences and the authenticity of his raw voice and lyrics, which are found in his early compositions before becoming world famous.

Chapter X

New Orleans, 1960s

Probation Violation
"The Cat's Meow"
"Tejano Rock, Funkadelic, Rhythm and Blues with a pinch of swamp pop"
"Satan and Disciples"

Out on parole (1963)

"From My Eyes" by Freddy Fender
I came out playing music!
My wife was not waiting for me; I had a little girl [Tammy] *I hadn't ever seen.*
The first thing I did when I got out of the penitentiary was
to drink a Coke and then divorce my wife.
I paid a lawyer $125 for the whole deal. I had to get my shit together!
(Professor Fred Hopkins. *Blue Suede News* #47. Summer, 1999.)

* * *

I write "born loser" songs. I absorb punishment, and it makes me very sad.
Instead of feeling bitter against whatever is causing this punishment, whether it's
society or my situation or whatever, I get really sad and put it into my songs.
(Cook and Greenberg. "*Tex-Mex Troubadour.*" Newsweek Music Magazine, 1975)

* * *

In July 1963, I headed for home from prison on a Trailways bus, but I would soon
have to come back to Louisiana, singing at Papa Joe's on
Bourbon Street in New Orleans until 1968.
It was there that I played music with such cats as Joe Barry, Herb Alpert,
Fats Domino, Joey Long, Skip Easterling, and Aaron Neville.

Freddie Fender and Eddie Con Los Shades: *Rhythm and blues/rock 'n' roll songs recorded in Spanish for Ideal Records: "El Hijo De Susie" ("Son of Susie"), "Despeinada" ("Hair Uncombed"), "Hay Un Algo De Tu Pensar" ("There Is Something on Your Mind"), "Camisa Negra" ("Black Shirt"), "No Estes Soñando" ("Don't Be Dreaming"), and "Desde Que Conozco" ("Since I Met You Baby")*
(Ideal label, 1964)

"From My Eyes" by Freddy Fender

In order for me to get paroled, I had to get a job, and so I asked Paco Betancourt, owner of Ideal Records, if he'd give me a job. My job went from sweeping the sidewalk in front of the store in the morning to sorting out records, to even recording other groups there. I learned to run a monaural Amex there.
I even recorded as a sound engineer, an album by the legendary Lydia Mendoza.
I also feel I recorded the best album that Tony De La Rosa ever had.
I remember when Lydia Mendoza came in; it was 1964, maybe early 1965.
She came into the studio to rehearse. It was just her and the guitar.
We knocked out the album in one or two days.

*I had learned a trick from her that has helped me tremendously.
She almost whispered her songs through the rehearsal; you could barely hear her.
I was puzzled as to what she was doing.
And then, when she was ready, her lungs opened up like giant amplifiers!
I couldn't believe the strength of this woman!
She knew her energy was very precious, and she was saving it for the right time.*
(Davia Nelson. Arhoolie Records. CD *Roots of Tejano Rock*, 1992.)

*Pancho Pechos, Despeinada, Interpreta El Rock, and Adios Muchachos
Freddy's greatest Tejano Rock albums recorded in English/Spanish.*
(Ideal label, 1963–1964)

"From My Eyes" by Freddy Fender

*I was probably the engineer on some of these sessions.
I would put the switch on and then run like hell to pick
up the guitar with the boys waiting for me.
We had Benny Méndez on the bass.
I played guitar, Lupe Hernández on the rhythm guitar and lead.
We had Robert Silva "El Turkey" on drums, Carlos Cantú on horns, and a couple
of other musicians from the* [Rio Grande] *Valley.*
(Nelson, Davia. *Rock 'n' roll, Eddie Medina con Los Shades*. 1950s–1960s.
Arhoolie Records. 1992.)

* * *

*When I came back from Louisiana, Mexico had really
gotten on the ball with Mexican rock 'n' roll.
So, we mostly kept an eye on the charts in Mexico and said,
"Okay, we gotta record this one or that one, it's hitting and we'll do it
in a Mexican American version."*

* * *

*As far as my liking the song "La Banda Está Borracha" ("The Band Is Drunk"), I
did want it on this collection for historical reasons because that is what was happening at
that time. Like a lot of us musicians, we grab on to what is happening to help our careers.
"Acapulco Rock," that was a big hit in Mexico, it was in the movies and everything. I
wrote that one. I wrote "Pancho Pechos." Benny Méndez helped me with the words. It's
about a crazy guy, a funny character. He was always strutting like a fighting rooster.
He had one eye. He was really a clown, just a goofy guy who was trying to be a hero all the time.
He had a shoot-out, but he shot his girlfriend instead because he couldn't see the other guy!*
(Davia Nelson. Arhoolie Records. CD *Roots of Tejano Rock*, 1992.)

*Fender's most romantic composition recorded in English/Spanish "The Magic of Love."
(Norco label, 1963)/Promotional Sign: Rio Theatre general admission only 25¢/
Spanish version "The Magic of Love" ("Majia De Amor") (Ideal label, 1963–1964)*

Interviewee:
Evangelina Muniz-Huerta
A Year after Freddy's Passing (forty-four years later), 2007

*Author Tammy L. Huerta Fender and mother Evangelina ride through
La Villita (The Town Talk) as Eva reminisces the pain of yesterday.*

Evangelina: ¿*Entiendes?* (Do you understand?) He was Freddy Fender! He couldn't do anything wrong in anybody's eyes. Everybody accepted him. I have never gotten to the point where I wanted to kill him. People always asked me, 'Didn't you want to kill him?' I said, 'No, never!' I never wanted to hurt him. My thing was to get away from him, but he always found me.

Tammy: Today, can you say you are glad he found you after all, Mama?

Evangelina: Today, yes! He gave me twenty-five bad years and almost twenty-five good years. Sometimes you think about how women go through this and what keeps women with these men. I don't know; I did try. I was always trying to leave. But I would just be black and blue. The last time was when he got out of prison; I was so beat up I had to put him in jail. I didn't want him back. I had no feelings for him. It had been too long. He was in jail. I liked my freedom, and I had two kids, I had you. You were the baby, and Doña Milagros [Sonny and Tammy's godmother] was taking care of you when he came to the house.

Paul [Eva's brother] was living with me, and Janie [Paul's wife]. Janie would sit behind the door, and she was very bashful. Paul was loud and loved to dance. He was a *pachuco*. When your dad came back into the kitchen, Paul went to go buy cans of food because there was nothing good to eat. But it was all cheap canned foods, and I didn't know what to do with it. We had a big fight over it! Nobody told him to go and look for me! He hit me so hard. He just kept on hitting me and hitting me until my ears were ringing. I can still hear them ringing today. He left me all scratched up and bruised.

It all started because he had all this anger bottled up in him, and he was just so messed up [drugged up]. He was also on probation. It was my baby brother, Paul, who called the cops. Then I had to face Doña Máge, and *"¿Y porqué, mi hijo?"* ("And why, my son?")

It was on the night he won $500 in the bingo [talent show] at the Rivoli movie theatre, Máge told him to divorce me. I had put him in jail that night, but I didn't press charges, but they could have put him back in prison. You have to thank me that I didn't do that! Mary got me and took me to Corpus Christi again. I was always *golpiada* (beaten). You were about two years old. I think he was let out in 1963. Your dad could have killed me many times. Once, he tried to run me over. But God was taking care of me. Your dad was so close that one time he shoved a knife in me. I knew that he had gone into the kitchen, and he was all messed up [drugged up]. Máge, Chencho, Porfirio, and Cáne were there. Freddy brought me in, in the wee hours of the morning, where I was in a *camison* [nightgown]. He had walked me from this end of the apartment on Robertson Street to where we used to live with Mary, through El Jardín, all the way to Máge's house. I went with him because I was scared. So, there I go once again, I am there. His mother says, 'What are you doing up so early in the morning?' and I didn't say anything because I was so quiet and shy. I felt him go into the kitchen because he was struggling with me. He knew I didn't want to be there. It was in the house at 631 Rossiter Street. So, when he came from the kitchen, I knew he had something already in his hand. Then he went so fast, and I sucked my stomach in and bent my upper body forward, and he pushed it in. I screamed, and everybody jumped on him! Yeah, he was always messed up! [The knife did not penetrate her body.]

I was living with two women in these apartments by Saint Benedict's Church, and he screwed them too. It happened in 1963–1964. Yeah, we were already married by then. He was always partying and being with women. He never took care of me. When he left me at Máge's house, she treated me fine, but when Balde was there, she treated me like a leper. He was always messed up (drugged up).

That is the thing. I don't think your dad remembers the things he did to me. Everybody saw him as Freddy Fender. Nobody knew what he did to me. Máge knew what he did to me. His brothers knew what he did to me, but it was a hush-hush thing. Freddy should have been in prison for what he did to me. I didn't have anybody to fend for me.

Now let me take you first down to Robertson Street, Tammy, to the Town Talk! I served beer to the guys and women there in the restaurant. They were very nice to me. I was very young and stupid, and nobody would hire me. I did not have any skills. I was working there before I was eighteen years old, when I was a minor. They paid me $20–$30. I did the best that I could. Your dad was in prison. He didn't feed me and did nothing. He couldn't. I did the best I could with what I had, and I never turned to prostitution. I was so shy. I could barely serve you or look at the customers. What do you do when you have no skills? You don't have anybody, and you have to eat! You have to pay bills and with two kids! I had to leave Sonny with Milagros, who took care of you all.

Tammy: You could have been dead just like your mom, Pauline! Right, Mom?

Evangelina: Yeah, exactly! (She looks around.) They had all these cheap bars around here. Here is the place where I used to work called The Town Talk [La Villita]!

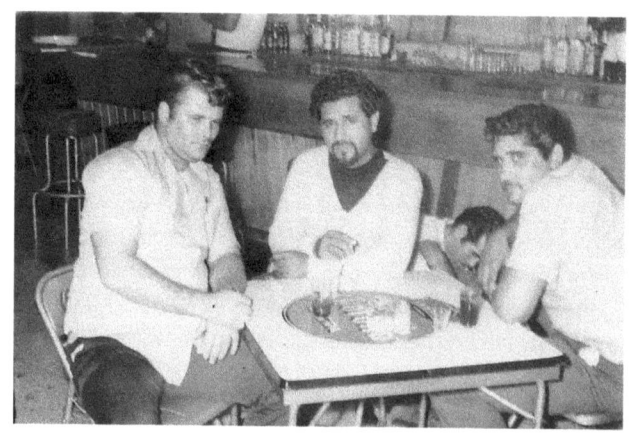

While on parole, Freddy crosses the border and is spotted with friends at a local cantina in Mexico. Freddy is accompanied by William "Billy" K. Jackson and friend having his shoes shined (1960s).

Freddy Hits the Newspapers Again: Probation Violation

Freddy started working again for drug lords in the Rio Grande Valley and was letting them use him to make the drug runs. He was driving back and forth over the Mexican border while singing and hauling their dope. He did it to earn a little extra money to provide for us.

Once again, Freddy's luck ran out. He was arrested at the checkpoint because he failed to register as a narcotics violator while passing through customs from Brownsville into Matamoros. This hit the local newspapers.

The courts returned him to Louisiana, and he found a job as a roofer in New Orleans. There was a lot of construction work because of the seasonal hurricanes from the Gulf of Mexico.

However, Freddy just couldn't stop partying, singing, or resist staying out of the honky-tonks, so he quickly went back to what was familiar and returned to the nightclub scene.

This time he focused on his love for music. The locals, as well as the tourists, loved hearing Freddy sing his blues away on Bourbon Street. It so happened that New Orleans became the perfect place for Freddy, because there he could express his musical talent wholeheartedly and without limitations.

That dreadful night of Friday the thirteenth in May of 1960 had not stopped Father dead in his tracks after all. If anything, it only fueled the fire within him to realize his true purpose.

In the French Quarter of the exciting city of New Orleans, Freddy would be able to pick up where he had left off. He used his heartfelt experiences and continued to develop his own unique voice, guitar, and rhythm and blues sound that would infuse the style of a more seasoned Freddy Fender.

Tammy Lorraine (Daughter/Author) The Spirit of Music Would become the Catalyst to Save My Father's Life!

As a toddler, Father was a shadowy figure to me. After his release in July of 1963 from DeQuincy's correctional facility, I first met him and lived with him in our hometown of San Benito. However, it didn't last long because, once again, he had to leave us, this time because he had broken parole. I just didn't have a clear picture of my dad yet because he was constantly in and out of our lives.

Few months later, Father sent for us to join him in New Orleans. It was there that I began to have a visual image of him; this is when I truly began to know my demanding, yet charismatic, cool hipster of a pop.

When we arrived, we stood in the middle of the bus station waiting patiently and quietly for him, when all of a sudden, my lower jaw dropped, leaving my mouth open. I'd been sucking on a nipple when my milk bottle had just been yanked right out of my mouth! I was stunned I tell you!

I thought to myself, *Could somebody please tell me what the heck just happened to me, and who is this stranger standing before me?*

Okay, I may have deserved that—I mean, I was almost five. I should have popped that nipple out myself sooner!

But it was no stranger; it was my dad who had walked up to greet us into his life again. We all looked up at him. We remained calm and awaited his next command.

My big brother, Sonny, knew our dad was in a foul mood. He was probably hung over from playing and drinking all night. But Mom tried to ignore his behavior.

"Having his family back, you would have thought Dad would have been content and pleased to see us," Sonny reflected when speaking of our lives in New Orleans.

As Dad led us out through the doors of the bus station, Sonny held on to the back of Father's pants to pull himself away from Mama. He was no sissy boy. We then followed Dad upstairs to a green-colored apartment on the French Quarter. We would come to live in many green apartments, a popular decorative color theme of the 1950s and 1960s.

I vividly remember us sitting around the kitchen table, quiet as a mouse, sitting on mama's lap. With apprehension, we waited to hear our father's next words, a string of continuous demands. And for the first time, I heard him holler, *"Y aqui, yo mando!"* ("And here, I am boss!")

(Wait for it—wait for it) "And she's already five years old!"

I was irked, and my little feelings were hurt. He had a point—I give him that! But why was my milk bottle such a big issue? Who cares! And why are we here, really? And why is this old man across from us, on the fifth floor, yelling out of his kitchen window? 'Oh, he's what, a wino.' Hmm, okay.

Memory Lane in New Orleans

Going through memory lane, I remember living on Charter Street near the French Quarter and going outside to play on a hill in front of our green-colored apartment. Next thing I know, some trash collector picked me up and took me upstairs to Mother. I was screaming all the way up the stairs! At this time, I had long wild black hair down to my knees like Cousin Itt, and I looked like a baby Sasquatch!

Well, as it turned out, I had huge fire ants all the way up to the tip of my head! Those ants were like those African ants that quietly crawl up all over you, from head to toe; they wait until that African queen gives the go-ahead to sting you all at once! I was red hot with welts. That hill was a doggone anthill!

Immediately, Mother placed me in bathwater. She was a good mommy and so very pretty. I loved combing Mother's hair and telling her in Spanish, *"Que chula, Mommy, que chula!"* ("How pretty, Mommy, how pretty you are!")

The nice thing I remember about my youth is that we were all very close as a family. And it was great to have my grandmother, Máge, along with my aunts and uncles (Sylvia, Elvia, Cáne, and Béke), come live with us for a while. We were all up in one tiny apartment like traveling gypsies as we slept on the hard-wooden floor.

Downstairs was Mr. Bird's grocery store and a warehouse where Mardi Gras beads were made and stored away. Dad would have gigs on the side singing on different shift changes to earn a few bucks during Mardi Gras season. Sonny Boy remembers us having to squat because of machine guns going off one year. At the time, Bourbon Street was open for passing vehicles; perhaps that is why the city sealed off the street to protect the bystanders.

There were a few times that the police had to bring me home because I would freely wander the streets alone on the French Quarter. I don't know how they knew where I lived, but they knew.

Dad already knew many people in Louisiana. A couple of bank robbers (husband and wife) named Valentine who had served time in prison for armed robbery had an acrobatic show at Lake Pontchartrain Amusement Park; we would go see the Valentines when they performed. This is where Father first discovered that his daughter (me!) loved music and was a natural born dancer.

As my family walked through the amusement park, I would lag behind because I would stop to sing and dance along with the bands. You couldn't even see my face because of my long thick hair swinging along my tiny body. After the band stopped playing, I would go to the next group of musicians and continue dancing. My family would just stop and watch me get my funky groove on, and wait for me. (Does this remind you of someone related to me, like Aunt Mary?)

Father knew what had gotten into me. It was the spirit of the music. Music is life to us. We felt free. We loved it there, and we fit in perfectly as a musician's family.

Freddy's Own Music Jambalaya: Tex-Mex Rock/ Funk/Rhythm and Blues with Swamp Pop

Freddy called for his musicians from the Lower Rio Grande Valley to accompany him on Bourbon Street. His cool bass player was a serious, large, heavyset dude named Benjamin "Benny" Méndez; his other outstanding badass drummer was Robert "Turkey" Sílva, who was tall, lean, and mean; a light-skinned Hispanic named Lupe "Lupillo" Hernández played a tight rhythm guitar, and Carlos Cantú, "La Cacahuata," who played a wicked horn (saxophone). When possible, the handsome and talented Cuban, Mando Peña, also accompanied Freddy on percussion.

Coincidently, if Mando wasn't playing drums for Freddy in New Orleans, he would be playing for Beatriz Llamas, "La Paloma del Norte" in the Rio Grande valley.

With the exception of Mando, his band members were intimidating and scruffy looking alley cats. But one thing is for sure, they enjoyed the excitement of hanging with Freddy, period. His band from the Rio Grande Valley also knew how to keep up. They were able to adapt to Freddy's most versatile musical demands and please audiences who enjoyed listening to Freddy perform rhythm and blues.

With no questions asked, they all agreed to follow Freddy Fender and continued again to perform as a band—in the musical, spirited, and wondrous city of New Orleans.

Freddy's drummer Armando "Mando" Peña playing drums for Beatriz Llamas "La Paloma del Norte" in South Texas (1960s).

Sonny and I agree that musicians like Benny, El Turkey, Lupillo, Carlos, and Mando were the real deal and closest to what our dad's style was really like. Father is originally a funk, rhythm and blues man. You can say my dad is more like a black soulful musician. No matter what music genre Father was singing, the sound of funk and blues is clearly heard in his voice and guitar playing.

However, Freddy had developed a rather unique and treasured mix; he intertwined Tex-Mex rock/funk/rhythm and blues with a swamp pop sound. Cajun culture, food, and music had also become part of Freddy's life; he even learned to speak Cajun and had a close rapport among the locals. He enjoyed singing tunes like "Jambalaya" and "Louisiana Woman." Freddy even wrote his own Cajun tunes, such as "Louisiana Blues" and "Cajun Stomp."

Our Father was just a real cool hipster and funkster type of dude and musician. He even wore a goatee. People don't realize how Dad really had it going on back in the 1960s. Freddy could sing any music genre he wanted. And he did!

On the weekends, I would see Dad sleeping late in the mornings, lying there with his big tummy out and mouth wide open while snoring. He'd be snoring so loud that the neighbors could hear him throughout the apartments. Snoring was one of the biggest problems we had living with Father. It was the most disturbing noise you ever heard. We had to leave and sleep across the house to try and avoid this horrific and unpleasant sound. Father worked long hours and partied hard, then he'd sleep it off.

The Rio Grande Valley alley cats all became carpenters by day, and by night, they became the cat's meow, showing off their wicked musical talent until dawn in the French Quarter. New Orleans was just one big party scene for them to pounce on. And believe me, they did.

These are some of the songs Freddy sang during the mid-1960s: "Little Mama," "Cool Mary Lou," "Three Wishes," "Bony Maroni" (by Larry Williams), and my all-time favorite "Ooh Poo Pah Doo" (by Jesse Hill). Listening to nothing but live music just became the norm for us from this point on. And when Dad played the lead guitar on a recording, we knew when it was him getting down on that funk and rhythm and blues.

Freddy's version of "Ooh Poo Pah Doo" and "Bony Moronie" (Norco label, 1963)

Freddy (with Benny Méndez) singing rhythm and blues at Papa Joe's Bar on Bourbon Street. (1968)

Wasted Days and Wasted Nights

"From My Eyes" by Freddy Fender

When the strippers went offstage at 3:30 a.m., we came on.
We would play until noon.
Sometimes we'd get a gig at night, sixty miles from New Orleans.
We'd drive for hours and play forty-five minutes.
We'd drink two or three beers, then we'd hit the sofa because we were knocked out.
Then they'd get us up again. We'd drive back to New Orleans and then start the whole thing all over again. I had no life. A balanced life is for people who have a brain. I'm a musician.
(Professor Fred Hopkins. Blue Suede News #47. Summer, 1999.)

Bourbon Street: "Papa Joe's" Bar

Papa Joe's bar was a small joint; yet, it was one of the most popular nightclubs to enjoy live entertainment on Bourbon Street. As you walked in the front doors it was nothing fancy. It had red carpeting, and there was a small bar to the right but no stage. The instruments and amplifiers were on the floor to the left side of the room. When the musicians played they had to be blowing music right out the door onto Bourbon Street. But where could you fit or sit all the people? So, the people would just linger outside trying to get a peek inside to see who was blowing their minds that night.

Sometimes Dad would take me to Papa Joe's so that he could handle some music business. I would sit myself on the bar stool, hoping the bartender would give me a Coke with lots of cherries on top. Then I would hope some more. Hoping to, that somebody would give me a dime to get some red pistachios out of the gumball machine. I really do miss those red-dyed shelled pistachios today.

I can't say that Dad kept having these "comebacks" when he truly never stopped recording and living out his dreams, even while serving time. I am pretty sure the jazz legends that came to know Freddy on Bourbon Street would agree that *Freddy Fender's* "prime" for his music career was clearly demonstrated in the 1960s (before he was star).

On many momentous occasions, jazz artists were only too happy to ask Freddy to join them on a late-night jam session; the lucky crowds would be captivated by talented New Orleans jazz and R & B musicians. Freddy kept Bourbon Street open for business until three or four in the morning.

Next, we moved closer to the Quarter, on Elysian Fields Avenue, parallel to Canal Street and smack dab in the middle of downtown. Our neighbors were a mixture of colorful races, such as blacks, Cajuns, Mexicans, and Puerto Ricans, but the odd thing was that there was a large white family down the street, which was unusual for our neighborhood, and they didn't speak French or Cajun.

One evening, at dusk, Mother and Benny Méndez's wife, Jesusa "Chucha," and I took a walk on Bourbon Street. Chucha was a very beautiful, tall young woman with jet-black hair. I walked behind the two of them while we listened to the live musicians. Then I saw a strange man began to serenade Chucha in her ear. He was singing aloud as we stood still in embarrassment. Thank goodness, Benny Méndez wasn't there, or else that guy would have been mashed potatoes on the pavement.

Father would also take me to recording studios. I remember having the sound engineer play a tune from Alvin and the Chipmunks, which was new to me. I do remember going to another recording studio in Downtown New Orleans where Mother and I had to wait in the lobby. If I am correct, it was under Lew Chudd's management with Imperial Records. We were told that Cher had recorded here under Lew Chudd's management and had been to that studio. I love her music. She is truly a rare jewel and rock star!

While I sat there, I flipped through the magazines and saw Cher with her long hair, bangs, and wearing her white go-go boots. Oh, how I always wished for a pair of white go-go boots so I could strut in them, sleep in them, and happily dance my life away while wearing them!

New Orleans was all about the people, food, music, dancing, and drinking. When Mother would take us there, I too, began to dance on Bourbon Street, as this was the norm. The tourists would throw pennies, nickels, and dimes at me. I didn't realize people were throwing me money because my little spirit was just so happy and free.

Like most little girls, I wanted colorful shoes and we didn't have bling-bling back then. However, the problem was that I could never find a pair of matching shoes at secondhand stores. I remember always feeling disappointed for not finding that second colored shoe.

Many years later, I asked Mother what she had done with the money I earned while dancing on the sidewalks on Bourbon Street. She told me she would sew dresses from patterns for me. I remember they were very pretty. She was just a very good mommy; I give her that.

Birth of Danny Boy: Like a Brown Pooh Bear

My grandmother and the rest of my relatives didn't stay with us for very long and moved back home to Texas. Then my parents had another one of their squabbles and separated once again. She took Sonny and me on a bus, and all three of us went back home to the valley. We moved into an apartment on Hayes Street in Harlingen.

Thereafter, Mother gave birth to our baby brother, Daniel, on December 22, 1966. All three of us were born in a house; we were all baptized and confirmed at Saint Benedict's Catholic Church in San Benito.

As a child, Danny was so cute and chunky and had curly brownish blond hair with light brown eyes. You just wanted to squeeze him like a brown Pooh Bear.

I have to tell you a cute story about Danny Boy. When he was little, he had gotten constipated, and Mother decided to wash his bottom out with an enema filled with soap and water. It must have helped to relieve some of his constipation because Danny began to blow real soap bubbles out of his bottom into mid-air. It was a sight that I'll never forget.

After Danny's birth, father came back for us and drove us back to New Orleans.

However, after one of the "off and on again" phases of their marital relationship, Father stole Danny Boy and drove away to see his family in San Benito for a few days. Dad said he prayed all the way on his ride there, hoping Danny wouldn't poop in his diaper because he wasn't about to change him. Father was very squeamish about things like that! In a way, I think Dad really favored Danny because he looked more Mexican than Sonny or I. Danny also has a temper, as well as a wonderful, contagious laugh like Father's. Today you can always tell when Danny Boy comes into a room, even from afar. His big beautiful smile, jokes, and laughter make you happy along with him.

We didn't even think much of the arguments during our parents' on-and-off separations because they just happened so quickly and ended so quickly. We just learned to move on and not dwell on yesterday—our norm.

Freddy holding son Daniel and Eva holding Benny Méndez's baby. Back porch of apartments on Elysian Fields Boulevard by the French Quarter (1967)

Tammy Lorraine Huerta Fender

"El Turkey" (drummer) holding "Danny Boy."

Freddy Fender at home in backyard of our apartment on Elysian Fields Blvd.

Our Daily Life and Our Neighbors in New Orleans: The Assassination of Rev. Martin Luther King Jr.

Mother worked part-time at Godchaux Clothing Co., which was located in downtown New Orleans on Canal Street. She worked at the gift-wrapping department and at the candy store. She really tried hard to care for us as best she could. One morning, while she was waiting for the bus to take us to school, she couldn't find any panties to put on me. She gave me one of her own underwear and placed a huge safety pin on it in order to fit me, and I happily went off to school.

Every single morning, Mother warned me that I better comb my long, tangled hair or else she would cut it off. I had one eye peeking out at you and walked around barefooted all day. Sonny and I were also very rambunctious, to say the least. However, I didn't take her seriously, and so I went off to play the next morning without combing my hair. Next thing I know I am wearing a pixie haircut. I looked like a boy, and Dad was not too happy with her; nor was I. She had taken my Latina mane away from me and left me feeling naked.

My brother Sonny was a tough boy, and I never saw him cry, not once. I remember that at least twice a week, he stepped on huge nails and bled all over the place. It was from all the nails Dad used to board up the windows during hurricane season. When the cops took away Sonny's firecrackers, he didn't cry, nor when his beagle dog got run over. I knew he hurt, but he never shed a tear. Crying was a sissy thing. I felt for him because he wouldn't or couldn't cry, but Sonny Boy had big shoes to fill.

Sonny had many neighborhood friends, and I was never allowed to talk or hang out with any of the boys. One time, I went next door to look for Sonny. He and his friends were playing in a tent. I asked for Sonny, and one of the boys peed on me. So, when I got home, mother punished me and placed me in the corner. She made me kneel down for a few hours because it was my fault for being with the boys.

The way Sonny and I bonded was during the holidays. During Halloween, he and I would go trick-or-treating together. Every year, we wore basically the same costume. I wore a mask of the Good Fairy. My mask was white, with blonde hair and red lips; my only prop was a wand. Sonny wore a sheet and dressed up as a ghost. Then Mother would give us both a large pillowcase, and the kids would start trick-or-treating at about 6:00 p.m. When the pillowcases filled up with candy and fresh fruit, we'd run back home and toss it behind the couch to hide it from each other. Then we'd race back out onto the streets and hit the same houses two or three more times. The adults masqueraded on Bourbon Street, and the kids enjoyed trick-or-treating until midnight—great times.

On Easter, Mother would buy a big chocolate bunny for Sonny and me. She would place the bunny on the mantle where we couldn't reach it. Sonny and I really looked forward to Easter Day so we could eat that chocolate rabbit.

The rest of the year, I'd race home after school and smack the bees away from our fig tree just so that I could enjoy sweet ripe figs. We loved fruits, but for the most part, I enjoyed spoonfuls of Hershey's chocolate powder in my mouth even more.

Sonny and I played a lot with Benny's daughter Mary. She was a year older and prettier than I was. She had very long and wavy hair. I must admit I was a little jealous. After all, I had no long hair left.

One afternoon, Sonny, Mary, and I began to play and do acrobatics together. Sonny placed his feet on her belly and flipped her over, and then I was next. But he didn't let go of my arm, and my bone snapped. He purposely broke my left arm! I cried so loud. We both went walking down the stairs back home. He then told me, "You're not going to die!"

I replied, "Yes, I am!" I knew he was scared, but of Dad!

I think this was probably the first time that Sonny ever got a good whipping with the belt. I felt bad for Sonny for getting beaten that night. I didn't see him get whipped because I was at the clinic, but I was told about it on my way back home. I had to wear an arm cast for six weeks.

Then came the time when Rev. Martin Luther King Jr. was assassinated on April 4, 1968. The city officials strongly recommended we place something black in front of our homes because the black people were retaliating and were burning houses down in New Orleans. I remember feeling the confusion. In the morning, I saw something black by our mailbox and I thought Mother had placed it there, but as it turns out, the black children in our neighborhood (who liked us) had placed the black cloth on our mailbox.

We were part of the majority of minorities, and that was cool of them to do this. The black folks saved our Mexican lives. That night, those who retaliated against society's prejudices set many houses on fire. We saw smoke in the air, and it was shown on television.

When Louis Moody once visited us, he brought a contraption he called a tape recorder, and Sonny had me singing with him. We still have the cassette. On it, you can hear Sonny telling me to sing. I gave him a hard time because I just wanted to dance to the music, but he knew I could sing too. I began to defy him, and you can hear Sonny telling me in Spanish, *"¿Tammy, y porqué peleas tanto, porqué peleas tanto?"* ("Tammy, why do you fight me so much? Why?")

Sonny spoke Spanish so sweetly. He took over and sang the theme song to *Batman*. He should have been the next musician and singer in the family. I too love singing, but I love dancing and acting silly even more.

Mary (Benny Méndez's daughter) and Tammy (with a pixie haircut) wearing her ballerina shoes

Sonny, Tammy, and their friendly neighbor Brian (American of African descendant)

Live Music: Our Own Rock 'n' Roll Star at Home:

All week long, Sonny and I got to enjoy Father and the band practicing in our front living room while I got to dance to his music and Sonny learned to play drums. We heard Father's English/Spanish rock singles and Ideal record albums over and over, like "Despienada," "No Está Aqui," "Mi Nena," "Si Si Rider," and "Acapulco Rock."

Sonny would stack books together and use spoons and forks as drumsticks. Then Dad would give him advice on how to keep a beat. Sonny even played the congas.

At the downtown Woolworth's store, Dad and Sonny saw a miniature drum set and purchased it for $49.99. They were perfect for Sonny. However, by the age of ten, Sonny had worn himself out playing drums.

Father also bought Sonny his first 45-rpm record. It was the *Wizard of Oz* and they would both lie back and relax while listening to their respective tunes together. Dad and Sonny have always had a very close father-and-son relationship.

After Father's passing in 2006, I came across an interview someone did with my father during which he was asked if his children were musically inclined. Father replied, "My son, Sonny, is a drummer, and my daughter, Tammy, is a dancer." That was awesome—the way he envisioned us. I had no idea he thought of us this way. Sonny and Danny played guitar and other instruments, but we all play drums.

Growing up, all our houses would be quite the same because with dad around, we had laughter and great live music. Yes, we had some drama and sometimes trauma!

Sonny commented, "I couldn't ask for our lives to be any better." And I agree!

He believes our grandmother really was a very good singer and that she was actually the one who had given Father the drive to be what he had become, a singer. Our grandmother just didn't flaunt it like her son.

As far as our education in New Orleans, Sonny and I went to McDonogh 39 and 42 Elementary School. There are several McDonogh schools. He was in the second grade, and I was in kindergarten. On certain days, it was a tradition to form a line in the hallways and sing patriotic and spiritual songs and even to pray.

At the end of the day, Sonny would pick me up after school. I would be waiting for him in the auditorium singing songs with my classmates. Then he'd grab hold of my hand and walk us to the bus stop. The bus dropped us off right in front of our home on Elysian Fields Avenue and within walking distance to Bourbon Street.

Sonny and Tammy (with a pixie cut) on Elysian Fields Boulevard

Satan and Disciples: The Cat's Meow

In the Quarter, psychedelic music and hallucinogenic drugs of all kinds were "in." New Orleans was a very exciting place, with many extracurricular activities, such as voodoo, love potions, and practicing satanic rituals. But as for Freddy, he just couldn't get enough of New Orleans' vibrant music scene.

In the 1960s, Father joined a cool and strange looking cat named R.O. Bates, who called himself Satan. Freddy extended the name to "Satan and Disciples," and man, would they put on one heck of a show! The music and lights alone would get you amped up and high. The long-haired, tall, skinny leader, who dressed up as Satan, wearing a red velour outfit, horns, and a long red tail, was very scary. Of course, the Disciples wore colorful Mexican ponchos and huge Mexican hats!

During the show, Satan would light up a stick, place it at the end of his mouth, and blaze fire toward the audience. Then Freddy would start singing, and everybody would just go crazy!

Father and R.O. Bates wrote and recorded a couple of cool songs called "Mummie's Curse" and "Cat's Meow." Anything and everything Dad was experiencing was being expressed through his music.

One night, about 3:00 a.m., Dad came in from working at Papa Joe's and woke us all up. We all had to get up as though it was Christmas or something special. Dad came in with a couple of foot-long chilidogs, and it was a real treat for us. Above all, we thought it was really nice of Dad to think about us like that.

I think Dad was just beginning to love us being around him as a family and not cramping his lifestyle. So, there we all were, with Father's bombastic persona, audacious Tejano rock, funkadelic, rhythm and blues with a pinch of swamp pop—blasting us away, every single day!

Satan and Disciples
Top: *Satan R.O. Bates* **Bottom:** *Benny, Lupillo, Freddy, and Mando (February 1968)*

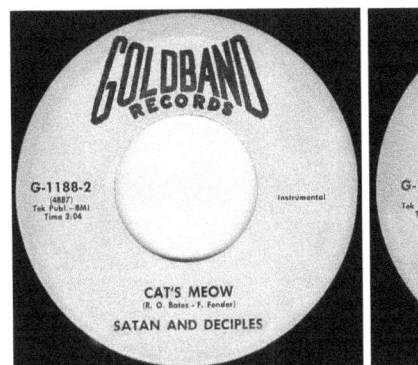

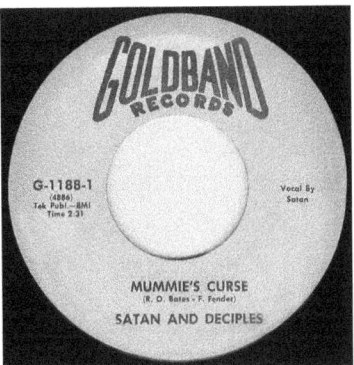

"Cat's Meow" and "Mummie's Curse"
(Goldband label, 1967-1968)

Satan and Disciples: (left to right) *Freddy, Benny, Satan R.O. Bates, Lupillo, and Mando (February, 1970)*

Wasted Days and Wasted Nights

Chapter XI

Home Again in the Magical Rio Grande Valley

"Aunque Me Hagas Llorar" ("Although You Made Me Cry")

Los Comancheros!
A Trade School
"Never forget your roots, brother!"

After a few years of living in the state of Louisiana, Father was paroled in the spring of 1968. Everyone, including the band, *Los Comancheros*, were thrilled to return home to the Rio Grande Valley. Our father's rock 'n' roll days had always reflected life on the beach at South Padre Island, and so would our upbringing. Father even taught us how to fish and even swim against the gulf currents as he had done in his youth. My brothers and I enjoyed swimming with Father, and we swam like fish without fear. He loved living by the Gulf of Mexico and enjoyed life as a beach rocker.

It was the day of my eighth birthday, September 6, when our family and relatives went to the beach in Port Isabel, a little town across from South Padre Island. The weather was perfect, with clear blue skies and beaches filled with tourists who were there to enjoy the many activities. They were there to see Father and his band perform at the outdoor pavilion.

That day, there was a cool breeze flowing through *la isla* (the island), kites flying high across the skies, and the palm tree leaves briskly blowing in the wind.

Before the show, I vividly remember staring at the golden, tanned backs of tall Anglos with long sun-bleached hair. The *Americanos* who came down south of the valley had never seen a cool, dark-skinned Mexican singing popular tunes in English, let alone Dad and his cool cats *Los Comancheros*! But there you have it!

Freddy Fender with Los Comancheros gave *el valle* a unique taste of their own Tejano rock/jambalaya mix. The band gave it their all and the party was back on—Rio Grande Valley style.

Our family, which included Amá Máge, Aunt Sylvia (nicknamed Chiva) and Aunt Elvia (nicknamed Pinga), sat attentively while Dad got his groove on. It was a perfect day because the whole Huerta family was together once again.

"The New Freddie Fender with his Newest Creations" (Dominante label, 1970)

Freddy with Los Comancheros *by the arroyo in the Rio Grande Valley. Lupillo Hernández, Benjamin Méndez, Armando Peña, and Freddy Fender*

Eva and the Children Need Stability: Freddy Enrolls in a Trade School

Freddy's struggles for fame, his continual late-night partying, and his infidelities did not sit well with Mother. His lifestyle was taking a toll on her, especially with three children to feed. *Eva was so unhappy that for several months she was unaware she was pregnant and carrying a lifeless fetus.* As an old-fashioned and responsible mother, this rollercoaster life with Freddy was filled with doubts and insecurities. Father also grew tired of fighting with Mother about not being a responsible stay at home husband and father.

Sure enough, Freddy finally gave in and decided to enroll at James Connally Technical Institute (of Texas A&M University). It was a trade school at an air base in Harlingen, Texas. This unique institute was one of the first organizations to help educate and benefit Mexican American and Anglo students by teaching them skills and preparing them to find jobs in the Lower Rio Grande Valley. While Freddy was enrolled, the trade school name was changed to Texas State Technical Institute (TSTI). There was a ground-breaking ceremony, and many local officials, including the students, celebrated this wonderful event. Today, it is officially known as Texas State Technical College (TSTC).

At the time, the students registered were 99 percent *Mexicanos* and 1 percent *Americanos*, and there were about fifteen trades offered to students—parts and auto body repair, diesel engine mechanics, carpentry, learning to be a cashier, and more. Some of the students even washed cars as part of their curriculum.

Each class would nominate a representative to attend a weekly meeting run by Mr. Griffin, who was head of the school, to see how each class was progressing and to discuss how to make learning even better. A classmate named Eugene "Gene" D. Martell had been nominated to represent his class, which was learning to paint the body parts of vehicles. Freddy was nominated to represent his diesel engine mechanics class. Even bass player Benny Méndez took auto body repair. While studying there, his classmates called him Benji; Martell vividly remembered him in his class.

Freddy would listen attentively to Martell when he made his report after every meeting and reported what they had learned to Mr. Griffin. He added that a local businessman, Victor Carillo, would bring the students material from his own body shop located in Pharr, Texas, so they could get started in school. Otherwise, the only work they had at the body shop class was washing cars.

Therefore, the students considered Victor Carillo a great man since the school was very limited on funds. And if it weren't for the personal involvement and contribution of Carillo, the school may not have been quite as successful as Martell recalled.

Martell, who knew of Freddy Fender, sat next to him at those meetings. However, he had no idea he was sitting next to the legendary Freddy Fender, whom he knew as Balde. At that meeting, they announced Freddy Fender was going to do a concert at their school auditorium.

On the night of the concert, Martell sat on the fourth row from the main stage. Martín Rosales, the voice of KGBT, introduced Freddy Fender to the audience, and when Martell saw Freddy onstage, dressed so nicely and singing to the students, he told himself, "*That is the guy that sits next to me at the meetings! I swear to God. I don't understand why Freddy is here. He is Hollywood. He is New York. He is Nashville. He is big time!*"

Shortly thereafter, Benny showed Martell the jacket sleeve from the album they were working on. Martell, who was very good in grammar, remembers looking at it and telling Benny that one of words on the song titles was misspelled. "Benji, this is all wrong," said Martell. The misspelled letter was on the album title of "Aunque Me Hagas Llorar" ("Although You Made Me Cry"). The word "Hagas" had been spelled with a letter "J" instead of H.

That weekend, a tall guy nicknamed Tiny drove Freddy, Benny, and Martell to see radio announcer Martín Rosales. On the way there, Freddy started to sing "Aunque Me Hagas Llorar" a cappella. After he sang a few bars, Freddy asked Martell, "*¿Qué piensas, bro?*" (What do you think, bro?)

Martell replied, "*Pues chingado* (well, damn), Freddy, I think it's good."

The guys weren't in favor of Freddy recording it and singing in English and Spanish, but Freddy always recorded that way.

Martell will never forget what he said to him: "Freddy, it is not the song. It's your voice that makes the song."

Freddy looked Martell right in the eyes and said, "This is the first time that someone has talked to me with sincerity."

Back in school, the student council was about to elect a new president during their weekly meeting on Friday because the existing president was moving away. Freddy was a born leader, and in school, he was considered to be an important man. So, if Freddy had someone go call you, you didn't say no to him. You had to go see him! He had power and fame even then, said Martell.

To start the wheels going with regard to his new goal, Freddy sent Benny to see Martell.

When he found him, Benny said, "Do you know they are going to elect a new president for the student body?"

"Yes, sir!" Martell answered.

"Well, I came to let you know that Freddy Fender wants you to be president of the student body."

Martell then told Benny that he would love to, but was moving to Chicago, adding, "It would not do me, or anyone any good, if I take the position and then vacate it." Benny went back to report to Freddy, and twenty minutes later, Benny returned.

"Freddy wants you to do him a favor and nominate him for president" Benny said.

"Well, I don't know anybody else better than Freddy. He has the charisma, and he has the fame," Martell responded.

"Well then, that's the way it's going down," Benny concluded.

At the next meeting, Griffin opened the nominations for the new president. Martell stood up and said, "I would like to nominate Baldemar Huerta."

When Griffin asked, "Are there any more nominations?" not one hand went up. Tiny got up to second the nomination, and that was it. Freddy was officially elected as the new president of the student council.

Shortly thereafter, Freddy and Benny went to thank Martell. He was washing cars to thank him. It was a big thing and an honor if Freddy Fender wanted to talk to you.

Freddy: I want to thank you, bro. I won't forget this favor.

Martell: You deserved it. If anybody should be president, it should be you.

[Then Freddy began to tell him about Huey Meaux and recording, commenting that if everything went well, he would live life with some success.]

Martell: I don't see why you are not up there already. You have a lot to offer, and you are bilingual.

Freddy: It is all about timing. Sometimes *la Raza* has to become educated.

[Freddy always told Martell, "You have to leave the valley so that you can come back a star!"]

Martell: All I am going to ask you, Freddy, because you said you owed me a favor, remember? So, I am going to ask you one thing. *Never forget your roots, brother, never forget where you came from, man, because that is what made you!*

Freddy: I promise I will never forget!

Martell: Everybody would always tell Freddy that and to never let it go to his head if he hit it big! Freddy, bless his soul, never forgot it. He never forgot the valley. He never forgot his people, their names, or the places he played. It never went to his head. I do not care what anybody says. The man I knew was the same man I knew from day one. He never changed!

Freddy performing at James Connally Technical Institute in Harlingen, Texas.

Freddy's band Carlos Cantú "La Cacahuata," Freddy, Robert Silva "El Turkey" (on drums), and Carlos Cantú (on saxophone)

NOTE: Freddy recorded as *Freddie Fender and the Streamliners*; *Freddy Fender and Los Barbarians*; *Freddie Fender and the Personalities*; *Freddie con Carlos Cantú "La Cacahuata;" Freddie Fender with* Conjunto *de Carlos Gonzales, and Freddy Fender con Los Comancheros,* which were Benjamin "Benny" Méndez, Lupillo Hernández, and drummers Armando Peña and Robert Sílva "El Turkey."

Martell Once More: "Never Forget Your Roots, Brother!"

Martell added that while living in Chicago (just a few years later—after Freddy's success in the mid-1970s), he was working in a car garage when he heard a song on the radio and shouted, "Hey, that's my friend, Freddy Fender!"

Another worker said, "Who?"

Martell said, "Freddy Fender from the valley, man!" They had not said his name yet on the radio. As soon as the song was over, the radio disk jockey, Mark Edwards, said, "And that was Freddy Fender from Texas! It is a new recording titled 'Wasted Days and Wasted Nights.'"

Two weeks later, when Freddy went to Chicago to do a radio interview at WJJD, the disc jockey said, "We have a surprise guest, and in a few minutes, you can talk to him."

When he announced it was Freddy Fender, Martell shouted, "That's my friend," and his coworkers would not believe him. The garage workers made a $5 bet; Martell said, "Make it $20!" Then he called the station as everybody, including the boss, listened in. When Edwards answered the listener line, Martell said, "Can I speak to Freddy Fender?"

[Funny, but Martell was mimicking Father's voice the whole time during our interview.]

While on the air, the disc jockey passed the phone to Freddy. "Hello?"

"¿*Qué te pasa, bro?* (What's up, brother?) It's me, Martell, from the valley!"

Freddy replied, "What's up, brother?" With that, Martell won the $20 bet.

Then Martell told Freddy once more, "Never forget your roots, brother!"

Freddy again responded, "No, Martell, I will never forget *mi Raza y La Villita de San Benito!*"

A struggling musician. A mechanic/digging ditches by day and singer by night. *(1970)*

"From My Eyes" by Freddy Fender

I used to call myself Johnny Potatoes—that's Juan Papas in Spanish. He is a guy who digs ditches all day long, and on the weekends, he's got on new clothes and shiny shoes, playing at some nightclub. I was greased up during the week, and on weekends dressed better than the mayor! That's what I was! I was trying to live a life of fantasy all weekend to escape the reality of home.

Fixing Cotton-Picking Machines!

In the Rio Grande Valley, Dad's first legitimate occupation that he actually enjoyed was working as a mechanic for Delta Spindle, a cotton gin in La Feria, Texas. He was fixing cotton-picking machines called Caterpillars and earning $1.60 an hour. By night, he would pick guitar for $28. In Dad's exact words, he did this "so that we wouldn't starve to death!"

Mother would pack him a lunch for his new job, but Freddy wasn't too crazy about American food, like sandwiches or salads. At work, Dad would trade his lunches with the other workers for their tacos.

One afternoon, Mother was late picking Dad up from Delta Spindle. She told me to heat up the beans, to keep stirring so that they wouldn't burn and dry out. So, I stood up on a chair to reach the stove and stirred the beans until she arrived back home. Then when Father was ready, he sat at the kitchen table and began to eat his meal alone. As I walked away, I heard and saw the plate fly against the wall. I saw salad and the macaroni and cheese scattered everywhere! He yelled something about can or boxed foods or other, and then I flew out of there.

And again, he yelled out, *"Aqui, yo mando!"* ("Here, I'm boss!")

Father wanted an authentic home-cooked meal as he had become accustomed to while growing up with his mother. I only saw this happen once.

Freddy got paid every two weeks; to keep him from spending his paycheck, Máge and Eva would quickly get on the bus and pick up Dad's paycheck and pay the bills. Máge also liked that Mother would take her out to eat with the extra income.

On one occasion, instead of taking the bus, Eva decided to drive Balde's vehicle. However, it has a stick shift and she didn't know how to drive it, so she wound up driving it all the way to La Feria in first gear. On their way back, the car stopped running and she had to pull over. Máge opened the hood, and Eva saw her take off her shoe and begin hitting the car battery. Sure enough, the engine immediately started back up again and they enjoyed a great lunch.

At work, Father moved up at Delta Spindle and learned to drive Caterpillars (tractors). He was so proud of working there that when we drove by, he pointed out his workplace to us. You could see the machinery was big.

Sometimes Dad would take us across the border into Matamoros. It was considered a special day for us, so he would order foods like *cabrito* and *menudo* (tripe soup).

Dad was sort of content to have a real day job. He enjoyed working with his hands, fixing machinery. I feel that having a normal and steady job boosted Dad's self-esteem.

After several months, Freddy's boss asked him to train a new guy to drive the tractor. Shortly thereafter, the boss gave Freddy's position to the new guy. Father felt let down after all his hard work learning the mechanics of the job. He did find himself another job digging ditches.

We were a family of five now. And with grandmother, Sylvia, and Elvia living with us, that made eight.

When Father came home from working, he would sit down, tired, and have us remove his work boots. He would have us turn around, place his boot between our legs, and gently push our butts with his other foot. I can still remember his fingernails, stained with black dirt and oil from working all those grungy odd jobs.

"From My Eyes" by Freddy Fender
I can say thank you, from the bottom of my heart (Delta Spindle), and I know if anything ever goes wrong with my career, I can always go back to fixing cotton-picking machines!

Our Sweet Uncle Béke

In 1969, our sweet uncle Béke, who had served time in the Navy, arrived back home from the Vietnam War. He had spent time in Cambodia on the patrol boats and had broken his leg. However, there were no other jobs for the men and our relatives. So, he went back to being a migrant worker along with everyone else in the barrio. On top of that, Uncle Béke had been feeling blue for a very long time because he had lost his wife and child while serving in the Vietnam war.

Hundreds upon hundreds of young, patriotic, South Texas born and bred Mexican Americans joined the military, never to return home. As a child, I remember hearing the mothers in El Jardín sadly wailing out loud, unbearable cries coming from the open kitchen windows of their home. They wept for their sons who had been killed or were missing in action. Rumors were that their mothers had gone mad.

Chapter XII

RGV Girl

Amá Máge and I
Childhood Dreams
The Magical Rio Grande Valley
Christmas Time in the Valley
La Parranda y La Pachanga
La Reseca Moon

Tammy Lorraine Huerta (1970)

Being a "valley girl" from the Rio Grande Valley (RGV) is something I treasure, and I am grateful for having been raised as one. I will always try to do my best in respecting that because it is where my true heritage lies. Today, the portrait of my father's kind-hearted face illustrated on San Benito's water tower is a sweet reminder of his undying love and the music he left behind for us to enjoy. A trip back home made on a regular basis to the RGV brings me much comfort. It embraces me just as my grandmother's bosom once did when I was a child. It is also clear to me that the townspeople, in all their charm and beauty, truly define my spirit and make me who I am today.

With all that said, I would like to share with you some extended stories of my barrio, El Jardín. It was a place and time when I was full of life, laughter, and hope; it was filled with many childhood dreams. I was sweet, cheerful, and innocent; therefore, I shall call this alluring and peaceful place *home*.

And because our family's future will take a drastic turn to the unknown within the abyss of "The Fall" (Part II), I will reflect upon that period in our lives first when we were all happy and united as a loving family.

However, I also believe that there shall be no darkness without the flicker of God's candlelight to see us through our journey here on earth.

Amá Máge (grandma) and I

We were now living back home, and in our dad's old stomping grounds. We moved into a two-room shack on Resaca Drive and Francisco Madero Street with Amá Máge, Sylvia and Elvia. It was at the end of the block kitty-corner to Business Highway 77. Our Aunt Minerva had married young and moved far, far away; my uncles lived nearby with their own families.

Amá Máge's humble home was by the back alley and in front of our little house lived Doña Santos. It was her home that faced *la resaca*. She was a nice lady. She used to call me *la muñeca azul* (blue doll); I never knew why, nor did I ask.

Our extended family slept together in one tiny room. There were two little cots, one for my mom and dad and the other for Amá Máge. We had a few Valley rats that also made themselves just as comfortable in our home. As a child, I really didn't mind the rats because they were part of our life. At night, I could feel one of them warm up to me, lying on top of my blanket between my legs, as it lay asleep with me.

We had an outhouse with a toilet and we also had a shower space. However, Amá Máge would place me in a galvanized tub that was set in the middle of the kitchen room for all to see. One pot at a time, she would heat water on the gas stove and pour it into the tub so that I wouldn't shiver. The grown-ups would just walk right by me. I loved how our families lived so close by.

I like to call *la resaca* our "lakefront property" because it is the best scenery we have and we are grateful for it. At that time, there was an empty lot on the corner of Francisco Madero from which we had a great view of people enjoying themselves at the park by the river. We cannot swim or have boats in *la resaca*, but we can definitely fish.

My hair grew back but I still refused to brush it. I felt untroubled, free spirited, and took great joy in roaming el barrio without my shoes on. I fit in perfectly. I can still hear Mother hollering at me as I walked down Francisco Madero like I owned the street, telling me to take my little hands out of the pockets of my red shorts, fearing I would grow up to be a tomboy and a *pachuca (girl gangsta)*.

My hair would provide a moment of further bonding between Amá Máge and her grandkids. Visualize my grandmother, sitting outside on the porch (on the floor), as we took turns having our lice pulled out, one by one. I think she really liked doing that for us. She was not embarrassed at all.

One day, Máge's friend Catarina "Cata" Galván-Briones came by to pierce my ears. I remember sitting on my grandmother's lap while she held me. After cleaning my ear with alcohol, Cata placed a hot needle on the gas fire and slipped it through my earlobes. I think they purposely did that to me to officially make me into a girl, and not a tomboy.

In the early mornings, we woke up to the sounds of roosters crowing and trains passing by on their way to bigger towns like Brownsville, McAllen, and Laredo. Then our grandmother would turn on KGBT-AM radio and listen to lively Mexican music as she anxiously awaited *las noticias* (news) from nearby and the tragedies from over the border. She also anticipated reading the Mexican papers and sharing their horrific stories with *las comadres* (female friends).

In my mind, I can still hear her singing songs like "Cucurrucucú Paloma," to which I too joined in, trying to be a sweet, happy Valley Girl. It was then that I began learning to speak our very own Tex-Mex lingo. Since my first language had become English while living in New Orleans. I now had to learn a little Spanish, which I mixed up with English, so I could communicate with my grandmother and relatives back home.

One afternoon, we drove to *la Azteca* warehouse to get low-priced dairy products that were available for low-income people. We picked up eggs, milk, cheese, butter plus molasses, sardines, and peanut butter. One of my favorite things was to pour clear white molasses or ketchup on a slice of bread or flour tortilla and eat it. Then on our way home, I turned back around to see my grandmother take a big chunk out of a stick of real butter. She was bold! I liked that about her.

Amá Máge would also take me along with her to *los montes* by the cemetery, to the same exact location where my dad is buried today. There, I just did what she did; I used the clothespin to hold the *nopal* (cactus) and a small razor blade to cut off the thorns. Then I would place the cactus into a paper bag. *Mexicanos* love to fry up *nopalitos* with scrambled eggs, onions, tomatoes, and beef.

When I got sick with a fever, Amá Máge would act as our *curandera* (healer). First, she would wipe my body down with pure alcohol. Then she would rub a cold-shelled raw egg all over my bare body while making the sign of the cross with the egg. You could hear her praying under her breath the Our Father and Hail Mary prayers repeatedly. When she was done healing me, she would crack the egg open into a clear glass. She looked at me to show me that it was slightly cooked and so my body temperature would go back to normal.

Before bedtime, she would light up her cigarette and smoke. Aunt Sylvia, Elvia, and I always slept together on the floor by Amá Máge's bed. Then she would begin to tell us chilling ghost stories. The girls and I would just follow the end of her lit cigarette in the dark while hanging on breathlessly to her next words. Nobody could tell scary folk tales like my Amá Máge would.

Another thing about this wonderful, charismatic, and maternal woman was that everyone just loved eating her cooking. She and her sister Lola made the best *salsa de chicharron* (pork skin) around town.

Above all, the best thing about our grandmother was how she enjoyed doting over Sonny, Danny, and me. She made us feel safe and truly loved; we were happiest when around her. We loved her laughter and the unconditional love she had for us. Oh, how I loved her dearly.

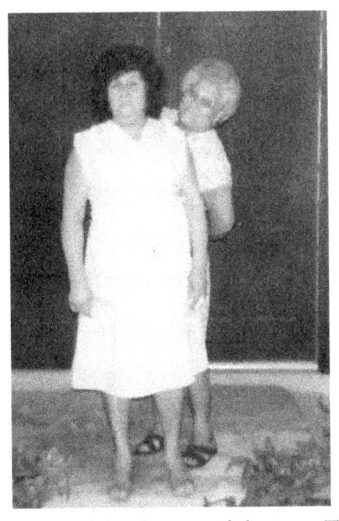

Doña Máge with her loving and shy sister, Tía Lola

Los Barrios

Resaca Drive was where I used to see Béke, Sylvia, and Elvia's father Manuelon "El Aventurero" (before Amá Máge left him). He'd park his truck in the back alley of Francisco Madero Street when he came to visit Máge and his children. I remember him stopping by to give his kids a fifty-cent piece or a dollar.

Since Manuelon was doing so well with his fruit markets, we would all get excited when he'd stop by to visit. He gave us sacks of fruits and melons, and we would take the watermelon across the street to *la resaca*, slice the watermelon on top of the picnic table and ravish it.

One of my best memories of the park by *la resaca* is when all my relatives from El Jardín came together to play the card game known as La Chalupa.

The neighborhood of El Jardín is only several short blocks in diameter, but that was plenty of room for me to explore and play. Everyone knows every barrio has its own personality. I knew my place, which meant not crossing over the railroad tracks into La Palma, Puente De Los Dos Amores, La Gallina, or other barrios. I also knew not to disturb the Anglo neighborhood across Business Highway 77, either. So, I had plenty of time to entertain myself by climbing trees for berries and pecans at *la resaca* where there were many pomegranates and papaya to enjoy as well.

During the summer, I spent afternoon with my cousin Amy (Uncle Chencho's daughter), and my Aunts Sylvia and Elvia. We sat and played alongside *la resaca*, getting our feet wet, fully aware that there were snakes, alligators and whatnot in the water.

Then without a word, Sylvia got up and ran across the street. We waited for her to return. I wondered why she was taking so long, but Elvia said she had gone to use the bathroom.

Then I heard a noise and looked over toward Doña Santos' house and saw an ambulance with a stretch bed out front. I asked Elvia, "Look, why is there an ambulance at Doña Santos?"

Elvia responded that Sylvia had eaten a whole jar of peanut butter the night before and her stomach hurt, and that's why she was being taken to the hospital. But Sylvia wasn't outside or on the bed at that point. Now, how would Elvia know the true cause when she was sitting with us?

I looked around for my tall, longhaired, quiet *prima* (cousin) Amy. Where was she? My question was answered when I heard water splashing. She was drowning in *la resaca*! So, I jumped in, swam after her, and pulled her out by the end of her long, beautiful hair.

Years later, Elvia admitted to placing a whole box of chocolate laxatives into the jar of peanut butter the night before the incident with Aunt Sylvia. While Sylvia is beautiful and reserved, Elvia, on the other hand, is mischievous like her big brother Balde; she has dreamy eyes just like him. Elvia also has an artistic handwriting that's all her own. I have never seen a more expressive and exotic penmanship than hers. Both Sylvia and Elvia were like sisters to me.

"Shimmy Shimmy Ko-Ko-Bop"

Next, we moved a few streets back to 549 Winchell Street. Since my parents withdrew Sonny and I out of school early in New Orleans, we both enrolled at Frank Roberts toward the last two months of the school term in order to complete our grade level. Sonny and Sylvia were the same age, and in the fifth grade. Sonny was very handsome with curly blondish brown hair, which attracted a lot of friends and attention. However, Sylvia vividly recounts how their teacher had to strap Sonny down to his desk on several occasions because he was so rambunctious.

Elvia and I were in the first grade when we joined the Brownies Girls Club and I was very proud to be a Brownie. I loved wearing my uniform, pins, badges, and cap; I took the Brownies very seriously, too, as we marched downtown on Sam Houston Road for San Benito's Parade. Dad had always teased me about my marching in the parade. He recalled that I thought I was "all that" because I was the smallest Brownie yet raised my legs up the highest while marching. I was so disappointed when school was over because I could no longer wear my Brownie uniform. But I was told I could join the Girl Scouts in the second grade and I looked forward to that day.

As far as my singing talent goes, I do love to sing, and though I may not have given myself an opportunity to pursue it as a career, I did get to enjoy a moment in the spotlight in elementary school. We were at our cafeteria getting singing lessons when the teacher chose me (after I raised my hand the highest) to get up and show off my talent. This was my second public performance other than when I would sing and dance on Bourbon Street.

I was sure to raise my voice and sustain the notes just long enough as I had been taught. Being the new kid at school, I was so eager to impress that I ran up onstage and quickly began singing a popular tune called "Raindrops Keep Falling on My Head." I didn't know all the lyrics, so I kept repeating the same verse and chorus. But what counts is that I got up and did it anyway!

I sang a whole lot, and I danced everywhere I went. I constantly entertained. In fact, I would look for total strangers and begin to sing to them in restaurants and city buses—tunes like Dionne Warwick's "Do You Know the Way to San José?" or "Shimmy Shimmy Ko-Ko-Bop," by Little Anthony and the Imperials. And sometimes, while we were out in public, Aunt Mary would pinch me hard and tell me to sit back down.

One day, as I walked in to our corner store on Winchell Street, I looked at the coloring books and boxes of crayons. I just loved colors so much that I memorized the largest box of 100 colored crayons. Then I heard the storeowner say, "If you sing for me, I will give you whatever you want." Why would he ask me such a thing? I am not a *real* singer; I'm a dancer! How does this man know me?

To me, Father wasn't a famous singer; he was just Dad! And because we were considered a little special in El Jardín, and I didn't know why, people liked asking me questions about my family. I was ignorant about the fact that my dad was El Bebop Kid (the Mexican Elvis) or Freddy Fender.

However, I could not resist the temptation and opportunity to show off again. So, I quickly sang "Shimmy Shimmy Ko-Ko-Bop" and shimmied for him but in the English language. I did my skit, and the storeowner gave me my box of crayons and coloring book. Then I ran out of the store.

My Dreams: Either a Ballerina or a Go-Go Dancer with White Go-Go Boots

Like every child, I too, had my dreams. But without a tutu, how was I supposed to become a ballerina dancer, or a go-go dancer without my white go-go boots, like Cher's?

One afternoon, Mother walked up to me while I sat on the porch and handed me a little petticoat, but where was the rest of the tutu? And where were my ballerina shoes? I did have a pair of ballerina shoes in New Orleans, but I had outgrown them. However, having to be without had never stopped Dad from learning music on a three-string guitar with no backside. It was clear to me; I was going to have to figure out a way to make my own dreams come true.

In the 1960s and 1970s, the Miss America pageant was a very popular show on primetime television. So, I would gather the girls in front of the porch and act as their pageant coordinator. I would place Sylvia and Elvia at each end of the corner porch. One by one, they would walk about, prancing gracefully and representing their states as I sang, "What's New Pussycat," a popular hit song by Tom Jones, which he may have performed once during the Miss America pageant.

Speaking of Tom Jones, he was a very steamy performer! Women would throw their panties and bras at him onstage. At times, Mother would have me sit by her and watch Tom Jones moving his hips on television and we'd hide from Dad when we watched him because Father was a very jealous man when it came to Mother.

On his humorous side, Dad caught us once and stood in front of the tube and flexed his own muscles (while wearing his boxers) to block our view. Sometimes he would even shut the television off. On one occasion, Father caught Mother watching Tom Jones again, so he grabbed the television and threw it out the back door. And that was that for Tom Jones!

(Years later, Mother and I did go see *Tom Jones Live* in the Corpus Christi Coliseum on Shoreline Boulevard while Dad was out on tour. Somehow, Tom Jones found out Freddy Fender's wife was at his show and he invited her backstage, but we knew if Father found out, we would be in big trouble. The Jackson 5 opened for Tom Jones that night, but we dared not go back where there were men. So, we sat and just enjoyed the show. It was just as well because Dad would have found out about it somehow—and then what?)

Tammy is happy to see Don Pacheco at his store again (30 years later). (1993)

Two decades later, Tammy visits Don Pacheco at his candy store in El Jardín (1993).

Storeowners at Every Corner: Candy, Candy, Candy

Pancho Galván's and Pacheco's are corner stores in El Jardín. I vividly remember buying my candy there as a child. The storeowners were very personable and kind to us. In el barrio, everyone knew each other's families. Every little store on every block sold a special kind of candy. I remember a thin, candy-shaped wafer that looked like a little spaceship was sold at Pancho Galván's. It tasted like the Holy Eucharist (communion bread). Inside were candy sprinkles, and when placed on the tongue, the wafer would dissolve with crunchy sweetness. Another popular candy I purchased at Galván's was a hardened sugar candy called *Peroline*. They were multicolored, layered candies that looked like a torpedo. It had a sharp point at the end, which if licked too eagerly could actually stab the back of your throat. But the *Perolines* were something special! They had something inside we all desired—a nickel or dime seen clearly in the middle of it. All one had to do was to lick it down for about three months or break it with a hammer to get to the coin.

However, Pacheco's store was my favorite. He was the kindest person to everyone and always had a smile for you. He enjoyed asking me about my relatives. One day, I remember riding my little red training bike up the sidewalk, when I spotted a quarter on the ground. I quickly grabbed it and raced to Pacheco's to buy me some candy. I wanted to buy a candy necklace and bracelet. I was so excited that I flew off my bike and began to walk into Pacheco's! Then I opened my little hand to check on my money, and my quarter was missing. I thought to myself that the quarter must have slipped through my little fingers while I was riding my bike! We have a saying in Spanish, *"El diablo se lo comio!"* (The devil must have eaten it!) Damn you, devil! Why? Why me?

Sonny Boy and Tammy: 549 Winchell Street

In our youth, Sonny and I didn't have many toys to play with, not that I am complaining, mind you. I didn't really play with dolls, either. I think I remember owning one Barbie doll I had gotten for Christmas. I mostly spent all day playing jacks with Sylvia and Elvia. And if we wanted paper dolls, we had to cut them out of the newspapers and magazines. Dad even showed us how to play the harmonica by placing plastic wrap over a hair comb and blowing air on top of its teeth. This is what we had to work with. Even so, Sonny did manage to teach himself how to play a real harmonica.

As a happy and self-entertaining little girl, I did enjoy crawling and playing under the house, digging for *cocanitas* (dirt bugs). I also loved collecting tadpoles, frogs, and especially scorpions. I had many scorpions and would scoop them up with a piece of paper into a large jar.

One late afternoon, I saw Sonny being dropped off in a car by his friend on Winchell. So, I ran up to his friend to show him my collection of scorpions. I thought he was going to look and admire them with me, but instead he told me to stand back and busted my jar in the middle of the street. Now all my scorpions were running loose! To top it all off, he yelled at me!

"Don't you know that they are dangerous?" he shouted. Then he backed up his car and ran over my scorpions! I just stood there in the middle of the street, stunned and speechless (just like when daddy pulled out the milk bottle nipple from my mouth)! They were my bugs! I wasn't fearful of anything! Why do people have to put fear into you? The angels took care of me. I was innocent! I was okay, back then!

Sonny and I were also very close as brother and sister. Sometimes we would bond over a large brown paper bag filled with multicolored popcorn. Mother would sprinkle the popcorn with Louisiana Hot Sauce as we often enjoyed eating in New

Orleans. Then we would sit together on the street curb, and watch the kids and cars go by as we quietly ate our popcorn.

After playing around midnight, we would walk through the pitch-dark back alleys to get home. We never feared anything or anybody; it just never entered our minds (not in San Benito, anyway).

Although we never knew what would come next living with our father, there wasn't anything that we couldn't handle. And you know what? I could swear that the full moon shining over El Jardín was watching over us the whole time! It cuddled us, keeping us safe as it followed us back home to 549 Winchell Street.

As for getting punished, I do not remember ever getting spanked, not really. My dad did grab me once by my skinny, little arms; as he began to swing his arm up high to spank me, I remember running around him in a circle trying to get away from him. I had Father going in a circle chasing me while I was screaming! I was petrified to get welts on my little bottom. He felt so bad for me because I was so tiny and frail. He thought I was going to break! He left me alone. He just laughed and couldn't get himself to do it. So, I never got spanked. But I was a good girl, most of the time.

As for Sonny, when he would get into trouble, Mom would tell Dad to take Sonny into the bedroom and beat him. One day, Sonny got into trouble of some sort, and Dad took him into the bedroom and shut the doors behind him. I heard poor Sonny screaming and crying and thought *Ooh, that's great! Well, he deserved it! After all, he did break my arm back in New Orleans, and on purpose! He told me so.*

I couldn't resist, so I peeked in to see Sonny get beat to hell. And when I looked up, I saw Dad's arm way up high, ready to swing at him once more. But Dad missed Sonny and hit the bed instead! But every time Dad was hitting the bed, Sonny would yell out loud and pretend he was in misery. They were in cahoots! I had caught them both red-handed! Dad just put his finger up to his mouth for me to be quiet, so I did. I just closed the door and left the scene of the crime.

Our Neighbors in El Jardín

Doña Theresa Tamayo was a lovely woman who lived across the street from us. She owned a *tortillera* and sold candy. Her specialty was a candy that was similar to a Kool-Aid package. It was sticky and gooey, tasted sweet yet bitter, and it stained your mouth and fingers into a deep purple color.

I got my first job at Doña Tamayo's at nine years old. I helped her prepare fresh corn tortillas. I placed large corn kernels into a large machine as big as me. Then she added ingredients on top of that. When the corn came out, it was raw, warm *masa* (corn dough). Afterward, she would heat fresh corn tortillas to sell. The customers outside could smell them as they walked by her store and the aroma drew them inside because they knew corn tortillas are best eaten hot with a little salt and butter.

One afternoon, I was dismissed (fired) because I gave away a free piece of candy to one of the Claudios' youngest sisters. The little girl said something in Spanish, and I didn't know what she meant, but it sounded like the word *free*. I mistook it to mean that she wanted it on her family's store credit as most people did back then. I was new in town and didn't speak much Spanish. Mrs. Tamayo asked me about the little girl, and I ratted myself out! She relieved me, and I went out to play instead.

Doña Tamayo had many wonderful grandchildren who would come by to visit her and keep her company. David, who was sweet, cute, and Danny's age, would visit the most.

One afternoon, when we were all sitting on our front porch with Dad eating ice-cold watermelon, we saw David across the street. We waved to him, motioning for him to come over and join us. He walked across the street, and Father gave him a big piece of watermelon to eat. David took it; he was so excited that he said he had to go tell his grandmother that he would be with us that afternoon.

As David was about to cross the street, Mother yelled out to him to make sure he looked to his left and then to his right! David did just that. He turned his head to the left and then to the right. Then he crossed the street. But as soon as he crossed the street, a car ran over him!

We jumped off the porch and ran toward him right away! Poor David was lying face down and was all scratched up. We didn't know whether to pick David up or what! What were we going to tell his grandmother, Doña Theresa Tamayo? We were all shook up!

All of a sudden, we heard him shouting, *"Mi sandia! Mi sandia!"* ("My watermelon! My watermelon!") David was more concerned about his watermelon.

You see, David had only turned his head while crossing the street; he hadn't looked with his eyes for vehicles passing by. He got scraped up in a few places, but no big thing! We bandaged him up, and Dad gave him another big piece of cold watermelon. We enjoyed the rest of the afternoon cooling off and eating valley watermelon. Life was great in El Jardín.

Doña Tamayo also had beautiful granddaughters and the girls invited me over one weekend to stay at their home, which was a farm on the outskirts of town. There, during my first sleepover, I saw huge pigs, and it was very muddy.

I was amazed with the girls because they taught me how to make mud dishes. I made saucers, bowls, and plates and was told to leave them overnight to dry. That morning, my mud dishes were hardened and ready to use as play dishes. I was impressed with the girls and my mud dishes. I thought they were very cool after that.

I thought I had the market cornered on imagination and creativity because I had always used natural products—mixing rocks, leaves, twigs, tadpoles, and dirt into a pot of rainwater like a potted stew. I felt like the witch in the story of Hansel and Gretel, making porridge and stirring it with a stick.

After it rained, playing with frogs and collecting tadpoles was one of my favorite pastimes. And in the Rio Grande Valley, it rains a lot! That is why we have such beautiful tropical plants and blooming flowers.

Doña Tamayo was already up in age, yet her mother was still alive. She too lived on Winchell Street and on the corner. This is another cool thing about the barrios in San Benito; everyone lives within a short radius of one another.

I was asked if I wanted to keep Doña Tamayo's mother company overnight; if I took the job, I would earn perhaps a quarter. Every Tuesday and Thursday, I would go across the street around 6:30 p.m. and most of the time, I would just sit there quietly with her in the kitchen while she cooked and boiled beans in *a jarro* (pot).

However, there were three things that bothered me about this job. One, there was the old-people smell, which is understandable. The second is that I wished I had never taken the job for money because I couldn't wait until morning to look for my change. I felt like a thief in the night, and would run out the door without saying goodbye. Third, I really wished I would have sang and danced for her. Of all people, she would have enjoyed me the most. In retrospect, I'm so glad I took the job after all. No one should ever be alone—no one, especially the elderly.

Migrant Workers: I, Too, Picked Tomatoes

I always liked following Amá Máge everywhere she went. So, one day, I decided to get up with her in the early morning. She made us potato and egg tacos for our lunch as we waited for *el troquero* to arrive!

We stood outside the curb and waited for our turn to be picked up. Then Amá Máge, Sylvia, Elvia, and I hopped in the back along with the rest of the migrant workers. The Claudio brothers were also in the back of the truck. They lived two streets back, closer to the projects. They were a large family of regular migrant workers. Then we all headed to *las piscas* to pick tomatoes.

The reason I went along was because I wanted to see what all the fuss was about and to join the grown-ups. As soon as I arrived, I was given a large flimsy cedar basket to fill up with tomatoes. I followed Amá Máge's lead and pulled the ripe valley tomatoes off the vines. I can still remember that strong scent of ripe, luscious red tomatoes. They were delicious! I filled up one basket, then two, and then *el troquero* would weigh it and in turn give me a chip. So, at the end of the day, when I collected my few coins, I had earned about $1.60.

During our lunch break, I noticed the handsome Rolando Claudio noticing me. I was only about ten years old and he was a couple of years older than me. But of course, we never spoke to one another. Plus, I didn't like boys because I thought they were kind of gross. After a hard day of work at the field, we were taken back home and dropped off one family at a time. But I noticed that the Claudio brothers were having fun throwing tomatoes at the migrant workers' homes. It was our turn to be dropped off, and they began to throw tomatoes at the house. This is when I realized that Rolando was about to throw a tomato at me as well! I ran around the truck to get away from him, and he ran the opposite way. Then I saw and felt a red tomato hit me hard in my eye! It hurt! Anyhow, my curiosity and career as a migrant worker was short lived, to say the least. And if that is the way that boys show their affection, well, then, forget it.

As for Sonny Boy, he learned to hustle for Amá Máge. San Benito was surrounded by vegetable fields; instead of picking tomatoes, she would have Sonny Boy pick corn or fruit from nearby fields, such as those by the Sunny Glenn Orphanage off Highway 77.

Meanwhile, Dad was also working as a migrant worker during the day, as were so many of our relatives. And for decades, there was a sign by the side of Highway 77 that read, "Welcome Home Valley Migrant Workers!"

Many times, the women and children would wait outside for their fathers and sons to come home. The quickest way to discover what fruits or vegetables were in harvest would be to watch what the neighborhood kids were eating because everyone in el barrio would be eating plenty of the same foods. Me, I would just hope it was sugarcane because I loved chewing on sugarcane sticks.

Christmas Time in the Valley

Meanwhile, Father was doing his best to appease Mother by working during the day, singing less, and staying home at night during the week. As a result, it was a little scarce under the tree during our valley morning Christmas. However, Sonny and I did look forward to decorating the tree with silver icicles. We could also depend on a great big peppermint stick and a ready-made stocking filled with candy and coloring books. The fruits gathered for the holiday season were tangerines and pecans.

Unfortunately, some of our Christmas and New Year mornings weren't without some drama or trauma! One morning, I woke up and heard loud noises. I realized I was in hysteria and couldn't stop myself from screaming because I heard one of my uncles and Dad fighting outside and I knew they would eventually bring it inside and knock down our Christmas tree as usual. I ran for cover into our parent's bedroom. But then Dad stormed in and rushed through his room, looking in Mother's sewing kit for a pair of scissors (something sharp). Then he went to the kitchen to look for a knife.

However, Dad loved his brothers very much and would never really hurt them. And I guess as long as nobody died that day, it was a good day. This was the norm for us growing up—seeing these fights, which were mostly fueled by tequila.

As for our New Year's tradition, Amá Máge would prepare us *buñuelos*! She would fry the flour dough (a tortilla) until it was crispy golden brown. Then she'd mix white powder sugar with cinnamon and sprinkle it on top and serve them to us at midnight. Today I make them the same exact way every New Year's Eve.

Nevertheless, the best part of our holidays was that we were all together. No matter what, we were a family. Aside from those drunken fistfights, our family traditions were the best ever!

"From My Eyes" by Freddy Fender
This guy was telling me about how hard he had it growing up!
He said that he sometimes had to wear his shoes to school without shoelaces.
So, I turned to him and said, "Oh really, vato (dude)—you had shoes? Wow!"

La Pachanga's en La Parranda del Jardín
("celebrations, entertainment, and cookouts")

San Benito's homes are all small and charming. The people are friendly and enjoy reminiscing, especially at night. It is here in our barrio where *la pachanga's* en la *parranda* del Jardín ("life's celebrations, entertainment, and cookouts") are frequently celebrated almost every weekend. Plus, you can actually see the people walking in the dark going from one house to another to visit each other. The residents take pride in their humble homes. Many have beautiful gardens filled with succulent tropical plants. My cousin Angelica Huerta (Lola's daughter), a missionary nurse, has a knack for growing tall, colorful bougainvillea and red poinsettias as tall as a house. It is truly an old-fashioned world filled with mysticism and folklore. To you, it may not look like much; but to us—it is everything meaningful in life.

Today, I like visiting my hometown and going to the cemetery to visit our ancestors. It is the most beautiful place I have ever been. It makes me feel welcomed and secure. I know it is eerie—okay, creepy to hear, but if you saw how the people partake in decorating their ancestors' gravesites as though it were a festive party, you would love it here too. I can't wait to linger about the cemetery place when it is my turn to go. I love it there; I feel like a free-spirited young girl running around playing, with lots of love around me. People can usually find me there during the holidays, roaming around, cleaning and decorating all my relatives' headstones. It brings me much peace and joy; it also puts my life back into perspective.

On New Year's Eve and the Fourth of July, the whole town gets involved as we wait for the townsmen to fill the evening sky full of fireworks. I don't think the police station has enough room in their jail to haul in the whole town for popping fireworks within the city limits. It's incredible to see everyone rejoicing at once! The skies are brilliantly lit from rockets that reflect off *la resaca and its moonlight*. The spirit of hope and gratefulness of generations of Americans of Mexican descent is what binds us together.

The Rio Grande Valley people (near the Mexican border) also love America and are so patriotic! San Benito expresses so much spirit, like nothing I have seen elsewhere. I wouldn't change a thing about her, ever. And I hope their city officials never try to attempt to turn it into a progressive city. It will surely lose all its enchanted magic, forever.

Moreover, I would never change a thing about myself. I am a true RGV girl, and I will always be one, no matter where I go or where my life leads me. We can always spot one another from afar because of our down-to-earth demeanor. Plus, our hearts are loyal and as big as the state of Texas.

Besides, I've got *la resaca* moonlight to guide me, just waiting for me to tell you another tale from the magical Rio Grande Valley.

Sonny and Tammy on Christmas morning at 549 Winchell Street.

Chapter XIII

The Border Diablos

Freddy's brother "El Tortillero"
"Poker run" and "Rocket-run"
"The Red-light District"

José Luis Garza Méndez (Freddy's brother, 1970)

Interviewee:
José Luis Méndez
(Freddy's half-brother)

In 1962, I was sixteen years old when I found out Freddy was my brother. All of Freddy's siblings knew that I was their brother. But part of the deal was that when Máge gave me away to the Méndez family, it was understood they were never to tell me. What was weird is that everybody else knew it in El Jardín, but the truth finally got to me. This guy came and told me, "Do you know Freddy Fender is your brother?" And I almost got into a fight with this guy!

The funny part is when I heard Freddy just starting out on the KGBT radio as El Bebop Kid, I told my adoptive mother that I had wished Freddy was my brother. Of course, I didn't know I was adopted at the time.

My mother just looked at me. I felt that one can only feel more or less something about one's own real blood relation.

So, the first guy that I approached was Cáne. I asked him, "Hey, I heard that you were my brother."

Cáne replied, "Yeah, but we're not supposed to tell you."

I said, "Oh, okay," and we shook hands.

Then Cáne asked me, "Do you want to meet your mom?"

I said, "Yeah, sure." Freddy was somewhere [in prison], but I met the rest of my siblings. I asked Máge, "Are you my mom?"

She said, "Yes." Then she explained to me what she had promised the woman when she gave me up, never to tell anyone. But now I know! My dad, Méndez, never told me that I was adopted. To his dying day, he never said anything. He had liked my real mother Máge when she was young and wished it were true, that he was my real dad, even when he wasn't.

I wanted to know who my real dad is, and I asked her. This is when she told me the name of my father, who was from a political family in South Texas last named De La Garza. [I chose to keep his first name anonymous; José Luis had never confronted him, either.]

When I first got to know Freddy, he was The Bebop Kid. And then I saw his records as Scotty Wayne, then Eddie and the Shades, as Eddie Medina. When he got out of prison as Freddy Fender is when I started to get to know my brother and family much better.

"Poker Runs" and "Rocket Runs"

The Border *Diablos* (Devils) was a motorcycle club in San Benito and not a real biker gang. They hung out together, just partying and playing games. Their club was about hanging out, having fun, messing around, partying, and playing games. They like to have a good time without the violence of rivalry toward other biker clubs, or having strippers as old ladies.

While they played games, some bikers smoked a little—well, okay, a lot—of marijuana and tequila. These were husbands, perhaps not perfect ones, but the club was mainly to pass the time away.

José Luis was twenty-two years old when they joined the Border Diablos. Lalo Soto was the president, José Luis was vice president, and Ted Ochoa was the treasurer; they had about thirty-three club members.

Freddy did not have a motorcycle when he joined, but Eva eventually gave in and let Freddy buy a used 1949 Harley Panhead, which the Diablos helped him reconstruct. Next, his brothers Cherín and Cáne also joined the club.

While they were fixing Freddy's bike, Soto, who was also a painter, told Freddy to sand the bike and he would then paint it for him, but when Freddy brought the bike to him, it was down to bare metal and Soto had a fit. Anyway, Soto and some other Border Diablos fixed it up and got it running for him.

At this time, Freddy was working as a mechanic for Delta Spindle in La Feria. On the weekends, he hung out with the Border Diablos; at night, he sang at the honky-tonks.

The Border Diablos' main activities were "poker runs" and "rocket runs." A "poker run" is basically a run during the day. There were five locations with a card at each site. The object was to pick up a card at each spot—around the arroyo and wooded area—come back to a designated area, and then they would see who had the best poker hand. Say you had thirty riders at $5 per person. Whoever would win that hand won about $150. That's a poker run!

A "rocket run" was held at night. In this game, they would throw rockets up into the air, and the object was to find those rockets on the other side of the arroyo. You had to ride your bike in the pitch darkness looking for them, and whoever found it would get a half-gallon of tequila or money. Whoever won the tequila would share. That was a rocket run.

"And believe it or not, the Border Diablos would get into a couple of fights," José Luis said. "People would mess around with us, and we would just take care of business. It was no big deal. We didn't kill anybody. It would just be a scuffle. It was just another night."

Freddy (wearing a mechanic's work rag in back pocket) meets-up with the Border Diablos after working at Delta Spindle: Ted Ochoa, José Luis, Freddy, and Tony Vásquez (1970s)

Wasted Days and Wasted Nights

Lalo Soto fixing Freddy's bike (top left), José Lemos, Ochoa, and Freddy (far right).

Freddy on far right in work clothes/Piece of wood is used as a kickstand for one of the bikers.

The Border Diablos
Freddy's brother Juan José "Cáne" is sitting as a bike passenger wearing only a jacket.

Ernest Chapa: "Take This and Defend Yourself"

Ernest "Chapita" Chapa, who got a government job as soon as he finished his military enlistment, liked hanging with Freddy and the Border Diablos. Though he was a small guy, he loved to fight and was always with Freddy at the clubs. He knew Freddy and his brothers all too well. Chapita, who met Freddy at school in 1951, was one of the closest friends to Freddy, Eva, and Moody.

Back then, Freddy and Chapita would go to the back entrance of the San Benito High School cafeteria, where a kitchen employee named Lupita Maldonado would ask them if they were hungry. Of course, they would say yes, and she would feed them leftovers and a can of fruit cocktail.

They may have been poor and hungry, but they were handsome, and self-absorbed. And because they were young, their only thought was of dressing up, getting ready for the next wild party, and meeting girls.

One day, Freddy went to Chapita's house and said, "Let's go because we are going to be late!"

"Well, how can we be late if we don't know where we're going?" Chapita asked.

It just so happened that Freddy was on his way to buy a suit for a performance at a nightclub. He wanted Chapita to take him to a secondhand store to shop for clothes. Afterward, he put on the suit and asked Chapita, *"¿Cómo la vez?"* ("How do I look?").

Chapita answered, *"No hombre, te queda a toda madre"* ("No, man, you look super cool").

Freddy was raised to shop at secondhand stores, like Goodwill. He never knew any better than that. At times Freddy would buy used tuxedos. That way if there was a fight and the tuxedo got ruined, he could just throw it away.

Chapita vividly remembers how, one night, Eva threw Freddy's clothes out of the window of their second-floor apartment. She then purposely throw an ashtray on top of Freddy's head to get his attention, and it really hurt him. She was angry because he was getting dressed up to go out clubbing when she had no money to pay the bills or buy food for his three children.

Chapita admits he and Freddy were crazy and they did not care about anybody. Freddy was so used to playing music in rough places that he even took his eldest son Sonny Boy (when he was young) to the beer joints. He took him all the way to Brownsville to a rough place called the Squeeze Inn, where sometimes there was gunfire, fights, and the like. There, they would fight for any stupid thing, like a game of pool or a broad or even if one gave an ugly look of disrespect. Yet, Freddy took Sonny Boy there and sat him down on a table while Freddy sang.

The Squeeze Inn club in Brownsville was a weekend gathering place for the entire Rio Grande Valley. The owner was a good friend of Freddy's, and many times Freddy would play without pay. It seemed that all the places Freddy would always end up playing at were packed with a rough crowd.

Whenever Freddy was playing in Brownsville, especially at the Squeeze Inn, every biker around would go there to see Freddy and join the party. Chapita also remembers that club owners would make a lot of money off of Freddy.

Big macho men from both sides of the border were always present and it was there that Chapita got into a bar fight. He politely asked someone for a cigarette; instead, he was punched out for it. Then someone handed him a pocketknife and said, "Take this and defend yourself!"

What was Chapita going to do against an entire mob? The guy who hit him was cold-blooded, and if a fight started, these types of men wouldn't hesitate to pull out a knife and slash you. This guy would fight with his own brother, his own bloodline. So why wouldn't he take him out? If someone picked on one's brother, then he'd be quick to defend his brother in a fight.

Balde's elder brothers were mean in their youth, Chapita added. His half-brothers were not as violent as Inocencio Ramirez, "Chencho"; Joe Méndez, "El Tortillero;" and Manuel, "Béke." The younger brothers would look to Freddy because they depended on Freddy a lot.

The funny thing is that after everything was over and done with, you could see the owner of the Squeeze Inn just mopping the floor (of broken glass and bloodshed) and taking care of business.

Chapita added that men were jealous of Freddy, and it was not his fault that he was young, and not a bad-looking man. He had talent, so women threw themselves at him and tried to make out with him. Then their jealous husbands would start fights.

A *pelionero de madre* (real mother at fighting), Chapita was a good fighter for a small guy, one of the fastest and toughest when it came to starting a fight.

Matamoros (across the border) had a nonstop night scene for everyone to enjoy. In the late 1950s–1970s, Freddy liked going to popular clubs like El Fox and Popeye's.

Of course, the *Red-light District* is known for their infamous *cantinas*, nude strippers, and prostitution, and they stayed open day and night, just like on Bourbon Street, but these *cantinas* were much wilder and unrulier.

Freddy knew everybody; when he would go across the border, Mando and his band would back up Freddy for free just to party and hang out with him. And Freddy would also entertain for free, but he didn't mind because they would give him free drinks.

A few hours of free drinks translated to the men getting drunk, which was often followed by a brawl. Freddy was no exception. So yes, Freddy once got into a fight at the red-light district in Matamoros. As the police truck drove him to jail, Freddy threw his wallet out the window to Chapita because he knew that in Mexico, the cops would not give you back your belongings. You also couldn't accuse the police of taking your belongings, either. You had to keep your mouth shut or they would go find you and do whatever they wanted to you.

There was one instance when Freddy was in the mood for *cabrito*. He took Duncan's black Cadillac and drove all the way to Brownsville to buy a baby goat from a guy, but he wasn't there. However, Freddy was determined to eat *cabrito*, and he was not going to go back home empty-handed. He saw some goats off the side of the road, caught one, and placed it in the back of the Cadillac. Back at the Starlight, Freddy, Chapita, and Mando killed it, cooked it behind the bar in a large galvanized tub, and ate it before show time.

Evangelina
Yes, he suffered, and they took advantage of him, porqué
el se dejo (because Freddy allowed it).
Yes, they used him and took advantage of not paying Freddy for his work and talent, but all Freddy wanted to do was to party and have fun!

Interviewee:
John Richard Vásquez
(Sergeant in Vietnam War and Ex-Joker motorcycle member)

In 1970, I was a hard-core member of the Jokers motorcycle club from Corpus Christi. I had just returned from two tours in Vietnam with the Eighty-Second Airborne. I was experienced with serious combat and had personally been a violent person while killing many enemies at war. I had been a sergeant, but I had killed some of my men because they raped women and children, so rather than take it to court, they dishonorably discharged me.

The Jokers were more of a motorcycle club, but I admit we were stupid and self-centered. And we had left our wives alone since the mentality of a biker was to be selfish and in full swing of the lifestyle of a biker. Our attitude was basically "f—k it!"

The Border Diablos would host the Jokers when they came into town. Host meant that the other club would take care of them while riding through town. They took care of the Jokers' bikes while they crossed over into Mexico so they wouldn't be stolen. The Border Diablos would also entertain us as well.

It was at a big park around August of 1971 that I first met or heard about Freddy Fender. He was singing "Mama Told Me Not to Come." I thought he had recorded the song, and I was impressed. I didn't talk to many people then, and I was very arrogant. But I walked up to him and told him I really liked the song.

I thought he had written it. Freddy mentioned that it wasn't him but rather the group Three Dog Night. We smoked our last joint with them and mainly just hung around with the Border Diablos that day. We would return the favor when the Border Diablos came up to Corpus Christi; the Jokers would host them.

Unfortunately, when the Border Diablos came to Corpus Christi once, the Banditos motorcycle gang held the Jokers up inside their garage on Gabrielle Street. The Jokers and the Border Diablos were all held at gunpoint.

The Banditos then was a very violent biker gang, and they were messing with us. They were thugs, and we had to rush one of our leaders named, or nicknamed, Gatcha to the hospital.

The president of the Border Diablos also had gotten hit on the mouth with a shotgun and was sent to the hospital. They hurt many members from the Diablos as they hit some of them with the butt of a shotgun and their faces were dislocated, smashed inward.

It was fortunate that Border Diablo members weren't shot because that was their (Banditos) style. Guns were drawn; it was bad, and it got real ugly.

Lucky for Freddy, he did not go this one time to Corpus Christi.

Freddy's brother, Juan "Cáne" Huerta, with guitar

(Left) *Cáne Huerta with sombrero and*
(Far right) *half-brother, Jose Luis, with sombrero*

Residing on Freddy Fender lane, José Luis holds a token of Freddy's brotherly love (2009).

NOTE:
Decades later, two months before Freddy's passing in 2006, Freddy stopped by to see all of his relatives in the Rio Grande Valley, including his half-brother José Luis. But not before stopping at a little thrift store and buying a small model antique motorcycle for himself. Freddy never planned anything in his life; whatever arose happened spontaneously. So, when Freddy saw José Luis, he told him that he had never given him anything. José Luis responded that he never asked for anything, either. In his own way, Freddy expressed his love and good-byes to his brother by giving him a tiny motorcycle as a small token of his feelings. I reckon it was for all the unforgettable memories they once shared, growing up as blood brothers and bonding while riding alongside the Border Diablos.

Chapter XIV

Broken Promises

A Single Parent
"We were a team, a family!"

Evangelina Huerta (1973-74)
(Still photo/quote: Film documentary The Life Story of Freddy Fender "Comeback")

Evangelina
He made me a lot of promises he couldn't keep.
But I just kept on giving in to him.

Mother left Dad in the Rio Grande Valley and moved us to be near her sister Mary in Corpus Christi, Texas. Amá Máge had kept the secret that Mother was planning on leaving Father; she also knew Mother had a day job packing grapefruits at a placed called La Bodega in Harlingen. Mother had gathered just enough money from her job to move us into a one-bedroom house on Seventeenth Street. However, she had to leave Sonny behind with Amá Máge until she got on her own two feet.

She reasoned that Father had gone right back into full swing mode as a singer and a musician's lifestyle. He played wherever he could find work, but mostly at a place called the Squeeze Inn, which was in Brownsville near the Mexican border.

Consequently, Mother felt as though Father had broken too many promises to her; the spirit of the music just wouldn't leave my father alone. Once again, Father's late-night partying began, nonstop, and at full speed ahead.

This was the second time mother had pulled me out of school before the term was up. Later, Elvia told me that my second-grade schoolteacher, Mrs. Thomas, was saddened by the news that I was gone. I didn't even get to say good-bye to my friends and cousins in San Benito. I was so happy and content living there. Unfortunately, I did not get a chance to join the Girl Scouts, either.

Soon after our arrival in Corpus, Mother enrolled Danny and me at T.G. Allen Elementary School; I was in the second grade and Danny was in preschool. She applied for government assistance for about a year or so, and that helped us get free lunch at school as well. Mother did get her life together and enrolled in nursing school; she became a licensed vocational nurse (LVN). She worked very hard on the graveyard shift and went to school during the day.

She got hired at the state school taking care of handicapped children. She even took us there to meet some of the patients. She wanted to show us how fortunate we were, so that we would be grateful that we weren't in a wheelchair or had brain damage. She also began to take us, along with our cousin Ruben (Aunt Mary's son), downtown to Saint Peter's Cathedral every Sunday.

Aunt Mary Dies: Good *Santeria* (Magic)

Aunt Mary had a day job working as a bartender at a local billiard place; the owner's name was Delia. She was Mary's friend and would sometimes babysit us. People just adored and loved Mary; she was still very beautiful and liked music and dancing. She especially enjoyed helping others.

However, a few years back, Mary had been in a terrible accident while driving on the highway. She and her friends, who had been drinking, had a head-on collision. One of her passengers died, and one was left in critical condition.

Mary was among the dead. Yes, she died. She had an out-of-body experience during which she heard the doctors talking after fifteen minutes of attempting to revive her.

When she heard them say, "Let's just sew her back up," Mary kept telling the doctors, "No, I'm not dead, I'm up here!" Fortunately, Mary lived, and her near-death experience was recounted in the Corpus Christi *Caller-Times*. The accident left her with a permanent scar across her forehead and further medical complications. However, Mary would come to show us that she was a survivor!

Following that miraculous experience, she began to speak in parables from the Bible. She became a very special human being; she stopped drinking and became very spiritual.

While Mother worked, Aunt Mary took care of us at her house. One night, she told me to place red polish on the mole that I had on the tip of my nose! She said it would permanently remove it. My mole looked cute on me, but I didn't want it there anymore.

I believed her, and I did what she told me. I put a dab of red polish on my mole and then went to bed. The next morning, I ran to the mirror and checked to see if my mole disappeared. The mole was still staring back at me.

Aunt Mary was into *Santeria* (old fashioned Mexican healing) to help and pray for people. She didn't charge anyone for intervening for them, either. People around the neighborhood would ask her to come and clean their houses by praying to the Lord Jesus Christ and the saints.

Mother told me a story about how Mary and her boyfriend became *curanderos* (spiritual healers). One day, Father had a painful toothache and she took him to visit the couple to see if they could help him.

"No problem, I will make it go away!" Aunt Mary said. Then she slapped Dad so hard on his cheek and loudly said, *"Se va! Se va!"* ("It's gone! It's gone!"). He just looked at Mother with shock. Then Aunt Mary and her boyfriend started to take turns slapping him on both cheeks. Back and forth, they slapped him; Father was getting so upset that he wanted to punch her boyfriend. Aunt Mary believed you could avoid suffering by feeling pain elsewhere. After they attempted to heal Freddy, he really had to hurry to the clinic. Freddy was worse off after seeing Aunt Mary.

Sonny Boy: Football Jock

Mother wrote and sent some money to Amá Máge asking her to put Sonny on the bus to come join us in Corpus. Weeks had gone by, and there was no sign of Sonny Boy's return. As a matter of fact, our grandmother wanted to keep both Sonny and Danny (the boys) with her. Mother wasn't going to allow that to happen, so she borrowed a car and went to pick up Sonny herself.

In San Benito, Sonny attended the Jr. High School and began to play football. Had he stayed behind a while longer, he would have helped their team win the football championship against Harlingen. I have nothing against the city of Harlingen since we lived there on several occasions, but the two are considered rivals back home. San Benito against Harlingen is like the story told in the Bible of David and Goliath.

Sonny loved football. He was fast to react, tall, and a big muscular guy. Upon arriving in Corpus Christi, he enrolled at Wynn Seale Junior High School and joined their football team.

T. G. Allen Elementary School

T. G. Allen Elementary School had both a football and a basketball team. In the fourth grade, my PE Instructor, Ms. Perez, asked me to try out for cheerleader. After the tryouts, she just so happened to handpick my closest girlfriends, Susie Solis, Melody Cook, and Laura Rangel. We were the first cheerleaders ever to start at T.

G. Allen. Our school colors were Kelly green and white. At first, we had to make our own pom-poms out of crepe paper until the school bought us real pom-poms. Of course, Mother sewed my cheerleading outfit for me; I wore black-and-white cheerleading shoes. We were T. G. Allen's mighty W-I-L-D-C-A-T-S!

When T. G. Allen had talent shows, I was so ready to entertain our school and do what I knew best—coordinate, delegate, and dance! Then I picked my girlfriends Susie, Melody, and next-door neighbor Liza Torrez to accompany me. As for my act, it took me a split second to come up with a theme and song for our routine. I also drew up a sketch of how I wanted the outfits to look. Then I showed it to Mother, and she found a sewing pattern just like it. It was a black-and-white checkered knickerbockers outfit. And I wore my matching black-and-white cheerleading shoes for the show.

Of course, I picked a funkadelic tune to dance to titled "Jungle Boogie" by Kool & the Gang! It was my baby, so I came up with the dance routine, and I rolled with it. We had a blast dancing and showing off that day. However, a brother/sister set of twins dressed as Frankenstein and Igor, who danced to "Monster Mash," had a great skit, and they won first place. They deserved it, but so did we.

For a different talent show, our PE instructor had the cheerleaders perform a team dance onstage in the cafeteria with our pom-poms. We dance to the great rock tune "We're an American Band."

And the best part is that my girlfriends and I were selected to be cheerleaders until we graduated from the sixth grade.

Summertime: Sonny, Tammy, Danny, and Ruben

Danny and I, who grew very close while living in Corpus, began to hang out with our cousin Ruben. Cousin Ruben found a short collie dog and named it Birdie. The dog followed Ruben everywhere, especially when he walked across town to visit us during the summertime. Eventually, Birdie didn't want to leave our front porch and refused to go back with Ruben. Mother kept whisking the dog away with the broom; however, when she found out that Aunt Mary was bathing the dog with bleach to get rid of his fleas, she felt sorry for Birdie and allowed him to be part of our family.

Sonny was well on his way to becoming a man, and he needed his own bedroom to sleep in. We moved to a small three-bedroom house on Eighteenth Street. There, Danny and I slept on twin beds, and Mother had her own room.

When we wanted bread or pastries, Mother would take us to Butter Krust Bakery on Ayers Street to buy day-old bread. And just for the record, Mother and I still go by there today to buy sweets.

During the Christmas holidays, Mother would borrow a car and take us to garage sales where we'd find presents for one another. During one of those years, I bought Sonny Boy a pair of sunglasses filled with assorted colored lenses. I knew he would like them because it was the early 1970s, and in this era, aviator glasses meant total coolness.

For Christmas, Sonny gave me a nail kit because he always teased me about biting my nails. If Sonny ever gives you something, it is given to you with all his heart and is a tender moment for him; that's a quality I like about him.

I finally got to join the Girl Scouts, and Mother helped me sell enough Girl Scout cookies to win first prize, but only because she sold cookies to her friends at nursing school and at work. She was such a good mom.

For fun, I had this thing about licking the ice off the sides of the freezer and one day, I told Danny Boy to join me and enticed him by telling him how tasty the ice was. So, we both stuck our heads in the freezer to lick the ice, when all of a sudden, neither one of us could get our heads out! We began yelling because both our tongues were stuck, and blood was on the ice. We tugged at each other finally ripping our tongues out! Then we looked and saw that some of our skin tissue was left on the ice, ouch.

On Saturdays, Mother and Aunt Mary would get rid of us while they were at garage sales by dropping us off at the movie theatre on Ayers Boulevard. This is where I saw my favorite all-time movie—*Jesus of Nazareth*.

On Sundays, Ruben, Danny, and I would walk all the way to the HEB swimming pool off Ayers Street while Sonny would go to the pool with his football buddies. There, we would dive off a twelve-foot diving board, swim like fish all day long, and because we had no money, we went without eating all day. We loved swimming so much that our hair was always sun bleached. Afterward, dripping wet, with red eyes from the chlorine and famished, we walked about a mile back home, just in time for supper. I remember we couldn't even wait for Mother to finish cooking and we devoured a whole loaf of white Rainbow bread before she served supper.

In the evening hours on Sundays, Ruben, Danny, and I would be dropped off at Gulf Skating Rink, which was on South Padre Island Drive. Mother always saw to it that there was just enough money for us to go to the skating rink where we had the time of our lives! Life couldn't get any better.

Furthermore, Danny and I were very competitive, and on weekdays, T. G. Allen's school cafeteria is where we spent our time playing ping-pong and tetherball. Our good friends and neighbors Liza and Richard Torrez were great opponents on doubles in ping-pong. We had the best of times playing during the summer.

As for Sonny Boy, well, he enjoyed torturing me when he came home after football practice as he grabbed my face and smeared it under his funky, sweaty armpits! Gross! Then he would pull me to the ground, sit on top of me, squash me, and tickle me nonstop while trying to make me pee in my pants.

He is still the same rambunctious Sonny Boy today! He is also one scary dude when he tackles you; you will seriously think it is the last breath of your life when he grabs hold of you from behind, pulls you down to the ground, and you don't know what to expect next.

Single Parent: *We Were a Team, a family!*

To fill in the void left by Father's absence and the lack of live music at home, Mother found me a portable record player at a garage sale. This is when I became a real record collector. I started my first record collection, but with stolen records. We came to know a juvenile delinquent named Richard, who was very cute. He sometimes lived with us (uninvited) back on Seventeenth Street. He would ask me what records I wanted from Woolworth's store. When I rattled off almost every pop song I knew and sang on the radio, he told me to just write him a list. I did, unaware he was going to steal them, until the police kept coming by to look for him. (I'm sorry, Mr. Woolworth!)

However, the best part of living without Father was that we now had our own lives, our own achievements, and individual identities to pursue. To a certain degree, we became part of the norm. And without Father in the picture, we could stick to our activities and complete them. We didn't have to be moving back and forth; we could also build relationships year after year and let our teachers and friends get to actually know us.

I assume Sonny was okay; he was busy being a popular football jock and fighting off the girls at school. He had a magnetic personality; even the teachers doted on him, so he basically had a free pass at Wynn Seale Jr. High to do what he pleased.

As for me, I was a teacher's pet; I especially enjoyed being asked to lead the class in our native Texas school songs every day. I also loved coloring and I would win first place on every single art contest in class. Funny thing, my school essays always seemed to be on the topic of big stars from the 1970s. In addition, I became a pitcher on the girls' softball team. I also didn't talk to boys and I was a very good girl.

Most importantly, I was only too happy to take good care of my younger brother, Danny. I tried protecting my baby brother from harm—by preventing him from sniffing paint, which many boys liked doing in our neighborhood. I adored him. He was a good kid, friendly, and very humorous. I really loved my baby brother with his golden curly hair and light brown eyes.

Even though our mother was a single parent, we felt okay without Father. She had taught us to place other people's hardships before our own. She had courage and worked hard, and we were proud of her! Our mom had built a secure life for us; she made that happen.

For almost three years, life was great in Corpus Christi, and we were happy! Our little lives were productive, calm, and secure. We lived life with direction and stability. No storms, no bolts of lightning, no unpredictable weather were in the forecast or upon us.

Each of us had a promising future filled with dreams and high hopes ahead of us. We finally were going be like everyone else—normal.

For the first time, people knew us for *who* we really were! There was Mom, Sonny, Tammy, Danny, and our new dog named Birdie. *We had a life. We were a team, a family!*

Sonny, Tammy, and Danny (1973-74)

Sonny and Tammy
Tammy wearing her name printed on beads given to her by her "secret love."

~212~ Tammy Lorraine Huerta Fender

Chapter XV

The Squeeze Inn

"The Squeezer"
Boom, boom, boom, bang, bang, bang!
"If you didn't have one [weapon], they'd give you one, two, three, or four!"

"From My Eyes" by Freddy Fender
I played at a place called the Squeeze Inn. It was a rough place.
They could only get dumb musicians to play there because it was so dangerous.
They used to kill three to four people during the week just to warm up for the weekend!
If you wanted to see me [Freddy Fender] for the weekend,
the bouncers would have to check you for weapons.
If you didn't have one, they'd give you one or two or three or four!
(Professor Fred Hopkins. *Blue Suede News* #47. Summer, 1999.)

In the late 1950s, Luis Moreno Garcia, a.k.a. Squeezer, from Primera, Texas, was a piano player in a professional band called "Professor Hernandez." Mr. Hernandez was also a music teacher.

When Garcia was in high school, his football teammates had nicknamed him Squeezer because he would squeeze the heck out of the other teams (and girls).

Later when he opened a few nightclubs in the early 1970s, he named them the Squeeze Inn I, II, and III. From this point on, Garcia was addressed as *Squeezer*.

Back in the 1950s, Squeezer was playing a gig at the American Legion in San Benito when a gentleman (Freddy) came up to him and asked, "Sir, can I do a couple of numbers?"

"What is your name?" Squeezer asked.

"Baldemar Huerta, but now they call me The Bebop Kid."

Squeezer then asked him, "What do you want to sing?"

"Be-Bop-A-Lula" responded Freddy.

Since Freddy didn't have a guitar with him, Squeezer accompanied him by playing the piano.

"He did the tune, and everybody was applauding because he was a real entertainer! Then he went into another song. He did about three or four songs with us, and as young as he was, he was terrific," Squeezer recalled.

"We just couldn't believe how talented he was. He wasn't playing the guitar, he just sang a cappella."

He did such an awesome job that Squeezer asked him for his contact information because he might have some other jobs for him in the future.

A few weeks later, he saw The Bebop Kid singing at a club that catered to blacks in Harlingen, and made a mental note of his wide appeal and acceptance by all cultures.

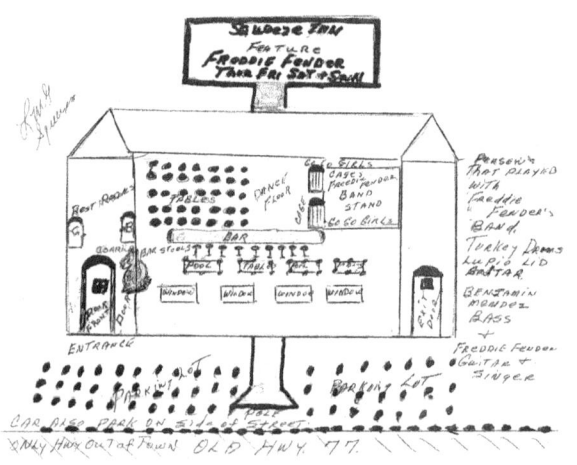

The Squeeze Inn nightclub "Feature Freddie Fender Thurs, Fri, Sat, Sun" (1960s-1970s)

The Marquee Read, "Freddy Fender Playing Tonight"

The first Squeeze Inn was at the site of the old Palmetto Inn off of Highway 77 and Military Highway in Brownsville. There was ample parking space on both sides of the street and since it was so large and paved entirely with gravel, the area grew to be known for its car races.

The main Squeeze inn was a brick building with six twelve-by-twelve windows. People would walk through the entrance, sit on the couch, and take pictures by a big statue of a gorilla. Inside, there were scantily clad go-go girls dancing inside cages.

The interior was a sight to behold because there were palm trees, a mirror between the band and five pool tables. The bar was smack dab in the middle and on the other side of the bar was the dance club; this is where Squeezer had his piano. "It was really a beautiful place," Squeezer recalled.

When Squeezer pondered over who would be the headline entertainer to hire for the grand opening, he immediately thought about Balde (Freddy). The Bebop Kid had been in the back of his mind all these years because he liked the way he sang, so Squeezer called him, and he accepted.

Freddy quickly rehearsed with his regular band members Lupe "Lupillo" Hernández, lead guitar; Benjamin "Benny" Méndez, bass; Robert "El Turkey" Sílva, drums, and his second drummer Armando Peña. When they had their routine down pat, Freddy told Squeezer, "We're ready."

The marquee read, "Freddy Fender Playing Tonight," and Freddy pulled in such large crowds that Squeezer hired them to play Thursday, Friday, Saturday, and Sunday from 9:00 p.m. to 12:00 midnight for $50 a night. However, Freddy would treat all his friends and run up a $100 beer tab. So, there were nights that Freddy wouldn't get paid.

With a repertoire such as "Majia De Amor" ("Magic of Love"), "Mean Woman," "The Wild Side of Life," "Jambalaya," "Sitting on the Dock of the Bay," "Crazy Baby," "Acapulco Rock," and, of course, "Wasted Days and Wasted Nights," Freddy would pack the Squeeze Inn beyond its designated capacity.

He also sang country and western tunes like "Together Again" and "Jealous Heart," Mexican songs like "Camisa Negra" ("Black Shirt") and "Hermosa Cariño" ("Beautiful Love"), plus some cha-cha-cha tunes.

For fun, when they performed "La Banda Está Borracha" ("The Band Is Drunk"), everybody played in the wrong key to purposely sound out of tune, and the crowd would start yelling, "Hey, get them off the stage, *corranlos* (run them off), boo, boo, boo, run them off."

It was something else to see them pretend to be drunken musicians. At the time, Freddy was only experiencing his art of music through what was truly transpiring in his life.

First Night First Killing: Freddy's Bass Player Becomes His Bodyguard

Fights often broke out around the stage, during which people would break chairs and tables and have their beer bottles thrown all over the place.

The first killing occurred as soon as Freddy opened up at the first Squeeze Inn. One of his friends was shot outside. His name was Guadalupe De León. They called him Big Guy, and he was from San Benito. It was said he had problems with somebody, and they shot him. It was probably one of his own friends that killed him.

"Oh my god, they shot Lupe, I don't think I'm going to play here anymore!" was Freddy's first reaction, but Benny was there to look out for him, and Freddy never did quit on anyone or himself.

Benny—who looked like a bouncer, was heavyset, and hardly smiled—became Freddy's bodyguard. He loved Freddy. In fact, when Benny once saw a guy bugging Freddy, he picked the guy up out of his chair, lifted him, and threw him across the club. He told him, "You leave him alone!" The guy had gotten jealous because his wife was making eyes at Freddy. But he was just playing his guitar, and that was Freddy's way. He would sing to the crowd; he didn't mean to flirt with anyone.

From the stage, Benny could see if any trouble was brewing on the dance floor. He would get down and tell the troublemakers, "That's enough of that, cut it out, or you're going to have problems with us!"

Squeezer would always tell his customers that if they were going to have a fight, they had better take it outside and not fight inside the club.

One-time Freddy actually had to use his fists when a Border Patrol agent put some quarters in the jukebox while Freddy was singing. He did Freddy dirty. The jukebox music overpowered Freddy's singing, and a big fight started right there and then. Benny jumped off the stage, ran, and grabbed one of them. Freddy was pissed, and from the bandstand, he swung his guitar! Then he and Turkey got down too and joined the fight. Everybody was going at it. They were swinging chairs, bottles were flying across the room, and bodies were thrown left and right.

Uncle Manuel "Béke" Salazar

I just got out of Vietnam, and this narc got his gun out and said he was going to kill my brother.
I started jumping from one table to another and started going after him.
But Freddy had his bass player Benny Méndez
get between them and hit the narc in the face with his bass.
Then Squeezer took out his gun and said, "Let's have a showdown right here!"
Thirty minutes later, we started playing and dancing again.
The guy was shooting at the bar as he drove off.
We would drive over the border after hours until five in the morning and that was part of life.
That was between 1969 and 1973.
There were Popeye's Club, Foxy's, and other honky-tonks across the border.

Squeezer's Drill: Alternating Freddy, one Squeeze Inn to the Next

Freddy was bringing in the crowds! After the gigs, Freddy and Squeezer would go across the border to Matamoros and entertain more people, but without charging the club owners a cent.

"That's what he was, a showman. He would accompany himself with a guitar, and that was it," said Squeezer.

"In the early 1970s, when Freddy had problems with his family, he would tell us, Well, I'm going to stay here tonight at the club." However, Benny, who looked after Freddy a lot, offered him a place to stay in Brownsville.

Because of the rowdy crowds and the excitement that Freddy brought into Squeezer's place, he would have to shift Freddy around from Port Isabel, on Garcia Street, to another Squeeze Inn on Cameron Park.

Freddy alternated playing at the three Squeeze Inns for several years. So, the drill was that he would perform for about an hour, then rush to entertain at one of the other inns.

In Port Isabel, Freddy performed with two talented black girls, BB, who played piano and Alice, who played saxophone. Squeezer would tell the crowd they had three black singers; Freddy was the third one since he sounded like a soul man.

Un Poco de Marijuana (A Little Marijuana): "Squeeze Out" Nightclubs!

Squeezer had many clubs because they were always closing him down for one reason or another. So, if one closed, he'd open up another to keep the customers happy. Then, when he started having trouble with the law, he quickly opened the "Squeeze Out" nightclubs!

No kidding! He was a "Squeezer" all right, and he booked the best bands in the Lower Rio Grande Valley.

There were times when Freddy would play at South Padre Island Beach and Anglo girls would get up on the stage and start hugging and kissing him, but he kept right on singing. Of course, their boyfriends would get jealous and try to pull Freddy offstage. But before that could happen, somebody in the audience always jumped up and pulled the troublemakers off Freddy so he wouldn't get hit. Freddy never got a chance to swing because there was somebody there to help him out. All because his audience just loved him, and they didn't want Freddy getting hurt.

Squeezer would also warn Freddy by saying, "Don't ever use your fists because your fists are for your guitar, and we don't want you to break a finger."

It was also no secret that Freddy enjoyed smoking a little pot and to play it safe, when he was performing, he would jokingly ask, "Are there any *narcos* (narcs) in the house?"

And everyone would yell out, "No!"

Then he would say, *"Bueno, entonces ahorita vengo, voy a fumar un poco de marijuana"* ("Good, then I'm going to take a little break and go outside to smoke a little pot").

"I thought he was joking," Squeezer said. "Then he would walk back in *risa y risa* (laughing and laughing)."

Invite the Border Diablos!

On special holidays, Freddy would ask Squeezer if he could invite the Border Diablos and allow them to gun their bikes inside the club while he sang for the partygoers. Squeezer would respond, "Do what you want to, Freddy!"

So, they moved tables around, and the Border Diablos would ride their motorcycles into the Squeeze Inn and let it roar as Freddy cranked out some rhythm and blues!

Everybody in the place became even wilder! Then, Squeezer would ask Freddy, "Do you have the guitar to hit somebody?"

Freddy answered, "No, I have my guitar here to protect myself with it if they jump on me!" [Laughing]

As for the shootings in the club, the shooting was normally among the customers that were drinking together. Sometimes they were guys making a drug deal at Squeezer's place; when a deal went sour, they had to do something about it, and they usually took someone out from their own group. Thus, Squeezer's place was a major hangout for many drug dealers from the Rio Grande Valley and Mexico.

A big plus for these events was that Freddy Fender was in the house; attendance would soar. And the people from the Rio Grande Valley, even the gringos, knew him intimately and viewed Freddy as their own Frank Sinatra.

New Year's Eve:

Boom, Boom, Boom, Bang, Bang, Bang!
Ajúa! Ajúa!

One New Year's Eve, Squeezer told Freddy to tell the people to get their *cuetes* (fireworks) out. Squeezer was at the bar stacking up drinks when Freddy was about to start the countdown. Over the microphone he told everybody, "If you don't have a *cuete*, Squeezer will get you one."

As the clock was about to hit twelve, Freddy shouts, *"Ahora si, ya va ser las doce de la noche, ya va ser el Año Nuevo"* y sacen sus cuetes. Y si no, Squeezer *no los va dejar volver."* ("It is almost midnight and almost the New Year! Take out your guns! If you don't get your guns out, then Squeezer is not going to allow you back in the club!")

What Freddy did not realize is that Squeezer was referring to firecrackers, but since the same word, *cuete*s is a slang word for guns —the crowd understood "guns." So, they pulled out their pistols instead.

When Squeezer saw the guns being pulled out, he shouted, "No! No! No!" over the PA system, but all he heard was *boom, boom, boom, bang, bang, bang*!

So exactly at midnight, everybody pulled out their guns and shot the hell out of the ceiling. "Ajúa"! "Ajúa"! ("Yahoo!") they shouted. They whooped it up, and the *bang, bang, bang* continued as dust and debris came down from everywhere.

When he saw the damage done to the ceiling, all he could utter was, "God Almighty, who is going to patch up all the holes?

"I mean, everybody was shooting holes inside because everybody had guns in there! It was just like the old Wild West. We were so happy-go-lucky," Squeezer recollected.

After that night, whenever Squeezer would see somebody with his, or her gun, inside his bar, he would say, "Please give me your gun." Eventually, he had to tell his customers to leave their guns in their car. If they did have a weapon in their possession, he'd take it and put it underneath the bar.

Then, at the end of the night, he would give them back their gun. Squeezer also got to know whose gun was whose. Thereafter, the customers got into the habit of checking in their gun at the door. However, he wasn't too sure about them sneaking and tucking their knives away.

Nonetheless, it wasn't always fistfights and shootings, he claimed. Like the night a lady caught Freddy's eye and he went up to Squeezer and said, "That woman is real nice. She's pretty, and I'd like to date her."

Squeezer said, "Yes, she's a very pretty woman."

"What's her name?" Freddy asked.

"Mary Kingsbury," Squeezer answered.

"Oh, she's beautiful," Freddy, continued. (Father was always attracted to soft-spoken, light-skinned women.) "Can you introduce me to her?" Freddy asked Squeezer.

"Sure, hey, Mary, can you come over here? Freddy Fender would like to meet you."

After she walked over to where Freddy and Squeezer were, Freddy said, "You're a very beautiful lady."

"Yeah, and I'm also Squeezer's wife," she answered.

Freddy became flustered and tongue tied as he tried to save face, "Oh no, hey, why didn't you tell me?"

"Well, Freddy, that just goes to show you, and because I wanted her to tell you," Squeezer told him.

That's the way it was. Other than that, Squeezer said he never saw him making *movidas* (the moves) on anybody else. He was just an ordinary guy, but an extraordinary entertainer.

Political Campaign at the Squeezer's: Again, Let's Invite the Border Diablos

The Squeeze Inn, on Cameron Park, was where Rey Ramon, who was running for county judge, would do his mixing and politicking. They made T-shirts and sold them from behind the bar. And Freddy, who would entertain for him, even wrote him a song, "Rey Ramon de Corazón."

One night, someone came in to steal the T-shirts and there was a big fight during which everyone was throwing chairs. In fact, Squeezer suffered a broken collarbone because he was determined that nobody was going to steal the T-shirts.

When Ramon won the election, he threw a big party for all his campaign workers and supporters to the club. That night Squeezer let the Border Diablos inside, and it was awesome. A big, tall guy nicknamed Tiny and Lalo Soto, president of the

Border Diablos, walked in wearing their bandanas and the whole scene appeared to be like something out of the movies!

"Now it all seems like a dream because things were so different then," Squeezer reminisced. "I remember loaning my guitar and amplifier to Freddy one night to go into Matamoros, only this time he came back with no guitar and no amplifier. When I asked him about it, Freddy matter-of-factly said, 'Oh, I hocked it because I needed some money.'

"I was mad, but I just had to laugh it off and said to him, 'Don't worry about it. You've already made enough money for me. But I'm not going to buy you any more guitars.'" Freddy was always losing his guitars.

"Oh, come on, I'm Daddy Blues," Freddy cooed.

"Yeah, I know the blues," said Squeezer.

"The way he would talk to me, I couldn't stay angry at him because he was real. After he talked to you two or three minutes, you would put your guard down because that's the way Freddy was. Freddy could charm you, and you'd believe him because he spoke with the truth and there was no bullshit with him!

"That's the way it always was with him—Freddy was brutally honest."

Squeezer! "They Robbed Your Crapper!"

One evening, as Squeezer was about to close up for the night, Freddy tells Squeezer he has to use the men's bathroom. "Okay," Squeezer acknowledged as he continued to lock up the club.

Then all of a sudden, he hears Freddy shouting, "Squeezer, Squeezer, *te robaron la crepa*" ("They robbed your crapper")!

"*¿Qué?*" ("What"?) Squeezer reacted as though Freddy was joking. "*¿Estas loco* ("are you crazy") Freddy?"

Freddy repeated, "*No, te robaron la crepa!*" ("No, they robbed your crapper!")

"Let me go look and check it out." When Squeezer saw the empty hole, he said, "*Ay Chihuahua*, son of a bitch, we've got a bunch of animals around here." He put an Out-of-order sign up and told all the men that if they needed to go, to go piss outside.

"*Sólo por cabrones* ("only for being sons of bitches") someone had pulled the commode and taken it outside," Squeezer complained.

On another momentous evening at the Squeeze Inn, Freddy was about to take a break and as usual asked, "*¿No hay narcos en el lugar?*" ("Are there any narcs here?") "*Bueno, entonces yo voy afuera para darme un tocazo*" ("Good, then I am going outside to take a little toke"). When he came back inside, Freddy went up to Squeezer and said, "You know that big statue you have out front?"

"Yes," Squeezer answered.

"Well, someone took it!" Freddy told him.

"You're crazy. It's too large and too heavy, Freddy!"

"Yeah, well, they just took your gorilla statue." And sure enough, it was gone!

Two weeks later, Freddy came in and said, "I know where your statue is at. It's at a club in Harlingen."

"No way, man, let's go check it out," Squeezer said.

They all got into his truck, went to the club, loaded the statue, and brought it back to the Squeeze Inn. From then on, it turned out to be an ongoing joke. Other club owners were taking it, and they would go and get it back; it went on and on like a joke. When they confronted the guy that was responsible for the joke, he said that they just wanted to borrow it for a few nights.

However, when things got too rowdy, and they had to quickly get out of the area for fear of the police, they would just go to one of the other Squeeze Inns or Squeeze Outs. Squeezer had a system and he took care of them all. Remember, all this happened over a period of five years. But everybody there had fun or was shot on the spot!

Hit Man Hired to Kill the "Squeezer"

At one point, someone had put a hit on Squeezer because he was involved in helping the unions out with a sensitive issue in Brownsville. So, the union flew him down to Mexico City for a couple of weeks until everything cooled down.

One late afternoon, a stout young man came into the Squeeze Inn wearing dark glasses. He was dancing with a young girl. The girl's cousin, a trucker, saw that the young man was dancing too close with his cousin, and he didn't like it. So, the truck driver told the young man to take his glasses off. But the guy told him he was wearing them because he was cross-eyed.

The trucker however thought the kid had talked back to him and slapped the young kid a few times. The kid was on the ground for a while and eventually got himself up and left.

Then the trucker went up to the bar and asked for another beer at which time Squeezer told him, "You already caused enough problems, go home." Squeezer then added that he had called the cops.

However, the guy refused to leave and insistently said, "No, just one more beer."

"Go home before that cross-eyed guy comes back," Squeezer said.

"Oh, that guy is just a little wimp, he won't come back," the trucker replied.

Twenty minutes later, he took another sip of his beer, and sure enough, the cross-eyed guy walked in and shot him in the back with a .351 Magnum.

The bullets had shattered the mirror behind him on the bar. Squeezer had blood all over him and local political friends of Freddy and Squeezer, like Eddie Lucio Jr., and all the other Lucios thought the Squeezer had gotten shot!

"They finally got Squeezer! They got you! They got you!" a customer yelled out.

Freddy who was hard of hearing, stopped singing and the music stopped. He turned to look at Squeezer and said, *"Oyé, ya te chingaron cuñado?"* ("Hey, they finally got rid of your ass, bro?")

"No, not me!" Squeezer said as he pointed to the trucker lying on the floor. "They got him!"

Squeezer had blood splattered all over his front chest from the guy who was on the ground.

Next, the trucker got himself up, looked at Squeezer and everyone else, and said, *"Voy a chingarle la Madre al vato*" ("I am going to beat the shit out of that guy") because he shot me." Apparently, he was still alive! Then he walked out the front door and dropped dead.

Freddy witnessed the first killing at the club—and the last murder.

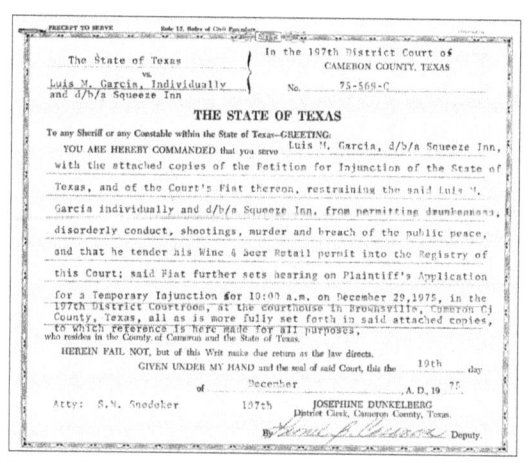

In December of 1975, the Squeeze Inn was commanded to close down immediately by the district court of Cameron County, Texas. The Squeeze Inn's had also lost its liquor license due to "drunkenness, disorderly conduct, shootings, murder and breach of the public peace" (1975).

Freddy Goes Home to His Family: Freddy's Luck is About to Change

In 1974, Freddy told Squeezer, "I'm going to be leaving and moving to Corpus soon."

Lupillo also confirmed to Squeezer how Freddy felt, "He must have gone back to his wife, Eva, and three kids because that's where Freddy said he belonged."

During those five years that Freddy played for him, Squeezer claims he never saw Freddy womanizing and only knew him to be a good person.

After their last performance, Freddy looked at Benny and said, "Just wait until I become famous, then Eva will come crawling back to me. Then I will stop, look at her, and say, 'Do I know you?'"

Squeezer added, "That was Freddy just talking and acting big with the guys, but you know what, the next day he was on his way to Corpus Christi to ask for forgiveness, once again, and on his knees."

Squeezer added, Benny just laughed because he knew how Freddy felt about Eva all those years. Freddy was easy to read because he was so vulnerable and honest with his feelings. He was never angry, just hurt and very sensitive. He just talked tough. He was mostly always silly and having fun with life and people. There was nothing serious about him. There was no doubt he loved and missed his wife, Eva."

Looking back, Squeezer recounts how he never saw a man like Freddy that could perform so well and was always on time. Freddy did a wonderful job singing, and he was just awesome! The man was a hardworking man! Whatever he did after that, that was his business, but he never missed a gig, Squeezer commented, never!

"That's all I can say about him, though sometimes Freddy would say he had another gig elsewhere, playing with black musicians in Harlingen. They liked him because he sung like a soul man."

Farewell, Squeeze Inn

A year later, in December, Squeezer and all his bartenders, go-go girls, waitresses, and band members gathered one last time for Christmas Eve party and exchanged presents. Even Freddy, who, in less than one year, had had his first two records hit the *Billboard* charts, took time off his busy schedule to be there for Squeezer and his RGV friends. They knew things were coming to an end and they would all have to move on.

Squeezer told Freddy, "You know, you played a lot of music for me. Thank you and Sonny Boy (drummer) for coming to play and to be with us. Have a Merry Christmas with your family."

They all shook hands on that night, knowing the club would be closing down. Freddy would no longer be playing rhythm and blues on New Year's Eve for the Squeezer. And never again would they blow the roof with real bullets or hang with the Border Diablos.

Squeezer is a man who is tough and rugged, just like Dad, yet sweet and cuddly like a teddy bear. They just act tough. But make no mistake; Squeezer will always be a legendary nightclub owner and band promoter of the ever so infamous "Squeeze Inn" and "Squeeze Out" nightclubs—north of the Mexican border.

Everything you can imagine that could happen in the South Rio Grande Valley happened right there! This was no Wild, Wild West movie rehearsal. No, they had to shut the Squeezer down—and for good reasons.

On a sad note, Benny Méndez drank a little too much, and on his way home from the Squeeze Inn, he crashed into a mailbox, which flew in through the windshield. He died instantly. Needless to say, Freddy and the rest of the band served as pallbearers at his funeral. His daughter Mary and I had been playmates in New Orleans; she was my only friend. We connected as children of music families.

Thereafter, Lupillo moved on. Mando continued to play drums for other great artists. And Turkey, the badass dude who was always loyal to Freddy, later became a minister and opened up a church in the building that once housed the Squeeze Inn.

As I sat at his home by the same pool table used at the main Squeeze Inn, Luis Moreno Garcia, a.k.a. Squeezer, wearing his standard black cowboy hat and boots, looked at me straight in the eyes as he articulated, "Isn't that something?" He sighed. "The Squeeze Inn turned into a good place after all!"

At the end of the interview, Squeezer asked me to sit next to him on the stool by his piano as he sang and played a few bars for me, knowing that the same piano and pool table in his den were used at the Squeeze Inn before Father became famous. At the time, I was still grieving heavily for Father while trying to keep my composure.

This was pretty much the end of an era for Freddy Fender's original group *Los Comancheros*. They were Freddy's original funk, rhythm, and blues band. Astonishingly, I could not locate any photo of Freddy taken at the Squeeze Inn. (A photograph of Squeezer and me can be viewed in back of the book under "Interviewees.")

Benjamin "Benny" Méndez with Turkey on drums.

"From My Eyes" by Freddy Fender
"The other side of my music [of country] has always been blues—rhythm and blues and shuffle.
I thoroughly love playing rhythm and lead guitar.
I played in the honky-tonks from the Squeeze Inn in Brownsville, Texas,
to Papa Joe's on Bourbon Street in New Orleans. Hey, "Get Down, Brother"!

Chapter XVI

"Before the Next Teardrop Falls"

"Wasted Days and Wasted Nights"
Huey P. Meaux, The Crazy Cajun
"He was a star, before he was a star!"

"From My Eyes" by Freddy Fender
I used to think I was the one making all of the sacrifices because I married her twice. But then I realized she married me twice, too. She made all the same sacrifices.

In 1974, Sonny was still a hotshot football player and fighting off the girls at Wynn Seale Junior High. And I was doing my girly things, being happy, while Mother was continuing her education to become a registered nurse (RN). Everything seemed to be going great for us without Father around.

That is, until the day when Danny was at the beach; he was on a field trip during which they were going to sculpt sand castles. Then out of nowhere, Danny heard a long roar coming from afar. As he looked up from the beach, he was blinded by the rays of sunlight glaring off the chrome. It was coming from hundreds of motorcycles off the expressway. They riders were coming across the Harbor Bridge over the Corpus Christi Port. As the noise kept getting louder, Danny noticed *montones* (many) of long choppers and hangers headed his way. He saw that some of the bikers were wearing mirrored aviator sunglasses with mustaches and long goatees.

"It was the Border Diablos!" Danny recalled. There were also several other biker clubs wearing their jackets.

As they arrived, the bikers parked on Shoreline Boulevard. Then quickly, the teachers began to round up the students, while the city police gathered around the bikers as well.

Then one of the bikers said aloud, "Come here, *mijito* (son)!" But the teacher quickly hung on to Danny.

"That's my son!" Freddy yelled out over the noise of the motorcycle engines.

That's when the rest of the Border Diablos got off their bikes.

The teacher answered, "Okay, he can go."

The chief of police just looked at Freddy and gave him a nod to proceed. Then the bikers placed Danny on Dad's motorcycle, revved up their bikes, and rode off.

Danny showed Dad where we lived and with that, he brought our long-lost Dad back home.

As of today, Danny doesn't know how Dad found him at the beach—perhaps it was fate.

Freddy Fender at home on Eighteenth Street, Corpus Christi, Texas. (1974)

"From My Eyes" by Freddy Fender
I picked cabbage as a migrant worker, I learned to mess with motors, and I went to Del Mar College in Corpus Christi. I was majoring in sociology, and my idea was that I would be able to help ex-cons when I got a degree.
But I always went back to my music!

"Dad's Back!"

We asked no questions, nor did Mother even ask us kids if we even wanted Dad back. Father must have saved up a little money because he bought Mother a new stove and furniture that we needed. He had also recorded two singles for Falcón, a single for ARV International, and a single for the Crazy Cajun label. This accounted for $1,000, half of which he gave to Mother. She used it to make a first down payment on a brand-new house located at 1530 Barcelona Street. Once again, Mother was swept off her feet, got weak, and allowed Father back into our lives.

I remember my dad lying in bed with his head against the headboard, thinking while smoking a cigarette. He seemed to be preoccupied, as if he were contemplating his next move.

Father and I played quietly like father and daughter, bonding together. I would place my ear on his chest to hear his heartbeat, and then he would listen to mine. We took turns as we softly spoke to one another with a smile.

However, the reason I really wanted to hear Father's heartbeat was that his chest was making a loud wheezing sound. He must have smoked many cigarettes, of all kinds, back then.

The Rogues Club: The Phantom

Father was searching for both day and nighttime employment in Corpus Christi. A nightclub owner of the Rogues Club, Sam Herro, let Freddy audition one night. He was a scary looking, big, tall, intimidating, Mafioso-type looking character also known as the Phantom. His club, as with most venues near Padre Island beach, was primarily geared toward hardcore rockers, beachcomber jammers, and local surfers. The nightclub featured heavy jitterbug and two-step dancing to rock 'n' country music.

When Father met the Phantom, he told him that he was Freddy Fender! But Herro didn't quite believe him. He did not know that Freddy Fender was a Chicano! Herro had related the song "Wasted Days and Wasted Nights" with an Anglo voice (Film Documentary "Comeback." Producer/Director Boon Collins. 1979).

Chicano or not, Freddy sang for him, and he got the gig. Thus, the Phantom became Freddy's new manager.

"From My Eyes" by Freddy Fender
I played at a place called the Rogues Club. The gentleman who owned it liked my voice and gave me a break. He forced the rock 'n' rollers there to back me up. So, I sang the song "Tutti Frutti," and the band just laughed at me! They started to play off-key. Well, the owner told them, "If you don't back Freddy the right way, I'm going to fire your asses!"

Freddy, Sam, and Huey go to Las Vegas!
The original Chicano, Freddy, with his road Manager, Sam "The Phantom" Herro

Interviewee:
Huey Purvis Meaux
(March 10, 1929–April 23, 2011)
Freddy Fender's Record Producer/Manager
Sugar Hill Record Studio, Crazy Cajun label of Music Enterprises

I'd heard of Freddy Fender all of my life and loved his voice! I had always wanted to produce Freddy. In 1962, Gene Marcantel, a guard who ran the kitchen at DeQuincy prison, came to me saying he knew Freddy. He knew I had to be big on record producing, so Marcantel brought me some of Freddy's material on tape. I heard it. "Yep, that's him all right!"

Marcantel responded, "He is good, Huey, and I can fix it up!"

However, I didn't want to be tied up with the prison system. I wanted Freddy to be clean when he got out. Wayne Duncan and I knew that Freddy was good, but Duncan had no real connections.

Duncan had taken Freddy to Imperial Records, but you have to be able to follow an act, and Duncan just couldn't do that with Freddy at that time.

The first time I ever really spoke or met with Freddy one-on-one was in Harlingen. It was 1963, right after Freddy got out of prison. I was a well-known freelancer in the record business. I had Sunny and the Sunliners and other local rising stars performing at the San Antonio Municipal Auditorium.

I had a couple of shows that night, and they were sold out. Back then, we used suitcases to pack up the money. I saw the club owners counting the money, and they were all $1 bills. Well, everybody down there [in Harlingen] was just so damn poor. I will never forget it.

Someone came up to me and said, "Mr. Meaux, Freddy Fender would like to meet you."

I said, "Oh, I'd love to meet him." Freddy was waiting for me, smoking a cigarette at the back door.

Freddy knew those guys in the valley area couldn't do any more for him, and he had gone as far as he could go. They just couldn't take him any further.

Then Freddy asked me, "Hey, man, so you are the great producer?"

"Well, I don't know about that, but I can make some hit records. Freddy, I always loved your voice. All you need is a good producer and the right song."

This was many years before I could ever have a chance to produce him. Freddy was real uptight about his parole, so we couldn't get together. But Freddy, he was just always on my mind. I saw him again in New Orleans when he was playing with Joe Barry on Bourbon Street.

Huey: You know why your father went to prison?

Tammy: Yes, for marijuana!

Huey: NO! Freddy went to prison because he had been set up, as explained to me by Edwin Washington Edwards, who served as governor of Louisiana. The governor is a good friend of mine. Freddy was set up from what other friends have also told me up in Louisiana. A political candidate for lieutenant governor back then was dating a blonde girl that Freddy started seeing. (At last minute, Miss Baton Rouge requested her name be left anynomous). They were very prejudiced in Louisiana, and they didn't want Mexicans anywhere around Louisiana.

They told him to get the f—k out!

"The Crazy Cajun" also becomes Freddy's personal hairstylist.

Wasted Days and Wasted Nights

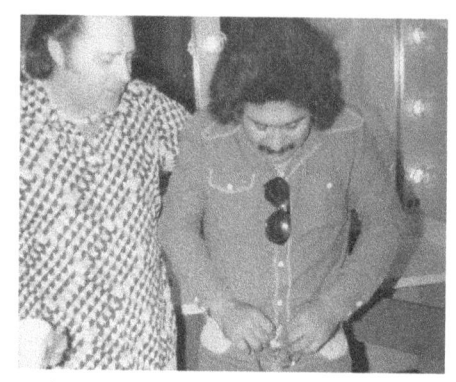

Record Producer and Manager, Huey "The Crazy Cajun" Meaux, trying to squeeze Freddy into a country and Western shirt attire before going onstage at a local gig.

"From My Eyes" by Freddy Fender

Huey once asked me, "Why do you want to record with me?"
I told him, "Because you and I are the same."
I knew he had served time in the joint, just like me. I said to him,
"I know what you went through." That's why we're alike.
(Professor Fred Hopkins. *Blue Suede News* #47. Summer, 1999.)

Interviewee:
Huey P. Meaux
Record Producer/Manager

When I saw Freddy again, it was in the fall of 1974 in Corpus Christi. I was there to see an attorney. The lawyer told me that Freddy was working around town somewhere. I told him, "I'd sure like to meet him."

I left and went to get my car washed. Then I heard someone singing, and I knew it was Freddy because nobody sung like Freddy—nobody! Freddy is one of a kind!

So, I followed the voice all the way to the front office. I could hear him singing back there. I thought to myself, *that is Freddy Fender, man!*

I asked him, "Are you Freddy Fender?"

He said, "Yeah!"

Then I said, "What are you doing here working at a car wash?"

Freddy answered, "Well, I am just getting a little paunchy."

I said, "Here is my card, call my secretary, Beth, and we'll get a contract together."

At this point of the interview, Huey paused, looked up in mid-air, grinned, and said, ***"He was a star before he was a star!"***

[At the time, I didn't quite understand what Huey's comment meant or implied until I dug deep into his past and swam deeper into my father's head. Now, Father was a star of astronomic proportions. So yes, I now understand precisely why "he was a star before he was a star."]

"I remember taking Freddy to New York to find some new material for him," Huey continued. I got some music from Tito Puente and tried Freddy on some salsa music, which didn't work out or even sound right. I then picked up a Jamaican track called "Out of Reach," and that record made Freddy no. 1 in New York.

Then we both returned to New York to visit my lawyers. And that's when I met a beautiful Jamaican girl who I met at the office through working with *Rolling Stone* magazine. Her name was Cheryl Brandt [and she later became a talent coordinator for Freddy's new album *Before the Next Teardrop Falls*].

I asked her to meet us on our next trip to New York, and that we would all fly to Jamaica. I fell in love with her. But then she later left me for another dude!

I knew Freddy had the right voice already, but he needed the right song just for him. I tried everything! That's when I got the song "Before the Next Teardrop Falls" (composed by Vivian Keith and Ben Peters).

Sonny was backing his father, Freddy, on drums [at Sugar Hill Studios]. Freddy was recording his own music, which he thought was cool for him. He just didn't want to record what I wanted!

The music Freddy chose for himself were songs that every Mexican had already recorded so many times before. And I knew they weren't going to hit!

I said, "Freddy, come do this for me? I am hurting right now, and my girlfriend done left me. Just do this for me?"

Freddy said, "Well, I can't sing that gringo shit, Huey!"

I was feeling it with this chick, you know! So, he sang it for me.

Freddy sang it just "once" and *bam!* He hit it!

We heard the playback, and Freddy said, "Man, that is the best record I ever made!" And it was.

Freddy Fender, smoking a Kool brand cigarette, Huey Meaux and Huey's Jamaican heartbreaker Cheryl Brandt (1974)

"From My Eyes" by Freddy Fender

I think it ["Teardrops"], had been recorded by Charley Pride. It was country whereas I was hip.

* * *

I knew Huey Meaux was my only real connection back to the recording business. Huey wasn't afraid to mix English/Spanish lyrics, so we did it ["Teardrops"] on one take!

ABC-Dot Records Reproduces and Distributes Final Cut: "Wasted Days and Wasted Nights"

Moving place to place, we continued on to a new address at 1530 Barcelona Street. It was a newly built two-bedroom house across town in both a Mexican and African American neighborhood. Most important, it would be a little closer to the airport because Huey Meaux, who lived in Houston, needed Freddy to keep up with their fast-paced and exciting new schedule.

Happily, our extended family was back together again, with Amá Máge and the girls. But our life was about to take a new twist. It would be the ride of our lives, one taken abruptly, courtesy of Huey P. Meaux, also known as The Crazy Cajun.

First photo op with the Huerta family at 1530 Barcelona Street, Corpus Christi, Texas.

Freddy, Eva, Sonny, Danny, and Margarita Huerta
(Photo by Jesus Garza. Permission to Reprint by *La Opinion, LA.* 1975)

"Wasted Days and Wasted Nights"
(ABC-Dot Records © *Universal Music Enterprises of UMG Recordings, Inc., 1975)*

Freddy listens closely to his reproduced record of "Wasted Days and Wasted Nights." The flip side was "I Love My Rancho Grande." (ABC-Dot labels, 1975)

I vividly remember Father in my bedroom staring at a 45-rpm single playing on my turntable, attentively listening to "Wasted Days and Wasted Nights" over and over. And I wondered to myself, what was the big deal about listening to himself sing on an old recording anyway?

Little did I know the original version of "Wasted Days," the one that should have given him national exposure and success at twenty-two years old (before imprisonment and before my birth), was about to be released all over again but on one of the biggest record labels in the world—ABC-Dot Records.

"Wasted Days and Wasted Nights" had been reissued several times already. However, this time, Freddy could hear that his raw and simple composition had been updated to marketing standards thanks to ABC-Dot. The gigantic mainstream label had engineered the final cut of "Wasted Days." This credit for this lies with his producer/manager Huey Meaux, who took Freddy to the next level. And, may I add, for a hell of a paycheck, too. Although Freddy was a purist about having everything kept in its original form, I think he really liked this newer, enhanced version of it just as well, if not better.

I can only imagine what he was really thinking about it all! Freddy's dream of becoming an established nationwide artist had become a reality. That must have been the look I kept seeing on his face (the sweet success around the corner) at home on Eighteenth Street, but I couldn't put my finger on it. For as long as I can remember, Father was always, always on the move!

Freddy hadn't given up! Here we were, unaware of his determination to fulfill his true passion and calling. We had been blind to the true nature of his being and identity, about who our father really was this whole time—a genuine music artist, who was about to open doors for other artists, and become a worldwide icon.

What was even more fascinating, Freddy wasn't even aware of how big "Teardrops" was hitting in the United States. To be honest, Father didn't really care as much because he was more attuned to his own composition of "Wasted Days."

Astonishingly, both "Teardrops" and "Wasted Days" simultaneously landed at the top of the charts on *Billboard*.

Finally, after twenty years of hustle, miss-and-hits, Freddy was literally being swept up into the stratosphere.

Scoreboard lights up; Freddy Fender's current single "Wasted Days and Wasted Nights" at Arlington Stadium baseball field in Texas.

Wasted Days and Wasted Nights

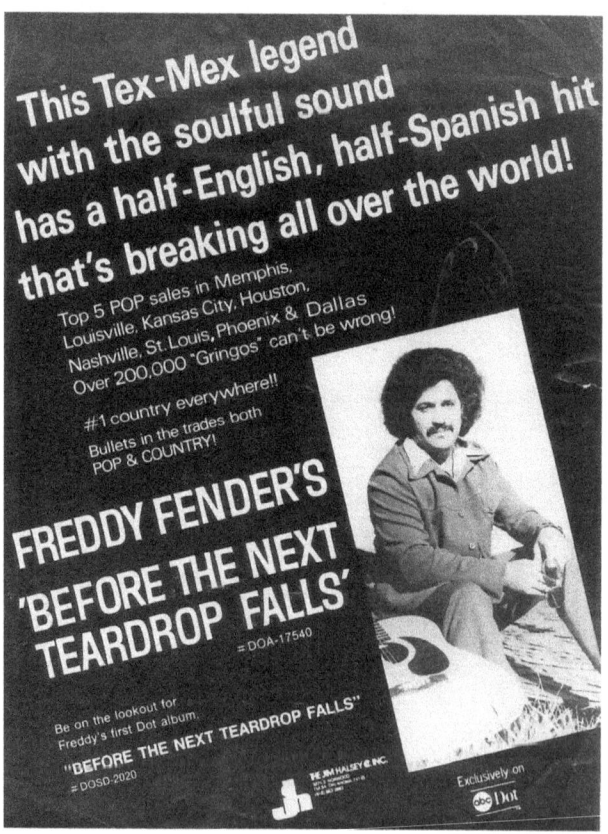

Over 200,000 "Gringos" Can't be Wrong!
(Permission to Reprint by Jim Halsey Agency, March 1, 1975)

Tammy Lorraine Huerta Fender

"From My Eyes" by Freddy Fender
Oh Lord, not again!

Still in the same suit "Fender Goes to Jail, But Just for a Visit"
(*Photo by Paul Blankenmeister. Permission to Reprint by Daily Texan and Texas Student Media. Austin, Texas. 1975)*

The day after arriving from Dallas, as a joke, two female sheriffs met Freddy at Robert Mueller Municipal Airport and handcuffed him. Freddy was given a summons to appear at the Travis County Jail in Austin, so he could sing for hundreds of jailbirds. (Writer Glenn Karish, photo by Paul Blankenmeister, *newspaper Daily Texan and Texas Student Media*. Austin, Texas, 1975.)

Freddy sings to comfort detainees at Travis County Jail in Austin, Texas. (Photo by Paul Blankenmeister. Permission to Reprint by Daily Texas and Texas Student Media. Austin, Texas. 1975)

Sonny Boy at Ray High School
On with Our Lives at School

Meanwhile, Sonny Boy was enjoying being a football star at W. B. Ray High School, while I was at Cunningham Junior High learning how to play percussion. I joined the entry level C band in seventh grade. This was after the band director, Mr. McElroy, heard me playing the timpani one afternoon and asked me how I had learned. I just shrugged my shoulders because I was too shy to talk. He later told the male percussionists in class that they should be ashamed that a girl was better than they were. He recommended that I take private classes so that I could play professionally, and gave me a phone number to call. It was embarrassing for all of us, and it put me in an awkward position. As a result, the boys had no mercy upon me, and paid me back by allowing me the honor of carrying the huge and heavy bass drum during practice every morning. Nonetheless, I led our school decadence and marched on the field for the duration of school term. But what the boys didn't realize was that I was a natural—I got this!

Father attended one of my performances during a competition held at the Del Mar College auditorium. I had the longest freaking three-timpani solo and I thought it was never end. Father said that my band director looked like the Frito Bandito because he wore a long curled red mustache. The director kept raising his baton up higher and higher as I had an extended drumroll. I thought Mr. McElroy would never place his baton down as the room rumbled like an earthquake.

However, it would have been nice to be a cheerleader again, but their team had already been selected from summer tryouts. So, I took a Home Economics class where I learned to cook and sew. I boiled frozen corn in a pot. The football players would come in after practice to help us eat our food and baked cookies. However, my biggest accomplishment was when I was elected class president for our class.

The Ghetto and Me: Plan A, B, or C?

Talking to boys or smiling, even with my cousins, was not considered ladylike. So, if I even got caught with a boy saying hello to me, I was immediately grounded. It didn't matter if he was the most handsome or popular boy in school. It's okay, because I was shy, a tomboy, and didn't talk much, anyhow.

Besides, how could I have boyfriends with my brothers humiliating me every minute? Sonny made fun of the way I held my beef tacos. He said I would hold them like drumsticks!

Sonny and Danny gave me the nickname, *chupa huesos* (skinny bones) because I was so skinny. I was so embarrassed that I wore two pairs of pants to school so I'd look filled out. As for my Father's nickname for me, he always called me Tomasa—Tammy in Spanish. (I naturally respond better to Tomasa.)

Then there were the pranks that Sonny would pull on me, like grabbing hold of my shorts and tearing them off me in public! Danny and I were always scared of Sonny Boy.

Living on Barcelona, the majority of our neighbors were black folks. On my way home, I would stop at the Circle K store to read *Spider Man* and *Archie* comic books. Then I'd buy a Coca-Cola and walk home.

One afternoon, on the way home, I heard a derogatory remark coming from behind me. Well, you know that life is like one big movie script anyhow, right? It's all about the acting and reacting with life's drama and trauma. Well, it is in my world, anyway.

So, my game plan (A) was to traumatize my tormentor; you know, to startle or sting her a bit. If that didn't work, I'd use plan (B), which was negotiation and bribery! And if all else failed, well, I surely had to use plan (C), and that was to run like hell for my life!

So, as soon as I finished my drink, I slowly stopped walking and then placed my books down. Then I quickly turned to my left, slammed my Coke bottle into the telephone pole, and broke it in two! I turned around and pointed it at her and said, all right, blankety blank, blank, blank! And wee, wee, wee, she ran all the way home! I shocked her like I knew I would.

I had to nip it in the bud because if not, it would have escalated into a gang of girls walking behind me the next day. After that scene, I made doggone sure she walked in front of me instead. I have a tendency to forget I was only 4'11" and weighed eighty-five pounds.

I was all talk, of course, but I had to stand my ground as I adapted to my new barrio—or, in this case, ghetto.

Tammy Lorraine Huerta Fender

Tammy (hair in ponytail) as a tomboy holding her drumsticks with family friend Jimmy "El Radio" Cortez. Tammy sits on Freddy's hog.

Tammy wearing "Are You Ready for Freddy" T-shirt with History/Coach teacher Rodriguez at Cunningham Jr. High

Chapter XVII

Star Makers

"Starring **FREDDY FENDER!"**
"One Night, One Take!"
Jim Halsey-Worlds Top Country Music Booking-Agency
Jim Foglesong- President ABC-Dot Records
Huey P. Meaux-Sugar Hill Studios

One Night, One Take! "An Overnight Sensation"
Freddy's first national debut at the Landmark Hotel in Las Vegas, Nevada. (1975)

Interviewee:
Jim Halsey
Artist Manager, Agent, and Impresario
Visiting Professor at HED Music College in Yehud, Israel
Halsey Learning Center of Music and Entertainment Business
Author of *Starmaker*, 2010
Board of Directors: Country Music Association (CMA), and the
Academy of Country Music (ACM)

There were many people involved in Freddy Fender's discovery. I would like to think I was part of that discovery, too. Jim Foglesong (president of ABC-Dot Records) was also very instrumental in Freddy's career during the time that I got acquainted with Freddy. I had a big group of superstars already! I had stars like Mel Tillis, Roy Clark, and Tammy Wynette.

I was producing shows in Las Vegas while running shows at the Landmark Hotel, called Country Music USA. I would change the stars every two weeks. It was like a production show. We would have a band, a comedian, a female singer, or a novelty act. Then we would put somebody else on, like Roy Clark or Jimmy Dean or someone like that to headline every two weeks.

One day, I got a call from Jim Foglesong while he was in Las Vegas. Foglesong said, "We got a guy that's got a record coming out, and he is going to be one of the biggest things that we ever had! Would you be interested in representing him?"

"Jim, I have never signed an act that I didn't see first or talk to and interview to see really where they wanted to go with their career in life."

Foglesong then said to me, "If you would take my word on Freddy Fender, then I guarantee ya, I can back up anything that I can say about him or that he can do. But we need to get this guy out there before big audiences, and they need to see him now because his record is shipping next week, and we need to have his representation in place!"

I had heard of Huey Meaux and knew of his work with other acts. I knew Huey was a credible producer. So, I said, "Jim, I am going to take your word on it. This is what I am going to do. I am opening a new show at the Landmark Hotel, and I don't have a headliner on it. Do you think he could headline?"

Foglesong replied, "Oh, absolutely! This guy is great, he's terrific!"

"Okay, we are going to put it in on the headline at the Landmark Hotel, of Country Music USA."

Some of the key facts about Las Vegas are that there are many transient people all the time. A lot of time they don't know who is coming or know who is on the shows anyway. But if the marquee has their name in big letters, they figure they know him or he is big and important.

So, we opened up Freddy as headliner, with his name in big, huge letters, twelve feet high, "Starring—**FREDDY FENDER**." Nobody in the world knew who Freddy Fender was at that time!

My guy Leo Zabelin took care of my press and PR. He went to the airport to pick up Freddy, and they opened that night. And this is how quickly all of this happened within a matter of a day and a few hours.

Walter Cane, now the head of the Howard Hughes Landmark Hotel walks in and tells me, "I am relying on you because I have never heard of Freddy Fender."

"I haven't either, but he comes so highly recommended through Jim Foglesong." And so, we were all just holding our breath.

The honest-to-God truth, the day of the opening, they are rehearsing the show; I am down at the rehearsal, and I had sent Leo, my guy, to go to the airport to pick Freddy up. I call him up, "Could you bring him right here because we have to rehearse the show?"

Leo gets to the airport, calls me back, and says, "Freddy's here. But all he has is the clothes on his back and wearing jeans and T-shirt. That is all he brought with him and, Jim, get this, his guitar was in a sack!"

I said, "Leo, before you bring him to rehearsal, you stop and get him some clothes!" So, when he first comes in and meets me, we instantly had rapport.

I instantly loved that guy because he was just himself. There was no star there. There was only Freddy Fender. Freddy Fender had warmth and heart.

So, they went to rehearsal, and I saw him, but I wasn't worried because I knew he was going to have the same effect on the audience that he had on me and with Leo and everybody else! We only met thirty minutes before rehearsal started. So, he was just Freddy. He was just a sensation that night! Everybody loved him. I brought some of my columnist friends, Joe Delaney from the *Las Vegas Sun* and Billy Willard from *Daily Variety News*.

God love 'em! They all loved Freddy; he told these stories and made them all laugh, and he just had a fantastic voice. It was God-given to him and that talent to play the guitar. He had this sense of humor, and how he was so infectious. When he was through that night, I knew we had another star in our hands! Before his engagement ended, that record "Before the Next Teardrop Falls" was no. 1 on all radio stations and all over America!

Freddy's debut makes history at the Landmark Hotel in Las Vegas

Tammy Lorraine Huerta Fender

Well, not only did it make a hero out of me with Walter Cane at Howard Hughes hotel, but it also proved that the magic and the power of any artist or star, if it is genuine, comes through. And Freddy got some good reviews. He was reviewed nationally. All of a sudden, he has this record, the hottest thing in America, but he was also being reviewed as a headliner of a show in Las Vegas!

At that time, Las Vegas was a real important show place, and I produced a lot of shows there at hotels. They were all my own artists.

We struck out a rapport with him. I got to know Freddy within those two weeks we were there. I called my associate in Los Angeles, Dick Howard, who ran my Los Angeles office. Primarily, he did television. I said, "This guy is so natural for TV. We got to get him on *The Tonight Show Starring Johnny Carson*. All the daytime shows we had to get him in, like *Mike Douglas, Merv Griffin*, and *The Dinah Shore Show*."

He was a talker. You get him on there, and those people are interested in somebody saying something, not just coming on to promote his record. Freddy always had some funny story, but it wasn't a joke. It was a real funny story. His stories were something related to him, of his life experiences, and in a very human way.

The next thing in building a star, because we knew we had a star in our hands, is that he had to be seen and heard by a lot of people. So, we put him out there on the road in front of a lot of other acts we were producing, and we would promote stars like Roy Clark. Roy put Freddy Fender in front of his show, and then Tammy Wynette put him in front of their show. Mel Tillis put him in front of his show. Jimmy Dean, even. All of these artists, we asked, "We need a favor because he has got the hottest record in the country now, but we need to put him out there in front of big live audiences!"

So, they all said, "Well, he can come open for ten or twelve days, or so."

Walter Cane booked him in Las Vegas. And so, we immediately brought him back to those huge hotels, which were the Landmark, the Sands, Stardust, Silver Bird, and the Frontier.

Dick Howard, a television expert associate of our company in the West Coast, loved him. I think Freddy did every talk show that was on the air at that time. Within a short period, Freddy Fender became a household name. Dick Howard included him in *Dean Martin, Tony Orlando, Flip Wilson Show, The Muppet Show, Dukes of Hazzard, Hollywood Squares*, and *Hee Haw*—too many shows to mention.

He was invited back repeatedly. They just couldn't get enough of him. Freddy Fender was booked in almost every daytime and nighttime show in the 1970s and 1980s more than any other entertainer. He was an overnight success!

But Freddy Fender was just so much more than any of that! Freddy just had these special gifts about him!

Dinah Shore Show at NBC Studios LA, 1975
With actors Ellen "Grandma Walton" Corby of the TV show *The Waltons*,
Dinah Shore, Robert Blake of the TV show *Barretta*, and Bernadette Peters
(Courtesy of NBC Entertainment-Studio. A division of NBC West, LLC.)

Dinah Shore Show at NBC Studios LA, 1975
Dinah Shore, Freddy Fender (smoking on set), and singer/TV actor Tony Orlando,
host of *The Tony Orlando Show*
(Courtesy of NBC Entertainment-Studio. A division of NBC West, LLC.)

The Tonight Show at NBC Studios
Starring Burt Reynolds and Freddy Fender
TV cohost Ed McMahon/Guest host Dallas Cowboy quarterback Don Meredith
(Courtesy of NBC Entertainment-Studio. A division of NBC West, LLC.)

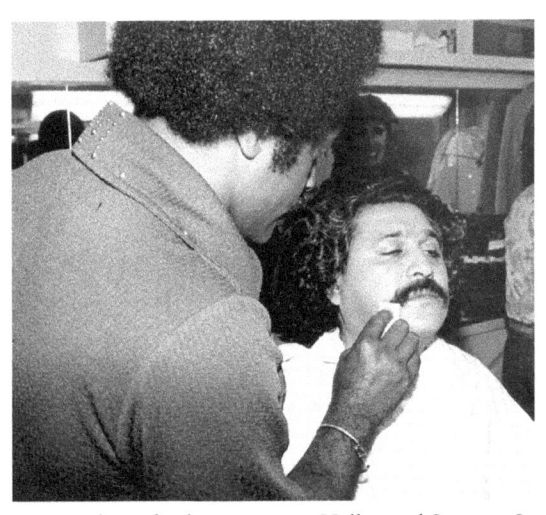

Freddy getting make up for the TV cameras Hollywood Squares *Game Show*

Hollywood Squares Game show with guest stars Bernadette Peters, Robert Fuller, Freddy Fender, Rip Taylor, Sandy Duncan, Tony Randall, Florence Henderson, and Marty Allen.

Interviewee:
James Staton "Jim" Foglesong
(July 26, 1922–July 9, 2013)
Director of the music business program at Trevecca Nazarene University
Adjunct professor at Vanderbilt University's Blair School of Music since 1991
President of Dot, ABC, Capitol and MCA Records/
Country Music Hall of Fame Inductee, 2004

I adored Freddy Fender, and when we signed Freddy, I was head of the company, president of the label. I was in California when my promotion man, Larry Baunach, called me and told me he had just spoken to Rick Libby, who was a local radio personality in Houston, and that they had a record on the Crazy Cajun label that was just lighting up the phones terrifically. Every time they played it, people called and wanted the radio station to play it some more. I said, "Well, I need to listen to this." He said it is half in English and half in Spanish. I just remembered that in Houston, there is a big Spanish population, and it may be something that was just a local hit, and not a national hit, and I got a copy of it the following day in Los Angeles. I listened to it, and I liked it. They gave me Huey's name, and I had known Huey Meaux for several years.

So, we made a deal and bought the product ["Before the Next Teardrop Falls"] from him. Of course, the rest is history, and he got it right out. It was a monster worldwide! It sold over a million copies.

Tammy Lorraine Huerta Fender

The second sale was "Wasted Days and Wasted Nights," and that sold even more than "Before the Next Teardrop Falls." The album sold over a million copies. It was a tremendously successful venture.

This was right before they started to recognize platinum records that awarded the artist for a million copies. Gold was as far as they went at that time. Then gold records were for five hundred thousand copies, and then they started with platinum for over a million copies.

I was also the producer of the record, although Huey wanted his name on it even though I did most of the producing.

I hadn't even met Freddy in person, yet I was very fond of Freddy. I found that we both had the same sense of humor. Freddy Fender taught me Spanish and how to pronounce it.

I am a former singer, and Freddy would often invite me onstage to sing the melody on "Before the Next Teardrop Falls."

In Tulsa, Oklahoma, at a ranch, was a Roy Clark Golf Tournament every year for a charity fund-raiser for a children's hospital in Tulsa. There were about fifteen thousand people there. It was sold out. There were a lot of different entertainers. Freddy was such a generous and compassionate fellow that if you were to ask him to do any benefits, he would have.

We had gone to do *Carnegie Hall* and record a live album with Roy Clark, Don Williams, and Hank Thompson, along with Freddy. It is a world-famous concert hall known for classical music. This was Jim Halsey's idea. These were artists from Jim Halsey's booking-agency. Jim Halsey booked all of them. It doesn't get more prestigious than Carnegie Hall in New York City. *There is no greater compliment than that!* It was for one night only, and it was sold out. It was a wonderful show. People drove from faraway places to attend. [On *Country Comes to Carnegie Hall*, the album has Foglesong's voice singing harmony with Freddy.]

They did not have a recording studio. Everything was in Texas with Huey then. The record company ABC-Dot played a huge role in making Freddy a star, publicizing him, selling the records. We always support our artists.

I got along great with Freddy. Most of the business he had was with Huey. Sam Herro [Freddy's road manager] was also part of that. Though a lot of the things that Huey said, I wasn't sure how well they communicated with Freddy, but they always delivered him when we needed him.

And when we got together, we had a good time. I am so glad that before he died, we had gotten together.

I had spoken to Stuart Dill [Freddy's manager in 1985] several times. Stuart Dill knew how fond I was of Freddy, and if he ever came to Nashville, I would love to meet him.

I teach music business courses now at two universities. One of them is at Vanderbilt University in Nashville. A year or two before Freddy died, Stuart Dill got Freddy to come over and speak at one of my classes.

It was a big thrill, and I even got to interview him. We talked about one another's experiences together, and Freddy answered the students' questions about his career. I was so glad. I wanted to get together with him. But every time I wanted to talk to him, he always had all these people around him. We rarely had much time alone. I just liked him. I liked his family. I used to call him at home, and everybody was so helpful. I felt a very warm relationship with him. Freddy and I had a lot of laughs. We both enjoyed humor.

Promotional Poster (and album) for Show *Country Comes to Carnegie Hall*
(Courtesy of Jim Foglesong with permission to reprint.)

Interviewee:
James Staton "Jim" Foglesong

Freddy Fender was a great performer and guitar player, able to mix rock, country, and Tejano yet with a very solid sound.

I never typed Freddy or categorized him into country, and that is what we were selling. Freddy was rock oriented. *He was rock 'n' roll!*

It was always such a unique experience to be with Freddy. You can hear Freddy Fender three or four times in a row and want to go back the fifth night to hear him perform. There is no greater compliment than that! God gave him a lot of talent, and he used it well.

There was never a problem between the two of us. I knew they partied when they came to town. But I was older, and they treated me more like a father. Like, "Dad is here, oh, oh, and Dad doesn't like that."

Eventually, ABC-Dot Records was sold to MCA.

Huey was a tough businessman, and whether I trusted him 100 percent, I am not real sure. [Foglesong chuckles.] Huey had a law firm in New York representing him and well-known accountants there that helped him stay out of trouble, which was very smart of him to do.

I wasn't sure that Freddy wasn't getting all that he should have gotten out of that relationship. It is really hard and sad, but I had no concrete evidence. But it was a feeling that I had with his management group. I do know that we delivered some big royalty checks down there to Texas, and I always hoped Freddy got his share of it. But my deal that we structured was with Huey Meaux to his company, to furnish his service of Freddy Fender.

We did not have a direct contract with Freddy. Huey had that. Freddy was assigned to Huey, and Huey was his manager. Their thing [record distribution agencies] was to deal with the manager and provide the services Huey needed.

There is nothing specific, but you can determine how much he should have received through an amount of a certain percentage that goes with what an artist should receive. Whether he received it is another thing, and I don't know what deal he had with Freddy. Huey is a tough businessman. He was very difficult to negotiate with. I considered Huey to be a friend of mine, and I liked Huey.

I know he probably wasn't paying Freddy top dollar. I doubt Freddy had anybody on his side to negotiate for him.

Jim Foglesong (ABC-Dot Records), Freddy Fender, and Huey "The Crazy Cajun" Meaux agreeably banking on their new recording star

Wasted Days and Wasted Nights

The Making of Freddy Fender at Sugar Hill Recording Studio in Houston, Texas (1975).

At Sugar Hill Studios: Sam Herro, Jim Foglesong, Freddy Fender, Huey Meaux, and Mickey Moody

Tammy Lorraine Huerta Fender

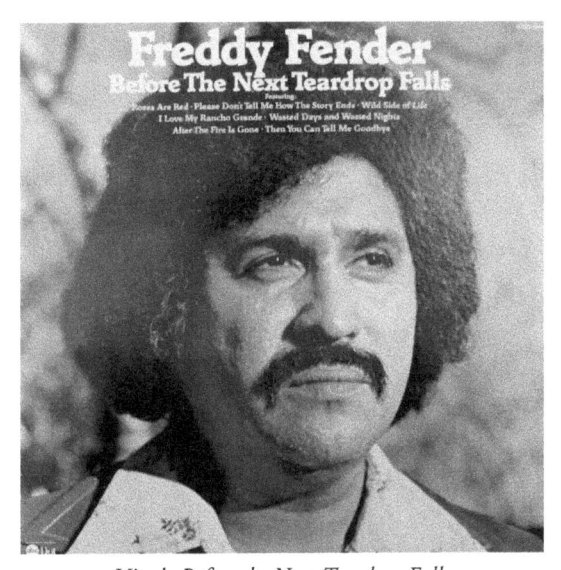

Vinyl: *Before the Next Teardrop Falls*
(ABC-Dot Records © *Universal Music Enterprises of UMG Recordings, Inc.*, 1975)

"From My Eyes" by Freddy Fender

I couldn't be prouder after twenty years of trying. I finally have my first national hit record! Thank you very much, Larry Baunach [vice president ABC Records], Sam Herro (manager), Bill and Wanda Harvey, and my friends Trini and Neto Bocanegra, my gratefulness. Thank you so much.
(Excerpt: ABC-Dot Records, Inc. Album "Before the Next Teardrop Falls," 1975)

"The Phantom" Freddy, and "the Crazy Cajun" rejoicing their overnight success at a hotel diner

Wasted Days and Wasted Nights

Interviewee:
Huey P. Meaux
Record Producer/Manager

I knew the minute I heard "Teardrops" sung by Freddy, it was a *hit* record! Some thought Freddy didn't have enough of a good voice, and it didn't sound country enough. But I did it anyway, even though he sounded different. It was first recorded as a 45-rpm and in the album *Before the Next Teardrop Falls* on Crazy Cajun label, then ABC-Dot.

Some disc jockeys said I had lost my ear, but I would tell them just to play the mother f—ker! I used to have to pay these bastards to play it! You had to do that with everything and everybody. If you don't put up the money, these disc jockeys won't play it.

I made the rounds even in Nashville, but nobody was buying it. KILT helped me, and another radio station in Rosenberg, Texas.

When I had my own radio show on KPFT on Friday nights in Houston, I would get drunk and play it. I'd dedicate the song for my mama and then play this one for y'all and then for myself. So that was three times in a row, and the phones would begin to light up!

I knew it was a hit! I was the biggest disk jockey there ever was! I didn't have any money either and I had an old van. It was on the way through Port Arthur [at a radio station], I'd stop and ask this guy to play it, and he told me, "Huey, you have done lost your ear, let me show you something you ought to hear." Then when Freddy hit it big, I went back and told the disk jockey, "Hey, you f—ked up!"

Anytime the lights light up like that, you know you have a hit. Well, after the phones kept lighting up with five lines, I had to start raising money. Freddy got hot enough to go to Vegas. I said, "Freddy, look here, buddy. I got this $500, and that's all I got. I am going to gamble it on you. If we go to Vegas, you may get very big."

He said, "Okay, I will gamble with you." So, we went to Vegas.

[Vice President] Larry Baunach, who worked for ABC then and worked for records distribution in Dallas, warned them about the song on the radio, that we couldn't press the records fast enough! It was five times the bank money to buy more promotion, you know. They gave it to me, and that is when ABC picked up, but they still didn't believe in him, until I had to make him so f—king big, they [the music industry] had to choke them to death, you know?

You see, the people in Nashville didn't like Mexicans in those days. So, when they saw Freddy Fender, it gave them reason; I didn't care whether they liked him or not. Freddy had outsold all them p—sys!

I had friends everywhere! I had some in Vegas from the music business and in New York. I didn't call them unless he had a hit record. I have many gold records and awards to show for my hard work producing many artists. I had hits with artists, like "Sweet Dreams," "She's About a Mover" by the Sir Douglas Quintet, "Talk to Me" by Sunny and the Sunliners, "I'm Leaving It All Up to You," "I'm a Fool to Care" by Joe Barry, "Don't Mess with My Toot-Toot" by Rockin' Sidney, including hits by Ronnie Milsap and B. J. Thomas.

I said, "What is it going to take?" and that is when Jim Halsey [Promoter/Booking-Agency] came in. He did those entire big rodeos, and that was good for Freddy.

Then Ed Salomon, a friend of mine in New York who owned a fifty-thousand-watt radio station, WHAN, had Freddy Fender's picture on the side of buses and on the subway.

The radio stations would call up the record shops and ask them which records had the biggest sales each week. I got a yellow cab and filled it up with Freddy's and B. J. Thomas' records. Then I would tell the record stores that when the radio station called, to tell them Freddy and BJ had the biggest sales.

I would never let Freddy go alone because when he did, he would f—k up!

Freddy would just say to me, "Just let me sing, Huey!"

Then when he was enormous, I tell him to just let me pick the songs and don't worry about nothing else. *Freddy, you are going to sing* "El Rancho Grande." *You watch and see that if you are not getting to those people, you kick it off with* "El Rancho Grande." *Then those white people will start getting on those tables and start pissing on those drinks, singing, "Ay, ay, ay, ay, ay! Allá en El Rancho Grande!" They don't know what the f—k you are saying. Then after that, you can go ahead and sing anything else after that!*

You got to know where to put that, you know! It is like a disc jockey. To have a big show, you have the first twenty minutes of music fast, fast, fast, and then you slow it down. You get them excited first!

I just had to make Jim Foglesong take Freddy. Freddy tore the place down. He brought the house down—I mean he showed them all up!

I know what I had when they heard Freddy sing. Freddy was already a superstar! And according to the white man, he didn't look good, but Freddy showed them different!

Freddy at The Los Angeles Palladium (1975)

Wasted Days and Wasted Nights

Interviewee:
Huey P. Meaux
Record Producer/Manager

I used to be a barber in Winnie, Texas. That is where I started making records, behind my barbershop. For publicity, I cut Freddy's hair in a jail in Austin, Texas.

I took Freddy to a lot of jails to sing voluntarily and some paying gigs like in Huntsville Prison in Texas. This was to show them that Freddy was no bigger than they were. If you do things like that, people feel from the heart, and I did that so that Freddy didn't ever forget who he was.

In the Huntsville Rodeo, they had some hardened criminals and over twenty thousand people attended the show. As soon as the prisoners saw Freddy ride in, they all got up and cheered. They even had themselves a Prison Rodeo Queen. But when W. J. Estelle, head of Texas Department of Corrections, stood up to greet Freddy, he asked him how he'd been. Freddy told him he was all right. "I've been staying out of here, haven't I?"

Freddy was playing at the Rogues Club. That's when Sam Herro leeched on to Freddy because I was going to make Freddy a star. I knew Sam Herro, "the Phantom," too, and so I made him Freddy's road manager; Sam was also a real gambler. I would give him [Freddy] all kinds of money, and Sam Herro would take it from him. He began to hustle Freddy on poker, and Freddy would lose all his money.

Major Riddle, who was from San Antonio, owned the Silver Bird and the Dunes [in Las Vegas]. He liked Freddy because he liked to see people come up from nothing into somebody. They told Sam Herro to stop gambling or he would be ousted.

I then had to go to Las Vegas and clear up a debt because they wouldn't let Freddy play there because of Sam Herro owing $50,000 before they could even get Freddy into Vegas.

Freddy always gave everything away. Like at the Astrodome, he saw a kid with only one leg, and he gave him his huge diamond ring. I also had to stop Freddy from giving one of his awards away to some young girl, too.

After this song, everybody wanted anything on Freddy Fender. I put everything back out that had not hit before "Teardrops," like "Crazy Baby."

I even went to buy all the songs in the Rio Grande Valley because I knew they were all going to be *piggyback* songs, you know.

Tammy: You are shrewd, Huey!

Huey: I am a good businessman. I know the business, and they definitely know me. I remember you, Tammy, when you all lived in a chicken coop in San Benito and the door wouldn't close. It kept swinging back and forth. I felt sorry. Vangie [Eva] was nursing then. I asked him how much he made that year. Freddy said about $3,000–5,000 a year. I said, "Freddy, is that all the money you all made?" Freddy thought it was a lot of money. I said, "Naw, Freddy, that ain't no money! Freddy, we are going to make more money than that."

The first check I gave Freddy, he went to go buy himself a big icebox and put all kinds of cow in it!

Freddy then placed floor carpeting in his new house on Barcelona in Corpus, and I walked in. I was stepping all over the kids that were on the floor. Ya'll had never seen carpet before.

[Huey chuckled and admitted that he was raised the same way too.]

"From My Eyes" by Freddy Fender

From Dolly Parton's lips, she was driving home one evening and heard "Teardrops" on the radio. She stopped to finish listening to the song. Then she stopped again to call the radio station to find out the name of the singer! The song led me to about two or three shows with her on TV. She had a show called Butterfly. *I did a duet with her on TV.*
We never got to record a duet together, though we wanted to.

Freddy Goes Country

"Before the Next Teardrop Falls" marked Freddy's shift to country and western music. It became a national hit because Huey pushed the single through a country music radio station rather than a pop or rock station in Houston.

Huey, The Crazy Cajun, quickly made revisions, having ABC-Dot take over (Crazy Cajun) productions and do an all-out promotional campaign by their marketing department. By the end of the year, it had made no. 20 on *Billboard*'s U.S. 200 Songs of the Year chart for 1974.

April 5, 1975, marked Freddy Fender's national television debut when we saw Father perform on Dick Clark's *American Bandstand*.

His second appearance on national television came shortly thereafter when Wolfman Jack hosted The *Midnight Special* in July 1975.

Less than a month later, on Thursday, August 7, 1975, Freddy sang "Before the Next Teardrop Falls" plus "Wasted Days and Wasted Nights" on *The Tonight Show*; before the month was over, Freddy also made a guest appearance on *The Mike Douglas Show*.

A classic example of his meteoric rise to the top occurred before the end of 1975, when he sang "Secret Love" and "Vaya Con Dios" during two appearances on *The Tonight Show*, and one more guest spot on *American Bandstand*.

Freddy's Formula for Success!

Overnight, Freddy became famous because of his distinctive, heart-warming voice; his formula in the studio of recording in both English and Spanish captivated listeners, and his ability to nail a recording on the first take was astonishing.

Huey Meaux, Jim Halsey, and Jim Foglesong are truly the "star makers". They just needed to get hold of Freddy Fender for just *one night* and *one take*.

"Just let me sing," Freddy said to Huey.

The rest is history!

While traveling, Dad would take raw *chorizo* (Mexican sausage) with him. The hotel cooks were only too kind to make his Mexican breakfast for him. Many times, Mother would make him lunch tacos instead of sandwiches to take on the plane. She became an awesome cook like her mother-in-law.

As for Doña Máge, she was having a ball in Las Vegas. She was nowhere to be found, and Freddy often had to page his mother during his nightly shows. It was not an act, nor a joke, when Freddy would ask the audience, *"If you see someone that looks exactly like me, but without a mustache, could you please remind her she has a son. And just who the heck brought her here to Vegas in the first place!"* The crowd couldn't help but embrace Father's sincerity, charisma, and natural humor. He had them eating right out of his hands. They weren't as tough critics as the crowd he had been used too. They were very kind to him and grateful. The country music lovers and the Anglo market allowed Freddy to be himself and let him sing, whatever and wherever, as long as he sang to them.

Doña Máge could be seen on the casino floors, wearing a bandage around her wrist. She had been using her wrist nonstop to pull back the lever from the slot machines. She eventually had to use her forearm to grab hold of it to pull the lever down. I don't think she ever found her way into the showroom too many times. Otherwise, she could have seen how big a star her son had become!

Freddy just made sure that there was always a bucketful of nickels and dimes to keep his mother happy. It was good enough for both of them.

"From My Eyes" by Freddy Fender
I had been shooting craps! But God must have rolled some sevens for me that day!

Chapter XVIII

The King of Tex-Mex

The American Dream
Rock 'n' Country Music Star!
"Piggybacks"
"Billboard Magazine, Congrats!"

He was no phony! Country music fans know when you are a true star and when you're not the real McCoy. They are familiar with hard times, and seeing others rise above from absolutely nothing to fulfill the American dream gives them hope with regard to their own goals. The many struggles and barriers Freddy had encountered while growing up led his fans to admire him; they were astonished to witness his triumph. His music and voice instantly captivated several generations of multi-cultural fans across the nation, and they literally began to fall in love with the man himself.

The outcome was that country-music lovers rushed to claim and embrace Freddy wholeheartedly as one of their own. They came to accept Freddy on a personal level, and that "golden throat" of his drew them into *his* world.

The large crowds responded to him easily, especially when he spoke his homegrown version of Tex-Mex lingo onstage, like "Get it on, *catche-ton!*" ("chubby cheeks") or *"Hecha-le, hecha-le!"* ("Give it more gas!"), and *"Ajúa! Ajúa!"* ("Yee haw!")

Freddy began to make the music industry happy, including Jim Foglesong, president of ABC-Dot record company, and their record promoter/distributer Larry Baunach. All began to take notice; their instincts had paid off.

Entertainment writer Jerry Flowers, who wrote the liner notes for the Freddy Fender album 'Freddie Fender" related a funny story. "Insiders at the company report that there were chuckles in an L.A. sales and promotion meeting when Baunach played the record and predicted it would be a monster . . . Baunach received a present from the officers of ABC Leisure Group I, the parent organization for ABC/Dot Records. Baunach was sent a nicely wrapped package by a Nashville taxi company. Inside was a badly battered auto fender, a concession that his judgment had been correct." (Flowers. Excerpt. "The Story of an Overnight Sensation" Album Freddie Fender. Reprint. THE MUSIC GIG. Pickwick International, Inc. LP. 1975)

Freddy Fender's name, voice, and persona began to carry much weight and mean something to the average folk, especially for those heavy weights in the music industry. Revitalized, they were delighted to carry their new rising star and have him on board.

Freddy was not only refreshing but also a new breed, a performer with multiple talents who could easily fascinate and charm people while speaking or singing on any platform and in any country in the world. All they had to do was put their best stallion in the front lines and just let him be nobody else but Baldemar Huerta aka Freddy Fender.

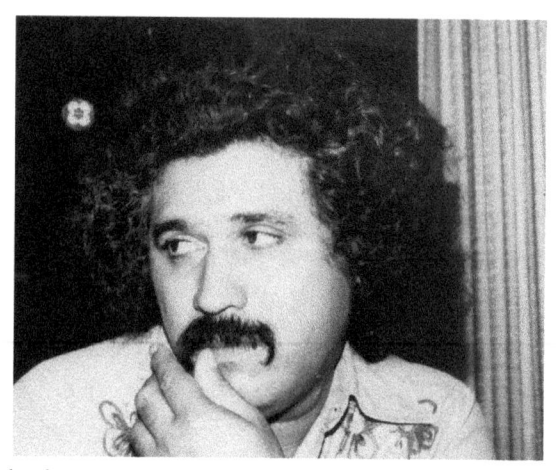

Freddy in a hotel room quietly listening in on a business meeting about his future career

Interviewee:
Huey P. Meaux

Sure enough, I had a hard time with a farmworker named César Chávez. Freddy and I were in East LA with some bad Mexicans there. I was the only white guy. Paul Rodríguez, a comedian, was performing at the club that night too, with Freddy. It was Chávez himself who came to see me in East LA [discussion at hotel room]. He asked me if we could do some political ads for him.

I told him that Freddy wasn't big enough [superstardom] yet. I turned him down, but I told him he had my word and that I wouldn't let Freddy do anything for anybody else either! So, he asked me if that was my word. I said, "Yes!"

I told Mr. Chávez, "I love what you are doing, but you don't understand. But if you give me a pass on this, I promise you, he will not do any other publicity for any other politician on this."

I was a white guy, and they were not scaring me; they were just telling me like it is, and they were powerful!

Tammy: Why did you feel you had to give Chávez your word or make a deal with him?

Huey: They were bad people. [Perhaps Influential; I don't know exactly what Huey meant by "bad."] Chávez was a good farmworker guy, but he did things he had to do. But Chávez didn't really know anything about the white people, and it would have killed him [Freddy's career].

The white people wouldn't have gone for that. We met in the middle, and I asked to bow out. I already had been through this political thing before Freddy came along. I knew how to handle this.

He took it that I was a man of my word, and I was! He kept his word, and I kept mine. It would ruin him [Freddy] in the pop market. I knew what was good for Freddy. They loved Freddy, but pop and country is where the money is. Chávez was smart enough to know that making Freddy in the music business was my business.

It was a rough thing for me because I was the only white man in that area, and I had to hold my ground. Yes, I was a little scared. So, I had to make a deal with Chávez.

Freddy met him in the hotel room. Freddy learned a long time ago to keep his mouth shut. He didn't speak. It was just an open-and-shut thing, a thirty-minute thing.

The one thing I can tell you about Freddy was that he was smart in history! He would go down to UCLA down in California to see all those professors, and Freddy would tell them about Maximilian and of other Mexican politicians.

The main thing about Freddy that he loved to do was cook. He showed me a few of his recipes. He liked to cook on the ground, placing a cow's skull and eating the tongue. He just loved *cabrito,* too.

In Mexico, they never really did like Freddy's singing too much. They liked those pretty voices singing. They didn't like Freddy there because he sounded too black.

However, a famous entertainer named Tony [Antonio] Aguilar had a party for Freddy in Mexico City. They had police officers for two blocks to keep people away from him. They placed Freddy up in a penthouse on the beach.

"From My Eyes" by Freddy Fender
I feel my costume is too lavish for me. I prefer and should
probably be wearing jeans for you tonight!
[On stage, Pasadena Convention Center, Los Angeles, California]

Goldmine: Redistributing Freddy's Old Compositions

The country music industry had a difficult time keeping Freddy Fender in their musical corral as Freddy's interpretations instantaneously crossed over into other *Billboard* music genres, from rock to rhythm and blues, pop, contemporary, and hot Latin charts.

The beauty of it was that there was no problem in marketing Freddy because he was already an original artist, with the talent to write his own melodies, lyrics, and play guitar. As a matter a fact, he had so much material that all they had to do was rerecord him in a mainstream sound studio, release the new version, and continue stacking more platinum records to the pile.

To cash in on his selling power, three labels—ABC-Dot, MCA, and Imperial—released "Wasted Days" in 1975 and 1976.

Imperial Records, who had shelved "Wasted Days" for sixteen years because Freddy was serving time, finally released the older version!

Not to be left out, Goldband Records also dusted off the former convict's in-prison production. They put out their *Recorded Inside Louisiana State Prison Power Pak* album a second time.

Suddenly Freddy was the goose that was laying the golden eggs; realizing that they had a goldmine of recordings on their shelves, Duncan Records leased or sold their original tapes to Vok Records and a label in Argentina. Falcón Records sister label, ARV International, also pulled their masters out of their vault, which they now treated as a goldmine and rereleased his entire set of raw, rare recordings from his early years.

Huey Meaux Quickly Retrieves "Piggybacks"

Huey Meaux did his best to outwit everyone by going to the lower Rio Grande Valley and Mexico and stripping record companies out of their masters. Then he went to the swamps of Louisiana to search for more of Baldemar Huerta, El Bebop Kid, Eddie Medina, Scotty Wayne, and other Freddy Fender original recordings, which Huey used as what he called piggybacks.

So, from 1974 to 1976, twenty more albums were released, many of them rehashed compilations of his early original works, and all worthwhile and lucrative to say the least.

Despite the market being saturated with Freddy's music singles and albums, other record labels were leasing rights to his music to leech off his vintage recordings.

There is no doubt that everything about Freddy's voice had the "Midas Touch," and it paid off big for ABC-Dot, who, after all was said and done, did not regret their decision to sign him up.

As for his secret musical recipe, Freddy always felt his music should be somewhat undercooked in order to be perfectly done. As an illustration of what I mean, when Father wanted *chorizo* and eggs for breakfast, it had to be stirred once ever so slightly, then tightly covered and left untouched to cook thoroughly for a minute. If he saw you do otherwise, he'd have you start from scratch. So, to avoid the heartache and waste of his time and food, he would rather cook it himself.

Freddy projected his raw and sincerest emotions in his voice; he sang his songs with pure perfection and articulated them in *one take*. No more, no less—it was ingenious.

Music Timeline by Music Archivist and Writer Ramón Hernández "Before the Next Teardrop Falls"

After almost two decades of recording for various labels, the year 1975 was Freddy's landmark year because that is when he achieved his first major national hit, "**Before the Next Teardrop Falls**."

The landslide of hits actually started when "Before the Next Teardrop Falls" made no. 1 on *Billboard*'s Country charts on March 8, 1975, and remained no. 1 on the charts for another fifteen weeks.

"Before the Next Teardrop Falls" also made no. 1 in the *World Record* Country Singles Chart on March 15, 1975. This is the same day that it also made no. 1 in *Cashbox* Country Top 75 Charts.

Upon reaching sales of a million copies, as certified by the Recording Industry Association of America (RIAA), Freddy was awarded a coveted gold record.

To top it off, it also made no. 1 on *Billboard*'s Hot 100 charts on May 31, 1975, and stayed on the charts for another fourteen weeks, ultimately coming in at no. 4 in *Billboard*'s end-year Hot 100 Songs of 1975, alongside legendary artists, such as Frankie Valli, Captain and Tennille, Glen Campbell, and Elton John.

If that was not enough, the single made no. 20 on the U.S. "200 Songs of the Year" chart for 1974.

Next, the Country Music Association (CMA) awarded this record "Single of the Year." The Music Operators of America also made it "Single of the Year" and in addition named Freddy "Artist of the Year."

Then, the Academy of Country Music (ACM) honored Freddy Fender as the "Most Promising Male Vocalist for 1975" (nineteen years after he recorded that first 78-rpm single).

The proof that this tune made Freddy a star in Europe and the South American continent is in the actual rerelease of "Before the Next Teardrop Falls" in Argentina, Spain, the Netherlands, and other countries. Huey Meaux had Freddy record a Spanish version—"Estare Contigo Cuando Triste Estas"—for his Crazy Cajun label and he leased that recording to the Hispavox label in Madrid (see 45-rpm label images). Meaux also leased his original recording to Talent Krijgteen in North Holland, the Netherlands, and a major label in the United Kingdom, where it also made no. 1. And in Mexico, many groups had already translated and covered this million-seller in Spanish.

Music Timeline by Music Archivist and Writer Ramón Hernández "Wasted Days and Wasted Nights"

Freddy's second international monster hit—better late than never—was **"Wasted Days and Wasted Nights."**

Fans wasted no time in buying it, and "Wasted Days" topped gross sales, making it to no. 1 on *Billboard*'s country charts for 1975 and staying on the charts for two weeks. It made no. 26 on *Billboard*'s U.S. Hot 100 Singles for 1975; it also made no. 1 on *Billboard*'s U.S. Country Song of the Year for 1975. It reached no. 8 on *Billboard*'s Pop Charts on July 19, 1975, stayed on the charts for another fourteen weeks, and also made Best Single of the Year in New York.

This resulted in Freddy being selected as recipient of a 1975 *Billboard* Trendsetter and for Establishing Tex-Mex Music in the National Pop Market, actually worldwide scale, since *Billboard*'s charts are the universally accepted standard.

At the end of 1975, he was also nominated for a 1976 *Grammy* award in the "Best Country Vocal Performance—Male" and "Wasted Days" was nominated for "Best Country Song."

Like fellow Americans of Mexican descent, Linda Ronstadt and Johnny Rodriguez, Freddy made country rock cool and was instrumental in inserting more rocking licks into country music.

From this point onward, Freddy Fender became an international household name because people could not get enough of his voice.

"From My Eyes" by Freddy Fender

"Wasted Days" and "Teardrops" had sold double platinum.
I remember the first Nashville show we did; we were in carriages. Little Tanya Tucker was there.
From behind, she said out loud "Freddy Fender when are you going to get off your big white horse!
Are you trying to corner the market or what?"
Of course, I was so ignorant about the music business.
I didn't know what she was talking about. She was real smart and a cute brat.
She was talking about my records being on all kinds of charts and cornering the market.
I had never heard that word before. I also shared a horse carriage with Donna Fargo.
Dolly Parton, Roy Clark, Marty Robbins, Conway Twitty, Charley Pride, and Don Williams.
The Oak Ridge Boys were like giggly kids; they were like twenty something.
(Wiseman, Mac. "Freddy and Tanya Tucker." KTTI Radio, Live R. J./Camp Springs, August 29, 1969.)

* * *

The type of country music I like is like rock and country.
I don't care how much rock 'n' roll you put into the country song.
You know by their voice it's still country.
The music and technique keep changing, but the roots of the tree are still on the ground and still thriving.
As long as the music is good—take off with it, man!

ABC-Dot Records Award

ABC-Dot Records, *Vice President/Promotor/Distributor, Larry Baunach, presents gold records to Huey Meaux and Freddy Fender for no. 1* Single of the Year, Before The Next Teardrop Falls *(Courtesy of Bev LeCroy © Grand Ole Opry Archives. October 1975.)*

Huey and Freddy elated about recording "Teardrops"
(Courtesy of Bev LeCroy © Grand Ole Opry Archives. October 1975.)

Country Music Awards

At CMA Awards, Billy "Crash" Craddock and Minnie Pearl present Freddy Fender with the award for Single of the Year "Before the Next Teardrop Falls." (Courtesy of Les Leverett. © Grand Ole Opry Archives. October 13, 1975.)

Freddy graciously accepts and thanks the Country Music Association and his fans for bestowing him with the CMA award for "Single of the Year"

Tammy Lorraine Huerta Fender

Freddy performs at the 50th Grand Ole Opry Anniversary with country legends such as Earnest Tubb, Marty Robbins, Johnny Cash, Tammy Wynette, Dolly Parton, Roy Clark, and Charley Pride, and many more stars. (1975)

Wasted Days and Wasted Nights

(BMI) Broadcasters Music Incorporated

BMI Broadcast Music Incorporated Country Awards Dinner. Shelby Singleton, Freddy, BMI's Frances Preston, John Singleton, and cowriters of single "Before the Next Teardrop Falls" Vivian Keith and Ben Peters (Courtesy of BMI, 1975)

Freddy Fender with BMI affiliates and guests (Courtesy of BMI, 1975)

BILLBOARD No. 1 Awards 1975:

*Billboard No. 1 Awards Event, 1975.
Huey Meaux, Freddy Fender, and comedian/actor Flip Wilson*

*Recipients Captain & Tennille, Olivia Newton-John, and Freddy Fender with Billboard's
No. 1 Award presented to them by television celebrity and comedian Flip Wilson*

Wasted Days and Wasted Nights

Music Timeline by Music Archivist and Writer Ramón Hernández "The Soulful, Blues-tinged Hit Singles"

Many more soulful, blues-tinged, rock 'n' country singles immediately followed his first two smash hits. Freddy's heartbreaking interpretation of "Vaya Con Dios" placed no. 6 on *CashBox*'s Top 100. But north of the border, in Canada, Freddy's south of the border song made no. 1 in *RPM* magazine, the Canadian equivalent of *Billboard* magazine.

"Secret Love" broke into *Billboard*'s Hot Country Singles on November 3, 1975. It reached no. 4 on *Billboard*'s Hot Country Singles on December 20, 1975, and it stayed on the charts a total of six weeks. In addition, it placed at no. 8 on its overall charts.

"**Since I Met You Baby**" came in at no. 19 on *Billboard*'s Hot Country Singles on December 20, 1975. Freddy's bluesy, soulful elements popped up when he recorded a country version of "You'll Lose a Good Thing" in 1975, which broke into *Billboard*'s Hot 100 at no. 32 on March 20, 1976, and it became his fourth no. 1 hit on April 3, 1976.

Freddy's hits ranked up there with Willie Nelson, Waylon Jennings, and other notables; both songs—**"You'll Lose a Good Thing"** and **"Wild Side of Life"** (No. 13 on *Billboard*'s Top Country Singles early in 1976) (https://en.wikipedia.org/wiki/The_Wild_Side_of_Life)—still ranked above George Jones, Jim Reeves, Charley Pride, Kenny Rogers, Conway Twitty, Mickey Gilley, plus the Charlie Daniels Band, Johnny Paycheck, Glen Campbell, Bill "Crash" Craddock, Eddie Rabbit, and Johnny Rodriguez.

By now, Freddy was an established star in South America, and Meaux also leased "Wild Side of Life" ("*Vida Salvaje*") and "Since I Met You Baby" ("*Desde Que Te Encontre Amorcito*") to MICSA Records in Argentina.

On the week of December 20, 1975, a look at *Billboard*'s Hot Country Singles chart shows that Freddy continued to lead over Hank Williams Jr., Ray Price, Johnny Cash, Waylon Jennings, Linda Ronstadt, Crystal Gayle, Tammy Wynette, John Denver, Dolly Parton, Anne Murray, Kenny Rogers, Barbara Mandrell, Donna Fargo, Tom T. Hall, Brenda Lee, and Moe Bandy.

"**Living It Down**," the first single from the *If You're Ever in Texas* album, made no. 1 in the Canadian *RPM* Country Tracks and peaked at no. 2 in *Billboard*'s Hot Country Singles chart and at no. 72 in *Billboard*'s Hot 100 chart—all in 1976 (https://en.wikipedia.org/wiki/Living_It_Down).

As icing on the cake, "**She Thinks I Still Care**" made no. 3 on *Billboard*'s Hot Latin LPs chart on January 3, 1976.

Freddy rocked country with "**The Rains Came**," the third single from his *Rock'n' Country* album. It also made no. 1 in Canada's *RPM* Country Tracks and peaked at no. 4 in *Billboard*'s Hot Country Singles (https://en.wikipedia.org/wiki/The_Rains_Came).

This archivist could go on and on in what would come across as the Bible's book of Numbers. With that in mind, suffice it to say that **"Loving Cajun Style," "Louisiana Woman," and "Sugar Coated Love"** were another handful of chart busters.

Music Timeline by Music Archivist and Writer Ramón Hernández "The Rockin' Country Hit Albums"

Freddy Fender gave the world a distinct taste of Tex-Mex music with two albums making it to the *Billboard* Album of the Year charts. His famous recipe of recording bilingual songs turned out to be a winning formula.

But there was more to his magic formula. As was evident, Freddy was not your typical country artist. He did not sing with a twang, but he did have a French Creole accent and that, plus his roots in rockabilly, blues, rock, swamp pop and Cajun music, are some of the traits that set Freddy apart from his country peers. And of course, his choice of Mexican standards and bilingual treatment of Anglo-Saxon lyrics also made this Chicano crooner stand out among others.

In 1975, the albums *Before the Next Teardrop Falls*, *Are You Ready for Freddy*, and *Wasted Days and Wasted Nights* albums all swiftly made no. 1 on *Billboard* Country Album charts; *Since I Met You Baby* peaked at no. 10.

A rock 'n' roller at heart, in 1976, Fender showed his true roots with the release of *Rock 'n' Country*, which peaked at no. 3 in the country charts and no. 59 in the year-end overall charts.

Henceforth, all *Billboard* Country Album chart numbers are listed at their peak chart positions. Thus, Freddy's *If You're Ever in Texas*, which contained the very Mexican "I Love My Rancho Grande," reached no. 4 and made no. 170 in *Billboard*'s year-end Top 200 Albums chart. U.S. and Canada's record buyers loved it, and it established Freddy's trend of international sales.

In 1977, *The Best of Freddy Fender* reached no. 4 in and also made no. 155 in *Billboard*'s Top 200 Albums of the Year; *If You Don't Love Me* made no. 34.

A year later, *Swamp Gold*, which brought Freddy's Cajun side to light, came in at no. 44.

Freddy's Selling Power

Freddy Fender was on top and among the no. 1 most-wanted performers in the world. As it turned out, music wasn't a waste of time for the original Tex-Mex superstar after all!

He was the people's choice for rock and country music for the next decade because of his continuous momentum in singles and platinum album sales.

On television, Freddy was in high demand. And aside from his highly successful commercial recordings, Freddy was swamped with requests to record PSAs, country-cooking programs for the Army Reserves, hoedown shows for the U.S. Navy Recruitment Command, plus tailor-written songs, like "Drive Like a Friend," for the Texas Governor's Office of Public Safety.

It was at Sugar Hill Studios that I remember hearing Father record the next theme song for the Houston Oilers football team. It was a very catchy tune, which Bum Philips requested he do, but was never released because the Oilers were moved out of Houston.

Each time Freddy sold one million albums, he received a gold record, and needless to say, he earned many gold records. But in 1979, the standards changed, and sales of one million units were now rewarded with a platinum record, with a gold record now representing sales of half a million albums.

As for Freddy's selling power, it had reached international proportions, and his fans considered him the King of Tex-Mex and country rock!

Playboy has a happy-birthday bash for music artist Mickey Gilley. Gilley introduces Freddy Fender at Gilley's Dancehall, where the movie Urban Cowboy was filmed in Pasadena, Texas. (Courtesy by Michael G. Borum, 1976)

Freddy singing at Mickey Gilley's Dance Club while Gilley plays piano. Three Playboy Bunnies are sent to Gilley's birthday party to entertain. (Courtesy by Michael G. Borum, 1976)

Chapter XIX

"To Our Favorite Son— Welcome Back Home!"

New Zealand Convict
Louisiana Governor Edwards Pardons Freddy
Surprise Home Coming Celebration

Interviewee:
Huey P. Meaux "The Crazy Cajun"

Freddy had an engagement in New Zealand and Australia to perform. That is where they used to send all the f—kups, you know? They didn't allow convicts in their country, and Freddy Fender was an ex-convict. (Google - *History of multiple prisons built, and criminals flown to the islands of New Zealand*).

The minister of Labor and Immigration agreed to contact Governor [Edwin Washington] Edwards from Louisiana and the Office of Business Affairs. They gave Freddy a quick full pardon, which cited him for being a good example as a citizen and humanitarian.

Freddy had done so many good deeds, showing up when he was asked to help those in need and singing without pay. Freddy never hesitated to sing for them, whether it was at a veteran's hospital, nursing home, the Ronald McDonald kids, or wherever they asked Freddy to appear. He was only too happy to sing for them. I know that is a fact!

But they prohibited Freddy from entering New Zealand at that time. Later, they allowed him back in. The governor from Louisiana was very nice to us, giving him the pardon.

At another special event, Bob Hope had their annual children's fund-raisers, and we were good friends. Every artist had two songs to sing at the Hollywood Bowl. The people got up, started clapping, and would not let Freddy off the stage! Bob Hope saw Freddy keep getting all this attention and asked me, "How does a guy that looks like that get so many standing ovations?"

I just laughed and told Bob Hope, "The people just love Freddy!"

So, Bob Hope asked Freddy to keep on singing. Then Freddy thanked the audience and told them, "Bob Hope is the one man in show business who believes in giving a beginner a chance."

"From My Eyes" by Freddy Fender
I crossed international borders all the time, and no one had ever given me any trouble before. I was sorry to disappoint my New Zealand fans. All my concerts were sold out. But after the way the authorities acted, I was very glad to be heading back to the good ole USA! The only thing that upset me was getting back on that airplane for twenty hours and mostly over water. I thought Jaws was waiting down below for me.

After being rejected in New Zealand, Freddy arrived at Houston International Airport, where Southwest Airlines had prepared a grand entrance for him with their stewardesses costumed in Western hats and vests. Then Father was placed onto another Southwest Airlines plane that he thought was headed back home to see us in Corpus Christi. Instead, the flight from Houston flew him straight to Harlingen and inflight, Lone Star Brewery executives served Freddy and his entourage free Lone Star Beer. Little did he know a pleasant surprise "WELCOME BACK HOME" festivity awaited Freddy!

Huey Meaux had coordinated an all-out celebration for him to return home to the Rio Grande Valley on Easter weekend. It was also a heck of an ingenious publicity opportunity. Huey Meaux coordinated this event every single step of the way; they had major sponsors like Lone Star Beer and Kentucky Fried Chicken, along with the San Benito Junior Chamber of Commerce (which included Huey's business agreements from photographers, T-shirt sales, and taco vendors).

So, imagine Freddy's surprise, after a long day's flight, when he stepped off the plane on Saturday, April 17, 1976, at Harlingen Airport, where he was warmly greeted by San Benito's mayor, César González, and a mob of fans who anxiously awaited him. San Benito city officials distinguished themselves by wearing blue coats, and the Harlingen officials wore red coats.

From the airport, he was quickly escorted to San Benito High School to greet all his hometown fans and family, who waited cheerfully at their football stadium. One-third of the Rio Grande Valley seemed to be related to him in some way or another. There was a huge banner in downtown across Sam Houston Boulevard that read, "To Our Favorite Son—Welcome Back Home!"

Next city officials gave Freddy a proclamation and the key to the city. And to top it off, as their favorite son, Balde's arrest warrants and traffic violation tickets that he had accumulated years prior were torn up by Constable Lalo Zepeda. After Freddy signed autographs at the football stadium, it was followed by a parade in his honor.

After the parade, Father was taken to the San Benito Community Building where all the dignitaries, Jess Coker, vice president of Southwest Airlines, the press, and special guests were entertained by mariachis while they waited for Freddy.

When Father arrived, he gave a speech and thanked everyone. He was overwhelmed and elated to see that everyone back home was pleased with him.

Lone Star Sponsorship Concert

That Easter weekend, there was a Rio Grande Valley Livestock Show in Mercedes, Texas where Freddy was to present donations to several worthy causes. He was to wear his big ten-gallon dude hat on stage and auction off the old one for a new customized hat.

However, before the grand finale, Freddy rode around in a Lone Star van, signing autographs at South Padre Island beach to promote his live performance. It was a concert sponsored by Lone Star featuring two legendary singers, Doug Sahm and Tommy McLain, who opened the show for him that evening.

On stage, Freddy mentioned how grateful he was to have the Lower Rio Grande Valley take part in celebrating his newfound success.

The townspeople were so proud of Father, they were just as happy as he was because they admired and needed Freddy more now than ever. He was (and still is) a reminder that dreams do come true, no matter one's nationality or their past.

Freddy had remained humble and true to his roots, just as he had promised his friend Eugene Martell, *la palomia y La Raza* (friends and race) *of La Villita* de San Benito.

"From My Eyes" by Freddy Fender
I never thought I'd see anything like this happen to me!
I was growing up in a one-room dirt-floor shack, sleeping with all my brothers and sisters,
and all of us working as migrant farm laborers to feed the family.
Well, I couldn't even have fantasized this! A whole day set aside just for me!

"Welcome Back Home Freddy!"

Compliments of Southwest Airlines, Freddy arrives in style to the Rio Grande Valley
(Courtesy by Tom Hendrix for all photos of event, *1976*)

Home-based fans anxiously wait to see Freddy Fender live

San Benito city officials (blue coats) on right/Harlingen city officials (red coats)

Freddy receives a customized Lone Star belt and hat made just for him

A baby (fan) *reaches out to touch Freddy*

The Rio Grande Valley paparazzi chases after that magical front page snapshot!

Freddy greets his fans at airport in Harlingen, Texas

San Benito Greyhound cheerleaders

Tammy Lorraine Huerta Fender

Lone Star and Southwest Airline Hosts

Mayor César González and a Lone Star executive ride along with Freddy while he signs autographs.

Courtesy of Kentucky Fried Chicken, Freddy is driven on a convertible to San Benito High School

Kentucky Fried Chicken convertibles making way for Freddy

Multiple Lone Star vans (filled with beer) trail Freddy leading the Easter party

San Benito High School fans wait for Freddy to arrive at football stadium.

Wasted Days and Wasted Nights

*Freddy receives the key to the city of San Benito from Mayor César González.
(Freddy's little sister Elvia sitting behind him on his left)*

Freddy thanks the Mayor and the hometown citizens of San Benito

Tammy Lorraine Huerta Fender

Tammy, Margarita, Danny on Freddy's lap, and wife, Evangelina

The Huerta Family

"WELCOME BACK FREDDY!"
San Benito civic center: Mayor González, Freddy, Huey, Sam Herro and wife Beverly

Lone Star executives with Freddy and his youngest son Danny, by his side.

Huey, Freddy's cousin Margarito Huerta, Freddy, and the eldest of two sons, Sonny Boy

Freddy riding in the Lone Star van on Easter weekend in Port Isabel, Texas

Wasted Days and Wasted Nights

Promoting Mercedes' Lone Star concert at the beach

In Port Isabel, Danny Boy sits on his father's lap. / Freddy signs autographs for the children inside the Lone Star van with plush carpeted ceiling.

Tammy Lorraine Huerta Fender

Freddy is mobbed by fans and signs autographs at Beach Pavilion in Port Isabel.

Wasted Days and Wasted Nights

Freddy smiles as he reads his own publicity bio on the Welcome Back Home Freddy program.

Doug Sahm gives tribute to Freddy's overnight success.
(Courtesy Images of "Welcome Back Home Freddy" by Tom Hendrix, 1976)

Freddy joyfully sings for the Rio Grande Valley.

Freddy's good friend Tommy McLain and Doug Sahm

Freddy gave the Rio Grande Valley a night to remember!

Tammy Lorraine Huerta Fender

Freddy's youngest sister, Elvia, scratching her face, Sylvia is in wonder, and Tammy (sitting behind Elvia on her right) has yet to process the reality that her father's real job is being a full-time singer and a superstar! The Huerta cousins are also in the audience.

Exitos Grandes de Freddy Fender *(with Danny Boy on the album cover)* (Starflite label, 1977)/Friends in Show Business *Freddy Fender and Tommy McLain* (Crazy Cajun label, 1978) (Courtesy of Demon Music Group Ltd., Music Enterprise Licensed.)

Chapter XX

The Mexican Hillbillies

Life into art
A cultural shock!
Sweethearts "My Secret Love"
Tammy's Identity Crisis

"From My Eyes" by Freddy Fender
I had the good fortune of recording a country song, and
all of a sudden, I'm a country entertainer!
If that's what puts the beans on the table, then that's what
I'm gonna stick with! I'd be an idiot if I didn't.

Our first family vacation was our best ever! We flew on a jet to Acapulco. There we stayed at the famous Las Brisas Hotel located on a mountaintop, where we had three individual villas and our own pool. The pool in my parent's suite began from the inside of their bedroom, and you could swim under the water to get to the main pool and out into the open deck. From our rooms, our view was of the aqua-blue-and-green Pacific Ocean. From there, if you looked down the mountain, you could see the pacific islands, boats, and city streets filled with life.

Every morning room service delivered fresh pastries, and our pools were dappled with fresh assorted flower petals. We had an amazing sunset and at night, one could feel as if you could reach up and touch the stars.

At the peak of the mountain is an enormous statue of a crucifix with our Lord and Savior of Souls, which can be seen glowing across the city at night. It is truly a beautiful and breathtaking view of Acapulco.

Father hired a tour guide from Las Brisas to drive us around in one of their hotel's pink-and-white jeeps. We stopped to watch the cliff divers as we had lunch at a nearby restaurant overlooking the deep sea. We didn't really shop much because we weren't in need of anything, and we weren't quite accustomed to extravagant material things just yet. However, I did buy an embroidered, flowered Mexican dress and an oversized sombrero to blend in. Then we rode around town and the outskirts of Acapulco, and even took a ride on a glass-bottom boat. Somehow, we didn't have the heart or stomach to watch the bullfights after eating so many barbequed cow heads.

It had been a pretty and hot sunny day, and Father needed another pack of Kool brand cigarettes to smoke. We were also thirsty and needed something cool to drink, so we had our driver pull over and stop at a local convenience store. Dad and Danny walked inside the store; suddenly, I saw Father grab hold of a guy's shirt and body-slam him into the wall. Dad said, "Don't ever go near my family again!" plus some cusswords, in his harsh warning!

I don't know exactly what the heck happened; I was in our pink-and-white jeep with Mother, being sweet and wearing my straw tourist hat. We didn't ask questions, but the guy must have approached Danny and asked him if he wanted to buy some marijuana. Dad got his smokes, we got our drinks, and we Scooby Doo'd outta there and continued our drive along the Pacific shorelines like regular tourist folks.

Tammy, Eva, Freddy, Danny, and Sonny, in Acapulco, Mexico (1975)

Tammy Lorraine Huerta Fender

Freddy Fender: Television Celebrity

The Dinah Shore *Show* was a popular television program during this time, and Father would often appear on her show. As they quickly became good friends, I would sometimes answer the phone when she called him at home just to chat. In fact, Dad even wrote a song for her called "You Came in the Winter of My Life." As my mother shared with me, Dinah once had a soft spot for actor Burt Reynolds, and that is why he wrote it for her. I don't think Reynolds ever knew how she felt about him. It's sad, yet beautiful. It really is one of the best and most beautiful love ballads Father ever wrote (okay, one of many).

On one of her shows, he wore a beautiful king-size Mexican straw *sombrero* (hat) that was decorated with frilly balls, dangling all the way around the edges. He was so proud of his Mexican heritage and enjoyed telling her so. From the audience, we saw Dad cooking Mexican *chorizo* (pork sausage) mixed with scrambled eggs and onions. Then he placed the mixture of ingredients in flour tortillas and fed the audience fresh *chorizo* and egg breakfast tacos.

The special guests that day were Cheryl Tiegs (a beautiful supermodel), LeVar Burton (a gentleman and wonderful actor who played the part of Kunta Kinte in the heart-wrenching television miniseries *Roots*), and a handsome young English actor by the name of Anthony Daniels (who played C-3PO in the *Star Wars* trilogy). He complimented me on how nice I looked up on the screen as the camera zoomed in on me. I am just glad Father wasn't around to hear him say that to me since Father was very strict with me about talking to boys.

I did fly a few times alone with Father during the hectic schedule laid out for him by Huey. On those (one-nighter) flights going from state to state, Father and I jumped on about a dozen planes within a few days. Most were small private planes; we were always running through airports and being chauffeured around so that Father would make it on time to his day and nighttime appearances. I felt cold on one landing and hot the next. We traveled mostly in the middle of the night while others lay asleep.

We once flew to Tulsa, Oklahoma, Phoenix and then to Orange, California. There I met up with a high school friend and spent the day talking to him while Father signed autographs with O. J. Simpson. They were there to attract customers for a new hardware store that stood up high on a hill.

Father also appeared on *The Tonight Show with Johnny Carson* at NBC Studios in Burbank, California, numerous times. On one of our Father and daughter trips, I was sitting in Father's dressing room when Mr. Carson came in and asked me where my father was. I told him Dad was in the makeup room. So, he (Johnny Carson) sat next to me and made small talk as we waited for dad. He politely asked me if I wanted something to drink. I politely answered, "No, thank you." Mr. Carson waited awhile, gave up and said, "Well, I guess I'll have to go look for the star!"

In 1975 alone, Freddy appeared on *The Tonight Show* three times within a four-month period. In fact, anytime Freddy made an unscheduled appearance on *The Tonight Show* with Johnny Carson as the host, a fill-in cohost, or even different guest hosts, the show would receive very high ratings.

I do remember Father talking about his past involvement with the law. At the time, I know Father didn't have a real PR person, other than Huey Meaux, coaching him about what to say or do. But Freddy could connect beautifully with the audience; he was just magnetic when he spoke with that big, pretty and friendly smile of his.

He also did not hide the facts about his past, either. He talked about his arrest and how he served time in prison. Father was just himself, as he knew no other way to be. He chuckled, and the audience laughed with him; they respected his sincerity, courage, and determination not to let the past interfere with his hopes and dreams.

From then on, Freddy continued to simply share his life stories from his barrio of El Jardín as his appearance on one show led to another and another.

Tammy with a huge straw hat, Eva, and Danny Boy at Los Angeles outdoor Food Market (1976)

Presents: Fancy Dolls & Indian Jewelry

When our father flew out of the country, he would bring back beautiful collectible dolls for me from Africa, Asia, Germany, Holland, India, Scotland, and Switzerland. He even brought back wooden shoes from Holland. Yes, I tried them on but they were very uncomfortable.

He also sang at many Indian reservations and brought home huge pieces of jewelry, like big gold nuggets and turquoise necklaces and bracelets with thick sterling silver. I mean these stones were enormous, nothing like you see today. The native Indians, who are very generous and selfless people, also gave him authentic large feathered hats and custom-made belts. During one of his performances, they even offered him a young native squaw to keep him company. Of course, he shared that funny part with Mother. The people, in general, always went out of their way to please Dad. The American Indians were especially kind and hospitable to Freddy throughout his life and musical career.

Father was invited to several political and historical events; these included dinners and luncheons at the White House, and a presidential inauguration ball. He also met dozens of world leaders, like African kings and queens.

However, Father's favorite and dearest friend was Minnie Pearl. She wore straw hats with the sales tag hanging off the side, as a part of her skits in the *Grand Ole Opry Show* in Nashville, Tennessee. And Father would often come back home wearing one of her crazy hats as well. She loved flying Freddy to her home on a regular basis to visit with her and her husband.

Freddy was also invited to the Smothers Brothers' and Liberace's home. Liberace was a famous pianist and showman whom I had the privilege to see perform in Las Vegas when I was eighteen years old. Father once commented about how he was taken aback when Liberace had served him breakfast at dinnertime rather than in the morning.

Following one of his many tours, Father chuckled as he sat and shared with us at the dinner table about how he had performed at a nudist colony and had seen bodybuilders there such as Arnold Schwarzenegger. They must have held a bodybuilding contest. Hehe.

No doubt about it, Father was in his comfort zone mingling and singing for fans (strangers) around the globe. And as the people would often say after meeting Freddy, "He is just a born natural!"

"From My Eyes" by Freddy Fender
I have no monopoly on struggling or suffering.
There are millions of people we'll never know about going through hell out there!
But I can reach them through my music!

More Than Plenty

Our mother was still being a great homemaker and wife. According to Mother, she felt she was not included in the "rise" of Freddy's career. It was not so much that she didn't want to be involved; she wasn't invited because she didn't fit in with Freddy and Huey's musical lifestyle and "wild side of life."

Mother has always been very shy and introverted. However, she did meet important people and celebrities like President Jimmy Carter, Presidnent George H.W. Bush, Dolly Parton, Minnie Pearl, Barbara Mandrell, Loretta Lynn, Engelbert Humperdinck, Rita Moreno, Tanya Tucker, Johnny Rodríguez, Glen Campbell, José Feliciano, Robert Redford, Christopher Walken, Benjamin Bratt, and many more.

She did make a special trip to England to accompany Father when he sang at the Old Wembley Stadium in London with other stars like Moe Bandy, Willie Nelson, George Hamilton, Joe Stampley, Tanya Tucker, Ronnie Milsap, and Roy Clark. A hardcover book covers this special event at Wembley Stadium, where Jim Foglesong appeared onstage singing with Freddy. She also went to Buckingham Palace and saw the Changing of the Guard with Sam Herro and his lovely wife, Beverly Herro.

In retrospect, she affirmed, "To have someone like Freddy in your life was more than plenty!"

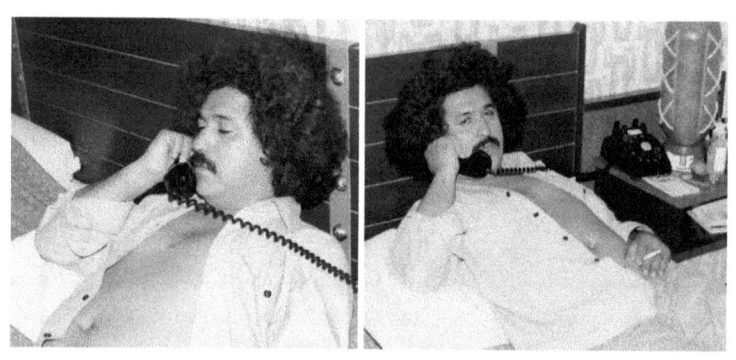

In his hotel room resting before show time

An All White (Anglo) Neighborhood

For our next geographical move, in 1976, Huey Meaux suggested we move to North Houston. The primary reason for the move was that Father needed to be closer to an international airstrip, like George Bush Intercontinental Airport. Huey had to deliver Freddy Fender on time around the world—in sixty days, if possible! We moved to an upper-middle-class subdivision known as Westador in Spring Branch, Texas. Our names had appeared in the local community newspaper, and we were told that the school kids were anxious to meet Freddy's children.

Sonny remained living with Grandmother and Aunt Sylvia in Corpus. He did not approve of our new lifestyle and thought it was too materialistic, so he stubbornly stayed behind. I think he made a wise decision, but Danny and I were younger, so we had no choice but to go along with our parents. Above all, Sonny was an established high school football player, the team needed him and he didn't want to disrupt his winning streak. Dad's little sister Elvia came to live with us, too.

Our home was not a mansion, but to us it was the biggest house we'd ever lived in. It was a four-bedroom house with a three-car garage. Our backyard was a wooded area with tall pine trees and I enjoyed walking through it. In the backyard of our new home, Father had a contractor build a heated pool, a fishing pond, and placed goldfish along with a bridge on top of the pond. Mom decorated our home very nicely with Finger Furniture from Houston. Elvia and I had two toilets and sinks in one bathroom all to ourselves. Danny had his own bathroom too. Mother had a beautiful vanity room in her large bedroom. There was a formal living and dining room, with a beautiful spiral staircase through the middle of our new home. We also had a huge, family-sized stone fireplace. And Father had his own library, where he enjoyed reading when he came home. It was an elegant home, and we now had plenty of food to eat, so what more could a family ask for?

Spring Junior High was only for ninth graders at the time because the school was brand spanking new. The classrooms were filled with different subjects being taught in large, open-air sectional rooms that were carpeted. There were also telephones attached to a few pillars, so you could stop and call out as you walked by. Our lunchroom was a huge sunken-in area. The auditorium bleachers would electronically come up and down. And while we walked from class to class, we listened to pop and rock music coming from the speakers. It was a nice school, I give them that.

On top of this, the children around the neighborhoods loved coming to our home to greet Father. If he wasn't home, they would just linger around until he came back. I understood everyone loved hanging out with Dad. I mean, he was a lot of fun to be around; he was cool like that. Even the elderly enjoyed his presence. But these kids thought of our home as theirs, and we didn't have the heart to ask them to leave. Besides, we didn't mind because we were used to having an overcrowded home.

Freddy's favorite pastime was cruising, so he would often ask the parents or grandparents if their kids wanted to ride along with him in his new RV. I don't know how he personally found the time to meet so many kind country folks, but I know we got a lot of fan mail from them.

Screaming Neighbor

One afternoon, I walked into the kitchen, and I saw this blonde-haired young girl coming out of the laundry room. Now the laundry room was very huge, almost as big as my bedroom. Then Elvia asked me, "Who was that blonde girl that ran out the front door?"

I answered, "I don't know, I have never seen her, why?"

"Well, because she just went screaming out the door and down the street." Then I swore to Elvia that I didn't touch her or say anything to her. I think Elvia assumed I had hurt the girl's feelings.

The next morning, it was all over the local community paper that Freddy Fender's family had a horse's head in his freezer! We kept an upright freezer in the laundry room and an even bigger one in the garage, along with Dad's fishing equipment, motorcycles, and pool table. It was all Dad's stuff. However, the freezers were packed with raw cow body parts! What she saw was a cow's head with its eyes and tongue still intact.

Father would take us to the nearby *matanza* (slaughterhouse) where they would use a sledgehammer to kill the poor cows. There, Father would buy fresh meat and/or order a whole side of a cow. He would preorder the meat over the phone a few days prior to his arrival and normally have it delivered straight to our house. We hadn't been able to buy meat of this quantity before. And it might be a taboo today, but if *la matanza* wasn't going to kill the cow, pig, or goat, Father would have.

Therefore, every single time he came back home from his worldly travels, we knew there would be a huge BBQ party coming up and that dad was the main and only chef. After the meat was seasoned, Father would place the cow's head, along with its tongue and eyeballs, either in the oven or barbeque pit. It was unlike having to dig a hole in the ground and cook it as before—but if he had had to, Father would have.

Tammy and Elvia (in back row) *enjoying handing out candy to trick-or-treaters in our new gringo neighborhood*

A Good Christmas

Christmas came, and each of us had one extravagant present. Dad bought Sonny a new yellow-and-black Camaro sports car; Danny got a new and expensive dirt bike; Mother got her new Lincoln Continental Towncar from Santa; Father got his first telescope; I got a fluorescent purple jukebox for my record collection. After listening to Christmas Carols, Father and I broke out my new records and played them on my jukebox. I remember us both enjoying listening to my record "Low Down" by Lou Rawls in his raspy and sensuous voice. The house was filled with loud music as our family loved to get down to that cool "funk" music. We also listened to hard rock and mainstream pop music. We were never into Spanish music; it just wasn't in our veins or lifestyle.

For New Year's Eve, I threw a last-minute party and played my records on the jukebox for the neighborhood kids while Mother and I fried up some *buñuelos (fried tortillas with cinnamon and white powdered sugar)*. This is our Mexican New Year's tradition. It was a great Christmas Holiday and New Year—and life was good. We were blessed.

Freddy during Christmas at Westador subdivision, in North Houston

Freddy, a Public Figure: Public Domain

During the winter, our heated pool emitted so much steam that some neighbors mistook the steam for smoke. Needless to say, they called the fire department because they thought the Freddy Fender house was on fire! Several fire trucks quickly responded to the call and helicopters were also dispatched to check out the fire, which in this case, was a false alarm.

Shopping malls were a new thing back in the 1970s, and Father came along with us during our first trip to the mall. However, we didn't get a chance to buy anything because, other than at concerts, it was our first public mob encounter. We saw people running toward us—correction, toward Father. We quickly moved aside and left poor Father alone to be trampled over.

It was then that we began to open our eyes and we realized Father was not ours to keep. He really never belonged to us, even way back when Mother had complained to him about his late hours staying out all night. Now Father was a public figure and hence, public domain.

At the mall, there were grandparents and children coming to greet Freddy. They came to hug and kiss him and take pictures of him and they really adored Father. And he was so happy to stop what he was doing and sign autographs for each and every one of his fans. He put them first and didn't exclude anyone from an autograph or picture. He didn't care how long it took or what important person was waiting for him. To him, his fans were always, always no. 1.

Eventually, we had to start going out and doing things on our own without Father because his fame was too disruptive for us. We had never known true normalcy before, but our "normal" wasn't normal anymore. It was almost dangerous.

"From My Eyes" by Freddy Fender
I have not had a bad life because I had nothing to compare it to.
I don't know how my mother did it. We got accustomed to hits and pain.
It gives you a strong backbone, life, and the spirit to accept life, and humor helped me.
I didn't get sad because I didn't realize the seriousness of my journey.
My music and voice had taken me through it.

* * *

We had worked as a family for $3 each a day, and there
were always at least five of us in the fields.
Fifteen dollars a day buys a lot of beans and tortillas!
It's not a life I'd want for my kids, but I don't regret having lived that way myself.
I spoil my kids Sonny, Tammy, and the baby Danny in some ways, but I'm strict in others.
America is my home, and we were all born here.
But I don't want them to lose the sense of their heritage.
I still want them to love their enchiladas!

News of Elvis' Death

It was midafternoon, August 16, 1977, when our chauffeur in Los Angeles was driving Mother and me around. We had several drivers as they had to make several shift changes with us. We were spending a lot of time in California because of Father's impossible television work schedule during the day, plus his massive concerts, singing at night. Father had his own driver taking him to his live appearances in Hollywood and going back and forth to Burbank Studios.

Our family began to spend much of our daily lives riding around in limousines without Father, and our drivers became very close to us. They would even invite us over to meet their families and have dinner.

One late afternoon, our driver stopped at a dry cleaner in LA so that Mother could pick up Father's rhinestone costumes. She went inside to retrieve them. So, I sat up front to talk with the driver a bit while we waited for her to return.

I asked him about a teenage Italian pop singer/idol named Tony DeFranco, on whom I had a crush. The chauffeur said he could take me to their home and arrange for us to meet together. All of a sudden, we heard the radio announcer in the limousine say that Elvis Presley had just died. What came into my mind—other than the shock—was that I clearly remember a conversation among Freddy's entourage figuring out Freddy's schedule so that he could meet with the great Elvis Presley that very month.

After his death, Father was told that his eight-track tapes were found lying around Elvis' home (on coffee tables). But unfortunately, this meeting never came to be. It would have been something special for Elvis to sing one of Father's songs or for them to record a duet together—Elvis and the Mexican Elvis—as both were humble and down-to-earth human beings.

I know they would have liked each other very much. They apparently listened to each other's music, so they probably would have partied hard together too and written some amazing new lyrics. And yes, this is how high Freddy's stardom had risen and how in demand he was. During this period, I had heard that Elvis listed the top ten singers he liked best in some magazine, and Freddy's name was on the very top of that list. However, I have never researched it. That would have been something.

Moving up a few decades, when Freddy was gravely ill, the wife of one of Elvis' band members e-mailed Mother to tell her how Elvis loved to listen to Freddy's music. During Elvis' road trips and after his shows, he would hop on his tour bus and have her insert Freddy's eight-track tapes. She also added how it would annoy the others on the bus because he would continue to play them over and over. Luckily, Freddy read her e-mail and was honored to know that the great Elvis Presley had enjoyed his music all along.

Shortly after Elvis' death, ARV International, a subsidiary of Falcón Records, reissued Freddy's records "No Seas Cruel" and "Jailhouse Rock" in memory of Elvis, "En Memoria a Elvis." Thus, the record label capitalized on both Elvis' death and Freddy's fame and selling power.

"In remembrance of the Great Elvis"
Freddy's first Spanish rock song, "No Seas Cruel" ("Don't Be Cruel") (ARV label)

Tammy's Identity Crisis

In the midst of it all, I somehow lost what little identity I had built for myself as a young girl living in Corpus Christi without Father in the picture. I had had steadiness, direction, plus kind and loyal school friends who liked me for who I was—just me, Tammy. That is the one thing that I never had a problem with—being popular and having lots of friends. Father's rise to fame and overnight success was a culture shock for my whole family. Regrettably, it affected me the most in the worst possible way!

I was trying to find my place to shine, so I tried cheerleading at Spring Junior High School, but they had their team members laid out already. I guess I could have asked to be accepted, but I was not in my element in an all-white school.

I was now in B band being groomed for A band, a marching band. I noticed on my first day of school that one cocky male student standing next to me was a pretty good and strong drummer. I realized he probably played a full set of drums, too. I didn't think I could measure up to him, and so I quit band the next day.

I was used to being the best, but instead of growing the balls to compete with the *gringo* drummer, I took my place as a young lady and found a different place to shine.

My economics class needed a class president, and since I had already been class president back at Cunningham Junior High, I wrote a speech in thirty seconds. I read it aloud, and I was elected. Yes, it may have been less dramatic and competitive than being a percussionist, and I did realize that withdrawing from band class was a cop-out. Therefore, I failed to excel and perhaps even learn from that student drummer.

Sweethearts "My Secret Love"

Before moving, I'd fallen madly in love with a teenage boy in Corpus Christi. He was my "secret love." His name was Victor Hernandez, and he attended a school district different from mine.

It was after graduating from the sixth grade at thirteen that I met my puppy love. Every Sunday afternoon, Ruben, Danny, and I would go to the Gulf Skating Rink, and this was where we met.

Victor had a lot of courage, and there was not a shy bone in his body. He was very charismatic, and I especially enjoyed him smiling at me. He was tall and thin, with shaggy black hair. He had an Afro and dark skin like Father. Victor had no fear, and that's what I liked about him. However, he hadn't met my parents yet.

I was uncomfortably shy, quiet, and naive when it came to boys. But what got my attention about Victor was that he was so self-assured about everything and so cocky about himself. He was inquisitive, and he just wouldn't stop talking to me as I sat quietly listening to him. He had a smile from ear to ear. He was very dreamy.

I enjoyed hanging on to his every word. The more I listened, the more he opened up to me. He was very intriguing to watch. I just responded to him so easily; I just got lost in him.

The music in the background was fast and loud. I don't think we skated to a slow song because Ruben and Danny were monitoring our every move. They both threatened to tell my parents if I didn't allow them to tag along with me everywhere. The lights were dim when a slow song played, and fluorescent lights reflected off a disco ball that surrounded us. It gave us a sense of warmth and romance. I had been caught in the middle of a whirlwind, and all that Victor had to do to get my attention was smile at me with his big pretty lips and teeth.

However, I was really worried and nervous because I was having these feelings for a boy without permission. He asked me to meet him next door at the bowling alley to get away and talk alone for a few minutes. I was so embarrassed I couldn't even look him in the eyes. He gently touched my chin upward to look at him. He made me feel special.

I escaped from my world into his. Victor allowed himself to be vulnerable and trust me. He also took pleasure in kindly teasing me.

Our second secret meeting was near our home at a drive-in burger-and-ice-cream place on the corner of Eighteenth and Ayer's Streets. He bought us an ice-cream soda, and he told me he had something special to give me. It was a beaded necklace with my name, Tammy. This was the fashion in the 1970s (as shown on an earlier photo of me and Sonny in the chapter titled "Broken Promises"). I think this was a way of saying that I was his girl. But the date lasted about twenty minutes. I told him I had to leave. I didn't want to get into trouble or have my family embarrass me in front of him. However, a bigger reason for my wanting to leave was that I saw a rat running in the shop (I know. How crazy is that?).

Once more, we secretly dated and met at a KCCT radio station outdoor event held on the outskirts of Corpus Christi on July 4. It was more of a Tejano music event with some Latin rockers. "Teardrops" had just come out on the market. My family and relatives had all attended the event. Father had just performed and was preoccupied with his new fans when Victor found me, so I sneaked away from the crowd and family to be with him.

We were finally together and alone, but lost among the crowd. Victor was just so full of life! Like every normal teen, he had so many hopes and dreams and knew just what he wanted. He bought himself a guitar and learned to play it in three months. He was so inspired that he wrote me a song.

Victor would serenade me at all hours of the night over the telephone. I remember talking until eight o'clock one morning. I feel these were the best times just listening to him over the phone telling me sweet nothings.

However, the hardest part of our relationship was keeping it a secret from my family. One Sunday evening, after Elvia and I returned from the skating rink, we got dressed up and went dancing at the Boys' Club (called the Record Hop), which was near our home on Barcelona Street.

I wore cowboy boots and a dress that was painted with the image of a lion with a full thick mane, like mine. I had a brunette Farrah Fawcett look-alike hairstyle going on back then.

I bought the dress in Los Angeles and had already worn it to *The Dinah Shore Show*. Victor told me he liked my dress, and we danced to a slow song called "Misty Blue," sung by Dorothy Moore.

After we moved to Houston, I missed Victor's voice. I couldn't get him out of my mind, and I became sadder and more depressed by the minute, and I just stuffed my feelings inward. Victor would call me and send letters. But my parents found out about my "secret love." Then my secret love was no more because my parents ended it.

Immediately after, I began to experience a lack of interest and disconnection from my family and social activities. I was spiraling downward, and my school grades soon reflected this development. It was then that my rebellious and negative behavior began to get the better of me.

I was being monitored while talking on the phone. Mother would hang up on Victor and humiliate both of us. Father, well, he was just stern. It was very embarrassing for us both.

As a result, I began to isolate myself in my room. It was so bad that Mother locked me out of my own room so that I wouldn't stay in there sulking all day. I didn't even want to come downstairs to eat. At nighttime, Mother would unlock my room, and I'd go to sleep. She had bought me this beautiful white bedroom set, which was lovely, but I was too miserable to enjoy our fortunate lives.

I'd sooner rot in my room and disappear from the face of the earth than to live without Victor. The saddest thing is that for two years, he tried so hard to reach me and fight for my parents' approval. Even his parents tried talking to Mother. We wanted our relationship validated but to no avail.

Do you think that perhaps Victor reminded Mother too much of Dad when he was the young and charismatic The Bebop Kid? Mother was so young when she fell in love and married Father?

But Victor was not clubbing me over the head. He was good to me. I don't think we ever disappointed one another. He never took advantage of me or demeaned me in any way. And he never said one unkind word or was rude. We also never held hands or kissed, nor did it cross our minds! We were that innocent.

To me, he was more than my sweetheart or puppy love; Victor was my life!

This is when my parents lost me, and I lost myself. All I know is that it broke my heart into bits and pieces. Why couldn't they have trusted me? They didn't give us a chance or a reason. I don't know why their decision was so final. I just couldn't accept it and go on. Why wasn't that good enough for me? I don't know why, but it affected me deeply.

It wasn't until recently (after Father's passing) that Victor told me he had wanted everything with me—a life with kids, a home, and a lot of music. Now, how romantic is that?

Father's stardom was also making things worse and shielding me from society even more. I just wanted to be normal again. Victor should have been my first of everything in life! He and I should have just eloped!

He was perfect for me. It was the perfect love. Though perhaps a puppy love, it was the sweetest and best-kept "secret love" that never came to bloom.

Victor and Tammy (Sweethearts and my Secret Love)

KCCT Hot Jalapeño radio station outdoor event (1975)
Presents! Welcome to the Neighborhood

The presents kept on coming to our family at Westador subdivision in Houston. Neighbors from far and near were so friendly, they brought Mother flowers, candles, and cookies. Even Elvia and I got a few packages of our own from some of the teenagers. We thanked them and shut the door, and then Elvia and I opened up our gifts. It was full of marijuana. We both just looked at each other. Far out!!! I guess the kids aimed to please us. Honestly, we didn't know what to do with it, so instead of giving it to Mother, I unscrewed the intercom in my bedroom and stuck some of my portion in there. The rest I hid in other places. I just left the bags of weed in there and forgot about it for a while. But the gifts kept on coming. I was hooked up for life!

One day, on the way to school, I was walking and saw some classmates in the woods smoking pot. I decided to join them and I took one toke, and then we walked to school. Smoking made me laugh but would also make me feel paranoid at the same time.

Much to my dismay, Mother was quick to smell the pot smoke on me. I kept getting caught smoking it and she would make Elvia and I—even Danny—blow on her face. Of course, I would be the one who got into trouble. Then she would look into our eyes to see if they were bloody red or glassy. Have you ever tried keeping a straight face while you're stoned? You can't help but to crack up laughing! I mean, look at whom she was married to? She had to have known my eyes were glazed!

One morning, Elvia and I attempted to take the school bus, and that was a mistake. A boy started to complain about how my little brother, Danny, didn't know how to ride his expensive dirt bike and that he had no reason to own one. How was my baby brother any of his business? How else is anybody supposed to learn if they don't get up and ride their bike? He then started in on me and shouted "jelly head!" in front of everyone. It meant pothead. That was the term back in the 1970s. That was a good one! I wasn't used to this kind of treatment and cruelty; I didn't have to endure it in our *barrios* or ghetto, so why here? I wished I had reacted to him because he was that same fool, the one in my band class, the drummer.

Had I stayed in B band, I would have shown him a thing or two. Instead, I let him get the best of me, twice. I allowed the *gringos* to make me feel intimidated or inferior to them. I just didn't like controversy, either. I wanted to be cheerful and active in school like I used to be. I was popular before, but instead, I now felt like a sideshow exhibition.

Okay, the way I saw it at the time, I figured if we were going to have to endure jealous and snobbish kids in our neighborhood every day, I was definitely going to have to continue to smoke weed before and after school just to tolerate them.

One day after school, Elvia, our friend Adrienne, and I walked home together. Elvia decided she wanted to take a shortcut home and walk through a ranch, so she crawled between the barbed-wire fence. Adrienne was next, and then I went in. But when we looked up, we saw Elvia running around and screaming. The bulls were chasing after her! We just stood there, watching her and laughing. I was so stoned that everything seemed to be in slow motion. We didn't know what to do about Elvia. She just kept right on screaming.

So, we quickly got out of there, and Elvia threw herself between the wires and ripped her jeans. We could see her underwear through the backside of her pants. It was definitely both hilarious and a total buzz-kill that day.

Caught in the Act

When we were children, Elvia and I would often fight with each other. When we were teenagers, a few of these fights had us rolling down the staircase, pulling each other's hair and whatnot. Believe it or not, these were still the good times!

One afternoon, the phone rang, and it was Dad calling from Switzerland. So, I thought, great! He is far away now, and Mother has to talk to him for a very long time. I answered the phone in her bedroom and called for her to speak with him.

Mother had been in our bathroom (mine and Elvia's), cleaning out the lower cabinets, which I found suspicious. I knew what she was looking for. She was looking for my marijuana stash. So, I panicked—and quickly made my move!

I immediately went to my bathroom and lifted up the sliding door on the wall that held the water heater, which was next to the toilet bowl. I grabbed my bag full of stash and quickly looked for another hiding place. Sure enough, there she was, standing at the door, looking at me holding on to my bag of weed. I had about eight joints rolled up and a lot more that was loose.

I forgot to lock the door! She just knew I had it in there. She was right as usual. Yup, I was busted! She told me to flush it down the toilet. I pretended to act stupid and replied, "What?"

She said, "You heard me."

I asked, "The rolled ones too?"

She said, "All of it!" Ouch!

At first, it was a lot of fun smoking pot because we laughed a lot. I used to go driving around with friends up and down the spiral ramp at Bush Intercontinental Airport. We couldn't tell if we were going up or down the garage parking levels anymore. It was insane! We were just having some innocent fun, or so we thought.

Then I found Dad's pills in the medicine cabinet. They were sedatives the doctor prescribed for him because he was working under so much stress and such a tight schedule. They were also for the anxiety Mother caused him as she pressured him for never being at home and being jealous about all the women.

Well, I got ahold of those pills, and I wanted out of there! I was hurting because Victor was gone out of my life. He had come to visit me, and I couldn't even sneak out to see him. We couldn't even write to each other.

I was now Tammy Fender to all my new so-called friends. I had left my true friends back home along with what little identity that I had built up. It was precious and valuable to me. I know I could have tried to fit in a little harder at school. Nonetheless, I felt misplaced, lost, with nowhere to shine. Then my emotions took over.

I took the pills and went to school that morning. I was in class when the principal came to get me. I dropped all my books on the floor, and I was staggering to my locker. Everybody could see me struggling and dropping my books because, as I said, it was an open area and there were many classes going on at one time.

The principal wanted to see if I had any drugs in my locker. I couldn't remember the combination. I stood there struggling while I was truly seeing double. I couldn't get it open, and I didn't have drugs on me, anyway.

I barely made it to the conference room. Mom and Dad were sitting there, waiting for me. They had an old friend visiting from Brownsville, and it was someone who was well connected into the drug ring in the Rio Grande Valley. Father wanted me to tell him what kind of drugs I had taken so that they would know what antidote to give me. I just made up some color and description. I was afraid and embarrassed to tell my parents the truth. I don't know why I couldn't tell them that they were just Dad's anxiety pills. I only took one or two. I didn't want to die; I just wanted to escape and not feel lovesick anymore.

Why couldn't I have communicated better with them? I was so miserable without Victor. I should have spoken up and fought for us as he had done, but instead I withdrew and was obedient to my parents' wishes. I felt helpless and hopeless when Mother put an end to it all.

As a result of my actions, I was suspended from school until I got a doctor's note stating that I had no drugs in my system. My parents took me immediately to the doctor's office and found nothing. However, the doctor asked me if I wanted to remove the cute mole on the tip of my nose. It took thirty seconds to remove it (so much for Aunt Mary's red polish *Santeria* cure).

I wished now I had never done those things to hurt my family and myself—but I did. Maybe I was asking for too much. And maybe, had my parents validated our relationship, I wouldn't have had the desire to see Victor anymore. But I guess we will never know that now, nor does it matter.

Mother had high expectations of me, and I was beginning to let my family down. I was their princess. I had so much talent, and I was a thoughtful, sweet girl. But now I was lying, sneaking around, and wanting to escape even further.

I just got lost so fast, and the ride was about to get even faster! I knew I wouldn't be able to hold on and endure it all! God help me.

I had been happy with my simple life. Why didn't they just leave me be, and allow me to live with Amá Máge? Why couldn't they grant me that one wish to be with my sweetheart? I was a good girl.

I could have gone back to Spring Jr. High, but Father thought it was best that we (for my sake) move back to Corpus Christi, right away! As long as I still didn't talk to boys we were okay. I know my parents did not do anything intentionally wrong to me, other than to protect me and give me a better life. However, my issues were not about Victor anymore. I now had to work on the broken trust and the relationship between my parents and me. But I always kept quiet and didn't know that I was allowed to have a voice and communicate. Plus, I didn't know how. Father was always the boss; we just followed his lead.

Back to Corpus Christi: "Adios, Wynn Seale Jr. High!"

Heading back to Corpus Christi brought us all much comfort. Nonetheless, I'm afraid that old friends can also change toward you after a certain lapse of time. It just wasn't the same anymore; everyone knew me as a mega star's daughter. I was also shunned for being the new girl in school, which is typical.

I finally made it to the A band at Wynn Seale Jr. High School. There was only six weeks left for me to complete the ninth grade, and I didn't finish the term at Spring Jr. High. Unfortunately, football season was over and I didn't get to march as much as I would have liked to.

Addressing the class, the band director told me to play a sheet of music on my own. I did what he told me, read the sheet music, and played the snare. After the last bar, I was too bashful to look up, but I heard him holler, "Now, that's the way it is supposed to be played!"

After class, a male band member approached me. He was very upset and angry; I didn't understand why. I didn't know him, but he thought I had just been showing off. After he had his say (words of cruelty), I went into the band director's office and started crying. I had not cried like that, ever! All that frustration I had been holding on to finally came pouring out in buckets. I had so much mucus dripping off my nose; I did not have any tissue to wipe my face, so I used the band director's music notes off his desk. I was a mess, and it wasn't going to get any better, not just yet anyway. I just stayed in his office for a whole hour. I was crying so loud. The instructor just left me alone. He didn't even try to console me. I felt like my mom, *La Califa*, when she was lost as a teenager. *I just couldn't figure it all out!*

Shortly thereafter, Wynn Seale Junior High got to march and play in the Corpus Christi Buccaneer Parade. If I remember correctly, we won first place in our ninth-grade division for our school district. My brother Sonny commented about how his friends would tell him how great a drummer I was. Danny even commented, "Yeah, we saw you marching, and you were twirling your sticks up in the air."

I said, "Oh yeah?" The truth was that the mallet flew out of my hand. I just got lucky and caught it, that's all! Oops! There it is!

I also remember having to wait to get into my own locker because other students had taken over my locker, using it to store their stuff in.

Then, a few days before school ended, a faculty member warned me that I was going to get beat up by several *chicas* (girls) on the last day of school. I had never had any real animosity toward anyone; no one had ever hated me before, or was jealous. Maybe I just thought everybody liked me. I liked them! I was just a happy-go-lucky girl! What happened to me?

Surprisingly, the girls approached me before the week was over, intending to beat me up. That is, until a stranger, a female student, intervened on my behalf. I don't know what she told them, but she talked them out of it.

If it weren't for her, I would have been beaten to a pulp. I wasn't scared, but I would have liked to know what I was fighting for, at least. I guess it didn't matter; I was the new girl and considered white, not Chicana or Mexicana anymore, by my own race. I didn't fit in there, not anymore, and not even in my old barrio.

That day, after school, my angel sat on the front steps of Wynn Seale, seeing me walk off the school grounds safely. I turned back and nodded at the girl who saved me that day; I didn't even get her name. I gave her the look like, "that's cool and thanks."

Mama didn't let me go back to school on the last day for fear of me getting the crap beat out of me. For old time's sake, Sonny drove me back to Wynn Seale in his new Camaro right over the lawn and up to the front steps. Like I said, Sonny could get away with it. He was handsome, boisterous, talented, and admired.

And as for all my band director's comments to the class, he was right! I was a badass drummer! Even if it was just for a moment, I got to shine as a percussionist after all! Adios, Wynn Seale!

From then on, I was no longer Tammy Lorraine Huerta. I was just Tammy Fender (Freddy Fender's daughter).

Chapter XXI

A Powerhouse

"Golden Poor-boy"
The Cripple Creek Band
Freddy's First Movie Role: Pancho Villa!
Live in Concert at Magic Mountain
"The High Point of My Life?"

Freddy and Eva cruising by their home front property on Ocean Drive in Corpus Christi (1979)

"From My Eyes" by Freddy Fender
I came from nothing. I never did have anything in my life.
We used to go riding around these beautiful homes, and I used to ask my wife, "Honey!
Which one of these houses do you want?" and she used to laugh!
(Film documentary *"Comeback,"* 1979)

Rich or poor, Father was always acknowledged as the family's patriarch. He was the eldest, the bread winner, and had an extraordinary, positive outlook on life. He also had a strong sense of self and pride—pride in his roots and who he truly was—Baldemar Huerta from San Benito, Texas. God had given Freddy not one, but many special gifts. Family and friends looked up to him, as he always made sure everyone around him was not without the bare necessities of life.

Now Father was making top dollar as an artist and could afford to buy Mother whatever house she chose. Mother, Danny, and I shopped around for a new home (a small mansion) to move into. After seeing a few elegant homes by Corpus Christi's bayside, Danny and I selected the most beautiful home yet for the Huerta family, located on the waterside of Ocean Drive.

While we lived there, Father would take us cruising around town and the outskirts of Corpus. The funny part is that when we were poor, he'd take us out cruising to the wealthiest neighborhoods to admire their big, fancy homes. And now he was driving us around cruising back to the barrios where we once lived.

Mother recalled a time when Freddy spotted a homeless man sitting down at a corner street, freezing out in the winter cold. She said that Father drove all the way back home just to grab one of his winter coats to give to the man so he wouldn't freeze to death. Now, anyone could have done that! But to Freddy, it meant a lot to him because he was now in the position to give, rather than need a used winter coat himself. He could never forget the hard times of his youth.

Only an original was good enough for Freddy!
A 1948 midnight blue Cadillac (1978)

Dad's Toy Collection

Father began to collect all kinds of classic show cars. He was also adamant about having their original parts intact. He had a 1938 green Pontiac with white walls, a 1939 burgundy Pontiac pickup truck, and a 1948 midnight blue Cadillac (shown above), which had a bullet hole on the side of the passenger door. It once belonged to George F. Parr and his wife, Dottie Parr. George was known as the Duke of Duval County in Texas, and they had their initials on the outside of the car doors. Freddy also had two decorative shining show cars, a 1956 Chevrolet and a 1957 Chevy. While filming a local Chrysler commercial, Father received a new vehicle from the Chrysler dealership as a perk, plus a replica of a red jeep (a miniature drivable toy car) that the character Tattoo used on the television series *Fantasy Island*. Danny often drove the little jeep in our backyard.

In addition, we had a small silver speedboat, one executive motor home for traveling, and a smaller RV for shopping and fishing. Oh, and of course, he had to have a motorcycle (a Hog). He also had two tour buses parked outside at times.

On one occasion, he traded his car for an older model while stopped at a red light with a total stranger. When in town, Dad would pick us up from school in his monster classics and embarrass the heck out of us.

Freddy and President Jimmy Carter

My baby brother, Danny, grew up to be handsome and charismatic, just like Father. He attended Cullen Jr. High along with many of the children of political families from Corpus Christi. Danny was very popular at school and some of the kids would linger at our home for hours just to wait for him to return. During Halloween, out of state politicians would bring their kids over to our house for a trick-or-treat party. Mother liked setting the dinner table with snacks and sweets for the children. She always went out of her way during the holidays to please everyone. She was such a good mom and enjoyed seeing us happy.

Father had the privilege of performing for several U.S. presidents during his lifetime. The first was for former president Jimmy Carter. Freddy was invited over for a special reception held at the White House, and President Carter enjoyed his company so much that he asked Freddy to join him for a personal one-on-one luncheon. During their conversation, the president asked Father what school his youngest son attended. Father told him that Danny went to Cullen Jr. High in Corpus Christi.

About a week later, Danny's school received a letter from President Carter; however, the school faculty didn't quite know for whom the letter was written. The school gathered that it must have been meant for some of the local political families' children who attended Cullen Jr. High. A few of the students at school were selected and given credit and news coverage. It had been an innocent mistake made by the school faculty, and Father told Danny to keep quiet so he wouldn't disappoint the children.

The students looked so happy when they took a photo-op for the local newspaper. It was posted on Thursday, October 25, 1979. The headline read "A Political Greeting Mystery at Cullen Jr. High." Several students held up an oversized printed copy of it (poster), handwritten and signed, "Greetings & Good Wishes to Cullen Jr. High, Corpus Christi, Texas October 2, 1979, Sincerely, President Jimmy Carter." We kept a copy of the newsprint.

The letter had been intended for Danny Boy, and he was a very good sport about the whole thing. Moreover, a United States president took the time to do something so thoughtful, to honor someone else's child and bestow a bit of prestige on their school. President Carter and First Lady Rosalynn were very kind to us, and our family enjoyed receiving their holiday cards throughout the years.

"From My Eyes" by Freddy Fender
We used to like the speeches of Jimmy Carter.
I remember when I was in the Marine Corps in the barracks.
We would sit around and listen to him talk on the radio.
He would sound like he was singing. We just couldn't believe how beautiful this man talked!

President Jimmy Carter and First Lady Rosalynn Carter greet Freddy Fender and road manager Sam Herro at a reception held at the White House. Freddy performed at gala. Salute to Country Music Gala at Ford Theatre, October 2, 1979.
(Courtesy of © President Jimmy Carter Library)

Freddy's Insight on Watergate Scandal

One of Freddy's keen gifts was that he had a photographic memory. It was amazing; he could remember every word, name, date, image, and every person he ever met, going back as far his childhood. He was also highly knowledgeable about world history, its political leaders, their military warfare tactics, geographic layout, and machinery such as tanks, planes, and other weaponry. He also enjoyed naming all the U.S. presidents backwards. We often asked him to recount the list over dinner.

When Freddy was not singing, he would read while he ate breakfast, lunch, and dinner. We had to keep multiple history books for him around the house to read because that was his personal pastime. There wasn't anything you could tell Freddy about world history that he didn't already know about and had examined. As a matter of fact, if you didn't have your facts straight (and regardless of whether a person was a history scholar or political leader) he would stop you and correct you immediately. Just like his music, this is one area that Freddy knew what he was talking about; otherwise, Freddy never opened his mouth unless he was asked and knew his facts first. Again, he was always a matter-of-fact kind of man.

Tammy Lorraine Huerta Fender

When a radio talk show host and political analyst named Dick Maurice took interest in Freddy while interviewing him on his show, Maurice asked Freddy about his opinion with regard to the Watergate scandal. As usual, Freddy spoke to him matter-of-factly.

During the interview, Freddy simply implied that former president Richard Nixon had just gotten caught! He felt that Nixon, like so many others, wouldn't be the first or the last president in our history to commit such an unethical and illegal act for the sake of their political party or for the security of America.

It was not that Freddy had condoned the unfortunate incident. Father was just being blunt, honest, and to the point about the reality of politics. To think otherwise was to be too gullible and closed-minded. Soon after, Nixon sent Father a letter thanking him, perhaps for shedding some objectivity about how some great leaders, whether here or around the globe, have practiced politics. He also autographed a biography for Freddy, titled *President Richard Nixon's Memoirs*.

All I'm saying is that Freddy knew his place in the world as a music artist. Yes, Freddy was a self-taught historian, and read thoroughly the biographies of world leaders, and not just about the United States; however, he didn't like commenting on politics much because that wasn't his arena or how he made a living.

And for the millions of people who came to personally know Freddy, they too felt his meekness, realness, and warmth. But they also realized that Freddy Fender (the man) was more than just a "rich poor boy" or a "golden throat"—he was someone they could trust and depend on—and who spoke from the core of his heart and meant it. He was selfless.

Moreover, when Freddy told you he would do something, there was no reason for a contract or handshake from him. Freddy's word was all you ever needed. No matter what, he never went back on his word—never.

RICHARD NIXON

LA CASA PACIFICA
SAN CLEMENTE, CALIFORNIA

March 7, 1979

Dear Mr. Fender,

I greatly appreciated your generous comments on the Dick Maurice radio show.

It occurred to me that you might like to have a copy of my Memoirs for your personal library and am sending one under separate cover, appropriately inscribed.

With warm regards,

Sincerely,

Richard Nixon

Mr. Freddy Fender
5626 Brock Street
Houston, Texas 77023

President Richard Nixon thanks Freddy for his impartial comments with regard to Watergate on the Dick Maurice radio show. (March 7, 1979)

Freddy Fender's Shining Era with The Cripple Creek Band: Billy Hogue (steel guitar, guitar, and vocals), Dennis Winton (guitar and vocals), Rick DeArmond (drums and vocals), Robert Hoffman (bass and vocals), and Sam Beck (harmonica, guitar, and vocals)

Interviewee:
Dennis Winton
The Cripple Creek Band, lead guitarist

Freddy was used to "pickup bands," all of his life. So, when in either the West Coast or the East Coast, he would have a band out there already standing by.

Jim Halsey, promoter and booking agent, had the most impressive country stables in the business. He was from Independence, Kansas, and was based out of Tulsa, Oklahoma. One of his artists was country legend Roy Clark, who had a bass player named Rodney Lay, a bandleader who played for Roy's band for twenty years. Lay had musicians like Sam Beck and me, and a few others, back up some of Halsey's acts, like Jodie Miller, Wanda Jackson, and Roy Clark. Not long after, their guitar player, Sam Beck, started his own band, and I was lead guitarist. They quickly attracted other talented musicians, like steel guitarist Billy Hogue and drummer Rick DeArmond.

Our name was the Cripple Creek Band! We were just a bunch of good old country boys from Tulsa, Oklahoma. Our job was to make sure that Freddy Fender shined like a true star during the peak of his success.

Our first job with Freddy was coming up at a festival known as Worlds of Fun in Kansas City, Missouri, around 1977. Rodney Lay had hired us to back up Freddy and go there. But the band didn't meet Freddy until thirty minutes before the show. Then Rodney Lay gave us Freddy's playlist.

We told Freddy we had been given the playlist and we were ready for the show! Freddy said to us, "Let me see the list!"

I handed him the playlist. Freddy looked it over and said, "This list is two years old, man. I am only doing four songs tonight!"

We just about had a stroke.

So, Freddy started naming off songs to us, and we never even heard of them. But that was Freddy's show! He named off another song, and I said, "Nah!"

Then Freddy names another song. Again, "Nah!"

Freddy reached down, opened his guitar case, and then opened a bottle of tequila. He took the lid off it, turned the bottle over, and just went *glug, glug, glug*! He looked up and said, "Boys, we're in trouble!"

He then named off another song, and once again, I said, "Nah."

Freddy went into that pool of songs and asked, "How about 'Rain, Rain, Rain'?"

In frustration, I hollered, "No!"

Freddy responded, "What's the matter? You're a bunch of rock 'n' rollers. This is my latest hit, man!" *Glug, glug, glug.* "Shit, man, we're in trouble!"

We did that first show, and it was pretty loose. After the second show, we got hold of some of Freddy's albums and tapes and went to a friend's home in Kansas City, Missouri. We spent the night at a friend's house and listened all night long to Freddy's songs, and it worked out.

When we had the next show, it was immensely better. If you make a mistake onstage, you don't let on; you just follow Freddy.

Freddy had been looking for a band to back him up in the Midwest, and that was going to be the Cripple Creek Band. After we did four or five shows together, Freddy decided he wanted to carry his own band from there on [The Cripple Creek Band].

First nights with The Cripple Creek Band, Worlds of Fun show, Kansas City, Missouri

Freddy's first two nights with The Cripple Creek Band at Worlds of Fun (1977).

Interviewee:
Dennis Winton

At another venue, while Freddy was hot on all the charts, we were in Las Vegas. We were there three times with him, and the first time was for a whole week; the second, two weeks; the third time was three weeks in a row in 1978.

The week before we got there, the entertainment director told Jerry Lee Lewis that he could use his grand piano, but to stay off it because Jerry gets on the pianos a lot. On the third night there, Jerry Lee got up on the piano, and the crowd loved it! It was a great show. But after the show was over, the entertainment director told him, "I told you to stay off that piano." So, Dennis thought they might have fired him for that.

A week later, we played at the same club and for the same entertainment director. And on the second time being booked there, opening night, Freddy shows up fried to the max!

He was in a trance, walked onstage, and stood about two feet away from Sam. Sam, his bass player, just stared at him. Freddy wouldn't start singing on cue. Finally, he turned around and started singing, but from behind the band members. Then Freddy is behind us, about half a major off, and stays that way through the whole song. We're telling ourselves, "Oh, don't let this be, this is opening night!" He was really waxed!

They get to the second song, which was quite appropriate. It was "Please Don't Tell Me How the Story Ends." Freddy was in his early stages of diabetes and had begun to take medication. He also had some sedatives given to him from his doctor because Freddy was having trouble at home with his wife, we thought.

So, Freddy's night didn't go well with mixing it with beer. He fell backward, and his head went right through the bass drum!

Then I stopped playing and reached down to give Freddy a hand, but he didn't take it. He rose himself up on one elbow, but his lower legs were still lying on the floor, and Freddy finished singing the song just like that, as though it was part of the show.

Then he got up and stumbled toward the crowd. I thought, *Oh, no, he is going to do a nosedive into the crowd!* Chairs started to clatter and bang; then people started to get out of the way. Jerry Walton, the band's manager/bus driver, ran out and grabbed the microphone away from Freddy. He said, "Here is the Cripple Creek Band!" and took Freddy off the stage. We went right into a song. That was at the Silver Bird Hotel in Las Vegas, and Wayne Newton was in the audience. The next day, it made Las Vegas headlines!

You would have thought there was a fire the way everyone ran out of there so fast! By the time they got finished with the first song, everybody came back in and sat down. Walton came back out and made a formal apology. He told the audience to take their time, go to the front door, and get their money back. We thought this was the end of us and Freddy because they just fired Jerry Lee Lewis a week before just for standing on the piano. [Of course, Mr. Jerry Lee's dismal incident is neither relevant nor a proven fact as he was never let go.]

The next morning, Walton and Freddy's band arrived at the entertainment director's office. Walton went in there to ask him to let them finish their engagement. The director said, "Yes," so Freddy Fender and the Cripple Creek Band did two great shows that night until they fulfilled their contract.

Wayne Newton returned the next night, and so did other big Las Vegas celebrities, to see Freddy perform again. But Freddy went all out and really made up for it! He did some great shows thereafter. Freddy got great reviews after that.

Sam Herro, who was a very big man, had no neck. He had big eyes and bushy eyebrows. Well, this one guy comes up to us [the Cripple Creek Band] and says, "We need to know what to do with these lights here, and we were talking to this Mafia-looking guy, and he told us to come talk to you." Well, the band and I knew right away who had sent him; it was the Phantom, Sam Herro.

Now for Walton, he had this thing about taking the band through the bad side of town and getting us lost. And it so happened that when we did get lost, it always was in that part of town. The band was always scared riding with Walton. But he was a funny and sweet character.

Bus driver Jerry Walton (splashing water at the band)

Freddy with The Cripple Creek Band and Jerry Walton

Wasted Days and Wasted Nights

Freddy and The Cripple Creek Band

Interviewee:
Dennis Winton

Once, we were in Canada riding (without Freddy) in his executive motor home, which we used when the bus broke down. It was about 2:00 a.m. Sunday following a Labor Day weekend show, when the fuel pump went out and we missed the first show. Freddy was already at the venue and did his show with somebody else's band. He told them he wouldn't do the second show until his band got there. People were real hot and upset when we got there so late. As we arrived, they were throwing beer bottles at the motor home because we were so late getting there.

However, when everybody was together in the bus traveling, it was a three-ring circus. When you're on a bus on a long journey, you get "rum dumb." You get giddy. Everything starts looking different, and everything starts looking just a little bit funny. The bus that Freddy owned was an old bus. It was a 1969 Flexible. Country singer Sonny James bought it brand-new, and then country singer Tanya Tucker took it over and drove the wheels off it. So, then Freddy wound up with it, buying everything used, as always.

But it was such a good price; he thought that something must be wrong with it, and there wasn't. Except later, he found out that the Flexible Company had gone out of business and you couldn't get the parts for it anymore. That is why he got it so cheap.

Somewhere in Ohio is where our band was driving through when the bottom of the bus had fallen out and the radiator was a goner. So, they wheeled her off the road and pulled into a warehouse. It just so happened that it was the main warehouse where the Flexible Company had once been in business. Walton went in there and asked them about Flexible Company because they needed a radiator. The guy told them that they were welcome to look out back. Guess what, lo and behold, they had a brand-new radiator. Our rotten luck turned into amazing good luck. Can you believe it?

At a show in Albuquerque, New Mexico, there were wall-to-wall people in Freddy's dressing room. We were told we had five minutes to get dressed. But there was no place to dress because it was filled with people. There was a big area, and then it narrowed down into a hallway about ten to twelve feet wide, going back about twenty feet. So, the band just walked all the way back, and we changed into our costumes. Freddy was standing there talking to the governor of New Mexico and his wife. Freddy was right there looking at us right over the governor's shoulder toward the hallway.

Sam was down there and mooning Freddy. So, here's Freddy trying to keep a straight face as he spoke to the governor and his wife. This was around 1980. The band members couldn't applaud Sam because the governor and his wife would have turned around. That was one incident Freddy didn't mention anything about, that night. Freddy always joked about his life experiences onstage.

Freddy entertains his audience in Las Vegas With The Cripple Creek Band (1978).

Freddy and The Cripple Creek Band in Las Vegas

At the Silverbird Hotel in Las Vegas!
With close good friend actor/comedian George "Goober Pyle" Lindsey from sitcom
The Andy Griffith Show/Major Riddle, owner of the Silverbird and
Dunes Hotel in Las Vegas, Freddy and Huey Meaux.

"*FREDDY FENDER: Also starring George Goober Lindsey*" at the Silverbird Album *The Tex-Mex—A Driving Force in Country Music*

Interviewee:
Dennis Winton

Another Freddy Fender moment happened on a rainy day, and we did not have a good turnout. Our bass player Robert needed to go pee really bad. They looked at the playlist and only "Teardrops" and "Wasted Days" were left. So, Robert thought he could make it through the end of the show. They got halfway through "Teardrops," and the bottom falls right out of the sound. It really just sounded terrible!

When the band looked around, they saw Jerry squatting down. He was pretending to play the guitar. Walton can't play nothing; he can't even play the radio! We found out later that Robert's electric bass had shocked him when he had stepped backward into a puddle of water. He was jolted by the shock! Robert starting peeing down his leg and couldn't stop peeing. That's why he quickly handed his bass to Walton and took off. Robert was just gone!

One thing that impressed me about Freddy was that he would wait and sign autographs until there was no one left to sign for. Freddy Fender fans are still Freddy Fender fans! It is just like Elvis Presley fans. They will always be his fans until the day they die.

Interviewee:
Rick DeArmond
The Cripple Creek Band, drummer

It was in Pennsylvania, and the fans stopped us. They were asking us for beer cans. "Yeah, we'll give you a beer," I said.

They said, "No, no, no! We don't want a full beer. We want the ones Freddy drank out of!" That was wild! He was a big deal to a lot of these people.

I remember two places the Beatles had played at. One was Shea Stadium in New York and the Cow Palace Arena in California. For us old country boys, that was real impressive.

At the Cow Palace, what impressed me was that I was expecting to see more of an older crowd of adults and cowboys, but they were young teenagers and a whole span of people.

And after every show, the women would line up and have him sign autographs. He was very big in the East and West Coasts, in California, New Mexico, Arizona, Colorado, New York, Pennsylvania, West Virginia, Ohio, and Florida. Freddy had fans in the country fields and rock fields. It was just amazing to see for us country boys from Oklahoma!

Gigantic Annual "Ranch Party" Freddy Fender and The Cripple Creek Band (1978)

Interviewee:
Billy Hogue
The Cripple Creek Band, steel guitarist

Freddy was like Elvis in some places. When the bus would drive into the venue or arena, everybody would just rush to it.

Tammy Lorraine Huerta Fender

Freddy and The Cripple Creek Band (1979)

Starring Freddy Fender as Pancho Villa!

Freddy always wanted to become a big Hollywood actor. He was extremely happy when asked to play the role of the infamous Pancho Villa in the movie *She Came to the Valley*, starring Ronee Blakley, Dean Stockwell, and Scott Glenn. The author, Cleo Dawson, recalls her childhood when she and her family befriended Villa and his soldiers. They would often feed and shelter them at their ranch in Mission, Texas, during the Mexican revolt of President Porfirio Diaz's last term.

We stayed at the beautiful and historic hotel La Posada, which is now named Casa de Palmas Renaissance in McAllen, Texas. (Even today, I often still like to visit their hotel because it brings me great memories of my late father and our family together.)

Our family got to meet Pancho Villa's fifth wife, Luz Villa. She was eighty-four years old and in a wheelchair. She made it clear and was vocal in stating that Freddy was not anywhere near as handsome as her late husband Pancho. I can relate; if anyone dared try to act like my father in a movie, Freddy would be a very tough act to follow, let alone to sing and look like him.

The production was filmed in Mission, Texas, and my grandmother and I got to play small parts as Villas' *banditas* (women bandits). And we were armed to the hilt.

I can be seen onscreen running past Dad as he shouts at me to hurry up and give aid to his soldiers. It was very exciting filming at night in the woods with horses, wagons, and actors while wearing Mexican military uniforms and carrying pistols.

Now that I was a teenager, I got to witness what Father was truly like in action other than what I knew of him as our strict dad at home. What was so neat about him was that he had this natural ability to enthuse others about his projects. They didn't care what it was about as long they got to be around Freddy.

Father even asked his ninth-grade math teacher, Mrs. Gosset, who lived in Mission, to play the character of a schoolteacher for the movie. In addition, the townspeople of Mission held a parade for this great historical event. During the event, Danny Boy rode on a horse with Father while waving back to the cheering crowd.

Of course, Freddy always made time to visit with his aunts and uncles in San Benito. He even drove through El Jardín in a pink convertible Cadillac as people, especially the elderly, came out of their homes and onto the street to greet him. Freddy had remembered every one of their names; he even asked about their relatives, and they were touched that Freddy had not forgotten them on his way to the top.

Two more albums were released with Freddy wearing his Pancho Villa attire, one on ABC-Dot labels and GCP-Stereo titled *Freddy Fender El Vino Al Valle*.

Freddy with Author Cleo Dawson "She Came to the Valley"
(Director/producer Albert Band and producer Frank Ray Perilli, January 11, 1979)

Freddy with Luz Villa (Pancho Villa's fifth wife) *in wheelchair. (January 11, 1979)*

Freddy in costume as the infamous Mexican soldier and bandit "Pancho Villa."

On the movie set, late at night—Oni Villarreal (Villa's soldier), Tammy (Mexican bandita), and Freddy (as Pancho Villa)

Also starring Margarita Huerta as Doña Máge (Freddy's mother), *playing one of Pancho Villa's most loyal and dangerous banditas*

Wasted Days and Wasted Nights

Huey Meaux and Tammy

While in the Rio Grande Valley, Freddy visits his uncles and aunts at Tía Lola's house.
Porfirio, Dolores, Freddy, Margarita, and Ovidio

Tammy wearing a Freddy Fender T-shirt at Magic Mountain, with candy-apple vendor

Super Stardom: Fans Await

Six Flags Magic Mountain is an amusement park in Valencia, California, and another of the many fun venues where Father would perform. Right after Father's shows, the first Freddy Fender memorabilia that would sell out (other than his eight-track tapes and T-shirts) were the assorted colors of ladies' panties with Freddy's face plastered on the booty side.

I was in my early teens at Magic Mountain when I witnessed a pregnant woman raise her blouse for Dad to sign his autograph on her huge belly. I was a little offended with her because that was my father sitting up on a platform being mobbed and hollered at; I was also very green. Like most teenagers, I was at an impressionable age, and a late bloomer, I must add. My father was a strict family man, especially with me, his only daughter, and I didn't appreciate her behavior. While traveling with Father, I saw many things that opened my eyes to the fast pace of his lifestyle—much more than I cared to know or admit.

After his second show, my family and I waited for him in the limousine in a dark isolated parking area behind the venue. We had our chauffeur at the wheel with the motor running. Father came inside, sat, and explained to Mother that he could not leave the premises just yet. He said that management wanted him to do a third show. Father wasn't happy about being put into a situation where the buyers demanded more of him other than what he originally agreed to on paper. Father always gave the crowd his very best and he always stayed behind to sign every single person's autograph—no matter how late, tired, or how sore his wrist was.

His concern was that if he didn't perform a third show, he might not be invited back to Magic Mountain.

The people from Las Vegas and around the state of California must have heard Freddy Fender was nearby and quickly jammed up the venue that weekend. So, Father took off to do his third show while Mother, Danny, and I went back into the park to amuse ourselves a while longer.

At ten years old, Danny took off without supervision to enjoy himself on the rides. And I bided my time by talking to a candy apple vendor.

Then I heard loud cheering, whistling, and applauding from afar. I could also hear The Cripple Creek band start to play Father's music. I could always distinguish Dad's guitar picking anywhere, because it was a cross between J. J. Cale and Stevie Ray Vaughan; Dad would also add his own funk, rhythm and blues, and Tex-Mex jambalaya!

However, it really hadn't sunk in for me yet as to why Father was in such high demand and hardly ever at home. But this time, instead of being shielded as usual by bodyguards (who would walk me to the bathroom and make me wait in a safe and hidden place away from the mob), I would have my chance to go alone and sit and view Father as others did. I could actually go see for myself what all the fuss was about—in the limelight!

Ladies and Gentleman, Here's Freddy Fender!

It was past ten o'clock at night, maybe later, and I was tired of walking around the amusement park alone. Then I made my way up the bleachers in the dark and found myself a vacant seat way up high.

There were many people seated at this outdoor, dome-like arena. I knew Mother was close by and must have been waiting for Dad backstage; she was introverted and preferred to be behind the scenes and away from the crowd. So, we each waited for Father's last performance as we saw fit.

The Cripple Creek band was playing "Jambalaya," a Louisiana tune turned into a national hit by Hank Williams. And I could see that the audience, as well as the band, were anxiously waiting for Freddy to appear on stage. Finally, he made his grand entrance with a big smile, waving at the folks. He wore a strikingly brilliant, iridescent country and Western rhinestone suit. For several years now, his tailor, Jim Harvey, designed an array of brilliant-colored suits for Freddy that were stunning. He was on the spindle top and he shined like a beacon.

Father started his show by riling up the crowd and sang the lyrics "Good-bye, Joe, me gotta go, me oh, my oh!" He gave them a few more upbeat Cajun songs like "Loving Cajun Style" and "Sugar Coated Love." Once he had them going, that's all he needed.

With a subtle change of expression, he then began to sing passionate love ballads such as "Holy One," "Thank You My Love," and "A Man Can Cry." Then he added "Mathilda," "Wild Side of Life," "If You Lose Me You'll Lose a Good Thing," "Tell It Like It Is," and "Vaya Con Dios."

Once again, he'd stir us up shouting his *"Ajúa's!"* and *"ay, ay, ay!"* and got people off their seats, jumping up and down with "I Love My Rancho Grande," stirring up the crowd as Huey had taught him. After that, he played the rock tune he wrote for Mother from the 1960s, "Mean Woman."

On each song, he made a habit of moving his head as he hit a low or high note, and as he did his big, kinky, salt and pepper Afro (which was one of his signatures, along with his thick Frito-bandito mustache) would bounce and move along with him.

A Global Scholar of Communication

The Cripple Creek band were in awe of Freddy. He sang and dominated the crowd. However, the tricky part about being a musician onstage with Freddy was that you didn't know where he was going to lead you from one night to the next with his playlist!

You had to keep up with him because Freddy was entertaining many different cultures here and abroad. He knew, only too well, how to enchant a crowd by playing different music genres. Freddy could play it all and had already done it all, as displayed in his early recordings; he knew exactly what the people demanded of him, and he aimed to please. Even when he sang half of his songs in Spanish the people just loved his voice. But Freddy had to roll like that! So, the band had no choice *but* to follow Freddy's lead and playlist from one gig to the next!

To give everyone a short break, Freddy would pause and speak with his audience. He put the crowd at ease by telling them a joke or two and shared his remarkable past and current life experiences. Amazingly, he spoke to them in their languages, such as Cajun, Chinese, Dutch, French, German, Italian, Japanese and other languages he taught himself while embracing, being intimate with, and befriending people around the world.

His fans might not have known the English language so well, but they knew Freddy's heart was genuine. And that is all they cared about, that he was one of them—a *real* and down-to-earth person.

"The Rains Came"

One of my all-time favorites of Father's is "The Rains Came." It is a heartfelt love ballad. When Freddy would sing the chorus to this song, Billy Hogue, the steel guitarist, would come in and follow. Hogue was seventeen years old with long, shaggy brown hair and blue eyes, and was therefore dreamy.

When you heard Father singing the chorus, "Rain, rain, rain, rain," you can hear the steel guitar repeat every note Freddy sang. Young Billy Hogue had the audience and I captivated. It was breathtaking to hear Father and the Cripple Creek play this tune because the whole band was beautifully synchronized.

During the middle of the show, Father would introduce the band one by one. And when it came down to Hogue, he would tell the audience, *"From Oklahoma, on steel guitar, here's Billy Hogue! And for you ladies out there that might be interested, he's still a virgin!"* Of course, that helped Hogue hook up with the ladies after the show, and Hogue thanked Freddy many times over.

Once, Hogue tried talking to me at our home on Ocean Drive when the band spent the night prior to a nearby performance, but Father cut him off "dead on the spot" with that Freddy Fender look that could kill. Father had warned him he would kill him if he ever spoke to me. He respected Freddy and was also scared of him. (In

2008, Hogue told me about that incident during his interview with me and we had a good laugh about it over the telephone. But we both knew that Father wasn't joking.)

My "Secret Love"

Next, the spotlight on Father was completely turned off and all you could hear in the background were the instruments and Hogue's steel guitar as they started to softly play "Secret Love" (music composed by Sammy Fain with lyrics by Paul Francis).

Suddenly, everyone got so quiet that I could honestly hear a pin drop. (I remember thinking this to myself.) The love ballad was being sung to us like a story being told in an opera, yet it was Freddy Fender, the balladeer. He was singing with immense feelings of distress as if it had just happened to him.

Then a romantic, deep-red light lit up Freddy's face and upper body while it slowly changed into an array of different colors. There he was, with his rhinestones glistening and dazzling all over the stage, curtains, instruments, and across the audience's faces. Dad looked downward with his dreamy eyes; for an instant, he shut them while holding on tightly with one hand to his microphone. On cue, he slowly opened his eyes and lifted his head high; he began to sing gently to us, like a bird with a burning desire to tell us of his passion and the agony of love.

As Freddy tenderly sang this lovely and delicate song, you could hear every note and word crystal clear. That is one thing people always noticed about Freddy's singing—that they could hear the emotion of the lyrics in his voice regardless of his strong and beautiful Mexican accent. But there wasn't any accent, only Freddy singing.

He was just gleaming as we all watched him steadily while trying not to blink and miss a beat. It seemed as if, for those few moments, time stood still for all of us as we sat there mesmerized.

That is when I looked around and saw the expression on people's faces. They seemed like they were in a trancelike state, just staring at my dad. I could see the questions on their faces! "Where did he come from? Who is he? Is he rock or country? Is he Mexican? Well, I thought he was Anglo! And how can he sing like that? Why does he sing with so much love and sorrow?" They seemed baffled! So was I!

You could feel in the air that something was about to happen; the music being played by the Cripple Creek Band carefully followed Freddy's voice. Everyone was on the edge of their seats.

My father was such a romantic person, and when he sang, he didn't care if men were in the audience. Without shame, he held nothing back! And when he sang the lyrics "I'm so in love with you," you could see in his face and eyes that he really meant it, as if he were telling her right then and there.

Freddy held his energy and breath (just as he learned to do from the Queen of Tejano, Lydia Mendoza). Then, he released it when he opened his mouth wide to reach the highest tenor note he could possibly sing. The song "Secret Love" is one of the most beautiful love ballads Freddy ever sang. *(Music composed by Sammy Fain and lyrics by Paul Francis Webster)*

But it was Huey Meaux who had pushed and pushed Freddy into reaching those higher notes to his fullest potential. Huey told him to do it! So, Freddy excelled and reached his maximum and just blew everyone away!

"Ay amor! No me dejes morir, ¿Qué! no miras lo que pasa en mi? Ven, y dame tu calor, que mi corazón se muere sin tu amor" ("Oh my love, don't let me die, don't you see what is happening to me? Come, bring me your warmth, because my heart is dying without your love. And my secret love is no secret, anymore.").

At the end of that song, Freddy slowly lifted his arms up high over his head while still holding his microphone. The thunderous applause, whistles, and cheers of "bravo" were just chilling. People called out his name while giving him a standing ovation, "Freddy! Freddy! Freddy!" The steel guitar was left to harmonize its closing notes, lights began to fade, and then total blackness again enveloped the arena.

I knew exactly what my dad was thinking because he had told me once before. It was an expression he often whispered under his breath for a job well done. Back home from one of his tours, he shared with me an incredible experience: "Tomasa, I was opening up for George Jones, and after I finished and was being driven away from the stadium in my limo, I could still hear them from a long distance away, 'Freddy! Encore! Encore!'" And then he told me exactly how that made him feel. "Oh yeah, baby! Just suck it up!" I just smiled along with Father.

Regardless of the hardships of his youth, sadness, struggles, and mistakes made while scratching his way up to the top for so long, he let us know what he was made of that night. There was nobody in the house to say otherwise.

All I know is what happened to me afterward—I had gotten goose bumps all over me. Well, let's put it this way, he left the crowd mesmerized, fascinated, awestruck, and speechless.

To close his show with a bang, he then hit us hard with one of his first platinum hit records, "Before the Next Teardrop Falls." And when the crowd roared, again he knocked it out of the ballpark with "Wasted Days and Wasted Nights!"

The crowd went wild, cheering for more, as Freddy shouted one last time *"Ajúa!" "Ajúa!" "Ajúa!"* and *"ay, ay, ay!"* Then he smiled so sweetly and pleasantly waved adios to his fans while the Cripple Creek played "I Love My Rancho Grande" as he walked off stage.

But the night wasn't quite over; we waited almost an hour for him to finish signing autographs again. He signed autographs three times that night after each show. Having to wait for Father had been well worth the experience. Everyone was pleased with Freddy's third performance, including Six Flags at Magic Mountain.

Freddy signs his autograph for every last person.

Just Let Me Sing!

From that point on, anyone who ever attended a Freddy Fender concert became a loyal forever Freddy fan! They didn't care if he was Mexican, Anglo, black, rock, or country, as long as he sang to them. On this night, I realized why we didn't have any more privacy in our lives and why Father always came first. I was so proud of him, so much so that I, too, was star-struck! Isn't that silly? But it hit me like a rock! I saw my dad for the very first time as a superstar! That wasn't my dad up there; that was Freddy Fender!

It was also true what Huey had clearly stated all along: *He was a star before he was a star!*

I give thanks to the Cripple Creek Band for backing up my dad, for helping him to shine at the peak of his success. If Freddy had had an orchestra backing him up throughout his career, there is no telling how much more iconic a superstar Freddy Fender might have become. Freddy had always been a balladeer, always. He sang with no reservations and allowed us into his world the way *he* had experienced it—*through his eyes!*

Freddy had known exactly what he wanted to do since he was child migrant worker picking both cotton and guitar. As I see it, Father had been living out his future that whole time and never wasted a moment of his life.

As for the Landmark Hotel, once owned by Howard Hughes and Walter Cane, it was Jim Halsey, Jim Foglesong, Huey Meaux, and even Sam Herro "the Phantom" who had believed in Freddy Fender. They helped expose him to the public, and he became an overnight sensation. All that Freddy needed was his well-known recipe of *one take* to show off his incredible talent. No doubt about it, Freddy created a historical landmark of his own the night Halsey and Foglesong took a chance on a "nobody" convict and put his name up in lights on the marquee in Vegas.

To me, this was a God thing beyond our control. It was supposed to go down like this. It was the hard way, but Freddy was going to make it there—regardless of obstacles—because God and the angels favored Freddy for his pure heart, his love for humanity and the unbelievable *will* to keep moving forth. No matter what was thrown at him, Freddy was destined to be a winner.

At last, Baldemar Huerta got to live out the great American dream, and he did it in front of the whole world. With every single note he could muster, Freddy selflessly and affectionately bared his genuine soul to us all.

"Let me sing," he kept saying. *"Just let me sing!"*

Balde and Eva "La Califa" (1979)

"From My Eyes" by Freddy Fender
Well, the high point of my life? —Is the hope I have for the future.
(Film documentary "Comeback," 1979)

Afterword

I hope you have enjoyed reading about "the rise" of my late father, Freddy Fender. Despite all of his obstacles, Freddy had the guts, strength, and spirit to live out the great American dream. It was not by fate or chance alone; I wholeheartedly believe God made this possible so that he could be an inspiration to all of us.

This massive project dominated my whole being for the past decade; I would go through it all over again for the love and respect I have for Father and what he accomplished, especially toward the end of his life. It is my way of paying tribute to him. Or perhaps it is just my way of saying goodbye to him.

However, there are many musical history matters that were important to Father that need to be addressed, updated, and recognized. He wanted me to clarify them and have you learn the facts as to his musical accomplishments. Hopefully, with your awareness and support, he will be acknowledged, especially by the Rock 'n' Roll Music Hall of Fame and the Country Music Hall of Fame and Museum.

Having been a trendsetter since his youth, he felt strongly that he had yet to be honored as a rock 'n' roll pioneer, as this early period in his life has never been officially recognized. Freddy was the first Hispanic artist to sing and record Rock music in Spanish. As an international star, he became known as "The King of Tex-Mex" and enjoyed cross over smash hits in rock 'n' country music genres, as evidenced on the Billboard charts. Therefore, I undertook this task for him because he deserves these accolades and then some.

Moreover, the trials and tribulations of Freddy's journey to success did not stop there. As a matter of fact, they had only begun. The second volume is a combination of "the fall" and "the redemption" of Freddy Fender. I will take you to a place nobody should ever see, wander into, or endure as we have. But I warn you, I shall take you to a place where the weather is treacherous and the waters are deep, choppy, and murky; blue skies are filled by pitch darkness. So, be prepared, for you may not be able to see, breathe, or withstand the layers of silt that lie within our abyss.

In "the fall" I describe in detail Father's shortcomings, his faults, and reveal his inner demons. It is unbearably brutal to take in and accept what Father did to himself, his career, and to us, his family. It is only four chapters long because that is all you may be able to withstand.

The "redemption" explores the extremes a man will go through to redeem himself in order to know his true God. The second book is truly my treasure, my prize, my masterpiece, as you shall see. It was also Father's last wish that a book be written about his incredible journey toward spiritual faith.

There are many interviews with my mother, and an entire chapter of her speaking to you about her husband, Freddy. She voices the reality of being the wife of a charismatic, world-wide music icon.

In addition, Father left his fans a voice message. It is called "Freddy's Farewell," and you can read it after the last chapter, "Vaya Con Dios," in the second volume. It is profound, yet short and sweet.

We do have a younger sister named Marla, who was adopted, and she will come into the picture in the second half of our lives. She was born on January 1, 1980. She would have a special role and place in Freddy's life.

We thank you from the bottom of our hearts for keeping Freddy's legacy alive since his passing on October 14, 2006. And if you knew our father as we did, Father would never, ever, want to rest in peace, as some might think. I just chuckle inside when people say, "Let Freddy rest in peace now." Freddy loved us fussing over him. He had always been a real diva! He just ate it up, and just kept on giving us so much more of that beautiful voice, smile, jokes, and the unconditional love he had for every single one of us.

Next, come with me, and see how Freddy travels through the fires of his own hell, and "rises" toward his true success of redemption.

Tammy Lorraine Huerta Fender
"The Tex-Mex Princess"

INTERVIEWEES

Evangelina and Tammy Huerta accepting an award for Freddy at the La Alameda Awards (six months after Fender's death)

Tammy with her Aunt Lola on Freddy Fender Lane (2012)

Tammy and Apolonia Galván-Briones at 550 Biddle Street (2011)

With Luann Matlock (2007)

With Teacher Mrs. Pat Gosset (2007)

Tammy with Ramón Piñon (2008)

Tammy with Ernest "Chapita" Chapa (2007)

Luis "Squeezer" Moreno Garcia by the Squeeze Inn's original pool table (2007)

Tammy and Record Producer Huey Meaux, (2010)

Acknowledgments

I first thank God and his son, Jesus Christ, for carrying me through the lonesome yet astonishing journey that was set before me to undertake, knowing I must tell what the Lord needed me to show you and not what I wanted you to hear. I did not sugarcoat anything, I just honestly told it like it was—no holds barred. I wrote about the hunger for success and the extremes that a man will go to in order to fulfill his life's passions, and the resulting pain and anguish those dreams can cause those who love him.

I will start by putting my family at the top of all the people I wish to thank. First, I thank my awesome spouse of nineteen years, William P. Mallini. He and Father had a wonderful and respectful relationship. He has been there for me in every way, throughout my grief and my passion to share the untold stories of Father's journey and of our life with him. Thank you for your selflessness and love for Father and me.

Next, I thank my mother, Evangelina Muñiz Huerta; my eldest brother, Baldemar Jr. "Sonny Boy" Huerta, and my baby brother, Daniel "Danny Boy" Huerta for their most heartfelt, intimate, and often painful interviews. For all of us, the mere mention of Father's name or the sound of his recorded voice was more than we could stand. Even today, his music is still difficult for us to enjoy listening to because we miss him that much.

For years, my family saw me with nothing more than my video camera, voice recorder, and laptop as I slept, ate, and breathed only to create his complete biography, from birth to death. Mother also worked incredibly hard to construct Father's discography; it can be viewed toward the back of the book.

Most importantly, our family wholeheartedly thanks the Forever Freddy fans from around the globe for buying his records, his CDs, and for attending his concerts. Numerous record companies recorded Freddy's music; they all released singles, albums, cassettes and compact discs – and others promoted the hell out of Freddy! However, all of their investments in those productions and efforts would have been wasted if it weren't for you, the fans. It was your hard-earned money that put food on everyone's table (since studios, record companies, and promoters ALL made money) and gave us a more fruitful life.

I thank my good friend, Ramón Hernández, who is a well-known music archivist, collector, and photojournalist; he knew Father well. Ramón was able to write the informative and historical Music Timelines for several chapters in the book that reflect Freddy's constant change of music genres. According to *Billboard*, Cashbox, and 100 Top Charts, Freddy broke many boundaries for singing the blues, rockabilly, and rock 'n' roll, and created the mold for rock-en-Español.

The list continues with Tex-Mex, country, and *boleros* (for which he won a few Grammy's), plus other prestigious awards throughout a musical career which spanned sixty years.

Alicia Villarreal made it possible for me to tell a beautiful story and keep the flavor of my Tex-Mex style. She was my sounding board and assisted in editing the complete biography of my late father. She helped this new writer to fulfill her vision for what this book should represent—the authenticity, validity, and integrity of his life. *Thank you for honoring his legacy. You gave me peace of mind. It was a dream of an extraordinary life that had to be revealed, because it was not meant for me to keep.*

Freddy is a fascinating subject to write about; however, the whole story line is actually bigger than Freddy. You, the reader, will come to understand this after reading the exclusive and complete history of his life—epic tale after epic tale.

Also important are the interviewees from my father's hometown of San Benito and everyone from the Rio Grande Valley who graciously and eagerly went back in time to recollect their personal memories; they helped paint the colorful picture of Freddy's childhood and his early beginnings as The Bebop Kid. Therefore, it is with all my heart that I thank our relatives: (Freddy's youngest brother) Manuel "Beke" Salazar; (Freddy's sister) Mínerva, "Míne"; (Freddy's brother) José Luis Garza Méndez; (Freddy's aunt) Dolores G. Huerta; (Freddy's cousin and his wife) Raul Castillo and Elvia Castillo, who assisted with the family tree; (Freddy's cousin) Ysaúle Ysasi, and (wedding godfather) Carlos Sifuentes.

I thank the musicians who were kind enough to share their experiences of Freddy as a young man. Their memories of him as a bigger than life character in the local clubs when he was The Bebop Kid singing Spanish/English rock 'n' roll in the 1950s–1960s are a priceless addition to this book. These musicians include Ruben Aguirre, Luis "Squeezer" Moreno Garcia, Rosendo "Chendo" Guillen, (Freddy's bass player and prison cellmate) Louis René Moody, Archie Pierce, and (Freddy's close family friend and musician) Ramón Piñon."

Additional thanks go to (Freddy's teacher) Pat Gossett, (Freddy's school friend*)* Ernest "Chapita" Chapa, (Neighbor) Apolonia "Pola" (Friends) Galván-Briones, Tomás Galván-Briones, Cipriano Galván, (Talent show contestant) Elida Andaverde, (Family friend) Rufina Alvarado, (Freddy's friend) Louis "Big Lou" Villarreal, (Anonymous) Baton Rouge—Beauty Pageant Queen, (School friend) William "Billy" K. Jackson, (Texas State Technical College [TSTC] school friend) Eugene "Gene" D. Martell, (Freddy's kind-hearted school friend and singer) Lou Ann Matlock, (Thank you for Freddy's pictures in the Border Diablos' motorcycle club) Linda S. Saldaña, (U.S. Vietnam Veteran and a "Jokers" Motorcycle Club member) John Richard Vasquez.

I would especially like to thank those who, with Freddy, served our country in the U.S. Marines Corps in Japan when Freddy was just sixteen years old: Carlos

Castillo, Pete López, and Leonard Encinas. The stories about Freddy really tell the tale of Freddy's state of mind at such an early age.

I thank the Museum of San Benito (Sandra Tumberlinson of the San Benito Historical Society and Rey Avila of the Conjunto Music Hall of Fame) for allowing me to use the images of Freddy's hometown; Arnaldo "Nano" Ramírez, Jr. and family for the use of 45rpm/Vinyl images of Falcón Records; Chris Strachwitz of <u>Arhoolie Records,</u> who loaned me ledgers which document Freddy's first recording sessions with Falcón Records, as well as Ideal record label images. I also thank Lisa Ann Wilson, granddaughter of Ideal's original owner, Paco Betancourt, for loaning me copies of prison letters my father had written to her grandfather. By reading those letters, we can now all experience what Freddy was feeling while incarcerated, during one of the saddest, most heartfelt moments of his life.

A special thank you to a beautiful woman and 1960s recording artist, Beatriz Llamas "La Paloma del Norte." She was so hospitable that she cooked dinner for me and I even spent the night at her house. Thank you for the photograph of both you and Freddy, taken during his rise to fame.

I am very grateful I had the opportunity to speak with Father's major record producer and manager, Huey Purvis "The Crazy Cajun" Meaux, before he passed away. I first met him when I was a young girl, and he was delighted to loan me photos for my book, as well allowing me to interview him on several occasions at his home in Winnie, Texas. We were close, like family. It was Huey Meaux who loved and pushed Freddy to the top, even when no one else would take a chance on an American of Mexican descent, let alone a convict.

My gratitude also extends to W. Sam Monroe and Leroy Lee Ashworth, who are the beneficiaries of a select number of photos given to them by Huey Meaux. I thank them for their generosity in loaning me the additional photos of Freddy, so that I may use them for my book in memory of both Huey Meaux and Freddy. I also thank Dan Workman, who took over Sugar Hill Studios after Huey's absence, for allowing me use of their studio photos.

Father must have heard me when I prayed and asked him to place the right people before me in order to write as straightforward and realistic a book as I possibly could. I was unbelievably blessed to get the opportunity to interview two major players who were only too happy to talk about Freddy's achievements and how much he personally meant to both of them. I was especially pleased since they were the ones who were responsible for turning Freddy into a mega star overnight. Thank you to two of the most talented and masterful music gurus of the music industry—Jim Halsey and James "Jim" Foglesong for believing in Father and his talent.

Jim Halsey, artist manager, agent, and impresario, is a visiting professor at the Halsey Learning Center of Music and Entertainment Business at HED Music College in Yehud, Israel. He is also the author of *Starmaker* and a member of the

Country Music Association (CMA) and Academy of Country Music (ACM) Board of Directors.

Jim Foglesong (July 26, 1922–July 9, 2013) was the director of the music business program at Trevecca Nazarene University; adjunct professor at Vanderbilt University's Blair School of Music since 1991; president of Dot, ABC, Capitol and MCA, Records, and was inducted into the Country Music Hall of Fame in 2004.

I also thank Polly Nodine, from President Carter's Library, for allowing me the use of a photo with Freddy and U.S. President Jimmy Carter.

I can't give enough thanks to Brenda Colladay, museum and photographic curator of the Grand Ole Opry Archives. The photos, taken at both the Country Music Academy and Grand Ole Opry annual birthday celebrations show Freddy at the peak of his success.

I am delighted to thank Kay Clary of BMI in Nashville for the use of the photos taken at the BMI Dinner honoring Freddy for his first no. 1 smash hit song, in which he is quite handsomely dressed in a white tuxedo.

A special thanks goes out to Tom Hendrix for the contribution of the most amazing and exclusive photographs ever taken of Freddy. I am sure the readers are going to enjoy these photos; they capture Freddy being his loving self (surrounded by devoted fans as he embraced them) at the airport in Harlingen, Texas. Hendrix's images truly bring Freddy back to life for us.

Another big thanks to The Cripple Creek Band, for making Father shine at the peak of his success. The band consists of Rick DeArmond, drums and vocals; Sam Beck, harmonica, guitar, and vocals; Robert Hoffman, bass and vocals; Billy Hogue, steel guitar, guitar, and vocals, and Dennis Winton, guitar and vocals. I enjoyed the wonderful and humorous road stories they told. People will enjoy reading about what actually occurred on the road in the life of a music legend. I also thank Rick DeArmond for the use of his photos.

Film producer and director Boon Collins allowed me the use of photos from "Comeback," a film documentary on my late Father's life up through 1979. It is the most spectacular and truest film ever made of Freddy. The essence of Freddy was captured, and the viewer is mesmerized in awe, joy, and in tears. I am also elated and grateful that he has given me the documentary film to use at my discretion. I can't wait to show it to the public. Thank you, my friend, for your selfless deed and generosity.

Thank you, everyone, for being a part of our lives and contributing to Freddy's biography, for helping to tell the tale of all that happened to him and what he went through to achieve the great American dream. God bless you and may the Lord provide you the inner strength and courage to fully experience and embrace life without fear, just as Freddy lived it—to his end.

FREDDY FENDER
HONORS AND AWARDS

HONORS:	
1995	Freddy Fender Lane (Street named after Freddy in San Benito, Texas)
1998	Ricardo Montalban's Golden Eagle Nosotros Award
1998	Chicano Music Awards
1999	Flying Pegasus Trophy for Country Western Music (Las Vegas)
1999	Miller Brewing Company Calendar
1999	Hispanic Cultural Calendar
1999	Austin Music Awards, Los Super Seven
2000	Los Angeles Orange County CA. Register Archives: 100 Most Important Latin Artist of the Century, Freddy Fender, no. 18
2000	United States Congressional Recognition for the Freddy Fender Scholarship Fund
2001	Honored by the Texas Senate and House of Representatives
2002	ALMA Pioneer Award, ABC Prime time
2003	International Entertainment Buyers Association, Nashville, Pioneer Award
2003	Top 100 Songs in Country Music History, "Before the Next Teardrop Falls," no. 86
2004	The 100 Best Texas Songs, "Wasted Days and Wasted Nights," no. 21 (*Texas Monthly*)
2004	Groundbreaking for a new water tower, bearing Freddy Fender's name in San Benito, Texas
2004	100 Greatest Country Love Songs, "Before the Next Teardrop Falls," no. 44

AWARDS:	
1975	Country Music Association, Single of the Year
1975	Academy of Country Music, Most Promising Male Vocalist
1992	Netherlands Gram Award, Texas Tornados
	Music Operators of America, Artist of the Year and Single of the Year
	Multiplatinum Sales Worldwide

HALL OF FAME/WALK OF FAME	
1986	Tejano Music Hall of Fame (San Antonio, TX)
1993	European Walk of Fame Star (Rotterdam, Holland)
1997	El Paso (Texas) Hall of Fame

1998	Hispanic American Entertainment Hall of Fame/Pura Vida Lifetime Achievement Award
1999	Country Music Hall of Fame and Museum (Nashville)
1999	Texas Music Hall of Fame
1999	Hollywood Walk of Fame Star
1999	Hispanic Walk of Fame Star (Phoenix, AZ)
1999	Nashville Sidewalk of Stars
2000	North America Country Music Association's International Hall of Fame
2001	Louisiana Hall of Fame
2002	Tejano Walk of Fame
2004	South Texas Music Walk of Fame (First to receive Star)
2007	Música Latina Hall of Fame (San Antonio, Texas)

GRAMMY NOMINATIONS		
1975	*Before the Next Teardrop Falls*	Best Single of the Year (Hollywood, California)
1976	*Wasted Days and Wasted Nights*	Best Song of the Year (New York, New York)
1991	*Zone of Our Own*	Best Country Duo or Group with Vocal
1993	*Hanging on by a Thread*	Tejano Country
1997	*A Little Bit Is Better Than Nada*	Best Mexican American Music Performance

GRAMMY AWARDS		
1990	*Texas Tornados*	Best Mexican American Performance
1999	*Los Super Seven*	Best Mexican American Performance
2002	*La Música de Baldemar Huerta*	Best Latin Pop category

VIDEOS:	
1989	"Spanish Harlem," Freddy Fender
1990	"Who Were You Thinkin' Of," Texas Tornados
1991	"Adios Mexico," "Laredo Rose," and "Rosa De Amor" with Texas Tornados
1992	"Is Anybody Goin' to San Antone" and "La Mucura" with Texas Tornados
1993	"Guacamole," Texas Tornados
1994	"Blanca Navidad" (White Christmas), Freddy Fender
1996	"A Little Bit Is Better Than Nada," Texas Tornados
2000	"Vertical Expression (of Horizontal Desire)," Bellamy Bros with Freddy Fender

FILMOGRAPHY:	
1979	*She Came to the Valley*, a.k.a. *Texas in Flames* (Scott Glenn)
1985	*Short Eyes* (Bruce Davidson and José Pérez)

1991	*Always Roses* (Lupe Ontiveros) and *La Pastorela* (Linda Ronstadt)
1992	*Who Will Sing Their Songs* (Vikki Carr)
1999	*Mi Amigo* (Mary Stuart Masterson)

TELEVISION:
Dick Clark's *American Bandstand*
Grand Ole Opry
The Merv Griffin Show
Mike Douglas Show
The Tonight Show
The Johnny Carson Show
Dinah Shore Show
Dennis Miller Show
Late Show with David Letterman Dolly Parton Show
Dolly Parton: Treasures
Crook and Chase
Dean Martin Christmas Special
The Dukes of Hazzard
Flying High
Hee Haw
Jerry Lewis MDA Labor Day Telethon
Hats Off To Minnie Pearl
Hollywood Squares
Nashville Now
Tony Orlando and Dawn Show
The Midnight Hour
Bobby Vinton Show
Austin City Limits
Wolfman Jack's *The Midnight Special*
Tom Brokaw's *Today Show*
Kiki Desde Hollywood
A Current Affair
Late Night with Conan O'Brien
Johnny Canales Show
El Show de Paul Rodriguez
Farm Aide '96
TNN'S *Salute to Texas Week*

Wildhorse Saloon	
Great Day America	
VH-1	
Country Music Association Awards	
CNN's *Farm Aide 1991*	
Entertainment Tonight	
E! Entertainment	
Sea World Television Special	
Legends of Country Music	
Prime Time Country	
Yesterday & Today	
Gold Guitar Awards (New Zealand)	
Good Morning Australia	
Showbiz Today	
MTV News	
Comeback: Freddy Fender/Baldemar Huerta Biography	
Latino Music Greats (1999)	
Years in Review Freddy Fender in Documentary	
Hispanic American (1999)	
ALMA Awards, ABC Prime time 2002	

NARRATOR:	
1996	*Storytime*
1996	*Songs of the Homeland*

SOUNDTRACKS:	
1979	*She Came to the Valley* (Scott Glenn)
1980	*Second-Hand Hearts* (Robert Blake)
1982	*The Border* (Jack Nicholson)
1990	*Silhouette* (Faye Dunaway)
1982	*Losin' It* (Tom Cruise)
1991	*Rush* (Sam Elliot)
1992	*Fire in the Sky* (D. B. Sweeney)
1993	*Son in Law* (Pauly Shore)
1993	*The Beverly Hillbillies* (Cloris Leachman)
1996	*Lone Star* (Matthew McConaughey)
1996	*Jack* (Robin Williams, Jennifer López)
1996	*Tin Cup* (Kevin Costner)

1997	*In Cold Blood* (Anthony Edwards)
1998	*Slums of Beverly Hills* (Natasha Lyonne)
2000	*The Prize of Glory* (Jimmy Smits)
2006	*The Three Burials of Melquiades Estrada* (Tommy Lee Jones)
2007	*The Astronaut Farmer* (Billy Bob Thornton, Bruce Willis)
2008	*Hancock* (Will Smith, Charlize Theron)
2008	*W.* (Josh Brolin, Elizabeth Banks)
2014	*Boyhood* (Ethan Hawke and Patricia Arquette)

COMMERCIALS:

Texas Department of Health Hepatitis C, Cellular One, Scott's Glass, Texas General Land Office, Pennies on the Dollar,

McDonald's Have a Coke and a Smile, El Chico Restaurants, Don't Mess with Texas, Diabetes Association, Pancho's

Restaurants, Chrysler Motors, Mello Yello, Miller Lite Beer, Pizza Hut

PRINT MEDIUM (Newspapers, magazines and tabloids:

Who's Who in South and Southwest (1997–1998)

International Who's Who

Who's Who in America

Look magazine

Photoplay Magazine

Playboy

Hustler

Newsweek

Newsweek en Español

USA Today

Stars and Stripes

Billboard magazine

People magazine

Rolling Stone

People Weekly magazine

Hispanic magazine

Texas Monthly

Vista Magazine

Easy Rider

Music City News

New York Times

Los Angeles Times

Chicago Tribune
Houston Chronicle
Country Music magazine
Country Style magazine
Country Weekly magazine
Country Weekly International
Nashville Reporter magazine
Blue Suede News magazine
San Antonio Express-News
Corpus Christi Caller-Times
LA's *Orange County Register* newspaper
Rona Barrett's Hollywood Magazine
"Above & Beyond," Former Marines Conquer the Civilian World (2004)

CAREER HIGHLIGHTS:	
1975	Macy's Thanksgiving Parade
Carnegie Hall and the Hollywood Bowl	
1979	The White House & Ford Theatre (Pres. Jimmy Carter)
1981/1986	Chicago Wrigley Field w/Chicago Cubs
1992	Inaugural Ball & Hispanic Gala at Ford's Theatre (Pres. George H. W. Bush Sr.)
Inaugural Ball (Ann Richards, Texas Governor)	
Inaugural Ball (Pres. Bill Clinton)	
Montreux Jazz Festival (Montreux, Switzerland)	

CD-ROMS:
1995 The Alamo

Freddy Fender Discography

BALDEMAR HUERTA (1947-1958), EL BE-BOP KID (1956-1962) AKA FREDDY FENDER (1958 to present) EDDIE MEDINA (1961), SCOTTY WAYNE (1962)

By: Vangie Huerta

Artist(s) Name	Name of Single	Label	Number	Year
Baldemar Huerta, El Be-Bop Kid	No Seas Cruel (Don't Be Cruel)/Ay Amor	Falcon Records	626	1957
Reissued		ARV International	5103	1958
Baldemar Huerta, El Be-Bop Kid	Puerta Verde/ Cantando Los Blues	Falcon Records	646	1957
Baldemar Huerta, El Be-Bop Kid	Los Ojos De Pancho/Si Estuviereas A Mi Lado	Falcon Records	656	1957
Baldemar Huerta, El Be-Bop Kid	En Medio De Una Isla/ Esa Sera El Dia	Falcon Records	717	1957
Baldemar Huerta, El Be-Bop Kid	Enriqueta/El Rock De La Carcel	Falcon Records	723	1957
Baldemar Huerta, El Be-Bop Kid	Adios A Jamica/Marianne	Falcon Records	666	1957
Baldemar Huerta, El Be-Bop Kid	Encaje De Chantilly/ Mala, Mala, Mala	Falcon Records	838	1958
Baldemar Huerta, El Be-Bop Kid	Botecito De Vela/El Twist	Falcon Records	1036	1960
Baldemar Huerta, El Be-Bop Kid	Jamas Corazon/ Rocanroleando	Falcon Records	1047	1960
Baldemar Huerta, El Be-Bop Kid	Te Esperare/Todo Termino	Falcon Records	1057	1960
Freddy Fender	Mean Woman/Holy One	Duncan	1000	1959
Reissued		Imperial Records	5659	1960
Freddy Fender	Wasted Days & Wasted Nights/San Antonio Rock (Inst.)	Duncan	1001	1959
Reissued		Talent Scott	1013	1960

Artist	Title	Label	Number	Year
Freddy Fender	Wild Side of Life/Crazy Crazy Baby	Duncan	1002	1959
Reissued		Talent Scout	1002	1960
Freddy Fender	Little Mama/Since I Met You Baby	Duncan	1004	1960
Freddy Fender	Wasted Days & Wasted Nights/I Can't Remember When	Imperial Records	5670	1960
Freddy Fender	Find Someone New & Lonely Night	Talent Scout	1007	1960
Freddy Fender	A Man Can Cry/Your Something Else	Talent Scout	1014	1960
Reissued		Argo	5375	1960
Scotty Wayne	Only One/I'm Gonna Leave	Talent Scout	1008	1962
Scotty Wayne	Sweet Summer Day/Pretty Baby	Talent Scout	1009	1962
Scotty Wayne	Something on Your Mind/You Got What It Takes	Talent Scout	1010	1962
Scotty Wayne	You Told Me You Loved Me/Roobie Doobie	Talent Scout	1011	1962
Freddy Fender	Love Light Is An Ember/The New Stroll	Norco	100	1963
Freddy Fender	Camisa Negra/Todos Dicen	Ideal	2212	1963
Freddy Fender	Never Trust A Cheatin' Woman/You Made Me Cry	Norco	102	1963
Freddy Fender	Going Out With The Tide/Comin' Home Soon	Norco	103	1963
Freddy Fender	Just A Little Bit/You Made Me A Fool	Norco	104	1963
Freddy Fender	Oop Poo Pah Doo/Three Wishes	Norco	106	1963
Freddy Fender/Oni Villareal	Bony Moronie/The Magic Of Love	Socko	107	1963
Freddy Fender	In The Still of The Night/You Don't Have To Go	Norco	108	1963
Freddy Fender	Donna./Lover's Quarrel	Norco	111	1963
Freddy Fender	Me He Quedado Solo/Dos Corazones	Discos Flecha	FL-110	1963
Freddy Fender	Donde Esta/Pinta Mi Mundo De Color	Discos Flecha	FL-107?	1963
Freddy Fender	llegando A Te/Viejos Amigos	Ideal Records	45-2087	1963

Artist	Title	Label	Cat. No.	Year
Freddy Fender	Todo Mi Amor/El Hijo De Susie	Ideal Records	45-2148	1963
Freddy Fender / Valerio Longoria	Escarcha/El Rosalito	Ideal Records	45-2255	1964
Freddy Fender / Valerio Longoria	Buscando Un Carino/Que Salarete	Ideal Records	45-2176	1964
Freddy Fender / Carlos Cantu	Anillo De Diamente/Majia De Amor	Ideal Records	45-2253	1964
Freddy Fender	No Estes Sonando/A Bailar El Perro	Ideal Records	45-2290	1964
Freddy Fender /Los Comancheros	Que Tal Amor/Porque Eres Tan Mala	Ideal Records	45-2355	1964
Freddy Fender	Carmela/My Train of Love	Goldband Records	1214	1964
Freddy Fender	Three Wishes/Me and My Bottle of Rum	Goldband Records	1272	1964
Ressued				1994
Freddy Fender	Bye Bye Little Angel/Oh My Love	Goldband Records	1264	1964
Reissued				1968
Freddy Fender	Te Quiero/Que Tristeza Hay En Mi	El Pato	EP-192	1966
Freddy Fender	Tu Amor Y El Mio/Fuiste A Acapulco	BEGO Records	BG-02	1966
Freddy Fender	Vagando Yo Voy/El Deseo De Los Dos	BEGO Records	BG-015	1966
Freddy Fender	Sin Decirte Adios/Ya Estoy) Pagando	BEGO Records	BG-322	1966
Freddy Fender	Cool Mary Lou/You Are My Sunshine	Pa Go Go	115	1967
Freddy Fender	Mummie's Curse/Cat's Meow	Goldband Records	1188	1967
Reissued				1968
Freddy Fender	Today's Your Wedding Day/Some People Say	Goldband Records	3332	1969
Freddy Fender	Wasted Days and Wasted Nights/Biding My Time	Pacemaker	1973	1969
Freddy Fender	Por Lastima/No Juegues Mi Amor	Disco Dominante, Mexico	DD-639	1969
Freddy Fender	Ahora Yo Voy/Me Siento Enamorado	Falcon Records	2053	1974

Artist	Title	Label	Catalog	Year
Freddy Fender /Los Hermanos Ayala	Quinto Patio/Amor Joven	Falcon	2027	1974
Freddy Fender	Crazy Arms/She Thinks I Still Care	ARV International	5083	1974
Freddy Fender	Before the Next Teardrop Falls/Crazy, Crazy Baby	Crazy Cajun	2002	1974
Reissued		ABC/Dot	17540	1975
Freddy Fender	Un Dia de Sol/La Costumbre(The Style)	ARV International	5102	1975
Freddy Fender	Pledging My Love	ARV Intertnational	NK	1975
Freddy Fender /Los Hermanos Ayala	El Roble Viejo (Yellow Ribbon)/Mi Corazon Tendras	ARV International	NK	1975
Freddy Fender	Esta Noche Mi Seras/ Vivo En Un Sueno	Starflite	SF-104	1975
Freddy Fender	Wasted Days & Wasted Nights/I Love My Rancho Grande	ABC/Dot	17558	1975
Freddy Fender	Since I Met You Baby/ Little Mama	GRT	031	1975
Freddy Fender	Go On Baby/Wild Side Of Life	GRT	039	1975
Freddy Fender	Secret Love/Lovin' Cajun Style	ABC/Dot	17585	1975
Freddy Fender	Secret Love/Wasted Days & Wasted Nights	MCA Records	P-2769	1975
Freddy Fender	A Man Can Cry/Your Something Else For Me	Talent Scout	1014	1975
Freddy Fender	Vaya Con Dios (Go With God)/No Soy El Mismo	Crazy Cajun	2019	1976
Freddy Fender	You'll Lose a Good Thing/I'm to Blame	ABC/Dot	17607	1976
Freddy Fender	Vaya Con Dios/ My Happiness	ABC/Dot	17627	1976
Freddy Fender	Livin' It Down/Take Her A Message	ABC/Dot	17652	1976
Freddy Fender	Wasted Days, Wasted Nights	Imperial	5670	1976
Freddy Fender	The Rains Came/ Sugar Coated Love	ABC/Dot	17686	1977
Freddy Fender	If You Don't Love Me/ Thank You My Love	ABC/DOT	17713	1977

Artist	Title	Label	Number	Year
Freddy Fender	Think About Me/If That's The Way You Want It	ABC/Dot	17730	1977
Freddy Fender	Christmas Time In The Valley/Please Come For Xmas	ABC/Dot	17734	1977
Freddy Fender	En Memoria a Elvis/In Memory of Elvis	ARV International	5146	1977
Freddy Fender	Cool Mary Lou/You Are My Sunshine	VOK	77102	1977
Freddy Fender	Talk to Me/Please Mr. Sun	ABC	12370	1978
Freddy Fender	Ella Vino Al Valle (She Came to the Valley) Mas Lagrimas	GCP	1002	1978
Freddy Fender	I'm Leaving It All Up To You	ABC	12415	1978
Freddy Fender	Sweet Summer Day/Walkin' Piece of Heaven	ABC	12453	1978
Freddy Fender	My Special Prayer/Turn Around	Starflite	4906	1979
Freddy Fender	Squeeze Box/Turn Around	Starflite	4904-4	1979
Freddy Fender	Yours/Rock Down In My Shoes	Starflite	4900-4	1979
Freddy Fender	If Your Looking For Love/Louisiana Woman	ABC	12339	1979
Freddy Fender	Please Talk To My Heart/Walk Under A Snake	Starflite	4908	1979
Freddy Fender	Goin' Out With The Tide/ Fannie Mae	Crazy Cajun	2037	1979
Freddy Fender	I Love My Rancho Grande/No Toquen Ya	Crazy Cajun	2014	1980
Freddy Fender	She's Still My Mexican Rose	Crazy Cajun	2057-A	1981
Freddy Fender	Across The Boderline/Before the Next Teardrop Falls	MCA	52003	1982
Freddy Fender	Chokin' Kind/I Might As Well Forget You	Warner Records	7-29794	1983
Freddy Fender	My Confession/Goin' Honky Tonkin'	Crazy Cajun	2060	1984
Freddy Fender	Pobre Viejo Papa (Poor Old Father)/Vaya Con Dios	Crazy Cajun	2077	1985
Freddy Fender	El Cofre/Nunca	Discos CBS International	ZSS-14002	1987
Freddy Fender / Janie C. Ramirez	Tu Y Las Nubes/Paloma De Donde Vienes	Hacienda Records	405	1988

Freddy Fender / Valerio Longoria	Ella Me Dejo Que No (She Said No)/Balance	Hacienda Records	409	1988
Freddy Fender/ Valerio Longoria	Amor Chiquitito (Little Love) Cartas Marcadas	Hacienda Records	7137	1989
Freddy Fender / Isidro Lopez	Tu Corazon Taidor	Hacienda Records	HAC-2205	1989
Freddy Fender / Texas Tornados	Who Were You Thinkin' Of/Soy De San Luis	Reprise/Warner	7-19787	1990
Freddy Fender / Texas Tornados	Adios Mexico/ Rosa De Amor	Reprise/Warner	7-19244	1990
Freddy Fender / Texas Tornados	A Man Can Cry/Hey Baby Que Paso	Reprise/Warner	7-19516	1990
Freddy Fender / Texas Tornados	Who Were You Thinkin' Of / Hey Baby Que Paso	Reprise/Warner	7-19521	1990
Freddy Fender / Texas Tornados	Is Anybody Goin' To San Antone/La Mucara	Reprise/Warner	7-19155	1991
Freddy Fender	It's All In A Game/Wasted Days & Wasted Nights	Reprise/Warner	7-19143	1991
Freddy Fender	It's All In The Game/Before The Next Teardrop Falls	Reprise/Warner	19143	1992
Freddy Fender / Texas Tornados	Guacamole/Hangin' On By A Thread	Reprise/Warner	7-18571	1992
Freddy Fender / Texas Tornados	Little Bit Is Better Than Nada/Amor De Mi Vida	Reprise/Warner	17587-2	1996
Freddy Fender / Texas Tornados	The Cibola Mixes (12" Maxi promo)	Reprise/Warner	PRO-A-8580	1997

Albums

Freddie Fender / Los Romanceros	El Unico Freddie Fender	Falcon Records	FLP2000	1959
Eddie (Medina) con Los Shades	Rock 'n' Roll	Ideal Records	ILP- 109	1961
Freddy Fender / Valerio Longoria	Adios Muchachos	Ideal Records	ILP-151	1963
Freddie Fender	Despeinada	Ideal Records	ILP-150	1963
Freddie Fender	Pancho Pechos	Ideal Records	ILP-158	1964
Freddie /Fender/ Baldemar Huerta	Interpreta El Rock!	Ideal Records	ILP-136	1964
Freddy Fender / Compilation	Freddy Fender and Friends At Goldband	Goldband Records	LP-7768	1964
Reissued				1968
Freddie Fender	El Nuevo Freddie Fender	Discos Dominante Mexico	DDM 1011	1970

Artist	Title	Label	Catalog #	Year
Freddie Fender	El Roble Viejo	ARV Initernational	ARV-1020	1974
Freddy Fender	The Freddy Fender Collection	Precision Records, Canada	TVLP-77025	1974
Freddy Fender / Compilation	Fanfarria Falcon Presenta "Exitos Enternacionales	Falcon Records	FF-3	1974
Freddy Fender	Fuera de Alcance - Out of Reach	Starflite	Starflite 2001	1974
Freddy Fender	Before the Next Teardrop Falls	Crazy Cajun	CC-LP-1008	1974
Reissued		abc Dot Records	DOSD-2020	1975
Reissued		MCA	37110 & 1635	1975
Freddy Fender	Antes De La Segunda Lagrima (Before the Next Teardrop	abc Dot Records	DOSS-2020	1975
Freddy Fender	Are You Ready For Freddy	abc Dot Records	DOSD-2044	1975
Reissued		MCA	636	
Freddy Fender	Since I Met You Baby	GRT Records	GRT 8005	1975
Reissued		Accord Records	SN7121	1981
Freddy Fender	Recorded Inside Louisiana State Prison	Power Pak Records	PO-280	1975
Freddy Fender	Freddy Fender	Pickwick International	JS-6178	1975
Freddie Fender	She Thinks I Still Care	ARV International	ARVLP-1030	1975
Freddy Fender	If Your Ever In Texas	abc Dot Records	DOSD-2061	1976
Freddy Fender / Compilation	The Wonderful World of Christmas	Specail Market/ Capital	SL-8025	1976
Freddy Fender / Josue	Freddy Fender & Josue	RIC	LP-8044	1976
Freddy Fender	Rocking' Country	abc Dot Records	DOSD-2050	1976
Freddy Fender	Recordando Los '50	ARV International	ARVLP-1034	1976
Freddie Fender	La Costumbre (The Style)	ARV International	ARVLP-1031	1976
Freddy Fender / Delbert McClinton	Sometime Country, Sometime Blues	Quicksilver Records	QS 1004	1976
Freddy Fender	Your Cheatin' Heart	Pickwick International	JS-6195	1976
Freddy Fender	Let The Good Times Roll	Pickwick International	PTP 2090-1A	1976
Freddy Fender	The Fabulous Freddy Fender	Suffolk Marketing	SMI FF 100	1976

Reissued		Brylen	4430	1984
Freddy Fender	The Best of Freddy Fender	abc Dot Records	DO-2079	1977
Reissued		MCA	3285, 835,11464	
Freddy Fender	If You Don't Love Me	abc Dot Records	DO-2090	1977
Reissued		MCA	699	
Freddy Fender	Merry Christmas-Feliz Navidad	Dot	DOSD2101	1977
Freddy Fender	Merry Xmas from Freddy Fender	MCA	15025	
Freddy Fender	Live	Carzy Cajun	CCLP-1039	1977
Freddy Fender / Compilation	Country Comes To Carniege Hall	abc Dot Records	DO-2087	1977
Freddy Fender	Exitos Grandes de Freddy Fender	Starflite	SF-2005	1977
Freddy Fender	Wasted Days And Wasted Nights	Starflite	FLP-2001	1977
Freddy Fender	His Greatest Recordings-Broadcasted for Military Bases	ABC/At Ease	MD 11108	1978
Freddy Fender / Tommy Mclain	Friends In Show Business	Crazy Cajun	CC-1100	1978
Freddy Fender	Ella Vino Al Valle	GCP Records	GCP-141	1978
Freddy Fender	Spanish Feelings	Capitol Records	SL-8107	1978
Freddy Fender	Swamp Gold	abc Records	1062	1978
Reissued		MCA	668	
Freddy Fender	The Texas Balladeer	Starflite	36073	1979
Freddy Fender	Let the Good Times Roll	51 West Records	Q-16011	1979
Freddy Fender	Love Me Tender	Crazy Cajun	CCLP 1011	1979
Freddy Fender	Tex-Mex	abc Records	AY-1132	1979
Reissued		MCA	37109	1979
Freddy Fender	20 Greatest Hits	Tee Vee Records, Inc.	TV-1020	1979
Freddy Fender / Compilation	Have a Coke and a smile	Coca Cola Company	None	1979
Freddy Fender	Together We Drifted Apart	Starflite	36284	1980
Freddy Fender / Sir Douglas	Reunion of the Cosmic Brothers	Crazy Cajun	CCLP-1013	1980
Freddy Fender	Freddy (Baldemar Huerta) Fender Canta (Sings)	Crazy Cajun	CCLP-1012	1980
Freddy Fender	Out In The Street	Album Globe	AG8137	1981

Artist	Title	Label	Catalog #	Year
Freddy Fender	Freddy Fender & Tommy McLain	Album Globe	AG8121	1981
Freddy Fender / Tommy McClain	Little Bitty Pretty One	B&B Records	AG-8121	1981
Freddy Fender	Enter My Heart	Picc-A-Dilly	PIC-3589	1981
Freddy Fender	You Made Me Cry	Great Sounds Records	TLA-50181	1982
Freddy Fender	Wasted Days - Wasted Nights	Andover Records	A 1009	1982
Freddy, Mickey/ Ronnie	Fender, Gilley & Milsap That Is	Pickwick Records-Canada.	JS-6196	1983
Freddy Fender	Christmas With Gusto	Gusto/CBS	P-17569	1983
Freddy Fender	Freddy Fender's 20 Gold Hits	Colorado/ Germany	CLP5-23018	1983
Freddy Fender	Siempre (Always)	RCA International	IL6-7521	1986
Freddy Fender	The Early Years... 1959-1963	Krazy Kat	KK-7437	1986
Freddy Fender	Greatest Hits	Black Tulip	555015	1987
Freddy Fender	Live! In Las Vegas	Crazy Cajun	LP 1106	1990
Freddy Fender / Texas Tornados	Texas Tornados	WEA Warner Bros	36251-2	1991
Freddy Fender / Texas Tornados	Los Texas Tornados	Reprise/Warner Mexico	26472-2	1990
Freddy Fender / Texas Tornados	Zone of Our Own	WEA Warner Bros.	26683-4	1991
Freddy Fender	Favorite Ballads	Warner Bros.	R10215	1991
Freddy Fender	The Freddy Fender Collection	Reprise/Warner	26638-2	1991
Freddy Fender / Texas Tornados	Hangin' On By A Thread	Reprise/Warner	45058-4	1992
Freddy Fender / Texas Tornados	The Best of Texas Tornados	Reprise/Warner	45511-4	1994
Freddy Fender / Compilation	A Tejano Country Christmas	Arista/Texas	18766-4	1994
Freddy Fender / Texas Tornados	4 Aces	Reprise Records	46197-2	1996
Freddy Fender / Compilation	Feliz Navidad	Delta Music Inc.	12-770	1996
Freddy Fender	Coming Home (Gospel)	Hacienda Records	HAC-7135	1996
Freddy Fender	With Love From Freddy Fender	Masters	003684	NK
Freddy Fender	"20 Greatest Hits"	Astan	20017	NK

Artist	Title	Label	Catalog #	Year
Freddy Fender / Compilation	Hit-Kickers Series Vol. 2 Texas Country Rock	NK	NK	NK

Cassettes

Artist	Title	Label	Catalog #	Year
Freddy Fender	Christmas Time In The Valley	MCA	MC 15037	1977
Freddy Fender	Merry Christmas From Freddy Fender/ Feliz Navidad	MCA	MCAC-15025	1977
Freddy Fender	Best Of Freddy Fender	MCA/1974, 1975, 1976	MCAC-835	1977
Freddy Fender	El Mejor De Freddy Fender Volume 1	MCA	MCAC-20413	1979
Freddy Fender	The Best Of Freddy Fender	MCA	MCAC 836	1980
Freddy Fender	50 Original Country Hits/ "You'll Lose A Good Thing"	Sessions	ARI-1024C-1	1981
Freddy Fender	Since I Met You Baby	Accord	SN-7121	1982
Freddy Fender	Before The Next Teardrop falls	Lucky	CLUC-017	1984
Freddy Fender	Before The Next Teardrop Falls	MCA/1974, 1975, 1976	MCAC 20257	1985
Freddy Fender	The Country Collection	Music World	CLUC 081	1985
Freddy Fender / Compilation	Tejanos For Hunger (Somos Hermanos)	Tejanos For Hunger	TFH 333	1985
Freddie Fender	Wasted Days 'N Wasted Nights	Big Star	BS 7063	1986
Freddy Fender	Sings Hank Williams	Hacienda Records	HAC-7088	1986
Freddy Fender	Mean Woman AKA Dirty Blues	Haceinda Records	HAC-7048	1986
Freddy Fender	"Reflections"	Vangie Records/ Vol II	NK	1986
Reissued		Freddy Fender Music	C-00022	1997
Freddy Fender	Thank You My Love	Vangie Records/ Vol I	NK	1987
Reissued		Freddy Fender Music	C-00012	1997
Freddy Fender	Siempre	Hacienda Records	HAC-7202	1987
Freddy Fender	El Cofre	Discos CBS International	ZMC-14309	1987
Freddy Fender	Aqui Estoy Yo	Hacienda Records	HAC-7290	1987
Freddy Fender/ Valerio Longoria	Ella Me Dijo Que No	Hacienda Records	HAC-7131	1988
Freddy Fender	Coming Home (Gospel)	Hacienda Records	HAC-1935	1989

Artist	Title	Label	Catalog #	Year
Freddy Fender & Valerio Longoria	Amor Chiquito (Little Love)	Hacienda Records	HAC-7137	1989
Freddy Fender	Greatest Hits 20 Songs	Hollywood	HT-407	1989
Freddy Fender / Texas Tornados	Warner-Reprise Country Hits/Who Were You Thinkin' Of	WB/Reprise	PRO-C-4483	1990
Freddy Fender / Texas Tornados	Zone of Our Own	Reprise	26683-4	1991
Freddy Fender	Favorite Ballads (Tape 1 & 2)	Warner/Time Life Music	R10215	1991
Freddy Fender	The Freddy Fender Collection	Reprise	26638-4	1991
Freddy Fender / Texas Tornados	Hangin' On By A Thread	Reprise	45058-4	1992
Freddy Fender/ Compilation	A Tex-Mex Conjunto Christmas	Hacienda Records	7372	1993
Freddy Fender	Canciones de Mi Barrio	Arhoolie/Ideal, 1961/1965	CS-366	1993
Freddy Fender	Sings Country	RoySales	RS-CS05	1993
Freddy Fender/ Compilation	Country Memories	MCA	MSC3-35429	1993
Freddy Fender / Texas Tornados	The Best Of The Texas Tornados	Reprise	45511-4	1994
Freddy Fender / Compilation	A Tejano Country Christmas	Arista/Texas	07822/18766-4	1994
Freddy Fender	El Hijo De Su	Hacienda Records	HAC-7283	1994
Freddy Fender	In Concert	Hacienda Records	HAC-7047	1995
Freddy Fender	King of Tex Mex	Laserlight	12519	1995
Freddy Fender / Texas Tornados	A Little Bit Is Better Than Nada	Reprise/Warner	CS-8213	1996
Freddy Fender / Texas Tornados	Tin Cup/Motion Picture/Little Bit Is Better Than Nada	Epic Soundtrac	ET 67609	1996
Freddy Fender / Texas Tornados	4 ACES	Reprise	R 4-46197	1996
Freddy Fender	Freddy Fender and Friends Live in Las Vegas	Hacienda Records	7426	1996
Freddy Fender/ Isidro Lopez	Sing Country	Hacienda Records	7084	1996
Freddy Fender	Great Hits	Public Music	9009	1996
Freddy Fender / Compilation	50 Number One Country Hits - Volume 1 & 2	MCA Records	MSC2-35952	1996

Artist	Title	Label	Catalog #	Year
Freddy Fender	Internacional - del corazon/from the heart	Freddy Records	FRC-1765	1997
Freddy Fender	Greatest Hits	ITC Masters	1114	1997
Freddy Fender	In His Prime	Edsel (UK)	516	1997
Freddy Fender	Rhythm & Blues & Me	Freddy Fender Music	C-00032	1997
Freddy Fender / Compilation	Lounge-A-Palooza	Hollywood Records		1997
Freddy Fender /Los Super Seven	Los Super Seven	RCA	07863-67689-4	1998
Freddy Fender / Compilation	Live at Gilley's...vol. 2 of 4	Q Records	Q10014	1998
Freddy Fender	20 Hits	Classic Sound	20012	NK
Freddy Fender	Have Yourself A Freddy Fender Xmas	Freddy Fender Music	CD00052CS	2000

Compact Disks				
Freddy Fender / Compilation	50 Number One County Hits – Volume 1 & 2	MCA Recrods	MSD2-35952	1996
Freddy Fender	Freddy Fender 20	Hollywood/ High land Music	HCD-407	1989
Freddy Fender	Before The Next Teardrop Falls	Blues Int. Inc./ Tokyo, Japan	PCD-2119	1989
Freddy Fender / Texas Tornados	Texas Tornados	Reprise	26251	1990
Freddy Fender	20 Track Collections	TRING INT'L	GRF-072	1990
Freddy Fender / Compilation	A Country Christmas to Remember	MCA	MCAD-20629	1990
Freddy Fender / Texas Tornados	Zone Of Our Own	WEA Warner Bros.	26683-2	1991
Freddy Fender	Favorite Ballads	Warner/Time Life Music	R10215	1991
Freddy Fender	The Freddy Fender Collection	Reprise	26638-2	1991
Freddy Fender / Texas Tornados	Los Texas Tornados (Spanish)	WEA Warner Bros.	26472-2	1991
Freddy Fender / Texas Tornados	Hangin' On By A Thread	WEA Warner Bos.	45058-2	1992
Freddy Fender / Compilation –Vol 17	Super Hits Of the 70's/Before The Next Teardrop Falls	Rhino	R2 71197	1993
Freddy Fender/ Compilation –Vol.18	Super Hits Of The 70's /Have A Nice Day/Wasted Days	Rhino	R2 71198	1993

Artist	Title	Label	Catalog #	Year
Freddy Fender	Canciones De Mi Barrio/Barrio Hits from 50's and 60's	Ideal/Arhoolie, 1961/1965	CD 366	1993
Freddy Fender/ Compilation	The Beverly Hillbillies/ Wasted Days And Wasted Nights	Fox/RCA	66313-2	1993
Freddy Fender	"Freddy Fender Sings Country"	Roy Sales	RS-CD-05	1993
Freddy Fender/ Compilation	Country Memories	MCA	MSD2-35429	1993
Freddy Fender	Before The Next Teardrop Falls	MCA	MCAD-20257	1994
Freddy Fender/ Compilation	A Tejano Country Christmas	Arista/Texas	18766-2-07822	1994
Freddy Fender / Texas Tornados	The Best of The Texas Tornados	WEA Warner Bros.	45511-2	1994
Freddy Fender	El Hijo De Su	Hacienda Records	HAC-7283	1994
Freddy Fender	Before The Next Teardrop Falls (Excesior Series)	MCA	20605	1994
Freddy Fender	King of Tex Mex	Laserlight	12519	1995
Freddy Fender	In Concert	Hacienda Records	7047	1995
Freddy Fender	The King Of Tex-Mex	Laserlight Digital Discos	12 519	1995
Freddy Fender / Texas Tornados	Tin Cup/Motion Picture/ Little Bit Is Better than Nada	Epic Soundtrack	EX 67609	1996
Freddy Fender / Texas Tornados	4 ACES	Reprise	46197-2	1996
Freddy Fender / Texas Tornados	Little Bit Is Better Than Nada	Reprise	PRO-CD-8213	1996
Freddy Fender / Compilation	Feliz Navidad/Christmas In The Valley	Laserlight Digital	12 770	1996
Freddy Fender / Compilation	Lone Star/Soundtrack Film/Desede Que Conosco	Daring/ Castle Rock	CD 3023	1996
Freddy Fender	Freddy Fender and Friends Live In Las Vegas	Hacienda Records	HAC-7426	1996
Freddy Fender / Texas Tornados	A Little Bit Is Better Than Nada	WEA Warner Bros.	46197-2	1996
Freddy Fender	Great Hits	Public Music Inc	9009	1996
Freddy Fender	Reflections Of My Life	Freddy Fender Music/'86	CD-00022	1997
Freddy Fender	Thank You My Love	Freddy Fender Music/'86	CD-00012	1997

Freddy Fender	Rhythm & Blues & Me	Freddy Fender Music/'96	CD-00032	1997
Freddy Fender	The Balladeer	Freddy Fender Music/'89	CD-00042	1997
Freddy Fender	Greatest Hits	ITC Masters	1114	1997
Freddy Fender	In His Prime	Edsel (UK)	516	1997
Freddy Fender	The Best OF Freddy Fender	MCA	MCAD-11464	1977
Freddy Fender / Texas Tornados	"Volver"/On The Border/ Honed On The Range	Texas Monthly	TMM-03-CD	1997
Freddy Fender	Internacional – del corazon/from the heart	Freddie Records	FRCD-1765	1997
Freddy Fender / Compilation	Lounge-A-Palooza	Hollywood Records	HR-62072-2	1997
Freddy Fender / Los Super Seven	Los Super Seven	RCA	RDAV67689-2	1998
Freddy Fender / Compilation	Live at Gilley's...Vol 2 of 4	Q Records (QVC)	Q10012	1998
Freddy Fender	The Best of Freddy Fender	Pegasus/UK	PEG CD 181	1999
Freddy Fender / Texas Tornados	Live From The Limo	BarbWire/ Virgin Records	47751 2	1999
Freddy Fender / TX Tornados Compilation	Rueda de Fuego (Ring of Fire) Movie "Price of Glory"	New Line Records	NLR 90002	2000
Freddy Fender	Have Yourself A Freddy Fender Xmas	Freddy Fender Music	CD00052D	2001
Freddy Fender	I Don't Want to Be Lonely	Freddy Fender Music	CD00053D	2001
Freddy Fender	Las Musica de Baldemar Huerta	Backporch/ Virgin Records	72438-11720-2-5	2001
Freddy Fender & Flaco Jimenez	Dos Amigos	Backporch/ Virgin Records	09463-39123-2-8	2005
Freddy Fender / Compilation	Three Burials of Melquiades Estrada (Soundtrack)			2006
Compact Disk - Singles				
Freddy Fender / Texas Tornados	A Man Can Cry - (single version, promo)	Reprise/Warner	PRO-CD-4527_	1990
Freddy Fender / Texas Tornados	Is Anyone Goin' to San Antone (remix, promo)	Reprise/Warner	PRO-CD-5029	1991
Freddy Fender / Texas Tornados	La Mucara (remix, promo)	Reprise/Warner	PRO-CD-5055	1991
Freddy Fender / Texas Tornados	Did I Tell You/Hey Baby Que Paso (promo)	Reprise/Warner	PRO-CD-5246	1991

Freddy Fender / Texas Tornados	Tus Mentiras (promo)	Reprise/Warner	PRO-CD-5707	1992
Freddy Fender / Texas Tornados	Guacamole (promo)	Reprise/Warner	PRO-CD-6032	1992
Freddy Fender / Texas Tornados	A Mover El Bote (promo)	Reprise/Warner	PRO-CD-6829	1994
Freddy Fender / Texas Tornados	Little Bit Is Better Than Nada	WEA Warner Bros.	437778-2	1996
Freddy Fender / Texas Tornados	Little Bit Is Better Than Nada (promo)	Reprise/Warner	PRO-CD-8213	1996
Freddy Fender / Texas Tornados	The Nada Mixes-Cyclone Step	Reprise/Warner	43826-2	1997

REFERENCES

Article and Liner Notes

Duncan, Wayne. "Duncan's Side of the Story on Freddy's Arrest." Since I Met You Baby. LP. © GRT Records, 1975. Print.

Karisch, Glenn. Staff writer. With Permission to Reprint. News article "Freddy's Arrest." *Daily Texan and Texas. Student Media.* Dallas, Texas. 1975. Print.

Flowers, Jerry. Reprint "The Story of an 'Overnight Sensation.'" Album *Freddie Fender. The Music Gig.* Pickwick International, Inc. LP. November 1975. Print.

Hernández, Ramón. Music Timeline by Music Archivist and Writer.

Nelson, Davia and Strachwitz, Chris. Arhoolie Records © & ℗1959 & 1993. Print. CD "*Roots of Tejano Canciones de mi Barrio,*" The Roots of *Tejano* Rock, 1992. Print.

The Advocate Paper. With Permission to Reprint. Historic New Orleans Collections/ East Parish Library. Baton Rouge, Louisiana. "Freddie Fender Slated for Trial on Dope Charge" and "Freddie Fender Facing Bail Jumping Charge." February 1960. Web. June 11, 2009 (n. ed.). Print.

The San Francisco Call Bulletin/San Francisco Examiner. With Permission to Reprint. "Father of 8 In S. F. Wife Murder-Slaying Suspect Returned." (n. ed.). February 4, 1955. Print.

Quotes: "From My Eyes" by Freddy Fender

ABC-Dot Records, Inc./© Before the Next Teardrop Falls. LP. 1975. Print.

Appling, Ron USMC Sgt. "Singer Recalls His Tank-Driving Days." *Japan Pacific Stars and Stripes* (Camp Hansen in Okinawa, Japan). December 18, 1982. Print.

Betancourt, Paco and Wilson, Lisa Ann. "Fender's Prison Correspondent Letters. 1961–1963.

Collins, Boon. Narrator James Whitmore. "The Life Story of Baldemar Huerta a.k.a. Freddy Fender." Film Documentary *Comeback*, 1979.

Cook, Bruce and Greenberg, Peter S. "Tex-Mex Troubadour." *Newsweek Music Magazine.* November 24, 1975. Albuquerque, MX. Print.

Fender, Freddy and Friends. "Are You Ready for Freddy." *Freddy Fender And Friends Souvenir Book.* "Freddy Salutes the Nation on this Bicentennial year. 1776–1976. Print.

Hopkins, Fred. *Blue Suede News*, no. 47, Summer 1999. Print.

Nelson, Davia and Strachwitz, Chris. Arhoolie Records © & ℗1959 & 1993. CD "Roots of Tejano Canciones de mi Barrio," The Roots of Tejano Rock, 1992. Print.

Nelson, Davia. "Rock 'n' roll, Eddie Medina con Los Shades." 1950s–1960s. Interview 1992. © & ℗ Arhoolie Records 2003. CD. Interview, 1992. Print.
Karisch, Glenn. Staff writer. With Permission to Reprint. News article "Freddy's Arrest." *Daily Texan and Texas. Student Media*. Dallas, Texas. 1975. Print.
Wiseman, Mac. "Freddy and Tanya Tucker." KTTI Radio, Live R. J./Camp Springs, August 29, 1969.

Websites: Freddy Fender Early Digital Recordings
http://frontera.library.ucla.edu/artists

Mexico's Artists/Movie Actors singing Freddy's songs
www.youtube.com/watch?v=IkLwDjzGoK0
www.youtube.com/watch?v=DR6tcL3sI_A
www.youtube.com/watch?v=ej-sTsx9UU4
www.youtube.com/watch?v=XyGGrtu8oik
www.youtube.com/watch?v=eVcfUAF7PGo
www.youtube.com/watch?v=8s7Ol5pod30
www.youtube.com/watch?v=OsN8yEHaeqM
www.youtube.com/watch?v=7n8HdiKW4UE
www.youtube.com/watch?v=cdX0u8sZb6g
www.youtube.com/watch?v=GdW08SECN-8
www.youtube.com/watch?v=eB8YVZ6sbEs
www.youtube.com/watch?v=UZBaJtzuPE4
www.youtube.com/watch?v=O_dwgd0DYCM

CREDITS

Book Cover

Courtesy by Joel Aparicio. Front cover "Freddy Fender at Palomino Club." N. Hollywood. August 1976.

Courtesy of Huerta Archives/Arnaldo "Nano" Ramírez Jr., Falcón Records/Chris Strachwitz of Arhoolie Records. Back cover "El Bebop Kid, 1957." Print.

Front Matter

Courtesy by Joel Aparicio. 2nd Title Page "Freddy Fender at Palomino Club." N. Hollywood. August 1976.

Courtesy of Huerta (Fender) Archives. "Freddy Fender with daughter Tammy during a movie film production *She Came To The Valley*." Mission, TX. 1979.

Courtesy of Museum of San Benito. Texas, Historical Society/Conjunto Hall of Fame. "Wagons in downtown, Sam Houston Rd." San Benito, Texas. 1900s.

Courtesy of Elvia Castillo and Tammy L. Huerta. "Baldemar Huerta, a.k.a. Freddy Fender, Family Tree."

Courtesy of Huerta (Fender) Archives. "Family."

Courtesy by Ramón Hernández. "Tammy L. Huerta early stages of research." 2009.

Courtesy by Les Leverett/Brenda Colladay Museum and Photograph Curator © Grand Ole Opry House Archives, 50th Birthday. "Freddy Fender singing on high platform." CMA Awards. October 13, 1975.

Interior Chapters:

I

Courtesy of Apolonia "Pola" Galván-Briones. "Baldemar Huerta at two years old." 1939.

Courtesy of Huerta (Fender) Archives. "Baldemar Huerta on horse." 1941.

II

Courtesy of Museum of San Benito, Texas. Historical Society/Conjunto Hall of Fame. "La Resaca." 1940s.

Courtesy by Boon Collins. Still Photos of "Freddy Fender's Childhood Home." Film Documentary of Freddy Fender's Life Story. *Comeback*. 1979.

III

Courtesy of Huerta (Fender) Archives. "*El Aventurero* (The Adventurer)." 1950s.

Courtesy of Museum of San Benito, Texas. Historical Society/Conjunto Hall of Fame. "Downtown Rivoli Movie Theatre." 1950s.

Courtesy of Huerta (Fender) Archives. "Doña Santos and Doña Máge on Resaca Drive, 1960s/Family, 1953."

IV

Courtesy of Huerta (Fender) Archives. "U.S. Marine at sixteen." 1954.

Courtesy by Hernández, Ramón. Music Timeline by Music Archivist and Writer. 2014.

U.S. Marine Corps Archive. "Platoon 422, 1954/ U.S. Marine Corps Private Huerta, 1956."

Courtesy of Carlos Castillo. "Cherry Club, April 27, 1955/N. Hollywood Palomino Club, 1990."

Courtesy of Huerta (Fender) Archives. "Marine buddy with Freddy holding guitar." (Marine name unk. and pho. unk.). 1955.

Courtesy of Pete López. "Marines Huerta, López, and Estrada (Freddy holding rifle)/ Freddy in cabin." 1956.

Courtesy of Huerta (Fender) Archives. "Balde squatting with U.S. Marine buddies." (Marines and pho. unk.). (1956).

V

Courtesy of Evangelina Nieto Muñiz-Huerta "Family Photos/Wedding Cards." 1940s-50s.

Courtesy by Photo by Ingwerson, Henry. *The San Francisco Examiner/Call Bulletin*. Permission to Reprint. "Father of 8 In S.F. Wife Murder-Slaying in Mission District." February 4, 1955. Print.

Courtesy by *The San Francisco Examiner*. Permission to Reprint. "Mate Held in Wife Killing." (pho. unk.). Feb. 5, 1955. Print.

Courtesy by *The San Francisco Examiner/Call Bulletin*. Permission to Reprint. "Slaying Suspect Returned/Wife-Killer Suspect Calm/Sneering Ex-Con Cold Over Wife's Slaying." (pho. unk.). February 5, 1955. Print.

Courtesy of Museum of San Benito, Texas. Historical Society/Conjunto Hall of Fame. "Evangelina and Mary's Apartment on 340 West Robertson Street/ Photo by Fernando Sanchez, La Villita (The Town Talk)/Photo by Fernando Sanchez, La Villita outdoor Dancehall and with Falcón Orchestra of Falcón Records." 1950s.

Courtesy of Carlos Sifuentes. "Baldemar and Evangelina in Matamoros, Tamaulipas, Mexico." Aug. 30, 1957.

VI

Courtesy of Arnaldo "Nano" Ramírez Jr., Falcón Records. *Falcón label*. 45rpms: "Baldemar Huerta Con Los Romanceros *Ay Amor* (Holy One), 1956/*No Seas Cruel* (Don't Be Cruel), 1956/El Twist, Mala, Mala, Mala, Botecito De Vela, Encaje De Chantilly, 1958-1960."

Courtesy of Museum of San Benito, Texas. Historical Society/Conjunto Hall of Fame. "Club 13 on Stenger Street/Grande Theatre." 1950s.

Courtesy of Huerta (Fender) Archives. "Balde and Louis both *rehearsing* and *performing* at the Grande Theatre, 1956/Baldemar with Chucho Hernández and his orchestra in Matamoros, Tamaulipas, Mexico," 1957.

Courtesy of Huerta (Fender) Archives. "Baldemar Huerta, The Bebop Kid." (pho. unk.). 1957.

Courtesy of Chris Strachwitz of Arhoolie Records. "Baldemar Huerta's Recording Ledgers with Falcón Records." *La Frontera Collection*. www.arhooliefoundation.org. 1956-1960.

VII

Courtesy of Louis René Moody. "*Los Romanceros* and friends at Civic Center/Club in Matamoros/Colorado Tour/The Senator Bar in Pueblo, CO./Three-man Band with Mando Peña." (1957).

Courtesy of Huerta (Fender) Archives. "Baldemar Huerta, The Mexican Elvis." (pho. unk.)/Envangelina, Baldemar Jr. "Sonny" Jr., and Balde." 1959.

VIII

Courtesy of Huerta (Fender) Archives. "Freddy Fender by Fender amplifier." (pho. unk.). 1959.

Wayne Duncan. *Duncan label*. 45rpms: Freddie/Freddy Fender. 1959-1960.

Courtesy of Arnaldo "Nano" Ramírez Jr., Falcón Records. Vinyl "El Unico! Freddie Fender!" (pho. unk.). 1959.

Courtesy by © Silicon Music PubCo. *Gene Summers Archives*. "Freddy Fender with Roy Orbison and The Tom Toms." 1960.

Imperial Records of © Universal Music Enterprises of UMG Recordings, Inc. *Imperial label*. 45rpms: "Holy One," "Mean Woman," and "Wasted Days and Wasted Nights." 1960.

Cashbox-Imperial Records. 2 Rock'n Swingin' Sides! Billboard Spotlight Winner. "Fender's Compositions 'Holy One' ('*Ay Amor*') and 'Mean Woman.'" April 9, 1960.

Cashbox Magazine Index. "Wasted Days and Wasted Nights at #82." July 23/30, 1960. Web. http://cashboxmagazine.com/archives/60s_files/1960.html. September 6, 2017.

Courtesy of Louis René Moody. "Baldemar Huerta, Wayne Duncan, and Louis René Moody at Intimo Club." 1961.

Courtesy of Chris Strachwitz of Arhoolie Records. *Ideal Label.* Vinyl: *Eddie Con Los Shades Rock 'n' roll,* 1961/ Ideal 45rpms: "Spanish Rock." 1960s.

IX

Wayne Duncan. *Talent Scout label.* "Freddy Fender, a.k.a. Scotty Wayne." 1960-1962.

Courtesy of LA State Penitentiary/State Officials: Perry Stagg/Gary Young. "Baldemar Huerta Headshots at Angola Prison." April 6, 1961.

Courtesy of Huerta (Fender) Archives. "Freddy and Convicts during the "Walk." (pho. unk.)/Freddy Fender, Louis René Moody and Family." DeQuincy, LA. 1961-1963.

DeQuincy (LCIS), Louisiana Correctional Industrial School. "Freddy, Convict headshots." (pho. unk.). 1962.

Courtesy of Lisa Ann Wilson-Paco Betancourt Family of Ideal Records. "Freddy Fender Correspondence to Paco Betancourt." June 20, 1961.

Courtesy of Huerta (Fender) Archives. "Baldemar Huerta and Family Letters." 1961-1963.

Courtesy of Edward Wayne Schuler. *Goldband label.* Vinyls: "Freddie Fender and Friends at GoldBand, 1964/Freddy Fender Recorded Inside Louisiana State Prison," 1975. 45rpms: "Freddie Fender Love Ballads" (1964).

Courtesy of Beatriz Llamas. "Freddy Fender and Beatriz Llamas 'La Paloma del Norte.'" (pho. unk.). 1975.

X

Courtesy of Huerta Archives. "Freddy out on Parole (pho. unk.)/Rio Theatre Admission Sign/ Freddy Crosses the Border/Family in New Orleans/Freddy and Benny Méndez at Papa Joe's/Satan and Disciples (pho. unk.)." 1963-1968.

Courtesy of Chris Strachwitz of Arhoolie Records. *Ideal label.* 45rpms: *"Freddie Fender-Spanish Rock and Blues* Records." Vinyls: *"Pancho Pechos/Despeinada/ Interpreta El Rock."* 1963-1964.

Norco Label. 45rpms: "The Magic of Love, Ooh Poo Pah doo, and Bony Moronie" Affiliated with Discos Dominante, Mexico and Falcón Records. 1963.

Courtesy of Beatriz Llamas/Hispanic Entertainment Archives/Ramón Hernández. "Armando 'Mando' Peña playing drums for Beatriz Llamas 'La Paloma del Norte.'" (pho. unk.). 1960s.

Courtesy of Edward Wayne Schuler. *Goldband label.* 45rpms: "Cat's Meow and Mummie's Curse." 1967-1968.

XI

Discos Dominante label. Mexico: 45rpm: *Aunque Me Hagas Llorar* ("Although You Made Me Cry"), 1969. Vinyl: *El Nuevo Freddie Fender Con Sus Nuevas Creaciones* ("The New Freddie Fender with his Newest Creations"). (pho. unk.) 1970.

Courtesy of Huerta (Fender) Archives. "*Freddy with Los Comancheros.*" (pho. unk.). 1969-1970/Baldemar Huerta - Archives/Fender performing at James Connally Technical Institute." (pho. unk.). 1970.

XII

Courtesy of Huerta (Fender) Archives. "Family." 1970/1993.

XIII

Courtesy by Linda S. Saldana. "*Border Diablos* Motorcycle Club/Freddy Fender/ José Luis." 1970s.

Courtesy by Tammy Huerta. "Uncle José Luis Mendez holding Motorcycle Toy Model." 2008.

XIV

Courtesy by Producer and Director Boon Collins. Still photo of "Evangelina," 1973. Film Documentary The Life Story of Freddy Fender, *Comeback.* 1979.

Courtesy of Huerta (Fender) Archives. "Family." 1973.

XV

Courtesy by Luis Moreno Garcia, a.k.a. Squeezer. Sketch "The Squeeze Inn Club/ Cameron Country Document" 1975.

Courtesy of Huerta (Fender) Archives. "Benjamin "Benny" Méndez with Turkey on drums." 1973.

XVI

Courtesy of © Demon Music Group Ltd., Music Enterprise Licensed. *Crazy Cajun label.* 45rpm: Freddy Fender "Before The Next Teardrop Falls." 1974.

Courtesy by Huerta (Fender) Archives. "Fender at home on Eighteenth Street/ Family/Freddy in Arlington Stadium." 1974.

Courtesy of Huey Meaux, Lee Ashworth and Sam Monroe, *Huey Meaux Selection.* "Fender and Sam Herro/Huey Styling Freddy's Hair/Fender buttoning shirt/ Fender, Meaux, and Cheryl Brandt"/Freddy Recording. 1974.

Courtesy by Jesus Garza, *La Opinion Newspaper.* Permission to Reprint. Photographer. "Fender Family Photo Op on Barcelona Street. 1974. Print.

ABC-Dot Records © Universal Music Enterprises of UMG Recordings, Inc. *ABC-Dot labels.* 45rpm "Wasted Days and Wasted Nights." 1975.

Courtesy by Jim Halsey. Permission to Reprint *"Over 200,000 "Gringos" Can't be Wrong!"* March 1, 1975. Print.

Courtesy by Paul Blankenmeister, *Daily Texan and Texas Student Media*, Austin, Texas. Permission to Reprint. "Freddy Goes to Jail but Just for A Visit/Freddy Sings for Inmates." Included: Permission to Publish use of Reproduction "Freddy Plays for the Inmates at Austin County Jail." Dolph Briscoe Center for American History, The University of Texas at Austin. Meaux (Huey) Papers. Image di_05206. 1975. Print.

Courtesy of Huerta (Fender) Archives. "Family." 1974-75.

XVII

Courtesy by Francesco "Frank" Valeri/Leo Ulfelder. Images "Freddy Fender at The Landmark Hotel in Las Vegas. 1975.

Courtesy of NBC Entertainment-Studio. A Division of NBC West, LLC. "*The Tonight Show/The Dinah Shore Show* starring Freddy Fender/Hollywood Squares Game Show." (pho. unk.) Dolph Briscoe Center for American History, The University of Texas at Austin. Images: "Freddy Fender on *Dinah Shore Show*, di_05186/Freddy Fender, *Dinah Shore, and Tony Orlando*, di_05207/ Freddy Fender and Burt Reynolds on *The Tonight Show*, di_05208/Freddy Getting Makeup, di_05209/Freddy on Hollywood Squares Game Show, di_05203." Meaux (Huey) Papers. (pho. unk.). 1975.

Courtesy by Jim Foglesong. Permission to reprint. Promotional Poster "Show Country Comes to Carnegie Hall." 1975. Print.

Courtesy of Lee Ashworth and Sam Monroe, *Huey Meaux Selection*/Sugar Hill Record Producer Dan Workman. Images: "Jim Foglesong, Sam Herro, Huey Meaux shaking hands/Sugar Hill Studio Crew/Sam Herro, Jim Foglesong, Freddy, Freddy Fender, Huey Meaux, and Mickey Moody. 1975.

ABC-Dot Records © Universal Music Enterprises of UMG Recordings, Inc. *ABC-Dot labels*. LP "Before The Next Teardrop Falls." 1975.

Courtesy of Huerta (Fender) Archives. "Sam Herro, Freddy Fender, and Huey Meaux rejoicing overnight success at diner." 1975.

Dolph Briscoe Center for American History, The University of Texas at Austin. Images "Freddy at The Los Angeles Palladium," di_05205, di_05196. (pho. unk). Meaux (Huey) Papers. 1975.

XVIII

Dolph Briscoe Center for American History, The University of Texas at Austin. "Freddy Fender with hand on face," di_05194. (pho. unk.). Meaux (Huey) Papers. 1975.

Courtesy by Bev LeCroy © Grand Ole Opry Archives. Images "ABC-Dot Records, Larry Baunach presents gold records to Huey Meaux and Freddy Fender. October 1975.

Courtesy by Les Leverett © Grand Ole Opry Archives. CMA Awards. Billy "Crash" Craddock and Minnie Pearl present Freddy Fender with the award for Single of the Year 'Before the Next Teardrop Falls'. October 13, 1975.

CMA Awards © Grand Ole Opry Archives. "Freddy graciously accepts and thanks the Country Music Association for Single of the Year" (pho. unk.)/Freddy performs at the 50th Grand Ole Opry Anniversary (pho.unk.)." Dolph Briscoe Center for American History, The University of Texas at Austin. Images di_05181, di_05187. (pho. unk.). Meaux (Huey) Papers. 1975.

Courtesy of BMI. Director of Media Relations, Kay Clary. (pho. unk.). "BMI Awards Dinner." 1975.

Billboard. Dolph Briscoe Center for American History, The University of Texas at Austin. "Billboard Number 1 Awards with Flip Wilson, di_05183 ((pho. unk.)/ Billboard Award recipients, Freddy Fender, Captain & Tennille, and Olivia Newton-John, di_051082 (pho. unk.)." Meaux (Huey) Papers. 1975.

Courtesy by Michael G. Borum, "Freddy Fender and Mickey Gilley." 1976.

XIX

Courtesy by Tom Hendrix. All Images: "Welcome Back Home Freddy." 1976.

Courtesy of Demon Music Group Ltd., Music Enterprise Licensed. *Starflite label/The Crazy Cajun label.* LP's: *"Exitos Grandes de Freddy Fender, 1977/Freddy Fender and Tommy McLain, Friends in Show Business."* 1978.

XX

Courtesy of Huerta (Fender) Archives. "Family." 1976

Courtesy of Arnaldo "Nano" Ramírez Jr., Falcón Records. *ARV label.* 45rpms: En Memoria A: Elvis! *"No Seas Cruel"* ("Don't be Cruel"). 1977.

Courtesy of Victor Hernandez. "Sweethearts, Victor and Tammy." 1974.

XXI

Courtesy by Producer and Director Boon Collins. "Freddy and Eva on motorcycle." Film Documentary *Comeback.* 1979.

Courtesy by Huerta (Fender) Archives. "1948 midnight blue Cadillac,1978.

Courtesy of © President Jimmy Carter Library. Nic13408.9a- "President Jimmy Carter and Rosalynn Carter greet country singer Freddie Fender at a White House reception." *Salute to Country Music Gala at Ford Theatre.* October 2, 1979.

Courtesy of Brenda Liles and Rick DeArmond. "The Cripple Creek Band/*Worlds of Fun*/ Freddy and band on the road/Freddy and The Cripple Creek on the road/ *Ranch Party*." 1977-1979.

Dolph Briscoe Center for American History, The University of Texas at Austin. "Freddy Fender at Silverbird," di_05165. (pho. unk.). Meaux (Huey) Papers. 1979.

Courtesy of Huey Meaux, Lee Ashworth and Sam Monroe, *Huey Meaux Selection*. ""Freddy Fender, George 'Goober Pyle' Major Riddle, and Huey Meaux at the Silverbird in Vegas (pho. unk.)/Freddy with author Cleo Dawson on horse/ Freddy in custom as Pancho Villa by clothing trailer." 1978-1979.

Dolph Briscoe Center for American History, The University of Texas at Austin. "Freddy Fender signing autographs," di_05198 (pho. unk.). Meaux (Huey) Papers. 1979.

Courtesy of Huerta (Fender) Archives. President Richard Nixon Letter to Fender/ Freddy Fender and The Cripple Creek Band in Las Vegas/Off-set filming movie *She Came To The Valley*, Freddy with Cleo Dawson, Freddy as Pancho Villa with Oni Villarreal, Tammy, Huey Meaux, and Margarita/Freddy with the widow of Pancho Villa/Freddy's aunts and uncles/Tammy at Magic Mountain/Balde and Eva." 1978-1979.

Back Matter

Courtesy by Tammy L. Huerta Fender. "Interviewees." 2007-2012.

Courtesy by Evangelina Muñiz-Huerta. *Freddy Fender Honors and Awards/ Discography*. 1956/2006.

Courtesy by Sandro Giorgi. About the Author. Headshot. 2014.

Disclaimer: Exercising great prudence, all efforts have been made to contact and release all publication infringements a related to copyrights and/or trademarks of other talents as mentioned with pictures in this book. Intent of this statement is to absolve the writer and publisher of infringement liability.

About the Author

Tammy Huerta, The Tex-Mex Princess

    Tammy keeps her father's legacy alive as an affiliate within the music industry as well as through social and political forums. She voices her genuine spirit and inspires others to challenge themselves in the belief that hope and courage may be achieved.

    Like her father, who achieved the American dream, Huerta wholeheartedly believes that others can overcome personal struggles and social injustice and persevere in the pursuit of their own destiny. Huerta believes this can be done with the spiritual aid of a Higher Power, and that it is within this realm where true happiness awaits.

Dreams are for the living!
When we stop dreaming, we give up on ourselves and those we love. My good fortune is wisdom; I learned it's never too late to live, love, let go and forgive— and to aspire to life's sweet dreams once again.
—Tammy Lorraine Huerta Fender

CPSIA information can be obtained
at www.ICGtesting.com
Printed in the USA
LVHW112025271021
701735LV00008B/206/J

9 781456 851057